Reading and Writing About Literature

Phillip Sipiora

University of South Florida

Prentice Hall

Upper Saddle River, New Jersey 07458

Library of Congress Cataloging-in-Publication Data

Sipiora, Phillip.
   Reading and writing about literature / by Phillip Sipiora.—1st ed.
     p. cm.
   Includes bibliographical references and index.
   ISBN 0-13-027974-9
   1. English language—Rhetoric—Problems, exercises, etc. 2.
Criticism—Authorship—Problems, exercises, etc. 3. Literature—History and
criticism—Theory, etc. 4. College readers. I. Title.

PE1479.C7 S63 2002
808'.0427—dc21

                                         2001033836

Editor-in-chief: Leah Jewell
Senior acquisitions editor: Carrie Brandon
Senior executive managing editor: Mary Rottino
Production liaison: Fran Russello
Editorial/production supervision: Bruce Hobart (Pine Tree Composition)
Prepress and manufacturing buyer: Sherry Lewis
Cover designer: Robert Farrar-Wagner
Cover image: "Light on Swimming Pool Surface, NJ"
  (photo by Marilyn Farrar-Wagner)
Marketing manager: Rachel Falk
Copy editor: Carol Lallier

This book was set in 10.5/12 Goudy by Pine Tree Composition, Inc.,
and was printed and bound by Courier Companies, Inc.
The cover was printed by Phoenix Color Corp.

For permission to use copyrighted material, please refer to
p. 335 which is hereby made part of this copyright page.

 © 2002 by Pearson Education, Inc.
Upper Saddle River, New Jersey 07458

Printed in the United States of America

10 9 8 7 6 5 4 3 2 1

ISBN 0-13-027974-9

Pearson Education LTD., London
Pearson Education Australia PTY, Limited, Sydney
Pearson Education Singapore, Pte. Ltd
Pearson Education North Asia Ltd, Hong Kong
Pearson Education Canada, Ltd., Toronto
Pearson Educación de Mexico, S.A. de C.V.
Pearson Education—Japan, Tokyo
Pearson Education Malaysia, Pte. Ltd.
Pearson Education, Upper Saddle River, New Jersey

For Cary, Jessica, Austin, and Phillip

Contents

Preface

Reading and Writing About Literature is a text that explores various approaches to interpreting literature. This book is intended to serve students in first-year English classes, introduction to literature classes, and other courses whose primary focus is the interpretation of literature.

There are several features that make this book unique, including the introduction of new interpretive approaches (ethical, civic, and cultural criticism, for example), as well as more established schools of interpretation (formalist, psychological, and deconstuctive schools, for example). Each chapter includes at least two literary readings, detailed instructions on reading and writing strategies, a sample essay, and Internet and library resources. Steps on how to write a research essay are treated in detail in Chapter 10, which also includes a sample research essay and comprehensive Internet and library research methods. *Reading and Writing About Literature* presents a systematic process and product approach to interpreting literature *and* composing essays about literature.

READING AND WRITING STRATEGIES

- **Reader-Response interpretation** focuses on the reader's personal background in approaching a literary text, particularly cumulative life experiences that philosophers refer to as forestructure.

- **Formalist interpretation** emphasizes the work itself rather than the author's intention, a reader's response, or other outside frames of reference. Formalist criticism searches for ironies and paradoxes within a work that come together to give a text overall unity.

- **Ethical interpretation** locates the center of meaning in the moral or ethical dimensions of a literary text, as represented in the personal interactions among characters.

- **Civic interpretation** explores literature for themes of moral values that have significance for individuals as members of communities.

- **Cultural interpretation** examines situations and contexts that give birth to a literary work. This approach may focus on the life of the author, the context (social, economic, and political) of the time the work was written, and various cultural representations contained within the work.

- **Feminist interpretation** looks at how patriarchal structures are reflected in literature and analyzes how structures based on dominance and submission affect economic situations, psychological and physical status, and interpersonal relationships.

- **Psychological interpretation** analyzes literary representations of mind constructions such as the id, ego, and superego, as well as the ways in which literary language represents characters' psychological profiles.

- **Deconstructive interpretation** investigates literary language for its ambiguities, gaps, silences, supplements, traces, and strategic metaphors, especially those that undermine unified interpretations of works.

UNIQUE FEATURES

- New interpretive strategies presented in accessible language.
- Literary readings selected for readability, diversity, and relevance to chapter perspectives.
- Detailed question and answer analytical exercises on two readings in each chapter.
- Organized sequence of steps in each chapter to assist students in writing interpretive essays.
- Sample essay in each chapter illustrating the respective interpretive approach.
- Internet and library resources in each chapter related to chapter topic and readings.

Reading and Writing About Literature is the result of a long struggle, never over, to learn how better to read literature. I have been reading literature a long time, going back to the days of my youth spent on a summer hammock in Grand Junction, Michigan, fascinated by detective stories about the Hardy boys, my brothers in adventure. Literature has always given me special pleasure, but at no time greater than today when I see literature through the various lenses of so many compelling theoretical approaches. Indeed, today's reader has a copious smorgasbord of critical perspectives to select from. Some readers, like myself, prefer to explore literature with an awareness of the strength in multiple interpretive perspectives. Like a voracious food connoisseur, I find it enriching to sample a little of everything before going back for seconds of those morsels I find most tantalizing.

Times have changed for readers of literature. Students of the new millennium have far more resources available to them for writing formal interpretations of literature than those of earlier generations. Indeed, today's readers are able to locate professional interpretations of nearly any major literary work with the click of a mouse. The ready availability of scholarly readings, however, does not assist today's student in organizing and writing interpretations of literary works. This book is an attempt to provide students with conceptual frameworks that will assist in the exploration, analysis, and evaluation of literary texts.

Many students reading literature soon realize a love for the process, which often grows with each new encounter. Although many readers may not realize it, we have built-in tools of interpretations that are already present in our intellectual and emotional systems. A reader may not be formally trained in psychological criticism, for example, but he or she often recognizes, intuitively, psychological elements at work in literature. Readers of literature are often touched personally by their encounters with literary texts, which sometimes set forth reactions that bring readers closer to their own personal experiences. This reaction is reader-response reading, although the reader may not have formal experience with this school of criticism. Readers are often aware of gender representations in literary texts, the terrain of feminist criticism. All schools of critical interpretation in this book represent, in some way, an outgrowth of intuitive reactions to literature. It is the goal of this book to present conceptual background and interpretive tools to generate responses to literature. Further, each chapter includes step-by-step suggestions to assist in the actual writing of essays about literature. *Reading and Writing About Literature* endorses both a product and a process approach to interpreting *and* composing about literary texts.

This book has many dimensions, as implied by its title, and none is more significant than the importance of being open to different ways of reading literature. Indeed, the critical perspectives we select say as much about ourselves and our intellectual constitutions and personal histories as they do about the qualities of a work of literature. For example, there are two chapters devoted to ethics, personal and public, which I consider critical in reading literature within a humanist tradition. The chapter on cultural criticism encourages you to think of multiple contexts in analyzing and evaluating texts. Deconstructive criticism attempts to show you how texts remain ambiguous, heavily figurative, and multi-layered, yet still open themselves up to meaningful interpretations. Formalist criticism offers the strategies of close reading and objective analysis, powerful tools for any theoretical approach. None of these critical tools will force a text to surrender its essential meaning, of course, but each one of them offers you strategies of interpretation. I encourage you to read each chapter with an open mind, willing to work with the tools of the trained reader and writer.

The writing sections of each chapter are intended to go hand in hand with the act of reading. I believe that reading inspires writing and writing is recursive. The more you write, the more ideas you will generate and the more you will want to write. For most writers, the hardest part of any project is getting started. The step-by-step sections on writing your essay are intending to assist you at each critical juncture in the writing process. Writing is difficult and painful, as many professional writers acknowledge, but the intellectual and emotional rewards are significant. And there can even be some fun in composing a literary analysis using the tools of the professional critic.

Acknowledgments

This book was inspired by many fine individuals, and it is impossible to mention them all. I have been blessed by having learned to read literature and language by superb teachers, beginning with Mrs. Long, my fourth-grade teacher at St. Priscilla, continuing in high school with Fenwick's Fathers Reynolds and Ryan, on to my Illinois undergraduate days with Louis Marder, Samuel Weiss, and Beverly Fields, and then to my Texas graduate study, working with Alan Friedman, Alan Gribben, Anthony Hilfer, Joseph Malof, Gayatri Chakravorty Spivak, Walt Reed, John Velz, Wayne Rebhorn, and James L. Kinneavy, my mentor and dear friend from whom I learned so much about reading, writing, and life. Each of these humanists has offered me special encouragement, and whatever interpretive skills I may have are the product of their intellectual acuity and infectious enthusiasm.

  Reading and Writing About Literature could not have been written without the encouragement, insight, and patience of Carrie Brandon, Senior Acquisitions Editor. Phil Miller, former President of the Humanities Division of Prentice-Hall, remains, as always, a solid source of wise counsel and support. Maggie Barbieri, Development Editor, has been a sharp eye and keen ear in shepherding this project through to its completion. Tom DeMarco is a consummate professional in expeditiously processing all documents. Bruce Hobart is a superb, efficacious project coordinator who was integral in bringing out this text in a timely manner. Carol Lallier is the finest copy editor that I have ever worked with and she has made a significant contribution in improving the readability of this book. Mary Dalton Hoffman is meticulous in securing permissions, indefatigable in tracking down copyright ownership in the murky haze of foreign authorship. Joyce Karpay, author of Chapter 7, Feminist Criticism, has been a continuous source of encouragement and insight from the beginning of the project. Gerald R. Lucas, author of "Research Sources" and "James Joyce's The Dead" in Chapter 10, is a keen-eyed reader of literature and more knowledgeable about literature and electronic pedagogy than anyone else I know. My USF colleagues Larry Broer, Sara Deats, Jack Moore, Tom Ross, and Steve Rubin, all superb readers of literature, have influenced me in more ways than they know. Lee Paver and Jackie Regan, USF English department staff members, have been particularly helpful in assisting with manuscript copying and preparation. I owe a debt of gratitude to Susan Friedman, USF English Department graduate research assistant, a promising scholar immune to fatigue and exemplary in the art of the literary sleuth. And a special nod goes to Pete Jordan, my dear friend with a patient ear and an eye for the aesthetic.

Anyone who has ever taught knows that a teacher learns much from his or her students. Over the past 20 years I have experimented with portions of this book in the classroom, sometimes to blank faces and looks of astonishment. Yet, at times, words of encouragement have come forth and have played an influential role in the shape that this book has taken. In every respect, this book is written for my students, past, present, and future.

I am most grateful to my mother, Florence Sipiora, for a lifetime of encouragement, support, and sustenance. Always in my memory is Julian Sipiora, my father and a scientist by training, forever an exemplary model in balancing reason and emotion. My late aunt, Helen Sipiora, an English teacher herself, stirred the early passions of reading in me as a toddler. My brothers Forrest Sipiora, Daniel Sipiora, and Bruce Sipiora and brother-in-law Alex Strobl, all good men, are consummate teachers of life. My parents-in-law, Walter and Lillian, continue to be sources of insight.

No one has inspired me more than my wife, Cary Ann Strobl, who has stood by me for more than 20 years as I struggle to learn from those texts I dearly love. My children, Jessica, Austin, and Phillip deserve so much for so many lost hours: Jessica without her Borders' companion, Austin without her swimming cheerleader, and Phillip without his batting practice pitcher.

Phillip Sipiora

chapter 1

Introduction

Western Wind, when wilt thou Blow,
The small rain down can rain?
Christ, if my love were in my arms,
And I in my bed again!
                —Anonymous, *Western Wind*

LITERARY READING AND WRITING

Reading and writing about literature has been an important part of Western civilization since at least the time of the ancient Greeks, and probably before that in earlier Egyptian civilizations. The ancients recognized what we sometimes take for granted today: The study of literature can be an uplifting experience that sharpens our minds, energizes our sense of the beautiful, and helps us to recognize what is good in literature and in life. The poem "Western Wind" suggests a poet in pain, anxiously waiting for the rain, but also yearning for his or her lover. This short poem of only two sentences contains powerful emotions, especially frustration, and reveals intense desire for a cessation of pain.

Reading literature like the poem above is not the same process as reading other kinds of writing. We often refer to fiction, poetry, and drama as "imaginative writing," because they call attention to the beauty, organization, and elements of the work itself. Other kinds of writing call attention to different things: Scientific writing (a technical report, for example) refers primarily to the subject matter under consideration; self-expressive writing (a diary, for example) calls attention to the writer; and writing that is explicitly persuasive (a letter promoting a credit card, for example) focuses on the reader, motivating him or her to do something. Literature draws in readers because of the pleasures it provides in reading beautiful language and stimulating ideas. Above all else, literature makes us think, both about ideas within literature and about issues in

1

our personal lives that are brought to the surface by reading literature. Literature is about human experience in its wide range of expressions. Reading and writing about literature is one of humanity's most poignant expressions of what it means to be human, including pain, suffering, joy, and intellectual growth.

When we read and write about literature, there are many fundamental contexts that influence interpretation: the reader's age, gender, and life experiences; knowledge of the writer's background; the context of the work; and the particular method of looking at reading the work, which is the subject of this book. Although each reader has a unique history of personal experience (which is called forestructure), what brings different readers together is looking at a work of literature from a common critical approach. All effective literary interpretation involves reading literature from one or more frames of reference. Indeed, the most rewarding readings of literature are those that are fully "interactive," in which the reader engages the text at the deepest levels of both text and reader. Intense, informed reading of literature can be a richly rewarding experience, and a major goal of this book is to introduce you to reading strategies that will enable you to read literature with significant insight.

Literary interpretation in the Western world has always been influenced by specific reading strategies. In ancient Greece, for example, students were taught to analyze and paraphrase key passages of literature (usually sections from Homer's *Iliad* and *Odyssey*). One of the major goals in classical literary interpretation was to teach students values and virtues, often represented through heroic characters such as Odysseus in Homer's epics. Values in literature, particularly ethical values, are an essential part of the humanities. Were literature devoid of values and ethics, there would be little to differentiate literature from various other kinds of writing. The goal of this book is not to teach you specific interpretations, but rather to introduce you to the tools of investigation, whereby you will be able to arrive at your own conclusions about values and ethics in *your* reading of a literary text. In order to make informed judgments about values and virtues in literature, you must first have the tools necessary to make those decisions with confidence that you can articulate your judgments.

LITERARY THEORY

Literary theory helps us to read literature by providing specific tools and strategies that increase our range and depth of interpretations, of which there are many valid and persuasive ones regarding any work of literature. Indeed, it is the rare literature teacher who would argue for one absolute reading of a work of literature. It is also important to remember that when we interpret literature, we are interacting with it. Our intellectual and emotional backgrounds intersect with the elements of literature (plot, character, voice, and metaphor, to name just some of the features in a short story). Each literary school in this book represents a different perspective on the complex matrix of text, reader, and the reference(s) of the work. The purpose of this book is to guide you to understand the principles and strategies of reading that underlie major schools of literary interpretation.

There are numerous schools of literary criticism, even going back to the ancient Greeks, and there are far too many to include every one in *Reading and Writing About Literature*. However, this book has attempted to represent the major schools of literary interpretation, along with some emerging approaches (such as cultural criticism) and other approaches that have reasserted themselves in recent times (ethical criticism, for example). Cultural criticism, for example, is particularly vibrant in revealing a set of principles that mirror changes in mores and ethical values that are an inevitable part of any society.

All approaches to literary interpretation rely upon the examination of fundamental components of literature. In the case of fiction, these elements include plot, character, theme, voice, metaphor, and other formal qualities of prose. In the genre of poetry, meter, rhythm, and symbol are particularly important, as are theme, voice, and other components. Dramatic literature contains all of these elements, emphasizing dialogue, action, and other aspects of theatrical performance. All of the critical approaches in this book can function as practical tools for interpretation, although it is often obvious that specific literary texts sometimes are more accessible to some schools of criticism than to others. In each chapter, I have attempted to select readings that open themselves up to the interpretative strategy that is the subject of that chapter. Each reading has been carefully selected to allow you to learn specific strategies of reading *and* writing about literature.

SCHOOLS OF INTERPRETATION

Reading and Writing About Literature introduces you to eight approaches to interpreting literature, as well as to writing a research essay about literature using electronic and traditional resources. Some of the interpretative strategies in this book may already be familiar to you. Other approaches, such as ethical criticism, literature as civic argument, cultural criticism, and reader-response criticism may be quite new to you.

Reader-response criticism examines how readers respond—intuitively, spontaneously, emotionally, and subjectively—to works of literature. This perspective emphasizes the reader's background as a significant frame of reference in the interpretive process. More specifically, you are introduced to the practice of examining literature from a personal experience that interacts with the backgrounds of other readers, as well as with the background of the text. The technical term for the reader's personal background is "forestructure" and you are encouraged to mesh your life experiences with those of others in locating common frames of reference. All college readers, for example, have gone through rites of passage, yet each rite of passage is a subjective experience and, therefore, the interpretation of these experiences in literature requires negotiating the personal with the literary.

Formalist criticism, or what is sometimes called New Criticism, focuses on the close reading and explication of literary texts according to formal textual patterns, which involve grammar, diction, syntax, and other elements of literary language. The formalist reader looks at literary works as unified, self-contained structures, and this method of interpretation of literature does not require biographical, historical, or other "outside" tools, other than a standard dictionary. The interpretive emphasis is on the text itself, without significant attention given to larger contexts of interpretation. As you will see in subsequent chapters, other approaches depend significantly upon larger contextual issues.

Ethical criticism introduces you to issues of values and morality in literature. Although there are many possible approaches to this issue, this chapter focuses on ethical values as illustrated in the relationships between individuals. You are encouraged to explore ways in which values are represented through characters' interactions with one another. This chapter includes a detailed discussion of the meaning of ethics and how one determines one's ethics through encounters with others. Literary authors use the words and actions of characters to create conflict, and an ethical critic examines the moral implication of literary conflicts.

Literature as civic criticism grows out of a long tradition in Western literature in which literature is interpreted for its treatment of social values and civil responsibility. Whereas ethical criticism emphasizes the personal, interactive nature of ethics, civic criticism explores morality from the larger perspective of the relationship between the individual and the community. Literature as civic argument reflects a very old tradition in which literature was the primary vehicle for analyzing a person's responsibilities to the larger environment of which he or she is an integral part. The same principles apply to contemporary students and this chapter encourages you to read literature from the perspective of your civic responsibility.

Cultural criticism, a form of historical criticism, seeks to explain a text by examining historical situations and contexts (social, economic, and political), which reflect the conditions that give birth to a literary work, including experiences of the work's author. All of these areas are important, although an emphasis on one or more of them may depend upon the work of literature and the particular interests of the cultural critic. This approach demonstrates how historical knowledge is critical to the interpretation of a text. Interpreting a literary text as a historical reader depends upon a general understanding of social, political, and economic events and movements, and may include a familiarity with the smaller cultural events in the life of the author and the work.

Feminist criticism examines how gender structures are reflected in literature and analyzes how structures based on dominance and submission affect all aspects of our lives: our economic situations, our psychological and physical well-being, and our interpersonal relationships. Feminist interpreters may question the effects of public institutions such as the educational system, the corporate world, and the medical profession, or it may probe social institutions and traditions such as marriage, motherhood, and the "beauty culture." Recent feminist critics insist that even our system of language privileges masculine thought (advantages for men and disadvantages for women as they exist in our language), and some feminists investigate ways in which women can become aware of these discrepancies, discover a distinctively feminine voice, and insert this specifically feminine voice into language.

Psychological criticism approaches literature from psychological perspectives, especially as articulated in the work of Sigmund Freud and Jacques Lacan. Particular areas of focus include the terrain of the subconscious, literary illustrations of the id, ego, and super ego, and the interaction of the imaginary and symbolic order, according to Lacan. The psychological approach is based on the assumption that psychological themes are important issues in a literary text. Psychological and psychoanalytic terms are defined and illustrated in ordinary language.

Deconstructive criticism involves the recognition and practice of the limitations of language. Deconstructive interpreters focus on multiple layers of interpretation made possible by a wide range of meanings of words. All language, for deconstructive critics, contains multiple meanings; all words refer to yet other words, whether we realize we are reading language as metaphoric or not. Deconstructive readers perceive language as open, ambiguous, and necessarily incomplete, rich in gaps, absences, and silences. Deconstructive critics challenge the possibility of objective truth, replacing objectivity by critically examining subjectivity, including the mind, culture, and beliefs of the individual. Deconstructive reading reveals not only what we can do with texts in interpreting them, but also how texts expose what they do within themselves. There are many strategies in deconstructive reading, but the concepts of supplement, trace, and metaphor are of particular importance.

A SAMPLE READING

"Babylon Revisited" by F. Scott Fitzgerald (1896–1940)

"And where's Mr. Campbell?" Charlie asked.

    "Gone to Switzerland. Mr. Campbell's a pretty sick man, Mr. Wales."

    "I'm sorry to hear that. And George Hardt?" Charlie inquired.

    "Back in America, gone to work."

    "And where is the Snow Bird?"   5

    "He was in here last week. Anyway, his friend, Mr. Schaeffer, is in Paris."

    Two familiar names from the long list of a year and a half ago. Charlie scribbled an address in his notebook and tore out the page.

    "If you see Mr. Schaeffer, give him this," he said. "It's my brother-in-law's address. I haven't settled on a hotel yet."

    He was not really disappointed to find Paris was so empty. But the stillness in the Ritz bar was strange and portentous. It was not an American bar any more—he felt polite in it, and not as if he owned it. It had gone back into France. He felt the stillness from the moment he got out of the taxi and saw the doorman, usually in a frenzy of activity at this hour, gossiping with a *chasseur* by the servants' entrance.

    Passing through the corridor, he heard only a single, bored voice in the once-   10
clamorous women's room. When he turned into the bar he travelled the twenty feet of green carpet with his eyes fixed straight ahead by old habit; and then, with his foot firmly on the rail, he turned and surveyed the room, encountering only a single pair of eyes that fluttered up from a newspaper in the corner. Charlie asked for the head barman, Paul, who in the latter days of the bull market had come to work in his own custom-built car—disembarking, however, with due nicety at the nearest corner. But Paul was at his country house today and Alix giving him information.

    "No, no more," Charlie said, "I'm going slow these days."

    Alix congratulated him: "You were going pretty strong a couple of years ago."

    "I'll stick to it all right," Charlie assured him. "I've stuck to it for over a year and a half now."

    "How do you find conditions in America?"

    "I haven't been to America for months. I'm in business in Prague, representing a   15
couple of concerns there. They don't know about me down there."

    Alix smiled.

    "Remember the night of George Hardt's bachelor dinner here?" said Charlie. "By the way, what's become of Claude Fessenden?"

    Alix lowered his voice confidentially: "He's in Paris, but he doesn't come here any more. Paul doesn't allow it. He ran up a bill of thirty thousand francs, charging all his drinks and his lunches, and usually his dinner, for more than a year. And when Paul finally told him he had to pay, he gave him a bad check."

    Alix shook his head sadly.

    "I don't understand it, such a dandy fellow. Now he's all bloated up—" He made   20
a plump apple of his hands.

    Charlie watched a group of strident queens installing themselves in a corner.

    "Nothing affects them," he thought. "Stocks rise and fall, people loaf or work, but they go on forever." The place oppressed him. He called for the dice and shook with Alix for the drink.

"Here for long, Mr. Wales?"

"I'm here for four or five days to see my little girl."

"Oh-h! You have a little girl?" 25

Outside, the fire-red, gas-blue, ghost-green signs shone smokily through the tranquil rain. It was late afternoon and the streets were in movement; the *bistros* gleamed. At the corner of the Boulevard des Capucines he took a taxi. The Place de la Concorde moved by in pink majesty; they crossed the logical Seine, and Charlie felt the sudden provincial quality of the Left Bank.

Charlie directed his taxi to the Avenue de l'Opera, which was out of his way. But he wanted to see the blue hour spread over the magnificent façade, and imagine that the cab horns, playing endlessly the first few bars of *La Plus que Lent,* were the trumpets of the Second Empire. They were closing the iron grill in front of Brentano's Book-store, and people were already at dinner behind the trim little bourgeois hedge of Duval's. He had never eaten at a really cheap restaurant in Paris. Five-course dinner, four francs fifty, eighteen cents, wine included. For some odd reason he wished that he had.

As they rolled on to the Left Bank and he felt its sudden provincialism, he thought, "I spoiled this city for myself. I didn't realize it, but the days came along one after another, and then two years were gone, and everything was gone, and I was gone."

He was thirty-five, and good to look at. The Irish mobility of his face was sobered by a deep wrinkle between his eyes. As he rang his brother-in-laws' bell in the Rue Palatine, the wrinkle deepened till it pulled down his brows; he felt a cramping sensation in his belly. From behind the maid who opened the door darted a lovely little girl of nine who shrieked "Daddy!" and flew up, struggling like a fish, into his arms. She pulled his head around by one ear and set her cheek against his.

"My old pie," he said. 30

"Oh, daddy, daddy, daddy, daddy, dads, dads, dads!"

She drew him into the salon, where the family waited, a boy and girl his daughter's age, his sister-in law and her husband. He greeted Marion with his voice pitched carefully to avoid either feigned enthusiasm or dislike, but her response was more frankly tepid, though she minimized her expression of unalterable distrust by directing her regard toward his child. The two men clasped hands in a friendly way and Lincoln Peters rested his for a moment on Charlie's shoulder.

The room was warm and comfortably American. The three children moved intimately about, playing through the yellow oblongs that led to other rooms; the cheer of six o'clock spoke in the eager smacks of the fire and the sounds of French activity in the kitchen. But Charlie did not relax; his heart sat up rigidly in his body and he drew confidence from his daughter, who from time to time came close to him, holding in her arms the doll he had brought.

"Really extremely well," he declared in answer to Lincoln's question. "There's a lot of business there that isn't moving at all, but we're doing even better than ever. In fact, damn well. I'm bringing my sister over from America next month to keep house for me. My income last year was bigger than it was when I had money. You see, the Czechs——"

His boasting was for a specific purpose; but after a moment, seeing a faint restiveness in Lincoln's eye, he changed the subject: 35

"Those are fine children of yours, well brought up, good manners."

"We think Honoria's a great little girl too."

Marion Peters came back from the kitchen. She was a tall woman with worried eyes, who had once possessed a fresh American loveliness. Charlie had never been sensitive to it and was always surprised when people spoke of how pretty she had been. From the first there had been an instinctive antipathy between them.

"Well, how do you find Honoria?" she asked.

"Wonderful. I was astonished how much she's grown in ten months. All the chil-   40
dren are looking well."

"We haven't had a doctor for a year. How do you like being back in Paris?"

"It seems very funny to see so few Americans around."

"I'm delighted," Marion said vehemently. "Now at least you can go into a store without their assuming you're a millionaire. We've suffered like everybody, but on the whole it's a good deal pleasanter."

"But it was nice while it lasted," Charlie said. "We were a sort of royalty, almost infallible, with a sort of magic around us. In the bar this afternoon"—he stumbled, see-ing his mistake—"there wasn't a man I knew."

She looked at him keenly. "I should think you'd have had enough of bars."   45

"I only stayed a minute. I take one drink every afternoon, and no more."

"Don't you want a cocktail before dinner?" Lincoln asked.

"I take only one drink every afternoon, and I've had that."

"I hope you keep to it," said Marion.

Her dislike was evident in the coldness with which she spoke, but Charlie only   50
smiled; he had larger plans. Her very aggressiveness gave him an advantage, and he knew enough to wait. He wanted them to initiate the discussion of what they knew had brought him to Paris.

At dinner he couldn't decide whether Honoria was most like him or her mother. Fortunate if she didn't combine the traits of both that had brought them to disaster. A great wave of protectiveness went over him. He thought he knew what to do for her. He believed in character; he wanted to jump back a whole generation and trust in char-acter again as the eternally valuable element. Everything wore out.

He left soon after dinner, but not to go home. He was curious to see Paris by night with clearer and more judicious eyes than those of other days. He bought a *strapontin* for the Casino and watched Josephine Baker go through her chocolate arabesques.

After an hour he left and strolled toward Montmartre, up the Rue Pigalle into the Place Blanche. The rain had stopped and there were a few people in evening clothes disembarking from taxis in front of cabarets, and *cocottes* prowling singly or in pairs, and many Negroes. He passed a lighted door from which issued music, and stopped with the sense of familiarity; it was Bricktop's, where he had parted with so many hours and so much money. A few doors farther on he found another ancient rendezvous and incau-tiously put his head inside. Immediately an eager orchestra burst into sound, a pair of professional dancers leaped to their feet and a maître d'hôtel swooped toward him, cry-ing, "Crowd just arriving, sir!" But he withdrew quickly.

"You have to be damn drunk," he thought.

Zelli's was closed, the bleak and sinister cheap hotels surrounding it were dark; up   55
in the Rue Blanche there was more light and a local, colloquial French crowd. The Poet's Cave had disappeared, but the two great mouths of the Café of Heaven and the Café of Hell still yawned—even devoured, as he watched, the meager contents of a tourist bus—a German, a Japanese, and an American couple who glanced at him with frightened eyes.

So much for the effort and ingenuity of Montmartre. All the catering to vice and waste was on an utterly childish scale, and he suddenly realized the meaning of the word "dissipate"—to dissipate into thin air; to make nothing out of something. In the little hours of the night every move from place to place was an enormous human jump, an increase of paying for the privilege of slower and slower motion.

He remembered thousand-franc notes given to an orchestra for playing a single number, hundred-franc notes tossed to a doorman for calling a cab.

But it hadn't been given for nothing.

It had been given, even the most wildly squandered sum, as an offering to destiny that he might not remember the things most worth remembering, the things that now he would always remember—his child taken from his control, his wife escaped to a grave in Vermont.

In the glare of a *brasserie* a woman spoke to him. He bought her some eggs and 60 coffee, and then, eluding her encouraging stare, gave her a twenty-franc note and took a taxi to his hotel.

II

He woke upon a fine fall day—football weather. The depression of yesterday was gone and he liked the people on the streets. At noon he sat opposite Honoria at Le Grand Vatel, the only restaurant he could think of not reminiscent of champagne dinners and long luncheons that began at two and ended in a blurred and vague twilight.

"Now, how about vegetables? Oughtn't you to have some vegetables?"

"Well, yes."

"Here's *épinards* and *chou-fleur* and carrots and *haricots*."

"I'd like *chou-fleur*." 65

"Wouldn't you like to have two vegetables?"

"I usually only have one at lunch."

The waiter was pretending to be inordinately fond of children. "*Qu'elle est mignonne la petite? Elle parle exactement comme une Française.*"

"How about dessert? Shall we wait and see?"

The waiter disappeared. Honoria looked at her father expectantly. 70

"What are we going to do?"

"First, we're going to that toy store in the Rue Saint-Honoré and buy you anything you like. And then we're going to the vaudeville at the Empire."

She hesitated. "I like it about the vaudeville, but not the toy store."

"Why not?"

"Well, you brought me this doll." She had it with her. "And I've got lots of 75 things. And we're not rich any more, are we?"

"We never were. But today you are to have anything you want."

"All right," she agreed resignedly.

When there had been her mother and a French nurse he had been inclined to be strict; now he extended himself, reached out for a new tolerance; he must be both parents to her and not shut any of her out of communication.

"I want to get to know you," he said gravely. "First let me introduce myself. My name is Charles J. Wales, of Prague."

"Oh, daddy!" her voice cracked with laughter. 80

"And who are you, please?" he persisted, and she accepted a rôle immediately: "Honoria Wales, Rue Palatine, Paris."

"Married or single?"

"No, not married. Single."

He indicated the doll. "But I see you have a child, madame."

Unwilling to disinherit it, she took it to her heart and thought quickly: "Yes, I've   85
been married, but I'm not married now. My husband is dead."

He went on quickly, "And the child's name?"

"Simone. That's after my best friend at school."

"I'm very pleased that you're doing so well at school."

"I'm third this month," she boasted. "Elsie"—that was her cousin—"is only about
eighteenth, and Richard is about at the bottom."

"You like Richard and Elsie, don't you?"   90

"Oh, yes. I like Richard quite well and I like her all right."

Cautiously and casually he asked: "And Aunt Marion and Uncle Lincoln—
which do you like best?"

"Oh, Uncle Lincoln, I guess."

He was increasingly aware of her presence. As they came in, a murmur of ". . .
adorable" followed them, and now the people at the next table bent all their silences
upon her, staring as if she were something no more conscious than a flower.

"Why don't I live with you?" she asked suddenly. "Because mamma's dead?"   95

"You must stay here and learn more French. It would have been hard for daddy to
take care of you so well."

"I don't really need much taking care of any more. I do everything for myself."

Going out of the restaurant, a man and a woman unexpectedly hailed him.

"Well, the old Wales!"

"Hello there, Lorraine. . . . Dunc."   100

Sudden ghosts out of the past: Duncan Schaeffer, a friend from college. Lorraine
Quarrles, a lovely, pale blonde of thirty; one of a crowd who had helped them make
months into days in the lavish times of three years ago.

"My husband couldn't come this year," she said, in answer to his question. "We're
poor as hell. So he gave me two hundred a month and told me I could do my worst on
that. . . . This your little girl?"

"What about coming back and sitting down?" Duncan asked.

"Can't do it." He was glad for an excuse. As always, he felt Lorraine's passionate,
provocative attraction, but his own rhythm was different now.

"Well, how about dinner?" she asked.   105

"I'm not free. Give me your address and let me call you."

"Charlie, I believe you're sober," she said judicially. "I honestly believe he's sober,
Dunc. Pinch him and see if he's sober."

Charlie indicated Honoria with his head. They both laughed.

"What's your address?" said Duncan sceptically.

He hesitated, unwilling to give the name of his hotel.   110

"I'm not settled yet. I'd better call you. We're going to see the vaudeville at the
Empire."

"There! That's what I want to do," Lorraine said. "I want to see some clowns and
acrobats and jugglers. That's just what we'll do, Dunc."

"We've got to do an errand first," said Charlie. "Perhaps we'll see you there."

"All right, you snob. . . . Good-by, beautiful little girl."

"Good-by."   115

Honoria bobbed politely.

Somehow, an unwelcome encounter. They liked him because he was functioning, because he was serious; they wanted to see him, because he was stronger than they were now, because they wanted to draw a certain sustenance from his strength.

At the Empire, Honoria proudly refused to sit upon her father's folded coat. She was already an individual with a code of her own, and Charlie was more and more absorbed by the desire of putting a little of himself into her before she crystallized utterly. It was hopeless to try to know her in so short a time.

Between the acts they came upon Duncan and Lorraine in the lobby where the band was playing.

"Have a drink?" 120

"All right, but not up at the bar. We'll take a table."

"The perfect father."

Listening abstractedly to Lorraine, Charlie watched Honoria's eyes leave their table, and he followed them wistfully about the room, wondering what they saw. He met her glance and she smiled.

"I liked that lemonade," she said.

What had she said? What had he expected? Going home in a taxi afterward, he 125 pulled her over until her head rested against his chest.

"Darling, do you ever think about your mother?"

"Yes, sometimes," she answered vaguely.

"I don't want you to forget her. Have you got a picture of her?"

"Yes, I think so. Anyhow, Aunt Marion has. Why don't you want me to forget her?"

"She loved you very much." 130

"I loved her too."

They were silent for a moment.

"Daddy, I want to come and live with you," she said suddenly.

His heart leaped; he had wanted it to come like this.

"Aren't you perfectly happy?" 135

"Yes, but I love you better than anybody. And you love me better than anybody, don't you, now that mummy's dead?"

"Of course I do. But you won't always like me best, honey. You'll grow up and meet somebody your own age and go marry him and forget you ever had a daddy."

"Yes, that's true," she agreed tranquilly.

He didn't go in. He was coming back at nine o'clock and he wanted to keep himself fresh and new for the thing he must say then.

"When you're safe inside, just show yourself in that window." 140

"All right. Good-by, dads, dads, dads, dads."

He waited in the dark street until she appeared, all warm and glowing, in the window above and kissed her fingers out into the night.

III

They were waiting. Marion sat behind the coffee service in a dignified black dinner dress that just faintly suggested mourning. Lincoln was walking up and down with the animation of one who had already been talking. They were as anxious as he was to get into the question. He opened it almost immediately:

"I suppose you know what I want to see you about—why I really came to Paris."

Marion played with the black stars on her necklace and frowned.   145

"I'm awfully anxious to have a home," he continued. "And I'm awfully anxious to have Honoria in it. I appreciate your taking in Honoria for her mother's sake, but things have changed now"—he hesitated and then continued more forcibly—"changed radically with me, and I want to ask you to reconsider the matter. It would be silly for me to deny that about three years ago I was acting badly——"

Marion looked up at him with hard eyes.

"—but all that's over. As I told you, I haven't had more than a drink a day for over a year, and I take that drink deliberately, so that the idea of alcohol won't get too big in my imagination. You see the idea?"

"No," said Marion succinctly.

"It's a sort of stunt I set myself. It keeps the matter in proportion."   150

"I get you," said Lincoln. "You don't want to admit it's got any attraction for you."

"Something like that. Sometimes I forget and don't take it. But I try to take it. Anyhow, I couldn't afford to drink in my position. The people I represent are more than satisfied with what I've done, and I'm bringing my sister over from Burlington to keep house for me, and I want awfully to have Honoria too. You know that even when her mother and I weren't getting along well we never let anything that happened touch Honoria. I know she's fond of me and I know I'm able to take care of her and—well, there you are. How do you feel about it?"

He knew that now he would have to take a beating. It would last an hour or two hours, and it would be difficult, but if he modulated his inevitable resentment to the chastened attitude of the reformed sinner, he might win his point in the end.

Keep your temper, he told himself. You don't want to be justified. You want Honoria.

Lincoln spoke first: "We've been talking it over ever since we got your letter last   155
month. We're happy to have Honoria here. She's a dear little thing, and we're glad to be able to help her, but of course that isn't the question——"

Marion interrupted suddenly. "How long are you going to stay sober, Charlie?" she asked.

"Permanently, I hope."

"How can anybody count on that?"

"You know I never did drink heavily until I gave up business and came over here with nothing to do. Then Helen and I began to run around with——"

"Please leave Helen out of it. I can't bear to hear you talk about her like that."   160

He stared at her grimly; he had never been certain how fond of each other the sisters were in life.

"My drinking only lasted about a year and a half—from the time we came over until I—collapsed."

"It was time enough."

"It was time enough," he agreed.

"My duty is entirely to Helen," she said. "I try to think what she would have   165
wanted me to do. Frankly, from the night you did that terrible thing you haven't really existed for me. I can't help that. She was my sister."

"Yes."

"When she was dying she asked me to look out for Honoria. If you hadn't been in a sanitarium then, it might have helped matters."

He had no answer.

"I'll never in my life be able to forget the morning when Helen knocked at my door, soaked to the skin and shivering, and said you'd locked her out."

Charlie gripped the sides of the chair. This was more difficult than he expected; he   170
wanted to launch out into a long expostulation and explanation, but he only said: "The night I locked her out—" and she interrupted, "I don't feel up to going over that again."

After a moment's silence Lincoln said: "We're getting off the subject. You want Marion to set aside her legal guardianship and give you Honoria. I think the main point for her is whether she has confidence in you or not."

"I don't blame Marion," Charlie said slowly, "but I think she can have entire confidence in me. I had a good record up to three years ago. Of course, it's within human possibilities I might go wrong any time. But if we wait much longer I'll lose Honria's childhood and my chance for a home." He shook his head, "I'll simply lose her, don't you see?"

"Yes, I see," said Lincoln.

"Why didn't you think of all this before?" Marion asked.

"I suppose I did, from time to time, but Helen and I were getting along badly.   175
When I consented to the guardianship, I was flat on my back in a sanitarium and the market had cleaned me out. I knew I'd acted badly, and I thought if it would bring any peace to Helen, I'd agree to anything. But now it's different. I'm functioning, I'm behaving damn well, so far as——"

"Please don't swear at me," Marion said.

He looked at her, startled. With each remark the force of her dislike became more and more apparent. She had built up all her fear of life into one wall and faced it toward him. This trivial reproof was possibly the result of some trouble with the cook several hours before. Charlie became increasingly alarmed at leaving Honoria in this atmosphere of hostility against himself; sooner or later it would come out, in a word here, a shake of the head there, and some of that distrust would be irrevocably implanted in Honoria. But he pulled his temper down out of his face and shut it up inside him; he had won a point, for Lincoln realized the absurdity of Marion's remark and asked her lightly since when she had objected to the word "damn."

"Another thing," Charlie said: "I'm able to give her certain advantages now. I'm going to take a French governess to Prague with me. I've got a lease on a new apartment——"

He stopped, realizing that he was blundering. They couldn't be expected to accept with equanimity the fact that his income was again twice as large as their own.

"I suppose you can give her more luxuries than we can," said Marion. "When you   180
were throwing away money we were living along watching every ten francs. . . . I suppose you'll start doing it again."

"Oh, no," he said. "I've learned. I worked hard for ten years, you know—until I got lucky in the market, like so many people. Terribly lucky. It didn't seem any use working any more, so I quit. It won't happen again."

There was a long silence. All of them felt their nerves straining, and for the first time in a year Charlie wanted a drink. He was sure now that Lincoln Peters wanted him to have his child.

Marion shuddered suddenly; part of her saw that Charlie's feet were planted on the earth now, and her own maternal feeling recognized the naturalness of his desire; but she had lived for a long time with a prejudice—a prejudice founded on a curious disbelief in her sister's happiness, and which, in the shock of one terrible night, had turned to hatred for him. It had all happened at a point in her life where the discouragement of ill health and adverse circumstances made it necessary for her to believe in tangible villainy and a tangible villain.

"I can't help what I think!" she cried out suddenly. "How much you were responsible for Helen's death, I don't know. It's something you'll have to square with your own conscience."

An electric current of agony surged through him; for a moment he was almost on   185
his feet, an unuttered sound echoing in his throat. He hung on to himself for a moment, another moment.

"Hold on there," said Lincoln uncomfortably. "I never thought you were responsible for that."

"Helen died of heart trouble," Charlie said dully.

"Yes, heart trouble." Marion spoke as if the phrase had another meaning for her.

Then, in the flatness that followed her outburst, she saw him plainly and she knew he had somehow arrived at control over the situation. Glancing at her husband, she found no help from him, and as abruptly as if it were a matter of no importance, she threw up the sponge.

"Do what you like!" she cried, springing up from her chair. "She's your child. I'm   190
not the person to stand in your way. I think if it were my child I'd rather see her—" She managed to check herself. "You two decide it. I can't stand this. I'm sick. I'm going to bed."

She hurried from the room; after a moment Lincoln said:

"This has been a hard day for her. You know how strongly she feels—" His voice was almost apologetic: "When a woman gets an idea in her head."

"Of course."

"It's going to be all right. I think she sees now that you—can provide for the child, and so we can't very well stand in your way or Honoria's way."

"Thank you, Lincoln."   195

"I'd better go along and see how she is."

"I'm going."

He was still trembling when he reached the street, but a walk down the Rue Bonaparte to the quais set him up, and as he crossed the Seine, fresh and new by the quai lamps, he felt exultant. But back in his room he couldn't sleep. The image of Helen haunted him. Helen whom he had loved so until they had senselessly begun to abuse each other's love, tear it into shreds. On that terrible February night that Marion remembered so vividly, a slow quarrel had gone on for hours. There was a scene at the Florida, and then he attempted to take her home, and then she kissed young Webb at a table; after that there was what she had hysterically said. When he arrived home alone he turned the key in the lock in wild anger. How could he know she would arrive an hour later alone, that there would be a snowstorm in which she wandered about in slippers, too confused to find a taxi? Then the aftermath, her escaping pneumonia by a miracle, and all the attendant horror. They were "reconciled," but that was the beginning of the end, and Marion, who had seen with her own eyes and who imagined it to be one of many scenes from her sister's martyrdom, never forgot.

Going over it again brought Helen nearer, and in the white, soft light that steals upon half sleep near morning he found himself talking to her again. She said that he was perfectly right about Honoria and that she wanted Honoria to be with him. She said she was glad he was being good and doing better. She said a lot of other things—very friendly things—but she was in a swing in a white dress, and swinging faster and faster all the time, so that at the end he could not hear clearly all that she said.

IV

He woke up feeling happy. The door of the world was open again. He made plans, vistas, futures for Honoria and himself, but suddenly he grew sad, remembering all the plans he and Helen had made. She had not planned to die. The present was the thing—work to do and someone to love. But not to love too much, for he knew the injury that a father can do to a daughter or a mother to a son by attaching them too closely: afterward, out in the world, the child would seek in the marriage partner the same blind tenderness and, failing probably to find it, turn against love and life.

It was another bright, crisp day. He called Lincoln Peters at the bank where he worked and asked if he could count on taking Honoria when he left for Prague. Lincoln agreed that there was no reason for delay. One thing—the legal guardianship. Marion wanted to retain that a while longer. She was upset by the whole matter, and it would oil things if she felt that the situation was still in her control for another year. Charlie agreed, wanting only the tangible, visible child.

Then the question of a governess. Charlie sat in a gloomy agency and talked to a cross Béarnaise and to a buxon Breton peasant, neither of whom he could have endured. There were others whom he would see tomorrow.

He lunched with Lincoln Peters at Griffons, trying to keep down his exultation.

"There's nothing quite like your own child," Lincoln said. "But you understand how Marion feels too."

"She's forgotten how hard I worked for seven years there," Charlie said. "She just remembers one night."

"There's another thing." Lincoln hesitated. "While you and Helen were tearing around Europe throwing money away, we were just getting along. I didn't touch any of the prosperity because I never got ahead enough to carry anything but my insurance. I think Marion felt there was some kind of injustice in it—you not even working toward the end, and getting richer and richer."

"It went just as quick as it came," said Charlie.

"Yes, a lot of it stayed in the hands of *chasseurs* and saxophone players and maitres d'hôtel—well, the big party's over now. I just said that to explain Marion's feeling about those crazy years. If you drop in about six o'clock tonight before Marion's too tired, we'll settle the details on the spot."

Back at his hotel, Charlie found a *pneumatique* that had been redirected from the Ritz bar where Charlie had left his address for the purpose of finding a certain man.

DEAR CHARLIE: You were so strange when we saw you the other day that I wondered if I did something to offend you. If so, I'm not conscious of it. In fact, I have thought about you too much for the last year, and it's always been in the back of my mind that I might see you if I came over here. We *did* have such good times that crazy spring, like the night you and I stole the butcher's tricycle, and the time we tried to call on the president and you had the old derby rim and the wire cane. Everybody seems so old lately, but I don't feel old a bit. Couldn't we

200

205

get together some time today for old time's sake? I've got a vile hang-over for the moment, but will be feeling better this afternoon and will look for you about five in the sweat-shop at the Ritz.

Always devotedly,

LORRAINE.

His first feeling was one of awe that he had actually, in his mature years, stolen a   210
tricycle and pedalled Lorraine all over the Étoile between the small hours and dawn. In retrospect it was a nightmare. Locking out Helen didn't fit in with any other act of his life, but the tricycle incident did—it was one of many. How many weeks or months of dissipation to arrive at that condition of utter irresponsibility?

He tried to picture how Lorraine had appeared to him then—very attractive; Helen was unhappy about it, though she said nothing. Yesterday, in the restaurant, Lorraine had seemed trite, blurred, worn away. He emphatically did not want to see her, and he was glad Alix had not given away his hotel address. It was a relief to think, instead, of Honoria, to think of Sundays spent with her and of saying good morning to her and of knowing she was there in his house at night, drawing her breath in the darkness.

At five he took a taxi and bought presents for all the Peters—a piquant cloth doll, a box of Roman soldiers, flowers for Marion, big linen handkerchiefs for Lincoln.

He saw, when he arrived in the apartment, that Marion had accepted the inevitable. She greeted him now as though he were a recalcitrant member of the family, rather than a menacing outsider. Honoria had been told she was going; Charlie was glad to see that her tact made her conceal her excessive happiness. Only on his lap did she whisper her delight and the question "When?" before she slipped away with the other children.

He and Marion were alone for a minute in the room, and on an impulse he spoke out boldly:

"Family quarrels are bitter things. They don't go according to any rules. They're   215
not like aches or wounds; they're more like splits in the skin that won't heal because there's not enough material. I wish you and I could be on better terms."

"Some things are hard to forget," she answered. "It's a question of confidence." There was no answer to this and presently she asked, "When do you propose to take her?"

"As soon as I can get a governess. I hoped the day after tomorrow."

"That's impossible. I've got to get her things in shape. Not before Saturday."

He yielded. Coming back into the room, Lincoln offered him a drink.

"I'll take my daily whisky," he said.   220

It was warm here, it was a home, people together by a fire. The children felt very safe and important; the mother and father were serious, watchful. They had things to do for the children more important than his visit here. A spoonful of medicine was, after all, more important than the strained relations between Marion and himself. They were not dull people, but they were very much in the grip of life and circumstances. He wondered if he couldn't do something to get Lincoln out of his rut at the bank.

A long peal at the door-bell; the *bonne à tout faire* passed through and went down the corridor. The door opened upon another long ring, and then voices, and the three in the salon looked up expectantly; Lincoln moved to bring the corridor within his range of vision, and Marion rose. Then the maid came back along the corridor, closely followed by the voices, which developed under the light into Duncan Schaeffer and Lorraine Quarrles.

They were gay, they were hilarious, they were roaring with laughter. For a moment Charlie was astounded; unable to understand how they ferreted out the Peters' address.

"Ah-h-h!" Duncan wagged his finger roguishly at Charlie. "Ah-h-h!"

They both slid down another cascade of laughter. Anxious and at a loss, Charlie shook hands with them quickly and presented them to Lincoln and Marion. Marion nodded, scarcely speaking. She had drawn back a step toward the fire; her little girl stood beside her, and Marion put an arm about her shoulder.

With growing annoyance at the intrusion, Charlie waited for them to explain themselves. After some concentration Duncan said:

"We came to invite you out to dinner. Lorraine and I insist that all this chi-chi, cagy business 'bout your address got to stop."

Charlie came closer to them, as if to force them backward down the corridor.

"Sorry, but I can't. Tell me where you'll be and I'll phone you in half an hour."

This made no impression. Lorraine sat down suddenly on the side of a chair, and focussing her eyes on Richard, cried, "Oh, what a nice little boy! Come here, little boy." Richard glanced at his mother, but did not move. With a perceptible shrug of her shoulders, Lorraine turned back to Charlie:

"Come and dine. Sure your cousins won' mine. See you so sel'om. Or solemn."

"I can't," said Charlie sharply. "You two have dinner and I'll phone you."

Her voice became suddenly unpleasant. "All right, we'll go. But I remember once when you hammered on my door at four A.M. I was enough of a good sport to give you a drink. Come on, Dunc."

Still in slow motion, with blurred, angry faces, with uncertain feet, they retired along the corridor.

"Good night," Charlie said.

"Good night!" responded Lorraine emphatically.

When he went back into the salon Marion had not moved, only now her son was standing in the circle of her other arm. Lincoln was still swinging Honoria back and forth like a pendulum from side to side.

"What an outrage!" Charlie broke out. "What an absolute outrage!"

Neither of them answered. Charlie dropped into an armchair, picked up his drink, set it down again and said:

"People I haven't seen for two years having the colossal nerve——"

He broke off. Marion had made the sound "Oh!" in one swift, furious breath, turned her body from him with a jerk and left the room.

Lincoln set down Honoria carefully.

"You children go in and start your soup," he said, and when they obeyed, he said to Charlie:

"Marion's not well and she can't stand shocks. That kind of people make her really physically sick."

"I didn't tell them to come here. They wormed your name out of somebody. They deliberately——"

"Well, it's too bad. It doesn't help matters. Excuse me a minute."

Left alone, Charlie sat tense in his chair. In the next room he could hear the children eating, talking in monosyllables, already oblivious to the scene between their elders. He heard a murmur of conversation from a farther room and then the ticking bell of a telephone receiver picked up, and in a panic he moved to the other side of the room and out of earshot.

225

230

235

240

245

In a minute Lincoln came back. "Look here, Charlie. I think we'd better call off dinner for tonight. Marion's in bad shape."

"Is she angry with me?"

"Sort of," he said, almost roughly. "She's not strong and——"   250

"You mean she's changed her mind about Honoria?"

"She's pretty bitter right now. I don't know. You phone me at the bank tomorrow."

"I wish you'd explain to her I never dreamed these people would come here. I'm just as sore as you are."

"I couldn't explain anything to her now."

Charlie got up. He took his coat and hat and started down the corridor. Then he   255 opened the door of the dining room and said in a strange voice, "Good night, children."

Honoria rose and ran around the table to hug him.

"Good night, sweetheart," he said vaguely, and then trying to make his voice more tender, trying to conciliate something, "Good night, dear children."

V

Charlie went directly to the Ritz bar with the furious idea of finding Lorraine and Duncan, but they were not there, and he realized that in any case there was nothing he could do. He had not touched his drink at the Peters', and now he ordered a whisky-and-soda. Paul came over to say hello.

"It's a great change," he said sadly. "We do about half the business we did. So many fellows I hear about back in the States lost everything, maybe not in the first crash, but then in the second. Your friend George Hardt lost every cent, I hear. Are you back in the States?"

"No, I'm in business in Prague."   260

"I heard that you lost a lot in the crash."

"I did," and he added grimly, "but I lost everything I wanted in the boom."

"Selling short."

"Something like that."

Again the memory of those days swept over him like a nightmare—the people   265 they had met travelling; then people who couldn't add a row of figures or speak a coherent sentence. The little man Helen had consented to dance with at the ship's party, who had insulted her ten feet from the table; the women and girls carried screaming with drink or drugs out of public places——

—The men who locked their wives out in the snow, because the snow of twenty-nine wasn't real snow. If you didn't want it to be snow, you just paid some money.

He went to the phone and called the Peters' apartment; Lincoln answered.

"I called up because this thing is on my mind. Has Marion said anything definite?"

"Marion's sick," Lincoln answered shortly. "I know this thing isn't altogether your fault, but I can't have her go to pieces about it. I'm afraid we'll have to let it slide for six months; I can't take the chance of working her up to this state again."

"I see."   270

"I'm sorry, Charlie."

He went back to his table. His whiskey glass was empty, but he shook his head when Alix looked at it questioningly. There wasn't much he could do now except send Honoria some things; he would send her a lot of things tomorrow. He thought rather angrily that this was just money—he had given so many people money. . . .

"No, no more," he said to another waiter. "What do I owe you?"

He would come back some day; they couldn't make him pay forever. But he wanted his child, and nothing was much good now, beside that fact. He wasn't young any more, with a lot of nice thoughts and dreams to have by himself. He was absolutely sure Helen wouldn't have wanted him to be so alone.

"Babylon Revisited" is one of the best well-known stories of F. Scott Fitzgerald, an influential American writer of the early twentieth century. In this story, Fitzgerald articulates the tragic experience of a flawed father attempting to reconcile himself with his daughter. It is a sad and compelling tale of failed dreams, wild excess, themes of the possibility of forgiveness, and the importance of fate in life.

Any interpretation of "Babylon Revisited" necessarily involves making judgments about the main character, Charlie Wales, as well as evaluating other major and minor characters. What are some of the steps you might take in interpreting this story? The answer will be dictated by the kind of approach, or critical perspective, that you bring to the work.

If you take a formalist approach, you might focus on the structure of the story and how the parts seem to fit together. You would examine very closely the words and actions of all the characters, but particularly of Charlie Wales. Your "close reading" would assume an organic integrity to the work; that is, everything in the story is tightly interconnected and absolutely essential to the narrative as a whole. Every image, metaphor, statement, and action is irreducible in coming together to give a meaning. The story might be summarized as "Charlie Wales' sad attempt to obtain custody of his daughter as he is thwarted by the ghosts of his own past irresponsible behavior coming out of the closet."

In an ethical approach to the story, you might see it quite differently. Charlie's fate is determined by his encounters with other important characters: Marion and Lincoln Peters, Honoria, Duncan Schaeffer, Lorraine Quarrles, and of course the ghost of Helen, Charlie's wife. Working from the perspective of "civic criticism" and personal responsibility, you might read the story as a commentary on the role of the individual (Charlie Wales) and the larger community around him, ranging from his troubled relatives, Lincoln and Marion, to his troubling "friends" from the past, Lorraine and Duncan. A civic perspective might examine Charlie's duties to his daughter, his relatives, and to the larger social order.

A cultural reading of the story might take into account some of the general economic and social conditions of the narrative: the wild swings of the stock market in the 1920s, social and sexual decadence in Paris, expatriation movements, and so forth. A new historicist perspective might look at smaller historical contexts: the setting of the Ritz bar as a hub of social and business life in the 1920s, the emergence of Prague as a center of business after the stock market crash, the significance of Charlie attending a performance of Josephine Baker, a symbol of Parisian decadence, and Charlie taking Honoria to see vaudeville at the Empire. F. Scott Fitzgerald's life experiences, including his carefree Paris days, surely played a role in the writing of the story. Many historical elements, large and small, play a role in shaping the interpretation of the story.

A psychological reading of "Babylon Revisited" might focus on the psychological dimensions of Charlie's stormy relationship with his wife Helen, as well as Charlie's evolving relationship with his daughter. Other psychoanalytic issues might include Charlie's attempts to come to grips with demons of the past (represented by Duncan, Lorraine, Alix, and Paul), as well as a range of desires, conscious and subconscious. A Freudian reading, for example, might examine Charlie giving Alix a note with the Peters' home address to pass along to Duncan as a subconscious attempt to remain connected with his days of debauchery (and thereby undermine his attempt to regain custody of his daughter). This powerful short story offers a rich weave of psychological issues for interpretation.

A feminist reading of the story might probe various images of the women in the narrative: Lorraine as a bothersome drunk, Marion as an unforgiving and narrow-minded shrew, Helen as a sympathetic victim of Charlie's excesses, and Honoria as an emphatic child caught between relatives in conflict. Further, a feminist reading might examine how the story is clearly told from Charlie's perspective and might consider how Charlie (and some of the other characters) represent images with explicit gender implications.

An ideological critic might look at the story in terms of how the material world is represented. Western capitalism (and its ups and downs) is a major topic in the narrative, as chronicled by Charlie's rise and fall on the economic ladder according to the dictates of the larger world economic order. Other characters, such as Lincoln and Marion, are depicted as representatives of the struggling middle class. And yet other characters, such as Duncan and Lorraine, appear to be insulated from the ups and downs of market conditions. The issues of money and financial success play major roles in many Fitzgerald stories, and "Babylon Revisited" is no exception.

A deconstructive critic reader might find much to say about this complex short story. Such a critic might begin with the opening sentence, which is a question about a character, Mr. Campbell, who plays no further role in the story, yet functions as the beginning of the end of Charlie's attempt to regain his daughter. The Ritz bar is clearly a strategic metaphor representing a way of life (past and present), a scene of triumph and failure, and a symbol of opulence and degeneration. Financial records at the Ritz represent the larger theme of "accounting" and "reckoning." Just as patrons reckon (or fail to reckon) their accounts, Charlie attempts to reckon his account with Lincoln and Marion, yet is thwarted when Duncan and Lorraine attempt to "reckon" with Charlie. A deconstructive critic could say much about the open-endedness of the story, including its ending in which Charlie speculates about what Helen would have wanted him to do. The conditional state of Charlie's mind is a metaphor for the uncertainty that surrounds him.

A reader-response critic considers his or her response to the short story, particularly the effect that the narrative has on him or her. This kind of reading is called a *subjective response* and it involves a reader's forestructure (or personal background) intersecting with the story. A reader-response critic allows his or her feelings, desires, emotions, and other interests to play a major role in interpreting the story. (And you might look at Charlie's background and examine how his "forestructure" has evolved. Charlie has changed, at least in his mind, from an irresponsible husband and father to a successful businessman who now leads a life of sobriety and productivity.) A reader-response approach does not suggest that all interpretations are equally convincing and rigorous, but suggests that life experiences play a role in articulating an interpretation that is grounded in the literary text as well as in the reader's life.

General Steps in Literary Interpretation

1) As you read a work for the first time, take notes about distinctive features of the text (qualities of characterization, critical turns in plot development, tone, voice, striking metaphors, and so forth).
2) After you have become familiar with plot, characters, and other features of the work, decide which interpretive strategies you wish to employ and reread the work with these tools in mind.
3) Once you have taken notes identifying qualities in the work that relate to the critical perspective, start to organize your interpretation in outline form.
4) After completing your outline, look for connections between your specific points (textual evidence) and your overall sense of the meaning of the text from your critical perspective.
5) Look for specific components of the text that do not fit in with your overall interpretation. Identify these issues as points for further inquiry. No interpretation is ever complete or final.

ELECTRONIC RESOURCES FOR F. SCOTT FITZGERALD

http://www.sc.edu/fitzgerald/index.html.   F. Scott Fitzgerald Centenary Homepage. Offers a guide to biographical, bibliographical, publishing, and textual information, and updates about recent reprintings of Fitzgerald's work. Also includes recordings of Fitzgerald reading poetry.

http://libweb2.princeton.edu/rbsc2/portfolio/fs1/index.html.   A very detailed guide to and criticism of Fitzgerald's life and work. There are dozens of links, including one to photographs from all phases of Fitzgerald's life.

http://www.angelfire.com/co/pscst/fitzgerald.html. Additional biographical information on F. Scott Fitzgerald.

http://www.angelfire.com/co/pscst/index.html.   An index with links to social, economic,
cultural, historical, and architectural aspects of American culture in the 1920s.

http://www.pbs.org/kteh/amstorytellers. A guide to film, video, and PBS documen-
taries on F. Scott Fitzgerald.

http://killdevilhill.com/fitzgeraldchat/wwwboard.html. F. Scott Fitzgerald bulletin
board.

http://www.netins.net/showcase/tdlarson/fsflinks.html. F. Scott Fitzgerald links page
(contains numerous links to critical, biographical, and cultural information).

http://infoshare1.princeton.edu:2003/libraries/firestone/rbsc/aids/fitz.html. An index to
all of the Fitzgerald papers at Princeton University.

To subscribe to the F. Scott Fitzgerald listserv, send an email message to *Majordomo@
mtu.edu*. In the body of the message write *subscribe Scottf-L*.

chapter 2

Reader-Response Criticism

Read anything I write for the pleasure of reading it. Whatever else you find
will be the measure of what you brought to the reading.

—Ernest Hemingway

Reader-response criticism is an approach to interpretation that locates the center of meaning in the reader and is based on the principle that each reader is motivated to better understand himself or herself through literature. You have seen that some critical approaches emphasize the literary text above all else (formalist criticism, for example), whereas other schools tend to emphasize references outside the text (historical criticism, for example). Reader-response criticism places meaning in the intersection where reader and text meet. All texts contain "blanks," and it is up to the reader to "fill them in" according to his or her life experiences. The reader's background is a significant frame of reference, as it combines with the energy of the literary text. You might say that the reader's forestructure, or cumulative personal experiences, catalyzes the text and makes it come to life in ways that are unique to each reader. Your reading consciousness changes and develops in directions that are often inexplicable when it interacts with works of literature.

As a reader-response critic, it is important to remember that the meaning you generate from a text is the result of your past meeting the present of the literary text. Whereas some schools of criticism (formalism, for example) ask you to ignore your intuitive responses to literature, reader-response criticism encourages you to release your instinctive responses, because you and your memory are strategic elements in the act of interpretation. Your past and your life experiences bring to life the present-time state of the literary text, no matter when it was written. Your personal experience and cultural environment provide the context for a "new" reading of the text. How you respond—intuitively, spontaneously, emotionally, and subjectively—to the work will depend on your ability to let your historical experience meet the text. Your interpretation is a result of the conversation between your personal past and the present time of your reading of the literary text. And just as you are never a fixed person, unable to change and develop, a literary work is not a "fixed" entity. It "changes," at least in terms of generating meaning, as a part of the dynamic interpretive process.

In Chapter 1 you observed the characterization of Charlie Wales, a fictive individual with an evolving forestructure. In the present time of the story, he is not the same person that he was in the wild Paris days of the 1920s, which come back to haunt him in the present time of the narrative. Other characters, such as the Peters, Duncan, Lorraine, and even Honoria, reveal a present-time mindset that also reflects past experiences. You too, in your interpretation of this story, profit by your evolving forestructure in responding to this powerful tale of sin and repentance. If you have had personal experience with a troubled marriage, custody conflict, or any of the other major issues in the story, you will respond differently than if you had no such experience.

The act of reading from a reader-response perspective involves our continually asking questions of ourselves during the process of reading. The process of "questioning while reading" is continuously triggered by elements in the text that evoke personal memories. In some texts, such as the primary reading for this chapter (Hemingway's "Indian Camp"), there is explicit attention given to a major character's evolving forestructure. This character is Nick, a doctor's son who experiences life in an Indian camp as he accompanies his father and uncle on a medical mission. What is particularly distinctive about reader-response criticism is its emphasis on the reader's bringing his or her "nonliterary" experiences into the arena of interpretation. To put it another way, our life experiences "make real" our literary experiences by bringing them into our personal lives. The act of reading is just as much the process of our entering literature as literature entering us. And reading literature is like many experiences in life—we are constantly in the process of making adjustments.

You might ask, "Does this kind of reading not make all acts of interpretation totally personal or subjective?" The answer is both yes and no. Yes, of course all readers have unique life experiences, and those memories will trigger individualized responses. However, many of our memories, the substance of our forestructures, involve the kinds of experiences that fall into general categories, which are not ours alone. All college readers have experienced some common rites of passage (reaching puberty, experiencing educational growth, perhaps falling in love, and so forth). Just like Nick in "Indian Camp," all of us have memories of experiences at the hand of a parent or other adult in our lives. It is these events (individual experiences that fall into common categories) that unite communities of readers. Our unique experiences make us what we are as individuals, but our collective experiences as members of cultures bring us together as readers with overlapping cultural experiences and make us members of a community of readers.

All readers of literature are concerned with values and themes in a text, and a reader engaged in reader-response criticism is no different. Indeed, the act of reading literature is a way of "ordering reality," of seeking stability in a world that may seem to teem with chaos. Literature often offers more structure than may be found in the average person's daily life. The act of reading may fill in some of the blanks in the reader's life. Although the personal experience of the reader is the triggering mechanism for searching for values and themes, those elements are located in the text, energized by the stored experiences of the reader. The images any reader carries around in his or her head are colorized by specific textual cues and events. (It is equally important to say that elements in a text colorize our images and memories.) The important issue is that reader-response reading is highly interactive.

The act of reading is necessarily an experience of always making adjustments to the text. Readers actively engage the text at multiple levels, because it is the nature of any literary text to open itself up to a wide range of interpretations. It might be suggested that readers recreate a text when they draw upon literary language and engage their interpretive matrix of personal experience and skills of formal analysis. To put it another way, meanings are made by readers, not found or discovered as if they were mysterious treasures buried deep within works of literature. A reader-response critic depends on his or her active participation in the creation of meaning.

As most readers of literature intuitively know, the process of interpretation is not stable and "set in stone." Our understandings (and the plural noun is important) are always in a state of development and change. Our moods and emotions will differ according to varying reading contexts. Our intellectual "filters" are always in a state of flux because of our development as readers. Even professional readers of literature, such as teachers, arrive at interpretations that differ from their own previous interpretations of the same material, due to changing conditions within themselves. The text remains stable—the words do not change—but we, as human beings, are never stagnant. Inevitably, we do change, and we bring these changes to all that we read. For example, when I first read Hemingway's "Up in Michigan" as a teenager, I was struck by the raw sensationalism of the story. As an experienced reader years later, I came to see nuances and subtleties in the narrative that I could not have perceived earlier because of my inexperience.

The acknowledgment that the more we read, the more we grow and develop does not mean that our interpretations are necessarily inconsistent and are always subject to our latest whims. Indeed, the changes we experience internally from time to time may evoke only subtle differences in interpretations. As we read (or take part in almost any language activity), we are constantly in a state of anticipation. When we engage a friend or stranger in conversation, our minds anticipate what the other person may say. We often quickly "program" ourselves to respond in certain ways according to the circumstances of the conversation. The same process occurs in reading literature, especially from the perspective of reader-response. We anticipate certain plot developments, character behavior, consistency of place and setting, a continuity of language style, and so forth. Again, the act of anticipation is the merging of our past experiences with the present time of our reading. If you know that you will read a story by Edgar Allan Poe, for example, you will probably anticipate certain conventions, such as gothic settings, strange characters, and predictable effects, such as feelings of fear and horror.

This chapter emphasizes your personal experiences in interpretation, but it is important to remember that personal experience is more than a collection of memories that represent fragments of our lives. Out of these many experiences, large and small, comes something like a "global perspective," or "world view," of human experience. As our particular experiences accrue, we develop attitudes toward many issues. Some individuals call this mindset our personal philosophy. What we call it is not important, but it is significant that when we come to a literary text as college readers, we bring our personal construction of "how things are." Reading literature helps us to "order reality" and make sense of human experience. (This is one reason readers often sympathize intensely with one or more characters. As we identify with literary characters, we sometimes live out their/our lives in the combined world of fiction/reality. As we follow their words and actions, we find our thinking, and perhaps our way of living, changing, sometimes strategically.)

If we are in earnest about developing intellectually, we will allow our mindsets to change and grow as we become exposed to new ideas, some of which we embrace and others, reject. This evolving world view is the sum total of our forestructures at any given time. To read Mark Twain's *Huckleberry Finn* at age 15 is usually a very different experience than reading it at age 25 or 45. We are different persons at different ages, and so too is the act of interpreting. What may seem fresh and straightforward to a younger reader may appear to be ironic and satiric to a more mature reader, as in the experience of reading James Joyce's *Portrait of an Artist as a Young Man*. (And one may well ask if the recently discovered irony and satire in this novel are as much in the reader's mindset as in the literary work!) In many important ways, experiences in literature can become our personal experiences and can change our lives in significant ways. Reading promotes a process of analysis and evaluation that makes us different—and more sophisticated—readers of all discourse.

Indeed, reading (and writing) involves confronting the text (whether a literary one or your interpretive text) as a series of "codes" that continually interact with one another. The code of the literary text changes as you read and confront it with your experience. The code of your essay changes as you create and edit text, in search of ways to improve its articulation and persuasiveness.

Readers are not the only part of the interpretive process that includes a world view. Literary texts, too, often reveal a mindset, a way of living, a philosophy of life that is sometimes quite explicit in some writers and very subtle in others. Ernest Hemingway, the author of "Indian Camp," is often associated with a certain philosophy, a "Hemingway code of living." Some literary works are quite explicit in their views. Upton Sinclair's novel *The Jungle*, for example, exposes abuses in the meatpacking industry. James Joyce's *Portrait of the Artist as a Young Man* chronicles the struggles of a young man as he thinks deeply about his family, religion, and country. All of these works produce certain effects on the reader, although specific effects will vary from person to person. Sinclair's novel may promote disgust and anger toward the meatpacking industry for its history of employee abuses. Joyce's novel may produce feelings of melancholy and nostaglia in some readers. Hemingway's story may evoke early childhood memories of a fear of the unknown. The specific effects of a work of literature depend significantly upon the reader's life experiences.

Reading from a reader-response perspective assumes that we are members of reading communities. Although your life experiences are unique from other readers in your class, you do share much in common as members of a community. Your instructor may ask the community to look for certain issues in an assigned reading. Further, the instructor may have lectured to the class about important trends, values, and themes that he or she finds in the text. Everyone in the class is reading for a common purpose: the interpretation of a literary text (although these interpretations will differ, of course). Class discussion of literary texts often provide a forum in which multiple readers form a consensus about certain issues in an interpretation, although not always. (For example, Macbeth, as a character, is usually read as a tragic character, but the character of Hamlet is sometimes interpreted as someone falling short of tragic status. He is arguably a different kind of tragic character than Macbeth.)

What is important to remember about reading communities is that the success of an interpretation depends upon a reader's ability to convince other members of the community (even if it is only one reader, the instructor) that an interpretation has credibility. This means that an interpretation must present textual evidence in support of a particular reading. Although a reader's life experiences are the triggering mechanism for generating meanings, the persuasiveness of interpretations depends upon readings that are well-organized, textually illustrated, sufficiently developed, and written (or spoken) in language that is clear, precise, and convincing. All interpreters of literature (even those interpreting only for themselves) have an obligation to explain meaning that is understandable and stands up to questioning. (The very best interpreters are often the most rigorous questioners of their own interpretations.)

The interpretation of literature, whether for personal pleasure and enrichment or for more formal reasons, such as educational advancement, calls attention to the fact that interpretation generates knowledge. A strategic assumption of reader-response interpretation involves the belief that knowledge is generated, not "found." An important underlying premise of this assumption is the belief that the act of observation (reading) changes what is being observed (literature). Other disciplines have accepted this belief; many scientists, for example, now embrace this perspective in relation to the acquisition of knowledge. In the act of interpreting literature, the needs of the community (classroom) will clearly play a role in the way in which consensual interpretations are made. Not only will generations of readers have different personal life experiences, but the forestructures of communities will change from generation to generation. Those individuals raised in the depression, for example, would bring one set of personal experiences to John Steinbeck's *The Grapes of Wrath*, whereas a reader born in the 1980s or 1990s would belong to a different community of readers, untouched by the communal experience of nationwide economic depression, at least in America.

Reader-response criticism is a point of departure for you to explore a literary text from your personal and communal experience. Reader-response criticism is not a rigid, dogmatic path to follow, and this approach requires no specific interpretation or response to a literary text. Indeed, for every reader there is a different interpretation (which of course should be suitable for presentation to a classroom community, if that is the context for your interpretive activity). If your life experiences have led you to approach social and cultural issues from a conservative orientation, then you may well interpret literary themes, values, and characters from this perspective. If your life has been characterized by sympathy for more liberal causes and beliefs, those sympathies will likely be reflected in your interpretations.

Reader-response criticism has no specific starting points or ideological assumptions, other than your subjective reading within a community of readers. As a reader-response critic, you will hone your analytic and evaluative abilities by addressing literature in the manner suggested in this chapter. Following Hemingway's "Indian Camp" is a series of reading and writing strategies to assist you in sharpening your reading and writing skills.

A SAMPLE READING

"Indian Camp" by Ernest Hemingway (1899–1960)

At the lake shore there was another rowboat drawn up. The two Indians stood waiting.

Nick and his father got in the stern of the boat and the Indians shoved it off and one of them got in to row. Uncle George sat in the stern of the camp rowboat. The young Indian shoved the camp boat off and got in to row Uncle George.

The two boats started off in the dark. Nick heard the oarlocks of the other boat quite a way ahead of them in the mist. The Indians rowed with quick choppy strokes. Nick lay back with his father's arm around him. It was cold on the water. The Indian who was rowing them was working very hard, but the other boat moved further ahead in the mist all the time.

"Where are we going, Dad?" Nick asked.

"Over to the Indian camp. There is an Indian lady very sick."   5

"Oh," said Nick.

Across the bay they found the other boat beached. Uncle George was smoking a cigar in the dark. The young Indian pulled the boat way up on the beach. Uncle George gave both the Indians cigars.

They walked up from the beach through a meadow that was soaking wet with dew, following the young Indian who carried a lantern. Then they went into the woods and followed a trail that led to the logging road that ran back into the hills. It was much lighter on the logging road as the timber was cut away on both sides. The young Indian stopped and blew out his lantern and they all walked on along the road.

They came around a bend and a dog came out barking. Ahead were the lights of the shanties where the Indian barkpeelers lived. More dogs rushed out at them. The two Indians sent them back to the shanties. In the shanty nearest the road there was a light in the window. An old woman stood in the doorway holding a lamp.

Inside on a wooden bunk lay a young Indian woman. She had been trying to have her baby for two days. All the old women in the camp had been helping her. The men had moved off up the road to sit in the dark and smoke out of range of the noise she made. She screamed just as Nick and the two Indians followed his father and Uncle George into the shanty. She lay in the lower bunk, very big under a quilt. Her head was turned to one side. In the upper bunk was her husband. He had cut his foot very badly with an ax three days before. He was smoking a pipe. The room smelled very bad. 10

Nick's father ordered some water to be put on the stove, and while it was heating he spoke to Nick.

"This lady is going to have a baby, Nick," he said.

"I know," said Nick.

"You don't know," said his father. "Listen to me. What she is going through is called being in labor. The baby wants to be born and she wants it to be born. All her muscles are trying to get the baby born. That is what is happening when she screams."

"I see," Nick said. 15

Just then the woman cried out.

"Oh, Daddy, can't you give her something to make her stop screaming?" asked Nick.

"No. I haven't any anaesthetic," his father said. "But her screams are not important. I don't hear them because they are not important."

The husband in the upper bunk rolled over against the wall.

The woman in the kitchen motioned to the doctor that the water was hot. Nick's 20 father went into the kitchen and poured about half of the water out of the big kettle into a basin. Into the water left in the kettle he put several things he unwrapped from a handkerchief.

"Those must boil," he said, and began to scrub his hands in the basin of hot water with a cake of soap he had brought from the camp. Nick watched his father's hands scrubbing each other with the soap. While his father washed his hands very carefully and thoroughly, he talked.

"You see, Nick, babies are supposed to be born head first but sometimes they're not. When they're not they make a lot of trouble for everybody. Maybe I'll have to operate on this lady. We'll know in a little while."

When he was satisfied with his hands he went in and went to work.

"Pull back that quilt, will you, George?" he said. "I'd rather not touch it."

Later when he started to operate Uncle George and three Indian men held the 25 woman still. She bit Uncle George on the arm and Uncle George said, "Damn squaw bitch!" and the young Indian who had rowed Uncle George over laughed at him. Nick held the basin for his father. It all took a long time.

His father picked the baby up and slapped it to make it breathe and handed it to the old woman.

"See, it's a boy, Nick," he said. "How do you like being an interne?"

Nick said, "All right." He was looking away so as not to see what his father was doing.

"There. That gets it," said his father and put something into the basin.

Nick didn't look at it.

"Now," his father said, "there's some stitches to put in. You can watch this or not, Nick, just as you like. I'm going to sew up the incision I made."

Nick did not watch. His curiosity had been gone for a long time.

His father finished and stood up. Uncle George and the three Indian men stood up. Nick put the basin out in the kitchen.

Uncle George looked at his arm. The young Indian smiled reminiscently.

"I'll put some peroxide on that, George," the doctor said.

He bent over the Indian woman. She was quiet now and her eyes were closed. She looked very pale. She did not know what had become of the baby or anything.

"I'll be back in the morning," the doctor said, standing up. "The nurse should be here from St. Ignace by noon and she'll bring everything we need."

He was feeling exalted and talkative as football players are in the dressing room after a game.

"That's one for the medical journal, George," he said. "Doing a Cæsarian with a jack-knife and sewing it up with nine-foot, tapered gut leaders."

Uncle George was standing against the wall, looking at his arm.

"Oh, you're a great man, all right," he said.

"Ought to have a look at the proud father. They're usually the worst sufferers in these little affairs," the doctor said. "I must say he took it all pretty quietly."

He pulled back the blanket from the Indian's head. His hand came away wet. He mounted on the edge of the lower bunk with the lamp in one hand and looked in. The Indian lay with his face toward the wall. His throat had been cut from ear to ear. The blood had flowed down into a pool where his body sagged the bunk. His head rested on his left arm. The open razor lay, edge up, in the blankets.

"Take Nick out of the shanty, George," the doctor said.

There was no need of that. Nick, standing in the door of the kitchen, had a good view of the upper bunk when his father, the lamp in one hand, tipped the Indian's head back.

It was just beginning to be daylight when they walked along the logging road back toward the lake.

"I'm terribly sorry I brought you along, Nickie," said his father, all his post-operative exhilaration gone. "It was an awful mess to put you through."

"Do ladies always have such a hard time having babies?" Nick asked.

"No, that was very, very exceptional."

"Why did he kill himself, Daddy?"

"I don't know, Nick. He couldn't stand things, I guess."

"Do many men kill themselves, Daddy?"

"Not very many, Nick."

"Do many women?"

"Hardly ever."

"Don't they ever?"
"Oh, yes. They do sometimes."
"Daddy?"
"Yes."
"Where did Uncle George go?"   60
"He'll turn up all right."
"Is dying hard, Daddy?"
"No, I think it's pretty easy, Nick. It all depends."

They were seated in the boat, Nick in the stern, his father rowing. The sun was coming up over the hills. A bass jumped, making a circle in the water. Nick trailed his hand in the water. It felt warm in the sharp chill of the morning.

In the early morning on the lake sitting in the stern of the boat with his father   65 rowing, he felt quite sure that he would never die.

ANALYZING "INDIAN CAMP"

Any approach to interpreting literature depends upon your understanding of characters, plot, point of view, imagery/metaphor, theme, and other formal aspects of literature. Before beginning a reader-response approach to "Indian Camp," it is important to consider the basic elements of the story. Once you have begun to feel comfortable with the literary elements of the story, the author's style, and the flow of the narrative, you will be in a better position to articulate your subjective reader-response. All readers reacts reflexively (even impulsively) to literature, of course, but the controlled interpreter uses the tools of the text to help build a reasonable and persuasive interpretation.

Style Issues

Ernest Hemingway begins his well-known story in typical Hemingway style: lean, hardhitting, athletic prose in which much is left beneath the surface (critics call this the *iceberg principle*). You may have observed that the story is characterized by understatement. The beginning, "At the lake," suggests a somewhat indefinite, unnamed place. The first two characters, never named, are identified as "The two Indians." The first action, Nick and his father entering the boat, is written in a very plain style with little ornamentation. Although we later learn that Nick's father is a physician, there is no hint of this at the beginning of the story. Uncle George too is described in minimal terms. We know little about him other than that he smokes cigars and displays a patronizing attitude toward the Indians in the story.

The dialogue in the story is very concise and taut, providing only as much information as the story requires to maintain its narrative rhythms. Although the story contains sensational subject matter—the unanesthetized delivery of a baby in a shanty and the suicide of the father—the style of the story is anything but sensational. Strategic moments, such as the suicide, are described in terse, journalistic fashion. (And it is worthwhile to know that Hemingway was a reporter for a number of years. Further, Hemingway was quite familiar with Native American culture and at times may have perceived himself as an "Indian," according to some critics.)

Character Issues

Nick is clearly the most pivotal character in the story; indeed, everything in the narrative revolves around his presence, participation, and perspective. However, we do not know very much about him: how old he is, if he has any brothers or sisters, what he does when away from his father, and so forth. What we do know is that he undergoes a painful and thought-provoking experience in the story. At the beginning of the story, Nick is like most any other boy accompanying his father on a short trip. By the end of the story, Nick has witnessed birth and death and is thinking about his own mortality, as illustrated by his questions to his father about death and suicide. Although the narrative is relatively short, Nick shows signs of change (perhaps even growth) by story's end.

The other major characters are a mixture of developed individuals and stereotypes, such as the portraits of Native Americans. Nick's physician-father is shown to be a callous man, somewhat insensitive to the birthing pains of the mother. Uncle George is portrayed as even more hard-hearted, referring to the Indian woman as a "Damn squaw bitch" after she bites him (in response to her pain in giving birth without anesthetic). It is not surprising that Uncle George disappears by story's end, something he has done before, as indicated by Nick's father's statement that "He'll turn up all right." The Native Americans are described by their actions (mother giving birth, father killing himself, Indians rowing boats, holding lanterns, etc.) but are not identified by name or given any personal traits. This textual lack of development, with distinct effects, turns the primary focus of the story to Nick and his two relatives. Nick's maturation depends very heavily upon his interaction with his father in observing how the doctor responds to pain and death. (Some critics have argued that Nick's father also experiences growth by the end of the story.)

Plot Issues

The plot or action of the narrative is fairly simple. A father takes along his young son to witness the delivery of a child, yet the son also witnesses the result of a suicide—the full cycle of life from birth to death, in just a matter of minutes. What is critical in terms of plot is not what happens to the other characters, but what happens to Nick as a result of his encounters. There is no question that Nick is a very different person by story's end, as the narrator describes Nick's innermost feelings: "he felt quite sure that he would never die."

Literary plot always involves cause and effect and change over time, and it is the sequence of causal scenes that constitutes the plot of "Indian Camp." Scene one depicts Nick and the others embarking for the Indian camp. Scene two involves their arrival at the camp. Scenes three and four chronicle the birth and the suicide discovery, and scene five reveals the conversation between Nick and his father, which shows how deeply Nick has been affected by what has happened. The traumatic events that take place in scenes three and four set the stage for Nick's confrontation with issues of life and death as he attempts to sort out what has happened. Nick will never be the same again, because his forestructure has been exposed to mind-altering and mood-altering experiences.

Point of View Issues

"Indian Camp" is written from the third-person, objective perspective. The narrator of the story knows a great deal, including what is going on in Nick's mind, as the concluding sentence reveals. However, it might be suggested that the "objective" narrator is sympathetic to one character (Nick) and unsympathetic to others (Nick's father and Uncle George). When a third person shows sympathy for a particular character and tells a story through that character's eyes, it is called the *Uncle Charles principle*, after a character in a James Joyce short story. Ernest Hemingway wrote a significant number of stories in which Nick Adams is the major character, and the portraits are almost always positive. It is fair to say that "Indian Camp" is told somewhat from the vantage point of Nick, even though Nick is clearly a boy. But Nick is a "good boy," listening to his father, doing as he is told, and refusing to flinch at the shocking sight of the bloody husband. The story concludes with Nick asking his father a series of very serious questions, and they are not naïve questions. It might be suggested that Nick attempts to avoid reality by feeling "quite sure that he would never die," but this is a story of a boy in the difficult stages of human development. It is not unusual or unnatural for Nick to deny to himself the implications of what he has seen and heard, which raises the issue of theme.

Thematic Issues

"Indian Camp," like most literature, offers a rich vein of themes that run through the narrative. Only a very narrow-minded reader would suggest that there is only one central theme or "message" to the story. Nick's development is surely a major focus of the tale, but the doctor's callous behavior toward the Indians is also part of the thematic texture of the work, as is Uncle George's behavior toward the Indians, including his giving them cigars. The portrait of Native Americans is also a significant subtext within the work. There are also suggestive motifs about birth and suicide, cycles of life and death. Why does the husband kill himself? There is no easy or obvious answer supported by the text. One might speculate that Uncle George is the actual father and that this realization is too much for the husband to accept. Perhaps the husband could no longer bear the suffering of his wife. Uncle George's disappearance at the camp fuels the fires of speculation about his role in Nick's introduction into "Indian life." Whatever thematic movement a reader attempts to explore, the strategic issue is to investigate such themes by citing textual evidence judiciously.

Metaphor Issues

All good literature contains rich metaphors and images. "Indian Camp" is no exception. The story begins by shrouding Nick and the other characters in the dark of night as they prepare for their journey. For Nick, this journey is into the unknown, ultimately to witness birth and death. Nick emerges from these experiences into the light of day (literally and figuratively). The contrasting metaphor of dark and light might be said to reflect Nick's movement from ignorance to insight (or at least knowledge). Nick's doctor-father refers to his son metaphorically as an "interne," a novitiate into the actual world of medicine, where pain and death are present. Nick's father is not only a medical man, but also a sportsman. Hemingway merges these identities in the striking metaphors of the doctor-fisherman medical equipment: He performs the cesarean section with a jack-knife and sews up the incision with fishing line, "nine-foot, tapered gut leaders." Other metaphors enrich the story—the rising sun, Uncle George's cigars, the shanty in the woods, a jumping bass, Nick's trailing his hand in the water, and so forth. Other metaphoric relationships (father and son, white man and Indian, middle-class and poor) serve important purposes in this compelling story.

Questions for Your Analysis of "Indian Camp"

1) What are some of your early impressions of the story?
2) What are your observations on the narrative's settings? Is there something from your personal experience that assists you in relating to any of the physical settings in the story?
3) How do you feel about Nick's father? Is he a good father? Should he have brought Nick with him to observe the operation and learn about life?
4) What kind of characteristics do you associate with the major characters, especially with Nick and his doctor-father?
5) What is your response to the portrait of Native Americans? Is the mother depicted unsympathetically? The husband? The guides? Why do you think the husband kills himself?

6) What is it that Nick learns from his experience (or perhaps he learns little and attempts to deny to himself the lessons of what he has experienced)?

7) What is there in your personal experience that resonates with some of the themes in this story?

8) How do you respond to the sensational elements of the plot, a birth coupled with a suicide? Do you feel that "Indian Camp" is a gruesome story, shocking in its basic plot?

9) Do you feel that the narrator prepared you for what happens in scenes four, five, and six? Was the suicide foreshadowed? Was Nick's development hinted at early on?

10) How do you react to the final thoughts of Nick: "he felt quite sure that he would never die"? Nick has changed, but has he grown?

The textual issues of this discussion can be appropriated to reader-response criticism, as well as to other interpretive approaches. Please read the following sample essay on "Indian Camp" as an illustration of one form that reader-response criticism might take. This essay, as you will see, focuses on changes in Nick's forestructure. Other reader-responses to the story might focus more heavily on the ways in which the story affects the reader's emotions and world view, or mindset.

Sample Essay on "Indian Camp"

"Indian Camp" has long been a favorite Hemingway short story for reading at multiple levels. There are many reasons for its popularity: its poignant depiction of a father/son relationship, its revelation of the "education" of a young man, its detailed description of Nick's sensitivity, and its treatment of two cultures interacting with one another. Although these themes invoke a number of interpretive questions, there is arguably a fundamental issue in understanding the story. This issue is context, especially the context of personal history (in this case, Nick's experience). Indeed, Nick's new independence from his father is emphasized by Nick's change in position in the boat for the return trip: He is in the circle of his father's arms on the way out, but sitting alone at the opposite end of the boat from his father on the way back.

The story begins with Nick, his father, and Uncle George boarding two rowboats. Nick is presented as an initiate, a raw child with no idea of where he is going or what is going to happen, and we know almost nothing of his background. Nick asks his doctor-father, "Where are we going?" as his father holds him securely in his arms, saying nothing more revealing than that they are headed for the Indian camp, where his father knows that he will deliver a baby. Nick is still groggy from sleep.

As Nick enters the birthing shanty, the Indian woman screams, and only then does his father tell him that "this lady is going to have a baby." Nick responds, "I know," although his father quickly corrects him by saying, "You don't know"—calling attention to Nick's inexperience. The doctor then proceeds to explain the process and dangers of childbirth. Nick's education has begun; his forestructure already has been altered in a critical way. I found this scene to be deeply compelling because it reminded me how little we know when we are adolescents. Nick's introduction to the "real world" of birth and death also reminded me how impressionable we can be at his age. First experiences, particularly under such traumatic circumstances, produce memories that last a lifetime. Nick is truly baptized into a new world.

As the woman screams out in pain, unaesthetized because the doctor has no numbing medications, Nick reveals his sensitivity as he asks his father to help her. Her screams are very important to Nick: "Oh, Daddy, can't you give her something to make her stop screaming?" Nick's father responds in a way that suggests Nick must become more hard-boiled, like his father: "No, I haven't any anaesthetic. But her screams are not important. I don't hear them because they are not important." To Nick they are very important, particularly because he has not heard them before. To the experienced, even callous, physician-father they are part of the everyday business of being a doctor, but to Nick they are frightening, and with good cause.

The doctor's "callousness" is further revealed in his explanation of the birth process, which says as much about the physician as it does about his patient: "You see, Nick, babies are supposed to be born head first but sometimes they're not. When they're not they make a lot of trouble for everybody." Nick's father then proceeds to perform a cesarean section. Uncle George, bitten by the woman, responds by yelling, "Damn squaw bitch!" Nick watches the operation as he holds a basin for his father. After the baby is born, the doctor says to Nick, "How do you like being an interne?" Nick had turned around, "looking away so as not to see what his father was doing." Nick says, "All right," but still refuses to look at his father or the mother. We are told: "Nick did not watch. His curiosity had been gone for a long time." It is clear to me that the doctor behaves in a patronizing manner: "Ought to have a look at the proud father. They're usually the worst sufferers in these little affairs." Nick gives no sign that he shares his father's attitude.

Nick's refusal to observe the process of birth signals his resistance to becoming part of his father's world, a world of hard-boiled stoicism, an ongoing scene in which one makes "tough" decisions based on a history of hard personal experience. The doctor says to George, "That's one for the medical journal. . . . Doing a cesarean with a jack-knife and sewing it up with nine-foot, tapered gut leaders." George responds, "Oh, you're a great man all right." I question whether this statement should be taken non-ironically and without sarcasm, and I can see how it might be read in at least two different ways and both make sense. But the important issue is that Nick is not ready for his father's world, as later events reveal.

The doctor pulls back the blanket from the husband's head, only to learn that the Indian had slit his own throat with a razor. This time, Nick observes the bloody mess, the result of the Indian's self-violence, in spite of his father's orders to have him taken out of the shanty in order to protect him from witnessing the dark side of life. Nick's forestructure has altered considerably in light of his new knowledge. Nick's development is revealed in his conversation with his father.

"Why did he kill himself, Daddy?"

"I don't know, Nick. He couldn't stand things, I guess." . . .

"Daddy?"

"Yes?"

"Where did Uncle George go?"

"He'll turn up all right."

"Is dying hard, Daddy?"

"No, I think it's pretty easy, Nick. It all depends."

The doctor has changed from a self-confident, pragmatic, knowing physician and father to a daddy who reveals that he cannot address his son's complex questions or, by implication, the complexities of life. Dr. Adams has changed from arrogant scientist to fumbling father, and now Nick must learn these things—lessons for living—for himself.

Nick's father's most important lesson is perhaps that he cannot give his son lessons in how to live. The narrative contains some ambiguities, to be sure, such as George handing out cigars after the birth of the child, perhaps in mock celebration of a culture for which he seems to have little regard, or maybe because George is the father of the child, as some critics have suggested. Whatever the meaning of these ambiguous moments in the text, the story is clearly about Nick's introduction (and indoctrination) into a world darker than that of most youths. It is clear that there is a change in Nick's consciousness as he attempts to come to grips with some shocking experiences in his young life.

The narrative concludes with Nick's thoughts: " . . . he felt quite sure that he would never die." Nick is in the grip of denial of essential human experience—especially the knowledge that all must die. In his attempt to "immunize" himself from life's darker experiences, Nick demonstrates that indeed he has experienced significant change in his personal context, his system of beliefs, his forestructure. Our forestructures, as readers, change as we observe Nick's experiences. After reading "Indian Camp," I could never read a story about Native Americans living impoverished lives in quite the same way. My personal and literary "bank of human experiences" has been enriched by Nick's experiences.

The hard experiences of difficult childbirth and suicide have taught him a way of living, which is to repress associating himself with such possibilities. Although his father has given him some assurance against suicide (including his own), Nick has developed an internal skin of resistance that will protect him, at least for now, from the horrors he has witnessed. This new defense system, the "growth" of Nick, is but one possible residue of this powerful short story.

Writing Your Essay From a Reader-Response Perspective

The following text, "Araby," is a short story by James Joyce. This story, like "Indian Camp," chronicles the experiences of a young man. It would be accurate to call it a coming-of-age narrative. This story is also told in the first-person voice of a narrator who is about 12 or 13 years old, and it is based on a bazaar that was held in Dublin about the time that Joyce was 12. It is quite likely that he visited Araby in 1894. Many critics have referred to *Dubliners*, the collection from which this story is taken, as ficitonalized biography. What is striking about this story is the author's attempt to capture the development and sensitivity of a young person whose hopes are dashed. What may seem to be an insignificant experience to an older, more mature person takes on grand proportions when experienced for the first time by someone coming of age. In that respect, the narrator of "Araby" and Nick Adams in "Indian Camp" share something in common. Following "Araby" is a series of steps to assist you in the analysis of the work, as well as in writing an essay from a reader-response perspective.

A SAMPLE READING

"Araby" by James Joyce (1882–1941)

North Richmond Street, being blind, was a quiet street except at the hour when the Christian Brothers' School set the boys free. An uninhabited house of two storeys stood at the blind end, detached from its neighbours in a square ground. The other houses of the street, conscious of decent lives within them, gazed at one another with brown imperturbable faces.

The former tenant of our house, a priest, had died in the back drawing room. Air, musty from having long been enclosed, hung in all the rooms, and the waste room behind the kitchen was littered with old useless papers. Among these I found a few paper-covered books, the pages of which were curled and damp: *The Abbott,* by Walter Scott, *The Devout Communicant* and *The Memoirs of Vidocq.* I liked the last best because its leaves were yellow. The wild garden behind the house contained a central apple-tree and a few straggling bushes under one of which I found the late tenant's rusty bicycle-pump. He had been a very charitable priest; in his will he had left all his money to institutions and the furniture of his house to his sister.

When the short days of winter came dusk fell before we had well eaten our dinners. When we met in the street the houses had grown sombre. The space of sky above us was the colour of ever-changing violet and towards it the lamps of the street lifted their feeble lanterns. The cold air stung us and we played till our bodies glowed. Our shouts echoed in the silent street. The career of our play brought us through the dark muddy lanes behind the houses where we ran the gauntlet of the rough tribes from the cottages, to the back doors of the dark dripping gardens where odours arose from the ashpits, to the dark odorous stables where a coachman smoothed and combed the horse or shook music from the buckled harness. When we returned to the street light from the kitchen windows had filled the areas. If my uncle was seen turning the corner we hid in the shadow until we had seen him safely housed. Or if Mangan's sister came out on the doorstep to call her brother in to his tea we watched her from our shadow peer up and down the street. We waited to see whether she would remain or go in and, if she remained, we left our shadow and walked up to Mangan's steps resignedly. She was waiting for us, her figure defined by the light from the half-opened door. Her brother always teased her before he obeyed and I stood by the railings looking at her. Her dress swung as she moved her body and the soft rope of her hair tossed from side to side.

Every morning I lay on the floor in the front parlor watching her door. The blind was pulled down within an inch of the sash so that I could not be seen. When she came out on the doorstep my heart leaped. I ran to the hall, seized my books and followed her. I kept her brown figure always in my eye and, when we came near the point at which our ways diverged, I quickened my pace and passed her. This happened morning after morning. I had never spoken to her, except for a few casual words, and yet her name was like a summons to all my foolish blood.

Her image accompanied me even in places the most hostile to romance. On Saturday evenings when my aunt went marketing I had to go to carry some of the parcels. We walked through the flaring street, jostled by drunken men and bargaining women, amid the curses of labourers, the shrill litanies of shop-boys who stood on guard by the barrels of pigs' cheeks, the nasal chanting of street singers, who sang a *come-all-you* about O'Donovan Rossa, or a ballad about the troubles in our native land. These noises converged in a single sensation of life for me: I imagined that I bore my chalice safely through the throng of foes. Her name sprang to my lips at moments in strange prayers and praises which I myself did not understand. My eyes were often full of tears (I could not tell why) and at times a flood from my heart seemed to pour itself out into my bosom. I thought little of the future. I did not know whether I would ever speak to her or not or, if I spoke to her, how I could tell her of my confused adoration. But my body was like a harp and her words and gestures were like fingers running upon the wires.

One evening I went into the back drawing-room in which the priest had died. It was a dark rainy evening and there was no sound in the house. Through one of the broken panes I heard the rain impinge upon the earth, the fine incessant needles of water playing in the sodden beds. Some distant lamp or lighted window gleamed below me. I was thankful that I could see so little. All my senses seemed to desire to veil themselves and, feeling that I was about to slip from them, I pressed the palms of my hands together until they trembled, murmuring: *O love! O love!* many times.

At last she spoke to me. When she addressed the first words to me I was so confused that I did not know what to answer. She asked me was I going to *Araby*. I forget whether I answered yes or no. It would be a splendid bazaar, she said; she would love to go.

—And why can't you? I asked.

While she spoke she turned a silver bracelet round and round her wrist. She could not go, she said, because there would be a retreat that week in her convent. Her brother and two other boys were fighting for their caps and I was alone at the railings. She held one of the spikes, bowing her head towards me. The light from the lamp opposite our door caught the white curve of her neck, lit up her hair that rested there and, falling, lit up the hand upon the railing. It fell over one side of her dress and caught the white border of a petticoat, just visible as she stood at ease.

—It's well for you, she said.

—If I go, I said, I will bring you something.

10

What innumerable follies laid waste my waking and sleeping thoughts after that evening! I wished to annihilate the tedious intervening days. I chafed against the work of school. At night in my bedroom and by day in the classroom her image came between me and the page I strove to read. The syllables of the word *Araby* were called to me through the silence in which my soul luxuriated and cast an Eastern enchantment over me. I asked for leave to go to the bazaar on Saturday night. My aunt was surprised and hoped it was not some Freemason affair. I answered few questions in class. I watched my master's face pass from amiability to sternness; he hoped I was not beginning to idle. I could not call my wandering thoughts together. I had hardly any patience with the serious work of life which, now that it stood between me and my desire, seemed to me child's play, ugly monotonous child's play.

On Saturday morning I reminded my uncle that I wished to go to the bazaar in the evening. He was fussing at the hall-stand, looking for the hatbrush, and answered me curtly:

—Yes, boy, I know.

As he was in the hall I could not go into the front parlour and lie at the window.   15
I left the house in bad humour and walked slowly towards the school. The air was piti-
lessly raw and already my heart misgave me.

When I came home to dinner my uncle had not yet been home. Still, it was early.
I sat staring at the clock for some time and, when its ticking began to irritate me, I left
the room. I mounted the staircase and gained the upper part of the house. The high
cold empty gloomy rooms liberated me and I went from room to room singing. From the
front window I saw my companions playing below in the street. Their cries reached me
weakened and indistinct and, leaning my forehead against the cool glass, I looked over
at the dark house where she lived. I may have stood there for an hour, seeing nothing
but the brown-clad figure cast by my imagination, touched discreetly by the lamplight
at the curved neck, at the hand upon the railing and at the border below the dress.

When I came downstairs again I found Mrs. Mercer sitting at the fire. She was an
old garrulous woman, a pawnbroker's widow, who collected used stamps for some pious
purpose. I had to endure the gossip of the tea-table. The meal was prolonged beyond an
hour and still my uncle did not come. Mrs. Mercer stood up to go: she was sorry she
couldn't wait any longer, but it was after eight o'clock and she did not like to be out
late, as the night air was bad for her. When she had gone I began to walk up and down
the room, clenching my fists. My aunt said:

—I'm afraid you may put off your bazaar for this night of Our Lord.

At nine 'clock I heard my uncle's latchkey in the halldoor. I heard him talking to
himself and heard the hall-stand rocking when it had received the weight of his overcoat. I could interpret these signs. When he was midway through his dinner I asked him
to give me the money to go to the bazaar. He had forgotten.

—The people are in bed and after their first sleep now, he said.   20

I did not smile. My aunt said to him energetically:

—Can't you give him the money and let him go? You've kept him late enough as
it is.

My uncle said he was very sorry he had forgotten. He said he believed in the old
saying: *All work and no play makes Jack a dull boy.* He asked me where I was going and,
when I had told him a second time he asked me did I know *The Arab's Farewell to His
Steed.* When I left the kitchen he was about to recite the opening lines of the piece to
my aunt.

I held a florin tightly in my hand as I strode down Buckingham Street towards
the station. The sight of the streets thronged with buyers and glaring with gas recalled
to me the purpose of my journey. I took my seat in a third-class carriage of a deserted
train. After an intolerable delay the train moved out of the station slowly. It crept on-
ward among ruinous houses and over the twinkling river. At Westland Row Station a
crowd of people pressed to the carriage doors; but the porters moved them back, saying
that it was a special train for the bazaar. I remained alone in the bare carriage. In a few
minutes the train drew up beside an improvised wooden platform. I passed out on to the
road and saw by the lighted dial of a clock that it was ten minutes to ten. In front of me
was a large building which displayed the magical name.

I could not find any sixpenny entrance and, fearing that the bazaar would be   25
closed, I passed in quickly through a turnstile, handing a shilling to a weary-looking
man. I found myself in a big hall girdled at half its height by a gallery. Nearly all the

stalls were closed and the greater part of the hall was in darkness. I recognized a silence like that which pervades a church after a service. I walked into the centre of the bazaar timidly. A few people were gathered about the stalls which were still open. Before a curtain, over which the words *Café Chantant* were written in coloured lamps, two men were counting money on a salver. I listened to the fall of the coins.

Remembering with difficulty why I had come I went over to one of the stalls and examined porcelain vases and flowered tea-sets. At the door of the stall a young lady was talking and laughing with two young gentlemen. I remarked their English accents and listened vaguely to their conversation.

—O, I never said such a thing!

—O, but you did!

—O, but I didn't!

—Didn't she say that?   30

—Yes I heard her.

—O, there's a . . . fib!

Observing me the young lady came over and asked me did I wish to buy anything. The tone in her voice was not encouraging; she seemed to have spoken to me out of a sense of duty. I looked humbly at the great jars that stood like eastern guards at either side of the dark entrance to the stall and murmured:

—No, thank you.

The young lady changed the position of one of the vases and went back to the   35 two young men. They began to talk of the same subject. Once or twice the young lady glanced at me over her shoulder.

I lingered before her stall, though I knew my stay was useless, to make my interest in her wares seem the more real. Then I turned away slowly and walked down the middle of the bazaar. I allowed the two pennies to fall against the sixpence in my pocket. I heard a voice call from one end of the gallery that the light was out. The upper part of the hall was now completely dark.

Gazing up into the darkness I saw myself as a creature driven and derided by vanity; and my eyes burned with anguish and anger.

Questions for Your Analysis of "Araby"

1) What are some of your early impressions of the story? What is the most striking aspect of the story, something that promotes an instant reaction in you?

2) This story is told in the first person by an unnamed narrator. What is your instinctive response to the narrator? Is he a particularly sympathetic figure to you?

3) What are your observations of the narrator's preoccupation with Mangan's sister?

4) How does the narrative's settings affect you? What is the significance of the story beginning with a description of the back drawing room where the priest had died? Is there a connection between the priest's death and the death of the narrator's dreams at the end of the story?

5) Is there something from your personal experience that assists you in relating to any of the physical settings in the story? How do you feel about the narrator's uncle, who clearly disappoints the narrator by coming home late and intoxicated?

6) What kind of characteristics do you associate with the narrator?

7) What is your response to the portrait of turn-of-the-century Dublin? This story contains much religious imagery and metaphor. How do these elements affect your reaction to the tale?

8) What is it that the narrator learns from his experience (or perhaps he learns little and is merely frustrated because of the way his trip to the bazaar turned out)?

9) What is there in your personal experience that resonates with some of the themes in this story?

10) Do you feel that the narrator prepared you for what happens in the last scene of the story, where the narrator suddenly realizes (called an *epiphany*) that he has been living a life of illusion?

11) How do you react to the final thoughts of the narrator: "I saw myself as a creature driven and derided by vanity; and my eyes burned with anguish and anger"?

STEPS IN WRITING A READER-RESPONSE ESSAY ABOUT ANY READING

1) Write down your first impressions of major elements in the text, whether fiction or poetry (theme, imagery, character, metaphor, tone, point of view).

2) Examine the qualities of the main character. Even if the reading is a poem and does not have characters, usually there are some elements in a work that are personified and can be treated as characters.

3) Consider the major movements in the reading and compare them with any personal experiences you may have had that relate to them.

4) Time is often an important component of literature, especially references to the past. Compare time experiences in the reading with your own past experiences, especially as they reveal change over time and cause and effect.

5) Identify major values that are represented in the reading and compare them with values in your system.

6) Analyze the ending of the poem or story in terms of your personal satisfaction. Consider whether or not you are comfortable with the ending. If you are not satisfied with the conclusion of the work, write down the specific reasons for your dissatisfaction.

7) A good general internet source to investigate the context of any literary reading is google.com. By typing in the title of the work in the Google search engine, especially if it is a well-known literary work, you will locate several sources that provide background information.

STEPS IN WRITING AN ESSAY ABOUT "ARABY"

Brainstorming Your Topic

1) Identify those elements in the text (character, plot, theme, metaphor) that prompt an immediate response from you. Write down whatever impressions you have of all major characters in "Araby."

2) Focus on the main character, the narrator. What is it about him that you do or do not like? Do you think that he is too shy in letting his feelings be known about Mangan's sister?

3) The narrator's emotional interest in Mangan's sister probably represents a first love, an intense emotional experience that individuals often remember for the rest of their lives. What is your reaction to his experience?

4) What personal experiences have you had that connect to parts of "Araby"? Have you ever been to a bazaar or traveling carnival?

5) Has the narrator been mistreated by the girl at the bazaar? Or is his disappointment primarily the result of his actions?

6) The story contains many references to the past. It might even be said that nostalgia is a major motif in the story. Write down the effect(s) these references to the past have on you.

7) Religion plays a role in the story. How does this emphasis affect your interpretive reaction?

8) Are you satisfied with the ending? Why or why not?

9) Unless your instructor insists that you not consult outside sources in brainstorming your topic, refer to the electronic sources for James Joyce listed at the end of this chapter. There are many good links that will connect you to biographical sources and detailed criticism. Any ideas and words drawn directly from outside sources should be properly cited, of course. Consult the appendix for documentation procedures.

Creating an Outline

1) Collect your answers to the brainstorming questions in short two-word or three-word categories and use them as preliminary "writing points."

2) Think about the points and consider whether they add up to a central idea (for example, the growth of the narrator in "Araby").

3) Identify five or six main writing points that support your central idea. These points should come from the main literary elements in the story (character, plot, theme, point of view, metaphor). All of the points should provide support for your controlling idea.

4) If you have more than five or six points, try to combine one or more of them. If you have fewer than five or six points, see if some of them can be used to generate additional points. You may have some large points that include smaller issues that can stand alone as paragraph topic sentences.

5) Look for transitional devices that connect your main points of support.

Preparing a Rough Draft

1) Now that you have created a working outline, you have already completed your major organizational work. Each major point is the topic of a paragraph, and your essay will have between 5 and 10 paragraphs, depending on development. These paragraphs need not be of equal length, but each one should sufficiently develop the topic sentence.

2) Now that you have your major writing points, assemble a preliminary draft by developing each topic idea with two or three sentences that discuss evidence from the text.

3) Focus on developing transitions between your paragraphs. Professional writers often begin a new paragraph with a direct reference to an idea expressed at the end of the preceding paragraph.

4) It is not too early to begin writing your concluding paragraph. Conclusions often summarize the main points of a central idea (but do not repeat word for word what has already been said). A conclusion may also refer to implications of what has been said (but what cannot be developed because of space limits).

5) Don't be afraid to include questions in your writing (see the sample essay on "Indian Camp"). No reader of literature can ever be absolutely certain of every observation that he or she makes, and perceptive observations often generate excellent questions, many of which are useful, even if unanswerable.

Editing Your Draft

1) At this stage, you should have a draft of a few hundred words. You have already done the most difficult work in thinking out your ideas, organizing them into an outline, and preparing a rough version of the final product. Look for ways to edit your paper that will strengthen the essay.

2) Search for repetitious wording and ideas. Do not repeat ideas, however important, throughout the essay. Use a thesaurus to locate synonyms for terms and ideas that reappear. Attempt to emphasize variety in your language.

3) If your instructor encourages peer editing, choose someone in your class, or perhaps a roommate, and solicit advice about how your essay reads. Is it articulate, compelling, insightful, and interesting? (All of these qualities are important.) Although your peer editor may not be taking a literature class, he or she may be a very good source of feedback on how effective your writing is. Professional writers often seek feedback from peers, and not only from professional colleagues.

4) Be open to make changes in your writing, both conceptually and in specific language. Professional writers know that writing is recursive (which means that the act of writing constantly generates new ways of looking at the topic), and student writers should also take advantage of changes in thinking *as they write*. Don't be afraid to make efficient and effective changes, especially in terms of cutting out words, phrases, and sections that may not be working very well in supporting your overall idea.

5) Proofread carefully for spelling errors, punctuation problems, run-on sentences, and ambiguous or awkward constructions. You should use a solid grammar handbook to assist you in these areas.

Final Checklist

1) Make sure that your central idea (sometimes called a *thesis statement*) appears in the first paragraph. It is important that your reader know what major point, or points, you are attempting to make.

2) Because this essay is a reader-response paper, check to see that the essay represents your subjective response to the reading. Your major points should be understandable, of course, to the community of readers to which you are writing.

3) Examine your essay for sufficient evidence. Each one of your major ideas will need illustration that comes from the text.

4) Review your conclusion to see if you have ended the essay in an effective manner, either summarizing what you have said (in different language) or suggesting some important implications of your reading.

5) Proofread one last time for errors, repetitious language, and awkward phrasing.

ELECTRONIC RESOURCES FOR ERNEST HEMINGWAY

http://www.cs.umb.edu/jfklibrary/eh.htm.   A biographical guide to the life of Ernest Hemingway.

http://www.literarytraveler.com/fall/midwest/ernestplaces.htm.   A guide to some of the important places in Hemingway's life as well as settings for his fiction.

http://www.atlantic.net/~gagne/hem/tim.html.   A timeline of the important events in the life of Ernest Hemingway.

http://www.hemingway.org/.   A virtual tour of Hemingway's birthplace.

http://members.aol.com/_ht_a/sbeegel/hemrev.htm.   Find abstracts of recent articles about Papa Hemingway and discover submission standards, editorial policies, and subscription details for *The Hemingway Review*.

http://www.usplanb.com/hemingway.cfm.   Read about a journalist's visit to the home where Hemingway spent the last two years of his life. Includes photos of the house and Hemingway's family.

http://www.cybernation.com/victory/quotations/authors/quotes_hemingway_ernest. html.   A list of Hemingway quotations on many topics.

http://members.aol.com/hta/sbeegel/hemsoc.htm.   Information on joining the Hemingway Society.

http://killdevilhill.com/hemingwaychat/wwwboard.html.   Ernest Hemingway bulletin board.

There is a listserv devoted to Ernest Hemingway. To subscribe, send an email message to Majordomo@mtu.edu. In the body of the message write subscribe Heming-L.

ELECTRONIC RESOURCES FOR JAMES JOYCE

http://www.levity.com/corduroy/joyce.htm.   A general page with numerous links to various Joyce sites.

http://www.TheModernWord.com/joyce/.   This site offers commentary on Joyce's works and also features other connections, such as forums.

http://www.grand-teton.com/cgi-grand-teton/jjoyce/omnisearch.cgi.   A concordance site containing references to all of Joyce's works.

http://www.robotwisdom.com/jaj/portal.html.   The James Joyce Portal, with dozens of connecting links.

http://www.ozemail.com.au/~caveman/Joyce/.   The James Joyce Web page.
http://www.facstaff.bucknell.edu/rickard/Joyce.html.   A comprehensive list of Joyce
    resources on the Internet.
http://lmmm.ccne.ufsm.br/users/guina/bloomsday/joyce.htm.   This site includes a con-
    nection to the International Joyce Society, as well as other links.

Further Readings in Reader-Response Criticism

Bleich, David. *Subjective Criticism*. Baltimore: Johns Hopkins UP, 1978.
Fish, Stanley. *Is There a Text in This Class?: The Authority of Interpretive Communities*.
    Cambridge: Harvard UP, 1980.
Flynn, Elizabeth, and P. Schweickart, eds. *Gender and Reading: Essays on Readers, Texts,
    and Contexts*. Baltimore: Johns Hopkins UP, 1986.
Iser, Wolfgang. *The Implied Reader: Patterns of Communication in Prose Fiction from Bun-
    yan to Beckett*. Baltimore: Johns Hopkins UP, 1974.
————. *The Act of Reading: A Theory of Aesthetic Response*. Baltimore: Johns Hopkins
    UP, 1978.
Tompkins, Jane, ed. *Reader-Response Criticism*. Baltimore: Johns Hopkins UP, 1980.

chapter 3

Formalist Criticism

Formalist criticism (or *New Criticism*, as it is sometimes called) is an approach to interpretation that locates the center of meaning in the text itself. The name comes from some of the formalist critics' practice of examining closely the form and structure of a work of literature, rather than looking for a particular message or attempting to discover the intended meaning of an author. Although formalist criticism has been practiced for a number of decades, it is still one of the major schools of literary interpretation practiced today. One of the principles of formalist criticism, the "close reading" of a text, is a routine analytical tool in nearly every school of interpretation.

As you saw in Chapter 1, some critical approaches locate meaning primarily in the reader (reader-response criticism, for example), or in a referential context primarily outside of the text (ideological criticism, for example). There are also schools of interpretation that locate meaning primarily in authorial intention (biographical criticism, for example). This is not to say that other factors, such as a reader's background, do not enter into the act of interpretation. Indeed, the personal background of the reader, cultural contexts, the "situation" of the interpretation (whether reading for personal meaning or for a classroom assignment), and other elements that are always present in any search for meaning do exist, even if they are not emphasized.

All approaches to literary interpretation grow out of contexts, and formalist criticism is no exception. Prior to the development of formalist criticism in the early part of the twentieth century, the interpretation of literature was dominated by a concern for the life of the author (biographical criticism) and the history of the creation of the literary work (historical criticism). Historical interpretations of Henry James' *The Portrait of a Lady*, for example, concerned themselves with James' personal life and various sources for the narrative (locating a house that served as a model for the novel's English mansion, for example).

Formalist criticism, in focusing on the text itself, is concerned particularly with structure and the relationships between the part and the whole. Each part of a poem or story, according to formalist critics, plays a critical role in the overall structure and meaning of the work. The parts of a literary work are not assembled arbitrarily, and they should not be interpreted arbitrarily. Each element of a literary text has a strategic connection with all other elements. As the reader examines a work's elements, he or she continuously establishes relationships and interrelationships that exist within the poem, narrative, or play.

One major principle of formalist criticism is the *integrity*, or overall unity, of the literary work. It is assumed that all parts of a literary work are necessary to the integrity and wholeness of the text. Further, the relationships of the component parts of a text are strategic to understanding the work. These parts (words, phrases, sentences, structure, tone, voice, ambiguities, themes, tensions, paradoxes, and so forth) constitute the "building blocks" of the work, and it is not possible, according to formalist criticism, to understand a work without understanding how its parts work together.

It is also important to note that formalist criticism is very concerned with the aesthetic qualities of a literary text. There is a certain beauty to a poem, story, or play that emanates from its very existence. Indeed, the primary value of a work of literature is its aesthetic quality, in contrast to, say, the political, ideological, or cultural overtones of a text. The beautiful dimension of a literary work also represents its "truth." Poetic truth is not like scientific truth, which is verifiable; poetic beauty is knowable only through intuition, resulting in the realization that something is inherently true. Part of this beauty, or aesthetic, is represented by the structure, or symmetry, of the work. Everything in the text is seen as being in harmony and proportion with the entire work. These three elements—harmony, symmetry, and proportion—are the essential properties of that which we call beautiful, and these are characteristics that we look for in well-constructed works of literature.

Although it may appear the practice of formalist criticism is relatively new, some underlying principles are very old, going back to the time of ancient Greece, where interpreters carefully examined the elements of a literary text in order to determine its overall meaning. It was always assumed that any worthwhile work of literature was unified, something the Greeks called *organic unity*. The formalist interpreter assumes the structural integrity and *objectivity* of the literary work. This means that the work itself—poem, story, or play—becomes an object of knowledge. You can see why formalist readers consider the "text itself" the most important part of interpretation.

There is no subjectivity or arbitrariness in arriving at the meaning of a work, according to formalist principles. Formalist readers perceive the act of interpretation as a careful process. Indeed, many formalist interpreters approach the literary text as something to be analyzed quite closely, almost as if one were in an interpretive laboratory. The primary tool is of course not a microscope, but a dictionary, coupled with the reader's skills of objective analysis and mature evaluation. To read closely means to read objectively and to consciously avoid making subjective and highly personal responses to a work of literature (exactly the opposite strategy of reader-response interpretation!).

Students of literature, according to formalist principles, should study literature itself, not about literature in terms of social, economic, and cultural history, or the personal history of the author. This is not to say that the goal of the formalist reader is to "solve" texts, but rather to read and interpret them in order to resolve, or make sense out of, textual paradoxes, tensions, and ambiguities. All great and lasting works of literature, for the formalist critic, leave a tiny residue of meaning that cannot be ultimately solved. This inexplicable "essence" or core of a literary text is what constitutes its greatness.

The formalist approach is not an exact theory laid out in careful and precise steps, but rather a way of judging a literary work. The early formalist critics of the twentieth century concerned themselves with writing practical judgments about specific literary texts rather than with writing detailed theoretical treatises. Some readers believe that the practical emphasis of formalist interpretation, without extensive abstract theory, is one of its greatest strengths.

Literary texts are not bound by culture, context, or time, but become interpretive opportunities that are timeless, as readers of most schools would agree. Indeed, many formalist interpreters see the literary text as the highest symbol of human value, a human artifact that is elevated to canonical status. Because the value of some literature is so important, not all literary works are deserving of such canonical status. Not all works of literature belong in the "long tradition" of Literature. It is the intrinsic properties of texts themselves that determine whether or not they are Literature.

In formalist theory it is not important to know much, if anything, about the author's life and intentions. Indeed, it can be distracting to know that an author intended that certain meanings or effects be produced by a text. When an author purposefully arranges a text to evoke a specific meaning, it is called *intentional fallacy*. When the text is arranged to produce a specific effect, it is called *affective fallacy*. They are important reminders that the formalist reader can be distracted by such misleading (and irrelevant) information. A literary work carries not its author's intention (intentional fallacy), but rather its own intention (the intention of the text). Effects generated by a text (affective fallacy) are not those necessarily intended by an author, but rather those generated when images, metaphors, and other parts of a work come together to produce an effect to be experienced.

Metaphor and image, fundamental building blocks of all literature, are especially strategic in interpreting literature from a formalist perspective. One of the reasons for the importance of metaphor and image involves the ways in which these elements often come together to make up fundamental tensions and even paradoxes in literary texts. Indeed, the analysis of tensions, paradoxes, and ironies, and the ways in which they combine to form an organic whole in literature constitutes one of the most important goals for the formalist reader.

All literary texts include concrete images, and the explication of these images is a particularly strategic part of formalist reading. These poetic devices, along with other elements, such as meter, rhythm, voice, diction, tone, and so forth, all come together to form a "stable text." Because the formalist emphasis is on neither the reader nor the writer, it focuses always and directly on the objective text itself. This perspective is in sharp contrast to many other approaches, as you will see in subsequent chapters.

Formalist critics have long called for a close reading of the text for effective interpretation. This emphasis does not mean that other approaches do not closely examine texts, but it does mean that the formalist approach pays particular attention to details and elements within a work that draw attention to the text itself. Whereas other approaches (feminist criticism, for example) may look to the ways in which texts refer to outside references (images of women or gender relations, for example), the formalist approach is always concerned with the text itself. Other approaches to literature believe that literature always reflects the culture within which it was created, but the formalist approach accepts literature as having been written for all time, with stable meaning that transcends cultural developments and historical movements. Even though a culture may change, the poem, story, or play will always retain its original integrity and organic unity.

As a formalist reader, it is strategic that you read literature for its coherence and structural integrity. You should explore texts as stable entities, rich in tension, paradox, and ambiguity, but nonetheless as works that hold together as a coherent whole. Works of literature, according to formalist principles, are experiences to be lived, not abstract activities to be read as references or discussions of someone else's experience. Formalist poet Archibald MacLeish concludes his 1926 poem "Ars Poetica" with these lines: "A poem should not mean / But be."

When we engage in close reading as formalist interpreters, we are in a continuous process of explication, which comes from the French expression *explication de texte* and means to examine the text very closely. We look carefully (and thoroughly) for meanings and nuances of meanings, allusions, denotations and connotations of words, connections among different parts of the work, overall structure and coherence, tensions and paradoxes that characterize and dramatize the work as a whole. We read a work not to arrive at an abstract, intellectual interpretation, but to "feel" the work in all its strength and meaning. Everything that we need for understanding is contained within the work and, with the aid of a good dictionary, there is no need for detailed library research or for a historical investigation of the author's life and times.

It is not an exaggeration to suggest that some readers are overpowered by the coherence and strength of the experience of reading a poem, story, or play—and often with lasting reverberations. To read from a formalist perspective is to see all of a work's complexities in an organized or unified manner, but the formalist reader can only arrive there by working closely with the details of the literary work.

Any interpretation of a work of literature involves a certain amount of summing up, or rephrasing meaning, in your own words. However, for formalist readers a paraphrase is not a substitution for a carefully articulated interpretation. A literary work is a complex weave of tensions, paradoxes, and ambiguities, and the simple restatement of a literary theme does not do justice to the rich, combined content and form of the work. The structure and meaning of a poem, story, or play must be worked out in careful detail, and paraphrase, when it is used sparingly, is only the beginning of an interpretation.

In approaches to interpretation, we sometimes look for an overall impact or effect to begin our interpretation (reader-response criticism, for example). Although there is more than one way to begin a formalist approach, a useful point of departure is to start by closely examining words and diction. Poets, prose fiction writers, and playwrights are very careful in the language they choose, and we should be no less precise in the way we interpret their words. All words have multiple meanings (depending on the context of the language and history of the terms) and words carry nuances and implications. We often examine words for their denotative (literal) and connotative (what they suggest or imply) meanings. Both denotation and connotation are very important in literary interpretation (and it is useful to bear in mind that sometimes the denotative and connotative meanings of words can contradict one another). As a formalist reader, it is important to remember that the goal of interpretation is to explain (as well as "feel") how the tensions, ambiguities, and paradoxes of the work can be reconciled in a unified interpretation. The overall goal of the formalist interpretation is to bring everything together into one cohesive whole.

Almost any work of literature includes language and other elements that are not clear upon a first reading. This confusion is particularly true for much of poetry. It is the role of the formalist reader to unravel the parts of the whole as soon as possible, which means to begin by carefully defining words. Although there is no detailed, exact process of interpretation handed down by the original formalist critics, there are some practical steps in developing your formalist sense of the work. In order to begin your analysis, I suggest the following steps:

1) Read the work at least twice, and think about ambiguities, tensions, and contradictions that strike you as significant parts of the text.
2) As you read the work again, look carefully at diction. Words are the building blocks of any story or poem, and it is important that you know their dictionary definitions (including historical information) as well as denotations.

3) Look for powerful images, metaphors, symbols, and allusions that resonate with meaning.

4) Pay particular attention to voice, tone, and point of view.

5) Examine the parts of the text and speculate about how they come together in forming a unified whole, where major tensions are reconciled. At this stage, you should be thinking about a central controlling idea or theme that unites the poem or story and brings the parts together.

As a formalist critic, you can hone your analytic and evaluative abilities by addressing literature in the manner suggested in this chapter. Following Emily Dickinson's "Because I Could Not Stop for Death," is a series of strategies suggested to assist you in sharpening your reading and writing skills.

A SAMPLE READING

"Because I Could Not Stop for Death" by Emily Dickinson (1830–1886)

> Because I could not stop for Death—
> He kindly stopped for me—
> The Carriage held but just Ourselves—
> And Immortality.
>
> We slowly drove—He knew no haste   5
> And I had put away
> My labor and my leisure too,
> For His Civility—
>
> We passed the School, where Children strove
> At Recess—in the Ring—   10
> We passed the Fields of Gazing Grain—
> We passed the Setting Sun—
>
> Or rather—He passed Us—
> The Dews drew quivering and chill—
> For only Gossamer, my Gown—   15
> My Tippet—only Tulle—
>
> We passed before a House that seemed
> A Swelling of the Ground—
> The Roof was scarcely visible—
> The Cornice—in the Ground—   20
>
> Since then—'tis Centuries—and yet
> Feels shorter than the Day
> I first surmised the Horses Heads
> Were toward Eternity—

ANALYZING "BECAUSE I COULD NOT STOP FOR DEATH"

Any approach to interpreting poetry depends upon your understanding of diction, tone, voice, and point of view, imagery, symbolism, metaphor, theme, plot, and other formal aspects of literature. Before beginning a formalist reading of "Because I Could Not Stop for Death," it is important to consider some of the basic elements of the story. Once you have begun to feel comfortable with the literary elements of the story, the author's style, and the flow of the poem and its tensions and ambiguities, you will be in a better position to articulate your objective interpretation. The controlled formalist interpreter uses the tools of the text to help build a reasonable and persuasive interpretation in which the parts of the poem come together into a unified, reasonable whole.

Diction

Emily Dickinson did not title her poems, so it would not be accurate to say that the title of this poem is anything other than the order in which the poem was numbered, 712. However, many readers have adopted the practice of referring to the poems by their first line, and this place is an excellent start in examining the poem's powerful diction.

The poem begins with the conjunction "Because," indicating a clear cause and effect relationship. The word "Because" tells us that the word and the rest of the clause relate to something else, another clause in fact ("He kindly stopped for me"). By deferring the key subject, "he," as death, the poem's introduction builds up suspense and mystery. Another important term, "Carriage," suggests courtliness, perhaps even aristocracy. There are connotations of gentility and civility. (Indeed, "Civility" appears at the end of the second stanza.) "Haste" is a noun that usually denotes intensity and urgency, but in this case, "no haste," it implies leisure and pace. "Children" normally evokes a sense of youth, vitality, potential of life (a paradoxical choice of diction in a poem about death). "Fields of Gazing Grain" suggests fecundity and fertility. The "Setting Sun" denotes the end of a cycle (a day), perhaps in preparation for the continuation of another turn in nature's process.

Word choices become more personal in the fourth stanza. "Gossamer, my Gown," identifies the speaker as female, as does "My Tippet—only Tulle." Yet there is a sense of sophistication in these terms. Gossamer evokes images of fine, delicate cloth. *Tippet* means a formal, elegantly embroidered shoulder covering, such as that worn by clerics, and suggests a religious formality (and gentility); a *tulle* is a fine, starched net of silk, used for a veil or bouffant grown.

The term "Cornice" also denotes a regal or majestic setting (a contemporary synonym would be "crown molding"). "Horses Heads" implies a journey, especially when directed "toward Eternity." Other terms, such as "Gazing

Grain," "Dews," and "Roof" carry special meaning that comes alive through the context and power of the poem, especially the ways in which they convey the complex relationship between life and death. Ironically, the speaker both experiences death and observes her death experience. Paradoxically, she is both inside and outside of her experiences.

Plot

This poem, like so many other narrative poems, tells a story. The poem begins by introducing the reader to the two main characters: the speaker/poet and Death, personified as a kindly, gentleman caller who arrives unexpectedly. The courtly carriage driver and the speaker travel through space and time (centuries no less!), traveling past fields, schools, and a cemetery. The characters are presented as a couple, as suggested by references to "we" and "us." Although one might expect a gentleman caller to arrive on a weekend, this one arrives in the middle of a day, indicated by "Children strove / At Recess"). This sense of timing is but another paradox in the poem.

Death is usually associated with despair, but this poem has a spirited rhythm to its plot development and the speaker does not describe herself as frightened or depressed in the least (an interesting paradox). Indeed, the speaker seems to have a vision of exuberant time-travel experience. The poem clearly conveys a sense of imaginative energy as the speaker travels through space and time with her courtly companion.

Tone and Point of View

The tone of this poem, detached and objective (in spite of the fact that it is a first-person narrator), is one of formality and gentility, which is first suggested by the use of the term "kindly" in describing Death's approach to the speaker. The figure of Death is a coachman, a suitor, an elegant footman. Although the poem is written in the first person, a narrating person, there is an elegance and civility between the two characters in their journey toward (and with) "Immortality." In spite of the first-person technique, however, the point of view is also somewhat detached and objective. The tension between the first-person perspective and the detached viewpoint are but one of several paradoxes in the poem. The poet speaks, for example, of her death with a detached equanimity.

Theme

There are many important thematic issues in this poem, including time, death, the world of the flesh, the world of the spirit, and also the speaker/poet's use of time and memory revealed in an almost meditative manner. Like so many of Emily Dickinson's poems, "Because I Could Not Stop for Death" calls attention to the tension between "reality" and the imagination. The speaker vacillates her focus between temporal, ordinary experiences and the eternal or infinite. One of the key passages in the poem, "Since then—'tis Centuries," reminds the reader that great periods of time have passed (almost infinite time), yet the speaker also reminds us of the mundane activities of daily living, "We passed the School, where Children strove." It is as if the speaker is calling our attention to two perspectives: the immediate and the eternal. Dying, for example, seems to be examined from both within and without. In death there are memories of life and in life there is the experience of death. To put it another way, one can only know death through life, and vice versa. The duality of these tensions, framed in a context of rich irony, stands again as one of many paradoxes in the poem.

Metaphor, Imagery, Symbol

It is probably obvious to most readers that "Death" in the personification of a gentleman suitor, almost comic, is a major metaphor in this narrative poem. There are many possible interpretations of this metaphor, of course, including reading death as a messenger from the heavens, sent to escort the speaker to a kind of heavenly marriage or reunion (note the emphasis on bridal clothing). Indeed, one might say that the poem has a Cinderella quality to it.

However one interprets "Death," the personification is clearly an attempt to make him/it a familiar and unthreatening experience. Indeed, one might even say that death is presented sympathetically. "Immortality" is an abstract personification that serves as both "witness" and context of time. Immortality is a place/experience toward which humans travel, but it is also something that can be known from a human perspective. The speaker comes to know immortality through life *and* death, as the centuries pass. There are other important images too, such as the journey motif; indeed, life and death are presented as parts of a connected, very long journey. The sequences of life are represented by the "Setting Sun," which brings together past, present, and future time. The cycle of one day symbolically represents the cycle of a human life, and the narrator's "consciousness" of this cycle becomes a major theme.

Questions for Your Analysis of "Because I Could Not Stop for Death"

1) Can you identify several important words in the poem, considering both denotations and connotations?
2) What are some of your early impressions of the overall structure of the poem?

3) What are the most important parts of the poem? How do these parts come together to form a unified whole?

4) What are your observations on the speaker's point of view? What tone do you
find in the poem?

5) What kind of characteristics do you associate with the personality of the narra-
tor/speaker, particularly as she tells her story of experiencing life and death?

6) How do you feel about the major topics of the poem: life and death, travel
through time and space, the experience of looking back at life after a long period
of time ("'tis Centuries")?

7) Many readers find that Emily Dickinson raises a range of questions in her poetry,
rather than present a clearly defined view of human experience that offers us
lessons on "how to live" or "solve problems," as do some other poets. What are
some of the strategic questions raised in the poem?

8) This poem contains numerous precise images and metaphors. Can you identify
some of these and explain how they come together to support some of the poem's
important themes?

9) Time is clearly a very important topic in the poem. What are the different perspectives on time?

10) The last stanza suggests, perhaps, that the speaker is an infinite state of travel,
with no end to her journey. What does this stanza say about the poem's resolution (or lack thereof)?

11) What are some of the main tensions or paradoxes in the poem?

12) How might these tensions and paradoxes be resolved in an overall reading that
takes them into consideration? Can you summarize the meaning of the poem in
one sentence?

The textual issues raised by these questions suggest that this poem is not
only a complex one, but that part of this complexity is due to the number of
polarities or oppositions addressed in the poem. The rich tapestry of diction,
images, and metaphors come together to create powerful effects, but they do
not follow a systematic and easily explained pattern. Please read the following
sample essay on "Because I Could Not Stop for Death" as an illustration of one
form a formalist interpretation might take. This essay, as you will see, focuses
on the critical elements of the poem. Other formalist interpretations to the
poem might focus more heavily on other tensions, paradoxes, images, and
metaphors that make up this dense, powerful poem.

Sample Essay on "Because I Could Not Stop for Death"

"Because I Could Not Stop for Death" is a powerful, haunting poem by Emily Dickinson that explores the complex mysteries of life and death, space and time, the natural
world and the spiritual world. It would be reasonable to characterize this poem as one
that also investigates the way we *think* about living and dying. The diction, rhythm, and
tone of the poem, along with a variety of images and metaphors, come together to illustrate themes of mortality and immortality, earthly existence and heavenly experience,

as well as the complex nature of time. There are a number of tensions, ambiguities, and paradoxes in the poem, but they come together to create an overall sense of what it feels like to be dead and alive, to transcend time and still be able to think about life's experiences within the context of human, daily time.

The poem begins with the speaker's announcement that a gentleman suitor came calling for her. The narrator implies that she had no time for death (is there ever a "right time" to die?), but he "kindly" came for her. The poem's atmosphere of gentility and formality is emphasized by the suitor's private "Carriage," reserved for the narrator, a silent observer; by "immortality"; and by the death-driver, who displays tenderness and "civility." The first two stanzas do much to emphasize, ironically, a nonthreatening portrait of death, a gentleman caller rather than a fearsome figure often portrayed as the "grim reaper."

The diction and tone of the beginning stanzas reveal a tension and ambivalence that runs through the entire poem. The first word, "Because" ("I could not stop for Death") tells us that this word and the rest of the clause relate to something else. By deferring the key subject, "he" as Death, the poem's introduction builds up suspense and mystery for the reader. Another important term, "Carriage" suggests courtliness, perhaps even aristocracy. There are connotations of gentility and civility throughout the poem. "Haste" is a noun that usually denotes intensity and urgency, but in this case it suggests "no haste," and implies leisure and pace. "Children" normally evoke images of vitality and emphasize the potential of life (a paradoxical choice of diction in a poem about death). "Fields of Gazing Grain" suggests fecundity and fertility. The "Setting Sun" denotes the end of a cycle (a day), perhaps in preparation for the continuation of yet another turn in nature's process. All of these words suggest a natural world that is unthreatening. Even the allusion to a cemetery plot, "A Swelling of the Ground," is portrayed as something ambiguous (it "seemed") and scarcely visible, perhaps as in a dream.

Word choices become more intense and personal in the middle of the poem. "Gossamer, my Gown," identifies the speaker as female, as does "My Tippet—only Tulle." Yet there is a sense of subtlety and sophistication, even royalty, in these terms. Gossamer evokes images of fine, delicate, expensive fabric. *Tippet* means a formal, elegantly embroidered shoulder covering, such as that worn by clerics, and suggests a religious formality (and again, gentility); a *tulle* is a fine, starched net of silk, used for a veil or bouffant gown. The narrator, through her choice of words, seems to be suggesting that her experience is one of majesty and solemnity.

The term "Cornice" also reinforces a regal or majestic setting (a contemporary synonym would be "crown molding"), yet paradoxically it also suggests a funeral mound in the poem. "Horses Heads" implies a journey, especially when directed "toward Eternity." Other terms, such as "Gazing Grain," "Dews," and "Roof" convey the complex relationship between life and death, the human and vegetable world. Ironically, the speaker both experiences death and observes her death experience. Paradoxically, she is both inside and outside of her experiences. This "double perspective" would seem to raise questions about the complex nature of seeing, knowing, and feeling.

Images of time dominate the poem, beginning with the speaker's description of "Immortality" as a person ("The Carriage held but just Ourselves / and Immortality"). The narrator and her suitor drive "slowly," passing schoolchildren, fields of grain, and the setting sun. The speaker seems unsure about where they are at any given time, as in "We passed the setting Sun— / Or rather—He passed Us—." The level of "not knowing" or not being able to know anything for certain is one of the major themes of the poem. The atmosphere and mood are relaxed, almost as if the travelers were on a long vacation, giving the narrator time to reflect on life. The travelers "pause" before swollen ground, which suggests vacationers visiting a cemetery. Indeed, I can see the two travelers on a vacation that never ends, "Immortality" their constant companion.

References to life and death are clearly important, yet they are not portrayed as links in a chain. On the contrary, life and death are part of the same cycle, not to be experienced as linear events, but rather as events that are inseparable. To live, according to the poem, is to be aware of death; to be dead is to observe life. These apparent contradictions come together as the "whole" of life. To put it another way, the knowledge of death makes living more intense, perhaps more joyful because we know that it is only temporary. And yet death is a release from life, which is not always pleasant. To die is to "live again" in a different form, as articulated by so many religions. This is not to suggest that there is a strong religious message to this poem, but rather to acknowledge that death is perhaps not so painful and is a continuation of life in another form.

The final stanza is perhaps the most complex and paradoxical section of the poem. The speaker tells us that centuries have passed since the arrival of her gentleman caller, but it feels less than the time she first realized that the "trip" was toward "forever." Time becomes a place (as well as a fellow traveler) in the mind of the speaker, and most of us do not think of time as place (or space). We do know that twentieth-century science has examined interconnections between space and time, and it appears that Emily Dickinson may have been ahead of her time in raising questions about relationships between space and time.

What are some of the major paradoxes and tensions in this complex poem? The narrator presents death as a kindly suitor, not a fear-inspiring, grotesque figure. Death is presented not as a departure from life, but rather as an extension of life (that includes life itself). Mortality and immortality, often portrayed as opposites, become indistinguishable from one another. Seeing and thinking become a way of death as well as a way of life. The tone of the poem is one of serenity and tranquillity, in spite of the theme of death.

How do these paradoxes come together and reconcile themselves into a unified, organic poem? I believe that there are several parts to the answer to this question. First, the narrator seems to suggest that everything that she experiences and thinks about contains the seeds of its opposite (death/life; mortality/immortality; limited time/unlimited time; ignorance/sudden insight). These "differences" reveal a tension in living that marks us as distinctly human. They reveal how we are able to overcome the limitations of being human. Second, everything in the poem suggests a narrator and her experience as being in perfect repose. There is no fear, danger, or threatening elements in the poem, not even death itself (perhaps the most basic human fear there is). Third, the rhythms of the poem suggest child's play, perhaps a nursery rhyme or games children play (symbolized by children playing in the ring at school). In order to understand life as a fully mature adult, one may have to rely on simple, almost childlike means of seeing and perceiving, through play. The "Cinderella" plot of the poem—a suitor carrying away his bride to the reaches of the universe—suggests a primitive experience that may reveal a very complex view of life and death, an epiphany that is reached by the narrator at the end of the poem.

WRITING YOUR ESSAY ABOUT A POEM FROM A FORMALIST PERSPECTIVE

"The Fish" is a poem by Elizabeth Bishop (1911–1979) that tells a story, as does Emily Dickinson's "Because I Could Not Stop for Death." "The Fish" focuses on themes of life and death, too, and is also narrated by a first-person persona who expresses new insight by the end of the poem, which some readers call an *epiphany*. In spite of these similarities, however, there are some major differences between these two poems, particularly the ways in which the poets use images, metaphors, and diction.

It would be accurate to suggest that "The Fish" is a poetic narrative about both a fish and the narrator or speaker of the poem. There is no question that it is a highly personal poem. Indeed, the poem contains nearly two dozen personal pronouns and the work is less than 80 lines long. What is striking about this story is the author's attempt to express the significance of what may appear to be a mundane event in the life of someone fishing. To catch a fish would normally appear to be an insignificant event, but Elizabeth Bishop is able to tell this story with such clarity, intensity, and personal involvement that it turns a common story into a memorable event, not only for the speaker but also for the reader. After you have read the "The Fish," there are a series of steps to assist you in your analysis of the work, as well as help you in writing an essay about this poem from a formalist perspective.

A SAMPLE READING

"The Fish" by Elizabeth Bishop (1911–1979)

I caught a tremendous fish
and held him beside the boat
half out of water, with my hook
fast in a corner of his mouth.
He didn't fight.   5
He hadn't fought at all.
He hung a grunting weight,
battered and venerable
and homely. Here and there
his brown skin hung in strips   10
like ancient wall-paper,
and its pattern of darker brown
was like wall-paper:
shapes like full-blown roses
stained and lost through age.   15
He was speckled with barnacles,
fine rosettes of lime,
and infested
with tiny white sea-lice,

and underneath two or three   20
rags of green weed hung down.
While his gills were breathing in
the terrible oxygen
—the frightening gills,
fresh and crisp with blood,   25
that can cut so badly—
I thought of the coarse white flesh
packed in like feathers,
the big bones and the little bones,
the dramatic reds and blacks   30
of his shiny entrails,
and the pink swim-bladder
like a big peony.
I looked into his eyes
which were far larger than mine   35
but shallower, and yellowed,
the irises backed and packed
with tarnished tinfoil
seen through the lenses
of old scratched isinglass.   40
They shifted a little, but not
to return my stare.
—It was more like the tipping
of an object toward the light.
I admired his sullen face,   45
the mechanism of his jaw,
and then I saw
that from his lower lip
—if you could call it a lip—
grim, wet, and weapon-like,   50
hung five old pieces of fish-line,
or four and a wire leader
with the swivel still attached,
with all their five big hooks
grown firmly in his mouth.   55
A green line, frayed at the end
where he broke it, two heavier lines,
and a fine black thread
still crimped from the strain and snap
when it broke and he got away.   60
Like medals with their ribbons
frayed and wavering,
a five-haired beard of wisdom
trailing from his aching jaw.
I stared and stared   65
and victory filled up
the little rented boat,
from the pool of bilge
where oil had spread a rainbow
around the rusted engine   70
to the bailer rusted orange,
the sun-cracked thwarts,

the oarlocks on their strings,
the gunnels—until everything
was rainbow, rainbow, rainbow!   75
And I let the fish go.

Questions for Your Analysis of "The Fish"

1) What are some of your early impressions of the poem? What is the most striking image in the poem, something that promotes an instant reaction in you?
2) This story is told in the first person by an unnamed narrator. Why would the poet choose an unnamed first-person narrator? What is the effect of this decision?
3) Can you identify several important words in the poem, considering both denotations and connotations?
4) What are the most important parts of the poem? How do these parts come together to form a unified whole, and how does the end of the poem fit into this structure?
5) What are some of your early impressions of the overall structure of the poem? What idea or ideas "hold" the poem together?
6) What are your observations on the speaker's point of view? What tone (or tones) do you find in the poem? (For example, is there a tone of sympathy for the fish?)
7) What characteristics do you associate with the personality of the narrator/speaker, particularly as she tells her dramatic story of interacting with the fish and determining his life or death?
8) How do you feel about the major topics of the poem: survival of the fish, his personal history, changes in the narrator after her encounter with the fish?
9) Many readers find that Elizabeth Bishop has taken a simple story of a person and a fish and made it into a larger tale of growth and sensitivity. What are some of the strategic questions raised in the poem?
10) This poem contains numerous precise images and metaphors. Can you identify some of these and explain how they come together to support some of the poem's important themes?
11) The personification of the fish is clearly an important part of the poem. When the narrator gives the fish human qualities, how does this affect your interpretation?
12) The last stanza suggests, perhaps, that the speaker has experienced an epiphany— sudden insight into herself. What does this stanza say about the poem's resolution (or lack thereof)?
13) What are the main tensions or paradoxes in the poem?
14) How might these tensions and paradoxes be resolved? Can you summarize the meaning of the poem in one sentence?

The textual issues raised by these questions suggest that "The Fish" is not only a complex poem (in spite of its superficial simplicity), but that part of this complexity is the change that appears to happen to the narrator as a result of her encounter with the fish. The striking diction, engaging plot structure, rich imagery and metaphors, and themes of insight come together to create powerful effects.

STEPS IN WRITING A FORMALIST ESSAY
ABOUT ANY READING

1) Write down key words in the story or poem, particularly strong nouns and active verbs.
2) Describe strategic moments and critical plot movements in the work.
3) Analyze the tone of the work and check to see if the tone changes. Identify key words or phrases that set the mood or atmosphere of the work.
4) Specify key themes in the work.
5) Flesh out important metaphors and images. Examine how they relate to one another and contribute to the overall structure of the work.
6) Identify central characters and their relationship to one another.
7) Examine any paradoxes or tensions in the work.
8) Consider the ending and determine whether it flows from what has taken place in the story or poem. Analyze whether the ending brings together the work as a unified whole.
9) A good general electronic source to investigate the context of any literary reading is google.com. By typing in the title of the work, especially if it is a well-known literary work, you will locate several sources that provide background information.

STEPS IN WRITING AN ESSAY ABOUT "THE FISH"

Brainstorming Your Topic

1) Write down key words, being careful to define them and write down possible connotations. (You might begin with some of these words: "tremendous," "venerable," "homely," "entrails," "medals and ribbons," "beard of wisdom" and "rainbow.")
2) Explain key moments in the poem when the plot seems to turn in important ways. (For example, "I looked into his eyes.")
3) Describe your impressions of the tone of the story and how the tone changes, if it does. (For example, "I admired his sullen face.")
4) Consider possible themes in the poem. (For example, "An old fish carries many war wounds.")
5) Observe key metaphors and images that appear, noting how they relate to one or more themes. For example, relate the image of the fish's "aching jaw" (line 64) with the narrator's response, "I stared and stared / and victory filled up" (line 65).
6) Focus on the two main characters, the fish and the narrator. Write down your impressions of the history of the fish (his survival of many battles) and of the narrator (her changing attitude toward the fish).
7) The narrator objectively describes a routine fishing experience. Write down what happens during that encounter that changes her mind.
8) Write down your reaction to her experience.
9) Write down any paradoxes and tensions that exist in the poem. (Is it a paradox that the narrator shows sensitivity to the fish? Is it paradoxical that the fish is described with human qualities?)

10) What personal experiences have you had that connect to parts of "The Fish"?

11) Are you satisfied with the ending? Why or why not?

12) Unless your instructor insists that you not consult outside sources in brainstorming your topic, refer to the electronic sources listed for Elizabeth Bishop. There are links that will connect you to biographical sources and detailed criticism. Any ideas and words drawn directly from outside sources should be properly cited, of course. Consult the appendix for documentation procedures.

Creating an Outline

1) Collect your answers to the questions above in short two-word or three-word categories and use them as preliminary "writing points" in your analysis of "The Fish."

2) Think about the points and consider whether they add up to a central idea (for example, the education of the narrator in "The Fish").

3) Identify five or six main writing points that support your central idea (one of these might be the battle-scarred history of the fish). These points should come from the main literary elements in the story (diction, plot, theme, point of view, metaphor). All of the points should provide support for your controlling idea, which should be stated in one sentence.

4) If you have more than five or six points, try to combine one or more of them. If you have fewer than five or six points, see if some of them can be used to generate additional points. You may have some large points (the long personal history of the fish, for example) that include other issues (images of the fish's immediate description) that can stand alone as paragraph topic sentences.

5) Look for transitional devices that connect your main points of support.

Preparing a Rough Draft

1) Now that you have created a working outline, you have already completed your major organizational work. Each major point is the topic of a paragraph, and your essay will probably have been 5 and 10 paragraphs, depending on development. These paragraphs need not be of equal length, but each one should sufficiently develop the topic sentence.

2) Now that you have your major writing points, assemble a preliminary draft by developing each topic idea with two or three sentences that discuss evidence from the text.

3) Focus on developing transitions between your paragraphs. Professional writers often begin a new paragraph with a direct reference to an idea expressed at the end of the preceding paragraph.

4) It is not too early to begin writing your concluding paragraph, which may involve the narrator's change of heart in releasing the fish. Conclusions often summarize the main points of a central idea (but do not repeat word for word what has already been said). A conclusion may also refer to implications of what has been said (but what cannot be developed because of space limits). Your conclusion should deal with the narrator's apparent change at the end of the poem.

5) Don't be afraid to include questions in your writing (as in the sample essay on "Because I Could Not Stop for Death"). No reader of literature can ever be absolutely certain of every observation that he or she makes, and perceptive observations often generate excellent questions, many of which are useful, even if unanswerable.

Editing Your Draft

1) At this stage, you should have a draft of a few hundred words. You have already done the most difficult work in thinking out your ideas, organizing them into an outline, and preparing a rough version of the final product. Look for ways to edit your paper that will strengthen the essay.

2) Search for repetitious wording and ideas. Do not repeat ideas, however important, throughout the essay. Use a thesaurus to locate synonyms for terms and ideas that reappear. Attempt to emphasize variety in your language.

3) If your instructor encourages peer editing, choose someone in your class, or perhaps a roommate, and solicit advice about how your essay reads. Is it articulate, compelling, insightful, and interesting? (All of these qualities are important.) Although your peer editor may not be taking a literature class, he or she may be a very good source of feedback on how effective your writing is. Professional writers often seek feedback from peers, and not only from professional colleagues.

4) Be open to make changes in your writing, both conceptually and in specific language. Professional writers know that writing is recursive (which means that the act of writing constantly generates new ways of looking at the topic), and student writers should also take advantage of changes in thinking *as they write*. Don't be afraid to make efficient and effective changes, especially in terms of cutting out words, phrases, and sections that may not be working very well in supporting your overall idea.

5) Proofread carefully for spelling errors, punctuation problems, run-on sentences, and ambiguous or awkward constructions. You should use a solid grammar handbook to assist you in these areas.

Final Checklist

1) Make sure that your central idea appears in the first paragraph. It is important that your reader know what major point, or points, you are attempting to make.

2) Because this essay is a formalist paper, check to see that the essay represents your objective response to "The Fish." Your major points should come together in a summary of the poem that explains its tensions and paradoxes.

3) Examine your essay for sufficient evidence. For example, your discussion may focus on both the narrator and the fish; give each of them adequate treatment. Each one of your major ideas will need illustration that comes directly from the poem.

4) Review your conclusion to see if you have ended the essay in an effective manner, either summarizing what you have said (in different language) or suggesting some important implications of your reading.

5) Proofread one last time for errors, repetitious language, and awkward phrasing. It is important that a formalist interpreter be clear in his or her writing.

ADDITIONAL READING

"The Necklace" by Guy de Maupassant (1850–1893)

She was one of those pretty and charming girls who are sometimes, as if by a mistake of destiny, born in a family of clerks. She had no dowry, no expectations, no means of being known, understood, loved, wedded by any rich and distinguished man; and she let herself be married to a little clerk at the Ministry of Public Instruction.

She dressed plainly because she could not dress well, but she was as unhappy as though she had really fallen from her proper station, since with women there is neither caste nor rank: and beauty, grace and charm act instead of family and birth. Natural fineness, instinct for what is elegant, suppleness of wit, are the sole hierarchy, and make from women of the people the equals of the very greatest ladies.

She suffered ceaselessly, feeling herself born for all the delicacies and all the luxuries. She suffered from the poverty of her dwelling, from the wretched look of the walls, from the worn-out chairs, from the ugliness of the curtains. All those things, of which another woman of her rank would never even have been conscious, tortured her and made her angry. The sight of the little Breton peasant who did her humble housework aroused in her regrets which were despairing, and distracted dreams. She thought of the silent antechambers hung with Oriental tapestry, lit by tall bronze candelabra, and of the two great footmen in knee breeches who sleep in the big armchairs, made drowsy by the heavy warmth of the hot-air stove. She thought of the long *salons* fitted up with ancient silk, of the delicate furniture carrying priceless curiosities, and of the coquettish perfumed boudoirs made for talks at five o'clock with intimate friends, with men famous and sought after, whom all women envy and whose attention they all desire.

When she sat down to dinner, before the round table covered with a table-cloth three days old, opposite her husband, who uncovered the soup tureen and declared with an enchanted air, "Ah, the good *pot-au-feu!* I don't know anything better than that," she thought of dainty dinners, of shining silverware, of tapestry which peopled the walls with ancient personages and with strange birds flying in the midst of a fairy forest; and she thought of delicious dishes served on marvelous plates, and of the whispered gallantries which you listen to with a sphinxlike smile, while you are eating the pink flesh of a trout or the wings of a quail.

She had no dresses, no jewels, nothing. And she loved nothing but that; she felt made for that. She would so have liked to please, to be envied, to be charming, to be sought after.   5

She had a friend, a former schoolmate at the convent, who was rich, and whom she did not like to go and see any more, because she suffered so much when she came back.

But one evening, her husband returned home with a triumphant air, and holding a large envelope in his hand.

"There," said he. "Here is something for you."

She tore the paper sharply, and drew out a printed card which bore these words:

"The Minister of Public Instruction and Mme. Georges Ramponneau request the   10
honor of M. and Mme. Loisel's company at the palace of the Ministry on Monday evening, January eighteenth."

Instead of being delighted, as her husband hoped, she threw the invitation on the table with disdain, murmuring:

"What do you want me to do with that?"

"But, my dear, I thought you would be glad. You never go out, and this is such a fine opportunity. I had awful trouble to get it. Everyone wants to go; it is very select, and they are not giving many invitations to clerks. The whole official world will be there."

She looked at him with an irritated glance, and said, impatiently:

"And what do you want me to put on my back?"   15

He had not thought of that; he stammered:

"Why, the dress you go to the theater in. It looks very well, to me."

He stopped, distracted, seeing his wife was crying. Two great tears descended slowly from the corners of her eyes toward the corners of her mouth. He stuttered:

"What's the matter? What's the matter?"

But, by violent effort, she had conquered her grief, and she replied, with a calm   20
voice, while she wiped her wet cheeks:

"Nothing. Only I have no dress and therefore I can't go to this ball. Give your card to some colleague whose wife is better equipped than I."

He was in despair. He resumed:

"Come, let us see, Mathilde. How much would it cost, a suitable dress, which you could use on other occasions, something very simple?"

She reflected several seconds, making her calculations and wondering also what sum she could ask without drawing on herself an immediate refusal and a frightened exclamation from the economical clerk.

Finally, she replied, hesitatingly: 25

"I don't know exactly, but I think I could manage it with four hundred francs."

He had grown a little pale, because he was laying aside just that amount to buy a gun and treat himself to a little shooting next summer on the plain of Nanterre, with several friends who went to shoot larks down there, of a Sunday.

But he said:

"All right. I will give you four hundred francs. And try to have a pretty dress."

The day of the ball drew near, and Mme. Loisel seemed sad, uneasy, anxious. Her   30
dress was ready, however. Her husband said to her one evening:

"What is the matter? Come, you've been so queer these last three days."

And she answered:

"It annoys me not to have a single jewel, not a single stone, nothing to put on. I shall look like distress. I should almost rather not go at all."

He resumed:

"You might wear natural flowers. It's very stylish at this time of the year. For ten   35
francs you can get two or three magnificent roses."

She was not convinced.

"No; there's nothing more humiliating than to look poor among other women who are rich."

But her husband cried:

"How stupid you are! Go look up your friend Mme. Forestier, and ask her to lend you some jewels. You're quite thick enough with her to do that."

She uttered a cry of joy: 40

"It's true. I never thought of it."

The next day she went to her friend and told of her distress.

Mme. Forestier went to a wardrobe with a glass door, took out a large jewel-box, brought it back, opened it, and said to Mme. Loisel:

"Choose, my dear."

She saw first of all some bracelets, then a pearl necklace, then a Venetian cross, gold and precious stones of admirable workmanship. She tried on the ornaments before the glass, hesitated, could not make up her mind to part with them, to give them back. She kept asking:

"Haven't you any more?"

"Why, yes. Look. I don't know what you like."

All of a sudden she discovered, in a black satin box, a superb necklace of diamonds, and her heart began to beat with an immoderate desire. Her hands trembled as she took it. She fastened it around her throat, outside her high-necked dress, and remained lost in ecstasy at the sight of herself.

Then she asked, hesitating, filled with anguish:

"Can you lend me that, only that?"

"Why, yes, certainly."

She sprang upon the neck of her friend, kissed her passionately, then fled with her treasure.

The day of the ball arrived. Mme. Loisel made a great success. She was prettier than them all, elegant, gracious, smiling, and crazy with joy. All the men looked at her, asked her name, endeavored to be introduced. All the attachés of the Cabinet wanted to waltz with her. She was remarked by the minister himself.

She danced with intoxication, with passion, made drunk by pleasure, forgetting all, in the triumph of her beauty, in the glory of her success, in a sort of cloud of happiness composed of all this homage, of all this admiration, of all these awakened desires, and of that sense of complete victory which is so sweet to a woman's heart.

She went away about four o'clock in the morning. Her husband had been sleeping since midnight, in a little deserted anteroom, with three other gentlemen whose wives were having a very good time. He threw over her shoulders the wraps which he had brought, modest wraps of common life, whose poverty contrasted with the elegance of the ball dress. She felt this, and wanted to escape so as not to be remarked by the other women, who were enveloping themselves in costly furs.

Loisel held her back.

"Wait a bit. You will catch cold outside. I will go and call a cab."

But she did not listen to him, and rapidly descended the stairs. When they were in the street they did not find a carriage; and they began to look for one, shouting after the cabmen whom they saw passing by at a distance.

They went down toward the Seine, in despair, shivering with cold. At last they found on the quay one of those ancient noctambulant coupés which, exactly as if they were ashamed to show their misery during the day, are never seen round Paris until after nightfall.

It took them to their door in the Rue des Martyrs, and once more, sadly, they climbed up homeward. All was ended, for her. And as to him, he reflected that he must be at the Ministry at ten o'clock.

She removed the wraps which covered her shoulders, before the glass, so as once more to see herself in all her glory. But suddenly she uttered a cry. She no longer had the necklace around her neck!

Her husband, already half undressed, demanded:

"What is the matter with you?"

She turned madly towards him:

"I have—I have—I've lost Mme. Forestier's necklace."   65

He stood up, distracted.

"What!—how?—impossible!"

And they looked in the folds of her dress, in the folds of her cloak, in her pockets, everywhere. They did not find it.

He asked:

"You're sure you had it on when you left the ball?"   70

"Yes, I felt it in the vestibule of the palace."

"But if you had lost it in the street we should have heard it fall. It must be in the cab."

"Yes. Probably. Did you take his number?"

"No. And you, didn't you notice it?"

"No."   75

They looked, thunderstruck, at one another. At last Loisel put on his clothes.

"I shall go back on foot," said he, "over the whole route which we have taken to see if I can find it."

And he went out. She sat waiting on a chair in her ball dress, without strength to go to bed, overwhelmed, without fire, without a thought.

He husband came back about seven o'clock. He had found nothing.

He went to Police Headquarters, to the newspaper offices, to offer a reward: he   80
went to the cab companies—everywhere, in fact, whither he was urged by the least suspicion of hope.

She waited all day, in the same condition of mad fear before this terrible calamity.

Loisel returned at night with a hollow, pale face; he had discovered nothing.

"You must write to your friend," said he, "that you have broken the clasp of her necklace and that you are having it mended. That will give us time to turn round."

She wrote at his dictation.

At the end of a week they had lost all hope.   85

And Loisel, who had aged five years, declared:

"We must consider how to replace that ornament."

The next day they took the box which had contained it, and they went to the jeweler whose name was found within. He consulted his books.

"It was not I, madame, who sold that necklace; I must simply have furnished the case."

Then they went from jeweler to jeweler, searching for a necklace like the other,   90
consulting their memories, sick both of them with chagrin and anguish.

They found, in a shop at the Palais Royal, a string of diamonds which seemed to them exactly like the one they looked for. It was worth forty thousand francs. They could have it for thirty-six.

So they begged the jeweler not to sell it for three days yet. And they made a bargain that he should buy it back for thirty-four thousand francs, in case they found the other one before the end of February.

Loisel possessed eighteen thousand francs which his father had left him. He would borrow the rest.

He did borrow, asking a thousand francs of one, five hundred of another, five louis here, three louis there. He gave notes, took up ruinous obligations, dealt with usurers and all the race of lenders. He compromised all the rest of his life, risked his signature without even knowing if he could meet it; and, frightened by the pains yet to come, by the black misery which was about to fall upon him, by the prospect of all the physical privation and of all the moral tortures which he was to suffer, he went to get the new necklace, putting down upon the merchant's counter thirty-six thousand francs.

When Mme. Loisel took back the necklace, Mme. Forestier said to her, with a   95
chilly manner:

"You should have returned it sooner; I might have needed it."

She did not open the case, as her friend had so much feared. If she had detected the substitution, what would she have thought, what would she have said? Would she not have taken Mme. Loisel for a thief?

Mme. Loisel now knew the horrible existence of the needy. She took her part, moreover, all of a sudden, with heroism. That dreadful debt must be paid. She would pay it. They dismissed their servant; they changed their lodgings; they rented a garret under the roof.

She came to know what heavy housework meant and the odious cares of the kitchen. She washed the dishes, using her rosy nails on the greasy pots and pans. She washed the dirty linen, the shirts, and the dishcloths, which she dried upon a line; she carried the slops down to the street every morning, and carried up the water, stopping for breath at every landing. And, dressed like a woman of the people, she went to the fruiterer, the grocer, the butcher, her basket on her arm, bargaining, insulted, defending her miserable money sou by sou.

Each month they had to meet some notes, renew others, obtain more time.   100

Her husband worked in the evening making a fair copy of some tradesman's accounts, and late at night he often copied manuscript for five sous a page.

And this life lasted for ten years.

At the end of ten years, they had paid everything, everything, with the rates of usury, and the accumulations of the compound interest.

Mme. Loisel looked old now. She had become the woman of impoverished households—strong and hard and rough. With frowsy hair, skirts askew, and red hands, she talked loud while washing the floor with great swishes of water. But sometimes, when her husband was at the office, she sat down near the window, and she thought of that gay evening of long ago, of the ball where she had been so beautiful and so fêted.

What would have happened if she had not lost that necklace? Who knows? Who   105
knows? How life is strange and changeful! How little a thing is needed for us to be lost or to be saved!

But, one Sunday, having gone to take a walk in the Champs Elysées to refresh herself from the labor of the week, she suddenly perceived a woman who was leading a child. It was Mme. Forestier, still young, still beautiful, still charming.

Mme. Loisel felt moved. Was she going to speak to her? Yes, certainly. And now that she had paid, she was going to tell her all about it. Why not?

She went up.

"Good day, Jeanne."

The other, astonished to be familiarly addressed by this plain goodwife, did not   110
recognize her at all, and stammered:

"But—madam!—I do not know—You must be mistaken."

"No. I am Mathilde Loisel."

Her friend uttered a cry.

"Oh, my poor Mathilde! How you are changed!"

"Yes, I have had days hard enough, since I have seen you, days wretched enough—   115
and that because of you!"

"Of me! How so?"

"Do you remember that diamond necklace which you lent me to wear at the min-
isterial ball?"

"Yes. Well?"

"Well, I lost it."

"What do you mean? You brought it back."   120

"I brought you back another just like it. And for this we have been ten years paying. You can understand that it was not easy for us, us who had nothing. At last it is
ended, and I am very glad."

Mme. Forestier had stopped.

"You say that you bought a necklace of diamonds to replace mine?"

"Yes. You never noticed it, then! They were very like."

And she smiled with a joy which was proud and naïve at once.   125

Mme. Forestier, strongly moved, took her two hands.

"Oh, my poor Mathilde! Why, my necklace was paste. It was worth at most five
hundred francs!"

STEPS TO ASSIST YOU IN WRITING ABOUT "THE NECKLACE"

Brainstorming Your Topic

1) Write down key terms, being careful to define them and write down possible connotations. (You might begin with some of these words: "dowry," "convent,"
   "usury," "attaches," "ruinous obligations," "Champs Elysées," and "paste.")
2) Explain key turning points in the story when the plot seems to turn in critical
   ways. (For example, when Mathilde decides that she must have jewelry for the
   ball.)
3) Describe your impressions of the tone of the story and how the tone changes, if it
   does. (For example, the narrator begins the story by introducing Mathilde as "one
   of those pretty and charming girls who are sometimes, as if by a mistake of destiny, born in a family of clerks.")
4) Consider possible themes in the story. (For example, "Do not try to be someone
   that you are not.")
5) Observe key metaphors and images that appear, noting how they relate to one or
   more themes. (For example, Mathilde's carefree spirit at the ball: "She danced
   with intoxication, with passion, made drunk by pleasure, forgetting all.")
6) Focus on the three main characters, Mathilde, her husband Mr. Loisel, and Mrs.
   Forestier. How does the author convey their personalities? To what end?

7) The narrator objectively describes an ironic situation of mistakes. Write down the reasons why Mathilde feels compelled to borrow the necklace and why she fails to tell Mrs. Forestier what has happened.
8) Think about what it means that the glittering thing Mathilde borrows—the life she envies—is fakery.
9) Write down any paradoxes and tensions that exist in the story. (You might begin with Mathilde's insistence on wearing jewelry to the ball or the confusion about the real value of the necklace.)
10) What personal experiences have you had that connect to parts of "The Necklace"?
11) Are you satisfied with the ending? Why or why not?

Creating an Outline

1) Collect your answers to the questions above in short two-word or three-word categories and use them as preliminary "writing points" in your analysis of "The Necklace."
2) Think about the points and consider whether they add up to a central idea (for example, the cost of creating an image to the social world).
3) Identify five or six main writing points that support your central idea (one of these might be the reasons why Mathilde borrows the necklace). These points should come from the main literary elements in the story (diction, plot, theme, point of view, metaphor). All of the points should provide support for your controlling idea, which should be stated in one sentence.
4) If you have more than five or six main points, try to combine one or two of them. If you have fewer than three or four points, see if some of them can be used to generate additional points. You may have some large points (the story's depiction of economic and social classes, for example) that include other issues (descriptions of social aspirations) that can stand alone as paragraph topic sentences.
5) Look for transitional devices that connect your main points of support.

For more development of your essay analyzing "The Necklace," refer to strategies of preparing a rough draft and editing a draft, and to the final checklist that appeared earlier in this chapter.

ELECTRONIC RESOURCES FOR EMILY DICKINSON

http://userweb.interactive.net/~krisxlee/emily. The Emily Dickinson Home Page.
http://userweb.interactive.net/~krisxlee/emily/#emweb. Email discussion list for Emily Dickinson.
http://town.hall.org/Archives/radio/IMS/HarperAudio/012794_harp_ITH.html. Audio recordings of Julie Harris reading poems by Emily Dickinson.
http://storm.usfca.edu/~southerr/emily.html. Essays on the work of Emily Dickinson.
http://tlc.ai.org/dickiidx.htm. A guide to the life and work of Emily Dickinson.
http://www-unix.oit.umass.edu/~emilypg/index.1.html. A site dedicated to the virtual Emily Dickinson.

ELECTRONIC RESOURCES FOR ELIZABETH BISHOP

http://iberia.vassar.edu/bishop/.   A site with links to Bishop resources, including membership information for the Bishop Society.
http://www.georgetown.edu/bassr/heath/syllabuild/iguide/bishop.html.   A guide to the work of Elizabeth Bishop, including links to other sites.
http://www.northshore.net/homepages/hope/engBishop.html.   Poems   by   Elizabeth Bishop.

ELECTRONIC RESOURCES FOR GUY DE MAUPASSANT

http://tlc.ai.org/demaupas.htm.   The Guy De Maupassant Teaching and Learning Center.
http://www.kirjasto.sci.fi/maupassa.htm.   A brief guide to the life of Guy De Maupassant.
http://www.selfknowledge.com/swgem10.htm.   Selected writings of Guy De Maupassant.

Further Readings in Formalist Criticism

Brooks, Cleanth. *The Well-Wrought Urn. Studies in the Structure of Poetry*. Metheun: London, 1986.
Brooks, Cleanth, and Robert Penn Warren, eds. *Understanding Poetry: An Anthology for College Students*. New York: Henry Holt, 1938.
Brooks, Cleanth, and Robert Penn Warren, eds. *Understanding Fiction*. New York: Appleton-Century-Crofts, 1943.
Ransom, John Crowe. *The New Criticism*. Norfolk: New Directions, 1941.
Richards, I. A. *Practical Criticism*. New York: Harcourt, 1929.
Wimsatt, W. K. Jr. *The Verbal Icon: Studies in the Meaning of Poetry*. Lexington: U of Kentucky P., 1954.
Wimsatt, W. K. Jr., and Monroe C. Beardsley. "The Intentional Fallacy." In *The Verbal Icon: Studies in the Meaning of Poetry*. 3–18.
Wimsatt, W. K. Jr., and Monroe C. Beardsley. "The Affective Fallacy." In *The Verbal Icon: Studies in the Meaning of Poetry*. 21–39.

chapter 4

Ethical Criticism

Ethical criticism is an approach to interpretation that locates the center of meaning in the moral, or ethical, dimensions of a literary text, particularly in the relationships characters have with others. The name comes from an emphasis on the ethical values that are present in all works of literature (literary texts may express, of course, quite different moral visions). Ethical criticism, like most of the schools of interpretation presented in this book, has been practiced in some form for a long time, at least as far back as ancient Greek times, when Greek children learned values and moral codes through the actions of the hero Ulysses in the epic tales the *Iliad* and the *Odyssey*.

Many schools of interpretation have principles that are easily identified and explained. Ethical criticism does not fall into this category, and there is not a body of common codes that can be easily summarized. This chapter attempts to explain ethical criticism in a way that you can practice it, and ethical criticism might be described in general terms as a way of reading literature for moral values and implications. While there are many possible approaches to this issue, this chapter will focus on ethical values as depicted in the relationships between individuals and you will be encouraged to explore ways in which values are presented through characters' interactions with one another, which create the opportunity for the emergence of new relationships (and ethical stances toward one another). There will be a discussion of the meaning of ethics (especially as it relates to personal responsibility, duty, and the burden of acting in good faith) and how our ethics are determined through encounters with others. (Chapter 5, "Civic Criticism," focuses on a broader sense of ethical criticism—examining literature for what it says about an individual's responsibility toward various communities.)

Characters in literature, whether clearly defined figures in short stories or speakers and/or abstract characters in poems (like the narrator and the fish in "The Fish"), always reveal qualities in themselves that have ethical dimensions. Like formalist criticism, ethical interpretation involves the close reading of a text in search of moral meaning as it is revealed through characters' words and actions. The things that characters say and do define what and who they are, at least from a moral perspective once referred to as *existentialism*. This view refers to the ability of all individuals to make free choices about what they do and say and to take responsibility for their actions and words. The choices that we make in our daily lives often have ethical consequences. Indeed, our words and actions define our ethical character, and the same concept holds true for literary figures.

A major principle in ethical criticism is the interaction, or encounters, between characters (for example, the "meeting" between the narrator and the fish in the preceding chapter). Characters' relationships with other characters reveal themes of morality (and possibly immorality or amorality). An ethical reading of a literary work considers how characters interface with others and accept their responsibilities. A character's ethical status is determined by how he or she relates to other characters. Some ethical critics suggest that characters show their true "faces," or ethical fiber, in their interactions with other characters. It is also true that we, as readers, interact with literary characters, and our own moral values influence the way we evaluate literary characters.

To read and interpret literature within an ethical context always means to judge characters by what they do (or choose not do not), as well as by what they say. It is important to judge characters as moral agents with responsibilities. In "Babylon Revisited," for example, all of the characters have responsibilities toward one another. Charlie Wales has obligations toward his daughter, the memory of his wife Helen, and his in-laws. Marion and Lincoln have a responsibility to look out for Honoria's welfare and treat Charlie fairly. Even Duncan and Lorraine have a responsibility to behave in a manner that does not adversely affect other people, such as Charlie. And it might be argued that all of these characters have a responsibility toward themselves to behave with fairness and dignity in their interactions with others. As you saw in Chapter 1, Charlie's loss of Honoria is partly his responsibility and partly the responsibility of others. It is by observing characters interacting with other characters that we are able to make ethical judgments.

In Chapter 2 you saw that the formalist reader looks for unity in a literary work; everything in the text (diction, plot, metaphor, theme) comes together to form a unified whole. Paradoxes and tensions, which surface in a text, often lend themselves to some kind of resolution or closure. An ethical interpretation of a literary work, on the contrary, does not seek out overriding unity, or wholeness. An ethical reading seeks to analyze human behavior for its moral dimensions, whether positive or negative. Since the beginning of literature, there have been agents of good and agents of evil, traditionally called protagonists and villains. Sometimes there are characters who are amoral, or without morality. And in some texts, particularly in modern literature, there are characters who behave morally in one set of circumstances and sometimes immorally (or amorally) under different circumstances. It is not always easy to make judgments about the morality of literary characters, but the primary goal of ethical criticism is to examine characters for the ethical dimensions of what they say and do in their encounters with others. In judging literary figures, we make judgments about ourselves and the values, duties, and responsibilities we hold dear.

Encounters between literary characters (which sometimes include a character's encounter with himself or herself, particularly in the case of a narrator) involve much more than words. The communication, or dialogue, between characters is strategic in analyzing the ethical elements of literature. In "Babylon Revisited," you saw how a verbal exchange among Charlie, Lorraine, and Duncan cost Charlie the guardianship of his daughter. The few words that were exchanged were pivotal in the turn of the plot, and they revealed much about the ethical faces of those directly involved. When characters speak to one another, they enter into relationships that often have serious ethical implications. Duncan and Lorraine had an obligation to speak cautiously in front of Charlie's relatives. Their careless, even reckless, banter cost Charlie dearly and their failure to observe an ethical responsibility is a key element for the ethical critic to consider. (There may have been a right time and place for their comments, but the setting of the Peters' home was clearly inappropriate.)

Conversations between characters are a two-way activity, of course, and they create an opportunity for readers to draw conclusions about all characters involved. Conversations (or dialogue) provide situations in which characters express themselves ethically (or unethically). An ethical reading of literary texts assumes that whatever we can know about a character comes through his or her dialogue and action. Characters do not have "essential" morality (or immorality); their ethical positions are revealed only through their encounters with others. The narrator of "The Fish" reveals an ethical stance, arguably, when she decides to release the fish after having thought about his past experiences. For her, it was the right thing to do (and perhaps some readers would agree), but she reached this decision only after encountering the fish *and* speaking/narrating about his experiences and circumstances. Her "ethical" decision is reached only after these contexts have been considered. In other words, the encounter set forth all of her actions, including her language about the encounter. The narrator's ethical decision is a personal one, involving only herself and the personified fish (and, of course, readers). Although we may draw larger conclusions about her decision to free the fish, it would not seem to relate to larger issues of community responsibility. "The Fish" is not a poem about the abolition of fishing.

Literary characters, like "real" individuals whom we encounter in our daily lives, are not presented to us as "finished" characters with finely polished, unchanging qualities. On the contrary, literary and real characters are understood, recognized, and interpreted by what they say and do, and sometimes their behavior is inconsistent, even contradictory. What this means is that a literary figure's ethical character is often "put into question" by his or her contact with other characters. In "The Fish," for example, the narrator apparently had never before considered the complex life of a fish. The encounter created the opportunity for ethical action, for a gesture of morality. The particular circumstance of "meeting" the fish created the opportunity for what the narrator takes to be a moral act. This is why these encounters are so important in literature (as well as in life): They reflect the conditions for making choices that have moral implications.

Ethical encounters in literature (and life) are sometimes called *face encounters*. This expression has at least two meanings. First, the choices characters make in words and actions reveal their "faces" to the world. The face is what others look at in encounters. In literary text we imagine the faces of characters. Second, "face" also means to interact with, as in a "face off." To face someone means to declare your values and allow another person to respond to those values. Charlie Wales, for example, presents a kindly, fatherly, dependable face to the Peters in order to secure the custody of his daughter. Yet Charlie also faces off with the Peters as he argues for the return of Honoria. Charlie's face, like all faces, has more than one profile.

Literary characters determine the right (or wrong) course of action in particular situations. And fictional figures, just like real individuals, sometimes do not know if their decisions are right or wrong until they experience the consequences of their decisions. Ethical decisions are not made according to an ironclad code, but rather are based on our perceptions of the right course of action according to contexts and circumstances.

One method of responding to the ethical judgments of characters is to ask whether they act in "good faith," which asks if they have sincerely and forthrightly attempted to "do the right thing" in words and deeds? To act in good faith requires characters to remain continually connected to their environments and situations, in spite of encounters with other characters that may produce the unexpected. Charlie Wales, for example, was not keenly aware of his situation when he gave out the Peters' address to Duncan and Lorraine. The narrator of "Because I Could Not Stop for Death" appears to be playfully in touch with the "circumstance" of her death (and knowledge of that experience). The narrator of "The Fish" is quick to recognize her changing perceptions of her captured fish as her encounter with him allows her to learn much about his past life. And in "Sonny's Blues," you will see how a brother comes to learn much about the circumstances of his own life because of his encounters with his brother Sonny.

It may appear obvious that literary characters always engage others, even if the "other" is himself or herself, as in the example of a story with only one character and his or her self-reflections. Characters often perceive (or fail to perceive) the context and implications of the circumstances and relationships they are in. Some characters act in good faith, whereas others do not. As we examine literary personae, it is especially important to judge them in terms of how they react to others. Do they proceed carefully with individuals they encounter, looking at others' personal qualities objectively? Or do they judge others through stereotypes and predetermined thinking, without giving others an opportunity to demonstrate that they have some things in common with other characters? "Sonny's Blues" is a powerful short story that illustrates some of these critical issues in ethical encounters.

In most literary texts, there are critical moments, or crises, when the plot turns dramatically and decisively. In "Babylon Revisited," for example, there is the moment at the Peters' home when Charlie's friend's comments dash Charlie's hopes of gaining custody of his daughter. In "Because I Could Not Stop for Death," the moment of recognition arrives when the narrator realizes her state of death and timelessness. The strategic moment comes in "The Fish" when the narrator begins to develop sympathy for the fish as she "looked into his eyes." All of these moments occur as narrators and characters experience the "ethical moment," a strategic or "special" time when there is a sudden insight into other characters, themselves, or both.

These ethical moments are often accompanied by characters' decisions to confront their responsibility for their actions. Sometimes characters accept responsibility for what they say and do, and at other times they do not. The important point in the ethical moment is the understanding that a "transaction" is taking place. Characters are interacting with other characters in ways that show their moral worth. (There may also be a similar moment in the transactions between the reader and literary characters. We react, sometimes strongly, to the moral implications of what characters say and do. Indeed, our reactions are one of our most important responsibilities as readers of literature.) The ethical moment is always a special time, a situation that is loaded with possibilities for literary characters (and this special time is for readers too, as we make critical judgments about characters' words and actions).

As we read literature for its ethical dimensions, especially as revealed by the interactions of characters, it is important to look at interactive scenes or encounters as an author's deliberate creation of "ethical opportunities." These opportunities depend upon characters making decisions and speaking in good faith, which means to act and speak honorably and truthfully and to take responsibility for their actions. As characters constantly engage one another, they must be held accountable for their actions, for the way they treat others, and for their success or failure in meeting their obligations. It is also important to consider characters' desire for ethical behavior. Authors use the words and actions of their characters to create conflict, and an ethical critic examines the moral implications of the conflict. The ethical critic makes moral judgments of the characters based on what they say and do, on how the characters respond to the moral conflicts they face. The desire to learn, ethically, whether for literary characters or readers, plays a role in the ethics of reading. And the only way that anyone, fictional character or reader, can come to know others is through interacting with them. Through these interactions, underlying motives behind ethical decisions become known. It is not an exaggeration to say that ethical encounters is a kind of moral summons, as we interact with characters, see their viewpoints, and project our own values into the situations they face. Through this interaction, we develop our ethical critique.

Whenever characters speak or act, they have made an ethical decision to do or say something (rather than saying or doing something else or remaining silent), and ethical criticism involves the evaluation of these actions, including their moral implications. As you will see in "Sonny's Blues," the issues of desire, responsibility, respect, and duty to family are major themes in the narrative, and they all come under the umbrella of ethical interaction occurring at ethical moments in the course of the story.

The overall goal of the ethical reader is to examine characters' interactions with others for their moral implications. Although there is more than one way to begin an ethical critique, a useful point of departure is to closely examine characters' words and actions, particularly as they occur in strategic moments of time. It is important to remember that literary characters are often depicted as evolving, and what they say and do at one point of time may be quite different from what occurs at another time. (This notion of strategic time is especially true in "Sonny's Blues.") Literary characters often change and grow, and sometimes learn from their experiences.

There is no formal body of ethical principles to guide the ethical approach, but there are some practical approaches in developing your ethical sense of the work. I suggest the following steps:

1. Read the work at least twice, and think about encounters between characters that strike you as significant parts of the text.
2. Look for instances in which characters say or do something that demonstrates responsibility and good faith (behaving honestly with good intentions toward others).
3. As you read the work for the second time, note moments that appear to be particularly important. These are the ethical moments when critical changes come about and characters come to know more about others (and themselves).
4. Pay particular attention to signs that characters are changing their thinking or attitudes because of a specific encounter.
5. Examine the text as a whole and speculate about the ethical encounters of the text that suggest larger themes in the text. Also be aware of changes that may come about in you as a result of your encounter with the text and its characters.

As an ethical reader, you can refine your own sense of ethical responsibility by examining literature in the manner suggested above. Following "Sonny's

Blues" is a series of reading and writing strategies suggested to assist you in sharpening your reading and writing skills.

A SAMPLE READING

"Sonny's Blues" by James Baldwin (1924–1987)

I read about it in the paper, in the subway, on my way to work. I read it, and I couldn't believe it, and I read it again. Then perhaps I just stared at it, at the newsprint spelling out his name, spelling out the story. I stared at it in the swinging lights of the subway car, and in the faces and bodies of the people, and in my own face, trapped in the darkness which roared outside.

It was not to be believed and I kept telling myself that, as I walked from the subway station to the high school. And at the same time I couldn't doubt it. I was scared, scared for Sonny. He became real to me again. A great block of ice got settled in my belly and kept melting there slowly all day long, while I taught my classes algebra. It was a special kind of ice. It kept melting, sending trickles of ice water all up and down my veins, but it never got less. Sometimes it hardened and seemed to expand until I felt my guts were going to come spilling out or that I was going to choke or scream. This would always be at a moment when I was remembering some specific thing Sonny had once said or done.

When he was about as old as the boys in my classes his face had been bright and open, there was a lot of copper in it; and he'd had wonderfully direct brown eyes, and great gentleness and privacy. I wondered what he looked like now. He had been picked up, the evening before, in a raid on an apartment downtown, for peddling and using heroin.

I couldn't believe it: but what I mean by that is that I couldn't find any room for it anywhere inside me. I had kept it outside me for a long time. I hadn't wanted to know. I had had suspicions, but I didn't name them, I kept putting them away. I told myself that Sonny was wild, but he wasn't crazy. And he'd always been a good boy, he hadn't ever turned hard or evil or disrespectful, the way kids can, so quick, so quick, especially in Harlem. I didn't want to believe that I'd ever see my brother going down, coming to nothing, all that light in his face gone out, in the condition I'd already seen so many others. Yet it had happened and here I was, talking about algebra to a lot of boys who might, every one of them for all I knew, be popping off needles every time they went to the head. Maybe it did more for them than algebra could.

I was sure that the first time Sonny had ever had horse, he couldn't have been much older than these boys were now. These boys, now, were living as we'd been living then, they were growing up with a rush and their heads bumped abruptly against the low ceiling of their actual possibilities. They were filled with rage. All they really knew were two darknesses, the darkness of their lives, which was now closing in on them, and the darkness of the movies, which had blinded them to that other darkness, and in which they now, vindictively, dreamed, at once more together than they were at any other time, and more alone.

When the last bell rang, the last class ended, I let out my breath. It seemed I'd been holding it for all that time. My clothes were wet—I may have looked as though I'd been sitting in a steam bath, all dressed up, all afternoon. I sat alone in the classroom a long time. I listened to the boys outside, downstairs, shouting and cursing and laughing. Their laughter struck me for perhaps the first time. It was not the joyous laughter which—God knows why—one associates with children. It was mocking and insular, its intent to denigrate. It was disenchanted, and in this, also, lay the authority of their curses. Perhaps I was listening to them because I was thinking about my brother and in them I heard my brother. And myself.

One boy was whistling a tune, at once very complicated and very simple, it seemed to be pouring out of him as though he were a bird, and it sounded very cool and moving through all that harsh, bright air, only just holding its own through all those other sounds.

I stood up and walked over to the window and looked down into the courtyard. It was the beginning of the spring and the sap was rising in the boys. A teacher passed through them every now and again, quickly, as though he or she couldn't wait to get out of that courtyard, to get those boys out of their sight and off their minds. I started collecting my stuff. I thought I'd better get home and talk to Isabel.

The courtyard was almost deserted by the time I got downstairs. I saw this boy standing in the shadow of a doorway, looking just like Sonny. I almost called his name. Then I saw that it wasn't Sonny, but somebody we used to know, a boy from around our block. He'd been Sonny's friend. He'd never been mine, having been too young for me, and, anyway, I'd never liked him. And now, even though he was a grown-up man, he still hung around the block, still spent hours on the street corners, was always high and raggy. I used to run into him from time to time and he'd often work around to asking me for a quarter or fifty cents. He always had some real good excuse, too, and I always gave it to him, I don't know why.

But now, abruptly, I hated him. I couldn't stand the way he looked at me, partly   10
like a dog, partly like a cunning child. I wanted to ask him what the hell he was doing in the school courtyard.

He sort of shuffled over to me, and he said, "I see you got the papers. So you already know about it."

"You mean about Sonny? Yes, I already know about it. How come they didn't get you?"

He grinned. It made him repulsive and it also brought to mind what he'd looked like as a kid. "I wasn't there. I stay away from them people."

"Good for you." I offered him a cigarette and I watched him through the smoke. "You come all the way down here just to tell me about Sonny?"

"That's right." He was sort of shaking his head and his eyes looked strange, as   15
though they were about to cross. The bright sun deadened his damp dark brown skin and it made his eyes look yellow and showed up the dirt in his kinked hair. He smelled funky. I moved a little away from him and I said, "Well, thanks. But I already know about it and I got to get home."

"I'll walk you a little ways," he said. We started walking. There were a couple of kids still loitering in the courtyard and one of them said goodnight to me and looked strangely at the boy beside me.

"What're you going to do?" he asked me. "I mean, about Sonny?"

"Look. I haven't seen Sonny for over a year. I'm not sure I'm going to do anything. Anyway, what the hell *can* I do?"

"That's right," he said quickly, "ain't nothing you can do. Can't much help old Sonny no more, I guess."

It was what I was thinking and so it seemed to me he had no right to say it.   20

"I'm surprised at Sonny, though," he went on—he had a funny way of talking, he looked straight ahead as though he were talking to himself—"I thought Sonny was a smart boy, I thought he was too smart to get hung."

"I guess he thought so too," I said sharply, "and that's how he got hung. And how about you? You're pretty goddamn smart, I bet."

Then he looked directly at me, just for a minute. "I ain't smart," he said. "If I was smart, I'd have reached for a pistol a long time ago."

"Look. Don't tell *me* your sad story, if it was up to me, I'd give you one." Then I felt guilty—guilty, probably, for never having supposed that the poor bastard *had* a story of his own, much less a sad one, and I asked, quickly, "What's going to happen to him now?"

He didn't answer this. He was off by himself some place. "Funny thing," he said,   25
and from his tone we might have been discussing the quickest way to get to Brooklyn, "when I saw the papers this morning, the first thing I asked myself was if I had anything to do with it. I felt sort of responsible."

I began to listen more carefully. The subway station was on the corner, just before us, and I stopped. He stopped, too. We were in front of a bar and he ducked slightly, peering in, but whoever he was looking for didn't seem to be there. The juke box was blasting away with something black and bouncy and I half watched the barmaid as she danced her way from the juke box to her place behind the bar. And I watched her face as she laughingly responded to something someone said to her, still keeping time to the music. When she smiled one saw the little girl, one sensed the doomed, still-struggling woman beneath the battered face of the semiwhore.

"I never *give* Sonny nothing," the boy said finally, "but a long time ago I come to school high and Sonny asked me how it felt." He paused, I couldn't bear to watch him, I watched the barmaid, and I listened to the music which seemed to be causing the pavement to shake. "I told him it felt great." The music stopped, the barmaid paused and watched the juke box until the music began again. "It did."

All this was carrying me some place I didn't want to go. I certainly didn't want to know how it felt. It filled everything, the people, the houses, the music, the dark, quicksilver barmaid, with menace; and this menace was their reality.

"What's going to happen to him now?" I asked again.

"They'll send him away some place and they'll try to cure him." He shook his   30
head. "Maybe he'll even think he's kicked the habit. Then they'll let him loose"—he gestured, throwing his cigarette into the gutter. "That's all."

"What do you mean, that's *all*?"

But I knew what he meant.

"I *mean*, that's *all*." He turned his head and looked at me, pulling down the corners of his mouth. "Don't you know what I mean?" he asked, softly.

"How the hell *would* I know what you mean?" I almost whispered it, I don't know why.

"That's right," he said to the air, "how would *he* know what I mean?" He turned   35
toward me again, patient and clam, and yet I somehow felt him shaking, shaking as though he were going to fall apart. I felt that ice in my guts again, the dread I'd felt all afternoon; and again I watched the barmaid, moving about the bar, washing glasses, and singing. "Listen. They'll let him out and then it'll just start all over again. That's what I mean."

"You mean—they'll let him out. And then he'll just start working his way back in again. You mean he'll never kick the habit. Is that what you mean?"

"That's right," he said, cheerfully. "*You* see what I mean."

"Tell me," I said at last, "why does he want to die? He must want to die, he's killing himself, why does he want to die?"

He looked at me in surprise. He licked his lips. "He don't want to die. He wants to live. Don't nobody want to die, ever."

Then I wanted to ask him—too many things. He could not have answered, or if   40
he had, I could not have borne the answers. I started walking. "Well, I guess it's none of my business."

"It's going to be rough on old Sonny," he said. We reached the subway station. "This is your station?" he asked. I nodded. I took one step down. "Damn!" he said, suddenly. I looked up at him. He grinned again. "Damn it if I didn't leave all my money home. You ain't got a dollar on you, have you? Just for a couple of days, is all."

All at once something inside gave and threatened to come pouring out of me. I didn't hate him any more. I felt that in another moment I'd start crying like a child.

"Sure," I said. "Don't sweat." I looked in my wallet and didn't have a dollar, I only had a five. "Here," I said. "That hold you?"

He didn't look at it—he didn't want to look at it. A terrible closed look came over his face, as though he were keeping the number on the bill a secret from him and me. "Thanks," he said, and now he was dying to see me go. "Don't worry about Sonny. Maybe I'll write him or something."

"Sure," I said. "You do that. So long."   45

"Be seeing you," he said. I went on down the steps.

And I didn't write Sonny or send him anything for a long time. When I finally did, it was just after my little girl died, he wrote me back a letter which made me feel like a bastard.

Here's what he said:

Dear brother,

You don't know how much I needed to hear from you. I wanted to write you many a time but I dug how much I must have hurt you and so I didn't write. But now I feel like a man who's been trying to climb up out of some deep, real deep and funky hole and just saw the sun up there, outside. I got to get outside.

I can't tell you much about how I got here. I mean I don't know how to tell you. I guess I was afraid of something or I was trying to escape from something and you know I have never been very strong in the head (smile). I'm glad Mama and Daddy are dead and can't see what's happened to their son and I swear if I'd known what I was doing I would never have hurt you so, you and a lot of other fine people who were nice to me and who believed in me.

I don't want you to think it had anything to do with me being a musician. It's more than that. Or maybe less than that. I can't get anything straight in my head down here and I try not to think about what's going to happen to me when I get outside again. Sometime I think I'm going to flip and *never* get outside and sometime I think I'll come straight back. I tell you one thing, though, I'd rather blow my brains out than go through this again. But that's what they all say, so they tell me. If I tell you when I'm coming to New York and if you could meet me, I sure would appreciate it. Give my love to Isabel and the kids and I was sure sorry to hear about little Gracie. I wish I could be like Mama and say the Lord's will be done, but I don't know it seems to me that trouble is the one thing that never does get stopped and I don't know what good it does to blame it on the Lord. But maybe it does some good if you believe it.

Your brother,
Sonny

Then I kept in constant touch with him and I sent him whatever I could and I went to meet him when he came back to New York. When I saw him many things I thought I had forgotten came flooding back to me. This was because I had begun, finally, to wonder about Sonny, about the life that Sonny lived inside. This life, whatever it was, had made him older and thinner and it had deepened the distant stillness in which he had always moved. He looked very unlike my baby brother. Yet, when he smiled, when we shook hands, the baby brother I'd never known looked out from the depths of his private life, like an animal waiting to be coaxed into the light.

"How you been keeping?" he asked me.   50

"All right. And you?"

"Just fine." He was smiling all over his face. "It's good to see you again."

"It's good to see you."

The seven years' difference in our ages lay between us like a chasm: I wondered if these years would ever operate between us as a bridge. I was remembering, and it made it hard to catch my breath, that I had been there when he was born; and I had heard the first words he had ever spoken. When he started to walk, he walked from our mother straight to me. I caught him just before he fell when he took the first steps he ever took in this world.

"How's Isabel?"   55

"Just fine. She's dying to see you."

"And the boys?"

"They're fine, too. They're anxious to see their uncle."

"Oh, come on. You know they don't remember me."

"Are you kidding? Of course they remember you."   60

He grinned again. We got into a taxi. We had a lot to say to each other, far too much to know how to begin.

As the taxi began to move, I asked, "You still want to go to India?"

He laughed. "You still remember that. Hell, no. This place is Indian enough for me."

"It used to belong to them," I said.

And he laughed again. "They damn sure knew what they were doing when they   65
got rid of it."

Years ago, when he was around fourteen, he'd been all hipped on the idea of going to India. He read books about people sitting on rocks, naked, in all kinds of weather, but mostly bad, naturally, and walking barefoot through hot coals and arriving at wisdom. I used to say that it sounded to me as though they were getting away from wisdom as fast as they could. I think he sort of looked down on me for that.

"Do you mind," he asked, "if we have the driver drive alongside the park? On the west side—I haven't seen the city in so long."

"Of course not," I said. I was afraid that I might sound as though I were humoring him, but I hoped he wouldn't take it that way.

So we drove along, between the green of the park and the stony, lifeless elegance of hotels and apartments buildings, toward the vivid, killing streets of our childhood. These streets hadn't changed, though housing projects jutted up out of them now like rocks in the middle of a boiling sea. Most of the houses in which we had grown up had vanished, as had the stores from which we had stolen, the basements in which we had first tried sex, the rooftops from which we had hurled tin cans and bricks. But houses exactly like the houses of our past yet dominated the landscape, boys exactly like the boys we once had been found themselves smothering in these houses, came down into the streets for light and air and found themselves encircled by disaster. Some escaped the trap, most didn't. Those who got out always left something of themselves behind, as some animals amputate a leg and leave it in the trap. It might be said, perhaps, that I had escaped, after all, I was a school teacher; or that Sonny had, he hadn't lived in Harlem for years. Yet, as the cab moved uptown through streets which seemed, with a rush, to darken with dark people, and as I covertly studied Sonny's face, it came to me that what we both were seeking through our separate cab windows was that part of ourselves which had been left behind. It's always at the hour of trouble and confrontation that the missing member aches.

We hit 110th Street and started rolling up Lenox Avenue. And I'd known this avenue all my life, but it seemed to me again, as it had seemed on the day I'd first heard about Sonny's trouble, filled with a hidden menace which was its very breath of life. 70

"We almost there," said Sonny.

"Almost." We were both too nervous to say anything more.

We live in a housing project. It hasn't been up long. A few days after it was up it seemed uninhabitably new, now, of course, it's already rundown. It looks like a parody of the good, clean, faceless life—God knows the people who live in it do their best to make it a parody. The beat-looking grass lying around isn't enough to make their lives green, the hedges will never hold out the streets, and they know it. The big windows fool no one, they aren't big enough to make space out of no space. They don't bother with the windows, they watch the TV screen instead. The playground is most popular with the children who don't play at jacks, or skip rope, or roller skate, or swing, and they can be found in it after dark. We moved in partly because it's not too far from where I teach, and partly for the kids; but it's really just like the houses in which Sonny and I grew up. The same things happen, they'll have the same things to remember. The moment Sonny and I started into the house I had the feeling that I was simply bringing him back into the danger he had almost died trying to escape.

Sonny has never been talkative. So I don't know why I was sure he'd be dying to talk to me when supper was over the first night. Everything went fine, the oldest boy remembered him, and the youngest boy liked him, and Sonny had remembered to bring something for each of them; and Isabel, who is really much nicer than I am, more open and giving, had gone to a lot of trouble about dinner and was genuinely glad to see him. And she's always been able to tease Sonny in a way that I haven't. It was nice to see her face so vivid again and to hear her laugh and watch her make Sonny laugh. She wasn't, or, anyway, she didn't seem to be, at all uneasy or embarrassed. She chatted as though there were no subject which had to be avoided and she got Sonny past his first, faint stiffness. And thank God she was there, for I was filled with that icy dread again. Everything I did seemed awkward to me, and everything I said sounded freighted with hidden meaning. I was trying to remember everything I'd heard about dope addiction and I couldn't help watching Sonny for signs. I wasn't doing it out of malice. I was trying to find out something about my brother. I was dying to hear him tell me he was safe.

"Safe!" my father grunted, whenever Mama suggested trying to move to a neighborhood which might be safer for children. "Safe, hell! Ain't no place safe for kids, nor nobody." 75

He always went on like this, but he wasn't, ever, really as bad as he sounded, not even on weekends, when he got drunk. As a matter of fact, he was always on the lookout for "something a little better," but he died before he found it. He died suddenly, during a drunken weekend in the middle of the war, when Sonny was fifteen. He and Sonny hadn't ever got on too well. And this was partly because Sonny was the apple of his father's eye. It was because he loved Sonny so much and was frightened for him, that he was always fighting with him. It doesn't do any good to fight with Sonny. Sonny just moves back, inside himself, where he can't be reached. But the principal reason that they never hit it off is that they were so much alike. Daddy was big and rough and loud-talking, just the opposite of Sonny, but they both had—that same privacy.

Mama tried to tell me something about this, just after Daddy died. I was home on leave from the army.

This was the last time I ever saw my mother alive. Just the same, this picture gets all mixed up in mind with pictures I had of her when she was younger. The way I always see her is the way she used to be on a Sunday afternoon, say, when the old folks were talking after the big Sunday dinner. I always see her wearing pale blue. She'd be sitting on the sofa. And my father would be sitting in the easy chair, not far from her. And the living room would be full of church folks and relatives. There they sit, in chairs all around the living room, and the night is creeping up outside, but nobody knows it yet. You can see the darkness growing against the windowpanes and you hear the street noises every now and again, or maybe the jangling beat of a tambourine from one of the churches close by, but it's real quiet in the room. For a moment nobody's talking, but every face looks darkening, like the sky outside. And my mother rocks a little from the waist, and my father's eyes are closed. Everyone is looking at something a child can't see. For a minute they've forgotten the children. Maybe a kid is lying on the rug, half asleep. Maybe somebody's got a kid in his lap and is absent-mindedly stroking the kid's head. Maybe there's a kid, quiet and big-eyed, curled up in a big chair in the corner. The silence, the darkness coming, and the darkness in the faces frightens the child obscurely. He hopes that the hand which strokes his forehead will never stop—will never die. He hopes that there will never come a time when the old folks won't be sitting around the living room, talking about where they've come from, and what they've seen, and what's happened to them and their kinfolk.

But something deep and watchful in the child knows that this is bound to end, is already ending. In a moment someone will get up and turn on the light. Then the old folks will remember the children and they won't talk any more that day. And when light fills the room, the child is filled with darkness. He knows that every time this happens he's moved just a little closer to that darkness outside. The darkness outside is what the old folks have been talking about. It's what they've come from. It's what they endure. The child knows that they won't talk any more because if he knows too much about what's happened to *them*, he'll know too much too soon, about what's going to happen to *him*.

The last time I talked to my mother, I remember I was restless. I wanted to get out   80
and see Isabel. We weren't married then and we had a lot to straighten out between us.

There Mama sat, in black, by the window. She was humming an old church song,
Lord, you brought me from a long ways off. Sonny was out somewhere. Mama kept watching the streets.

"I don't know," she said, "if I'll ever see you again, after you go off from here. But
I hope you'll remember the things I tried to teach you."

"Don't talk like that," I said, and smiled. "You'll be here a long time yet."

She smiled, too, but she said nothing. She was quiet for a long time. And I said,
"Mama, don't you worry about nothing. I'll be writing all the time, and you be getting
the checks. . . ."

"I want to talk to you about your brother," she said, suddenly. "If anything hap-   85
pens to me he ain't going to have nobody to look out for him."

"Mama," I said, "ain't nothing going to happen to you *or* Sonny. Sonny's all right.
He's a good boy and he's got good sense."

"It ain't a question of his being a good boy," Mama said, "nor of his having good
sense. It ain't only the bad ones, nor yet the dumb ones that gets sucked under." She
stopped, looking at me. "Your Daddy once had a brother," she said, and she smiled in a
way that made me feel she was in pain. "You didn't never know that, did you?"

"No," I said, "I never knew that," and I watched her face.

"Oh, yes," she said, "your Daddy had a brother." She looked out of the window
again. "I know you never saw your Daddy cry. But *I* did—many a time, through all these
years."

I asked her, "What happened to his brother? How come nobody's ever talked   90
about him?"

This was the first time I ever saw my mother look old.

"His brother got killed," she said, "when he was just a little younger than you are
now. I knew him. He was a fine boy. He was maybe a little full of the devil, but he
didn't mean nobody no harm."

Then she stopped and the room was silent, exactly as it had sometimes been on
those Sunday afternoons. Mama kept looking out into the streets.

"He used to have a job in the mill," she said, "and, like all young folks, he just
liked to perform on Saturday nights. Saturday nights, him and your father would drift
around to different places, go to dances and things like that, or just sit around with people they knew, and your father's brother would sing, he had a fine voice, and play along
with himself on his guitar. Well, this particular Saturday night, him and your father was
coming home from some place, and they were both a little drunk and there was a moon
that night, it was bright like day. Your father's brother was feeling kind of good, and he
was whistling to himself, and he had his guitar slung over his shoulder. They was coming down a hill and beneath them was a road that turned off from the highway. Well,
your father's brother, being always kind of frisky, decided to run down this hill, and he
did, with that guitar banging and clanging behind him, and he ran across the road, and
he was making water behind a tree. And your father was sort of amused at him and he
was still coming down the hill, kind of slow. Then he heard a car motor and that same
minute his brother stepped from behind the tree, into the road, in the moonlight. And
he started to cross the road. And your father started to run down the hill, he says he
don't know why. This car was full of white men. They was all drunk, and when they

seen your father's brother they let out a great whoop and holler and they aimed the car straight at him. They was having fun, they just wanted to scare him, the way they do sometimes, you know. But they was drunk. And I guess the boy, being drunk, too, and scared, kind of lost his head. By the time he jumped it was too late. Your father says he heard his brother scream when the car rolled over him, and he heard the wood of that guitar when it give, and he heard them strings go flying, and he heard them white men shouting, and the car kept on a-going and it ain't stopped till this day. And, time your father got down the hill, his brother weren't nothing but blood and pulp."

Tears were gleaming on my mother's face. There wasn't anything I could say.   95

"He never mentioned it," she said, "because I never let him mention it before you children. Your Daddy was like a crazy man that night and for many a night thereafter. He says he never in his life seen anything as dark as that road after the lights of that car had gone away. Weren't nothing, weren't nobody on that road, just your Daddy and his brother and that busted guitar. Oh, yes. Your Daddy never did really get right again. Till the day he died he weren't sure but that every white man he saw was the man that killed his brother."

She stopped and took out her handkerchief and dried her eyes and looked at me.

"I ain't telling you all this," she said, "to make you scared or bitter or to make you hate nobody. I'm telling you this because you got a brother. And the world ain't changed."

I guess I didn't want to believe this. I guess she saw this in my face. She turned away from me, toward the window again, searching those streets.

"But I praise my Redeemer," she said at last, "that He called your Daddy home   100 before me. I ain't saying it to throw no flowers at myself, but, I declare, it keeps me from feeling too cast down to know I helped your father get safely through this world. Your father always acted like he was the roughest, strongest man on earth. And everybody took him to be like that. But if he hadn't had *me* there—to see his tears!"

She was crying again. Still, I couldn't move. I said, "Lord, Lord, Mama, I didn't know it was like that."

"Oh, honey," she said, "there's a lot that you don't know. But you are going to find it out." She stood up from the window and came over to me. "You got to hold on to your brother," she said, "and don't let him fall, no matter what it looks like is happening to him and no matter how evil you gets with him. You going to be evil with him many a time. But don't you forget what I told you, you hear?"

"I won't forget," I said. "Don't you worry, I won't forget. I won't let nothing happen to Sonny."

My mother smiled as though she were amused at something she saw in my face. Then, "You may not be able to stop nothing from happening. But you got to let him know you's *there*."

Two days later I was married, and then I was gone. And I had a lot of things on   105 my mind and I pretty well forgot my promise to Mama until I got shipped home on a special furlough for her funeral.

And, after the funeral, with just Sonny and me alone in the empty kitchen, I tried to find out something about him.

"What do you want to do?" I asked him.

"I'm going to be a musician," he said.

For he had graduated, in the time I had been away, from dancing to the juke box to finding out who was playing what, and what they were doing with it, and he had bought himself a set of drums.

"You mean, you want to be a drummer?" I somehow had the feeling that being a   110
drummer might be all right for other people but not for my brother Sonny.

"I don't think," he said, looking at me very gravely, "that I'll ever be a good drummer. But I think I can play a piano."

I frowned. I'd never played the role of the older brother quite so seriously before, had scarcely ever, in fact, *asked* Sonny a damn thing. I sensed myself in the presence of something I didn't really know how to handle, didn't understand. So I made my frown a little deeper as I asked: "What kind of musician do you want to be?"

He grinned. "How many kinds do you think there are?"

"Be *serious*," I said.

He laughed, throwing his head back, and then looked at me. "I *am* serious."   115

"Well, then, for Christ's sake, stop kidding around and answer a serious question. I mean, do you want to be a concert pianist, you want to play classical music and all that, or—or what?" Long before I finished he was laughing again. "For Christ's *sake*, Sonny!"

He sobered, but with difficulty. "I'm sorry. But you sound so—*scared!*" and he was off again.

"Well, you may think it's funny now, baby, but it's not going to be so funny when you have to make your living at it, let me tell you *that*." I was furious because I knew he was laughing at me and I didn't know why.

"No," he said, very sober now, and afraid, perhaps, that he'd hurt me, "I don't want to be a classical pianist. That isn't what interests me. I mean"—he paused, looking hard at me, as though his eyes would help me to understand, and then gestured help-lessly, as though perhaps his hand would help—"I mean, I'll have a lot of studying to do, and I'll have to study *everything*, but, I mean, I want to play *with*—jazz musicians." He stopped. "I want to play jazz," he said.

Well, the word had never before sounded as heavy, as real, as it sounded that af-   120
ternoon in Sonny's mouth. I just looked at him and I was probably frowning a real frown by this time. I simply couldn't see why on earth he'd want to spend his time hanging around nightclubs, clowning around on bandstands, while people pushed each other around a dance floor. It seemed—beneath him, somehow. I had never thought about it before, had never been forced to, but I suppose I had always put jazz musicians in a class with what Daddy called "good-time people."

"Are you *serious?*"

"Hell, *yes*, I'm serious."

He looked more helpless than ever, and annoyed, and deeply hurt.

I suggested, helpfully: "You mean—like Louis Armstrong?"

His face closed as though I'd struck him. "No, I'm not talking about none of that   125
old-time, down home crap."

"Well, look, Sonny, I'm sorry, don't get mad. I just don't altogether get it, that's all. Name somebody—you know, a jazz musician you admire."

"Bird."

"Who?"

"Bird! Charlie Parker! Don't they teach you nothing in the goddamn army?"

I lit a cigarette. I was surprised and then a little amused to discover that I was   130
trembling. "I've been out of touch," I said. "You'll have to be patient with me. Now.
Who's this Parker character?"

"He's just one of the greatest jazz musicians alive," said Sonny, sullenly, his hands
in his pockets, his back to me. "Maybe *the* greatest," he added, bitterly, "that's probably
why *you* never heard of him."

"All right," I said, "I'm ignorant. I'm sorry. I'll go out and buy all the cat's records
right away, all right?"

"It don't," said Sonny, with dignity, "make any difference to me. I don't care
what you listen to. Don't do me no favors."

I was beginning to realize that I'd never seen him so upset before. With another
part of my mind I was thinking that this would probably turn out to be one of those
things kids go through and that I shouldn't make it seem important by pushing it too
hard. Still, I didn't think it would do any harm to ask: "Doesn't all this take a lot of
time? Can you make a living at it?"

He turned back to me and half leaned, half sat, on the kitchen table. "Everything   135
takes time," he said, "and—well, yes, sure, I can make a living at it. But what I don't
seem to be able to make you understand is that it's the only thing I want to do."

"Well, Sonny," I said, gently, "you know people can't always do exactly what
they *want* to do—"

"*No,* I don't know that," said Sonny, surprising me. "I think people *ought* to do
what they want to do, what else are they alive for?"

"You getting to be a big boy," I said desperately, "it's time you started thinking
about your future."

"I'm thinking about my future," said Sonny, grimly. "I think about it all the
time."

I gave up. I decided, if he didn't change his mind, that we could always talk about   140
it later. "In the meantime," I said, "you got to finish school." We had already decided
that he'd have to move in with Isabel and her folks. I knew this wasn't the ideal
arrangement because Isabel's folks are inclined to be dicty and they hadn't especially
wanted Isabel to marry me. But I didn't know what else to do. "And we have to get you
fixed up at Isabel's."

There was a long silence. He moved from the kitchen table to the window.
"That's a terrible idea. You know it yourself."

"Do you have a *better* idea?"

He just walked up and down the kitchen for a minute. He was as tall as I was. He
had started to shave. I suddenly had the feeling that I didn't know him at all.

He stopped at the kitchen table and picked up my cigarettes. Looking at me with
a kind of mocking, amused defiance, he put one between his lips. "You mind?"

"You smoking already?"   145

He lit the cigarette and nodded, watching me through the smoke. "I just wanted
to see if I'd have the courage to smoke in front of you." He grinned and blew a great
cloud of smoke to the ceiling. "It was easy." He looked at my face. "Come on, now. I bet
you was smoking at my age, tell the truth."

I didn't say anything but the truth was on my face, and he laughed. But now
there was something very strained in his laugh. "Sure. And I bet that ain't all you was
doing."

He was frightening me a little. "Cut the crap," I said. "We already decided that you was going to go and live at Isabel's. Now what's got into you all of a sudden?"

"*You* decided it," he pointed out. "*I* didn't decide nothing." He stopped in front of me, leaning against the stove, arms loosely folded. "Look, brother. I don't want to stay in Harlem no more, I really don't." He was very earnest. He looked at me, then over toward the kitchen window. There was something in his eyes I'd never seen before, some thoughtfulness, some worry all his own. He rubbed the muscle of one arm. "It's time I was getting out of here."

"Where do you want to *go*, Sonny?"   150

"I want to join the army. Or the navy, I don't care. If I say I'm old enough, they'll believe me."

Then I got mad. It was because I was so scared. "You must be crazy. You goddamn fool, what the hell do you want to go and join the *army* for?"

"I just told you. To get out of Harlem."

"Sonny, you haven't even finished *school*. And if you really want to be a musician, how do you expect to study if you're in the *army*?"

He looked at me, trapped, and in anguish. "There's ways. I might be able to work   155
out some kind of deal. Anyway, I'll have the G.I. Bill when I come out."

"*If* you come out." We stared at each other. "Sonny, please. Be reasonable. I know the setup is far from perfect. But we got to do the best we can."

"I ain't learning nothing in school," he said. "Even when I go." He turned away from me and opened the window and threw his cigarette out into the narrow alley. I watched his back. "At least, I ain't learning nothing you'd want me to learn." He slammed the window so hard I thought the glass would fly out, and turned back to me. "And I'm sick of the stink of these garbage cans!"

"Sonny," I said, "I know how you feel. But if you don't finish school now, you're going to be sorry later that you didn't." I grabbed him by the shoulders. "And you only got another year. It ain't so bad. And I'll come back and I swear I'll help you do *whatever* you want to do. Just try to put up with it till I come back. Will you please do that? For me?"

He didn't answer and he wouldn't look at me.

"Sonny. You hear me?"   160

He pulled away. "I hear you. But you never hear anything *I* say."

I didn't know what to say to that. He looked out of the window and then back at me. "OK," he said, and sighed. "I'll try."

Then I said, trying to cheer him up a little, "They got a piano at Isabel's. You can practice on it."

And as a matter of fact, it did cheer him up for a minute. "That's right," he said to himself. "I forgot that." His face relaxed a little. But the worry, the thoughtfulness, played on it still, the way shadows play on a face which is staring into the fire.

But I thought I'd never hear the end of that piano. At first, Isabel would write   165
me, saying how nice it was that Sonny was so serious about his music and how, as soon as he came in from school, or wherever he had been when he was supposed to be at school, he went straight to that piano and stayed there until suppertime. And, after supper, he went back to that piano and stayed there until everybody went to bed. He was at the piano all day Saturday and all day Sunday. Then he bought a record player and started playing records. He'd play one record over and over again, all day long some-

times, and he'd improvise along with it on the piano. Or he'd play one section of the record, one chord, one change, one progression, then he'd do it on the piano. Then back to the record. Then back to the piano.

Well, I really don't know how they stood it. Isabel finally confessed that it wasn't like living with a person at all, it was like living with sound. And the sound didn't make any sense to her, didn't make any sense to any of them—naturally. They began, in a way, to be afflicted by this presence that was living in their home. It was as though Sonny were some sort of god, or monster. He moved in an atmosphere which wasn't like theirs at all. They fed him and he ate, he washed himself, he walked in and out of their door; he certainly wasn't nasty or unpleasant or rude, Sonny isn't any of those things; but it was as though he were all wrapped up in some cloud, some fire, some vision all his own; and there wasn't any way to reach him.

At the same time, he wasn't really a man yet, he was still a child, and they had to watch out for him in all kinds of ways. They certainly couldn't throw him out. Neither did they dare to make a great scene about that piano because even they dimly sensed, as I sensed, from so many thousands of miles away, that Sonny was at that piano playing for his life.

But he hadn't been going to school. One day a letter came from the school board and Isabel's mother got it—there had, apparently, been other letters but Sonny had torn them up. This day, when Sonny came in, Isabel's mother showed him the letter and asked where he'd been spending his time. And she finally got it out of him that he'd been down in Greenwich Village, with musicians and other characters, in a white girl's apartment. And this scared her and she started to scream at him and what came up, once she began—though she denies it to this day—was what sacrifices they were making to give Sonny a decent home and how little he appreciated it.

Sonny didn't play the piano that day. By evening, Isabel's mother had calmed down but then there was the old man to deal with, and Isabel herself. Isabel says she did her best to be calm but she broke down and started crying. She says she just watched Sonny's face. She could tell, by watching him, what was happening with him. And what was happening was that they penetrated his cloud, they had reached him. Even if their fingers had been a thousand times more gentle than human fingers ever are, he could hardly help feeling that they had stripped him naked and were spitting on that nakedness. For he also had to see that his presence, that music, which was life or death to him, had been torture for them and that they had endured it, not at all for his sake, but only for mine. And Sonny couldn't take that. He can take it a little better today than he could then but he's still not very good at it and, frankly, I don't know anybody who is.

The silence of the next few days must have been louder than the sound of all the music ever played since time began. One morning, before she went to work, Isabel was in his room for something and she suddenly realized that all of his records were gone. And she knew for certain that he was gone. And he was. He went as far as the navy would carry him. He finally sent me a postcard from some place in Greece and that was the first I knew that Sonny was still alive. I didn't see him any more until we were both back in New York and the war had long been over.

He was a man by then, of course, but I wasn't willing to see it. He came by the house from time to time, but we fought almost every time we met. I didn't like the way he carried himself, loose and dreamlike all the time, and I didn't like his friends, and his music seemed to be merely an excuse for the life he led. It sounded just that weird and disordered.

170

Then we had a fight, a pretty awful fight, and I didn't see him for months. By and by I looked him up, where he was living, in a furnished room in the Village, and I tried to make it up. But there were lots of people in the room and Sonny just lay on his bed, and he wouldn't come downstairs with me, and he treated these other people as though they were his family and I weren't. So I got mad and then he got mad, and then I told him that he might just as well be dead as live the way he was living. Then he stood up and he told me not to worry about him any more in life, that he *was* dead as far as I was concerned. Then he pushed me to the door and the other people looked on as though nothing were happening, and he slammed the door behind me. I stood in the hallway, staring at the door. I heard somebody laugh in the room and then the tears came to my eyes. I started down the steps, whistling to keep from crying, I kept whistling to myself, *You going to need me, baby, one of these cold, rainy days.*

I read about Sonny's trouble in the spring. Little Grace died in the fall. She was a beautiful little girl. But she only lived a little over two years. She died of polio and she suffered. She had a slight fever for a couple of days, but it didn't seem like anything and we just kept her in bed. And we would certainly have called the doctor, but the fever dropped, she seemed to be all right. So we thought it had just been a cold. Then, one day, she was up, playing, Isabel was in the kitchen fixing lunch for the two boys when they'd come in from school, and she heard Grace fall down in the living room. When you have a lot of children you don't always start running when one of them falls, unless they start screaming or something. And, this time, Grace was quiet. Yet, Isabel says that when she heard that *thump* and then that silence, something happened in her to make her afraid. And she ran to the living room and there was little Grace on the floor, all twisted up, and the reason she hadn't screamed was that she couldn't get her breath. And when she did scream, it was the worst sound, Isabel says, that she'd ever heard in all her life, and she still hears it sometimes in her dreams. Isabel will sometimes wake me up with a low, moaning, strangled sound and I have to be quick to awaken her and hold her to me and where Isabel is weeping against me seems a mortal wound.

I think I may have written Sonny the very day that little Grace was buried. I was sitting in the living room in the dark, by myself, and I suddenly thought of Sonny. My trouble made his real.

One Saturday afternoon, when Sonny had been living with us, or, anyway, been in our house, for nearly two weeks, I found myself wandering aimlessly about the living room, drinking from a can of beer, and trying to work up the courage to search Sonny's room. He was out, he was usually out whenever I was home, and Isabel had taken the children to see their grandparents. Suddenly I was standing still in front of the living room window, watching Seventh Avenue. The idea of searching Sonny's room made me still. I scarcely dared to admit to myself what I'd be searching for. I didn't know what I'd do if I found it. Or if I didn't. 175

On the sidewalk across from me, near the entrance to a barbecue joint, some people were holding an old-fashioned revival meeting. The barbecue cook, wearing a dirty white apron, his conked hair reddish and metallic in the pale sun, and a cigarette between his lips, stood in the doorway, watching them. Kids and older people paused in their errands and stood there, along with some older men and a couple of very tough-looking women who watched everything that happened on the avenue, as though they owned it, or were maybe owned by it. Well, they were watching this, too. The revival was being carried on by three sisters in black, and a brother. All they had were their voices and their Bibles and a tambourine. The brother was testifying and while he testified two of the sisters stood to-gether, seeming to say, amen, and the third sister walked around with the tambourine out-stretched and a couple of people dropped coins into it. Then the brother's testimony ended and the sister who had been taking up the collection dumped the coins into her palm and transferred them to the pocket of her long black robe. Then she raised both hands, striking the tambourine against the air, and then against one hand, and she started to sing. And the two other sisters and the brother joined in.

It was strange, suddenly, to watch, though I had been seeing these street meetings all my life. So, of course, had everybody else down there. Yet, they paused and watched and listened and I stood still at the window. *'Tis the old ship of Zion,"* they sang, and the sister with the tambourine kept a steady, jangling beat, *"it has rescued many a thousand!"* Not a soul under the sound of their voices was hearing this song for the first time, not one of them had been rescued. Nor had they seen much in the way of rescue work being done around them. Neither did they especially believe in the holiness of the three sis-ters and the brother, they knew too much about them, knew where they lived, and how. The woman with the tambourine, whose voice dominated the air, whose face was bright with joy, was divided by very little from the woman who stood watching her, a cigarette between her heavy, chapped lips, her hair a cuckoo's nest, her face scarred and swollen from many beatings, and her black eyes glittering like coal. Perhaps they both knew this, which was why, when, as rarely, they addressed each other, they addressed each other as Sister. As the singing filled the air the watching, listening faces under-went a change, the eyes focusing on something within; the music seemed to soothe a poison out of them; and time seemed, nearly, to fall away from the sullen, belligerent, battered faces, as though they were fleeing back to their first condition, while dreaming of their last. The barbecue cook half shook his head and smiled, and dropped his ciga-rette and disappeared into his joint. A man fumbled in his pockets for change and stood holding it in his hand impatiently, as though he had just remembered a pressing ap-pointment further up the avenue. He looked furious. Then I saw Sonny, standing on the edge of the crowd. He was carrying a wide, flat notebook with a green cover, and it made him look, from where I was standing, almost like a schoolboy. The coppery sun brought out the copper in his skin, he was very faintly smiling, standing very still. Then the singing stopped, the tambourine turned into a collection plate again. The furious man dropped in his coins and vanished, so did a couple of the women, and Sonny dropped some change in the plate, looking directly at the woman with a little smile. He started across the avenue, toward the house. He has a slow, loping walk, something like the way Harlem hipsters walk, only he's imposed on this his own half-beat. I had never really noticed it before.

I stayed at the window, both relieved and apprehensive. As Sonny disappeared from my sight, they began singing again. And they were still singing when his key turned in the lock.

"Hey," he said.

"Hey, yourself. You want some beer?"   180

"No. Well, maybe." But he came up to the window and stood beside me, looking out. "What a warm voice," he said.

They were singing *If I could only hear my mother pray again!*

"Yes," I said, "and she can sure beat that tambourine."

"But what a terrible song," he said, and laughed. He dropped his notebook on the sofa and disappeared into the kitchen. "Where's Isabel and the kids?"

"I think they went to see their grandparents. You hungry?"   185

"No." He came back into the living room with his can of beer. "You want to come some place with me tonight?"

I sensed, I don't know how, that I couldn't possibly say no. "Sure. Where?"

He sat down on the sofa and picked up his notebook and started leafing through it. "I'm going to sit in with some fellows in a joint in the Village."

"You mean, you're going to play, tonight?"

"That's right." He took a swallow of his beer and moved back to the window. He   190
gave me a sidelong look. "If you can stand it."

"I'll try," I said.

He smiled to himself and we both watched as the meeting across the way broke up. The three sisters and the brother, heads bowed, were singing *God be with you till we meet again.* The faces around them were very quiet. Then the song ended. The small crowd dispersed. We watched the three women and the lone man walk slowly up the avenue.

"When she was singing before," said Sonny, abruptly, "her voice reminded me for a minute of what heroin feels like sometimes—when it's in your veins. It makes you feel sort of warm and cool at the same time. And distant. And—and sure." He sipped his beer, very deliberately not looking at me. I watched his face. "It makes you feel—in control. Sometimes you've got to have that feeling."

"Do you?" I sat down slowly in the easy chair.

"Sometimes." He went to the sofa and picked up his notebook again. "Some peo-   195
ple do."

"In order," I asked, "to play?" And my voice was very ugly, full of contempt and anger.

"Well"—he looked at me with great, troubled eyes, as though, in fact, he hoped his eyes would tell me things he could never otherwise say—"they *think* so. And *if* they think so—!"

"And what do *you* think?" I asked.

He sat on the sofa and put his can of beer on the floor. "I don't know," he said, and I couldn't be sure if he were answering my question or pursuing his thoughts. His face didn't tell me. "It's not so much to *play.* It's to *stand* it, to be able to make it at all. On any level." He frowned and smiled: "In order to keep from shaking to pieces."

"But these friends of yours," I said, "they seem to shake themselves to pieces   200
pretty goddamn fast."

"Maybe." He played with the notebook. And something told me that I should curb my tongue, that Sonny was doing his best to talk, that I should listen. "But of course you only know the ones that've gone to pieces. Some don't—or at least they haven't *yet* and that's just about all *any* of us can say." He paused. "And then there are some who just live, really, in hell, and they know it and they see what's happening and they go right on. I don't know." He sighed, dropped the notebook, folded his arms. "Some guys, you can tell from the way they play, they on something *all* the time. And you can see that, well, it makes something real for them. But of course," he picked up his beer from the floor and sipped it and put the can down again, "they *want* to, too, you've got to see that. Even some of them that say they don't—*some,* not all."

"And what about you?" I asked—I couldn't help it. "What about you? Do *you* want to?"

He stood up and walked to the window and remained silent for a long time. Then he sighed. "Me," he said. Then: "While I was downstairs before, on my way here, listening to that woman sing, it struck me all of a sudden how much suffering she must have had to go through—to sing like that. It's *repulsive* to think you have to suffer that much."

I said: "But there's no way not to suffer—is there, Sonny?"

"I believe not," he said and smiled, "but that's never stopped anyone from trying." He looked at me. "Has it?" I realized, with this mocking look, that there stood between us, forever, beyond the power of time or forgiveness, the fact that I had held silence—so long!—when he had needed human speech to help him. He turned back to the window. "No, there's no way not to suffer. But you try all kinds of ways to keep from drowning in it, to keep on top of it, and to make it seem—well, like *you*. Like you did something, all right, and now you're suffering for it. You know?" I said nothing. "Well you know," he said, impatiently, "why *do* people suffer? Maybe it's better to do something to give it a reason, *any* reason." 205

"But we just agreed," I said "that there's no way not to suffer. Isn't it better, then, just to—take it?"

"But nobody just takes it," Sonny cried, "that's what I'm telling you! *Everybody* tries not to. You're just hung up on the *way* some people try—it's not *your* way!"

The hair on my face began to itch, my face felt wet. "That's not true," I said, "that's not true. I don't give a damn what other people do, I don't even care how they suffer. I just care how *you* suffer." And he looked at me. "Please believe me," I said, "I don't want to see you—die—trying not to suffer."

"I won't," he said, flatly, "die trying not to suffer. At least, not any faster than anybody else."

"But there's no need," I said, trying to laugh, "is there? in killing yourself." 210

I wanted to say more, but I couldn't. I wanted to talk about will power and how life could be—well, beautiful. I wanted to say that it was all within; but was it? or, rather, wasn't that exactly the trouble? And I wanted to promise that I would never fail him again. But it would all have sounded—empty words and lies.

So I made the promise to myself and prayed that I would keep it.

"It's terrible sometimes, inside," he said, "that's what's the trouble. You walk these streets, black and funky and cold, and there's not really a living ass to talk to, and there's nothing shaking, and there's no way of getting it out—that storm inside. You can't talk it and you can't make love with it, and when you finally try to get with it and play it, you realize *nobody's* listening. So *you've* got to listen. You got to find a way to listen."

And then he walked away from the window and sat on the sofa again, as though all the wind had suddenly been knocked out of him. "Sometimes you'll do *anything* to play, even cut your mother's throat." He laughed and looked at me. "Or your brother's." Then he sobered. "Or your own." Then: "Don't worry. I'm all right now and I think I'll *be* all right. But I can't forget—where I've been. I don't mean just the physical place I've been, I mean where I've *been*. And *what* I've been."

"What have you been, Sonny?" I asked. 215

He smiled—but sat sideways on the sofa, his elbow resting on the back, his fingers playing with his mouth and chin, not looking at me. "I've been something I didn't recognize, didn't know I could be. Didn't know anybody could be." He stopped, looking inward, looking helplessly young, looking old. "I'm not talking about it now because I feel *guilty* or anything like that—maybe it would be better if I did, I don't know. Anyway, I can't really talk about it. Not to you, not to anybody," and now he turned and faced me. "Sometimes, you know, and it was actually when I was most *out* of the world, I felt that I was in it, that I was *with* it, really, and I could play or I didn't really have to *play*, it just came out of me, it was there. And I don't know how I played, thinking about it now, but I know I did awful things, those times, sometimes, to people. Or it wasn't that I *did* anything to them—it was that they weren't real." He picked up the beer can; it was empty; he rolled it between his palms: "And other times—well, I needed a fix, I needed to find a place to lean, I needed to clear a space to *listen*—and I couldn't find it, and I—went crazy, I did terrible things to *me*, I was terrible *for* me." He began pressing the beer can between his hands, I watched the metal begin to give. It glittered, as he played with it, like a knife, and I was afraid he would cut himself, but I said nothing. "Oh well. I can never tell you. I was all by myself at the bottom of something, stinking and sweating and crying and shaking, and I smelled it, you know? *my* stink, and I thought I'd die if I couldn't get away from it and yet, all the same, I knew that everything I was doing was just locking me in with it. And I didn't know," he paused, still flattening the beer can, "I didn't know, I still *don't* know, something kept telling me that maybe it was good to smell your own stink, but I didn't think that *that* was what I'd been trying to do—and—who can stand it?" and he abruptly dropped the ruined beer can, looking at me with a small, still smile, and then rose, walking to the window as though it were the lodestone rock. I watched his face, he watched the avenue. "I couldn't tell you when Mama died—but the reason I wanted to leave Harlem so bad was to get away from drugs. And then, when I ran away, that's what I was running from—really. When I came back, nothing had changed, *I* hadn't changed, I was just—older." And he stopped, drumming with his fingers on the windowpane. The sun had vanished, soon darkness would fall. I watched his face. "It can come again," he said, almost as though speaking to himself. Then he turned to me. "It can come again," he repeated. "I just want you to know that."

"All right," I said, at last. "So it can come again. All right."

He smiled, but the smile was sorrowful. "I had to try to tell you," he said.

"Yes," I said. "I understand that."

"You're my brother," he said, looking straight at me, and not smiling at all.   220

"Yes," I repeated, "yes. I understand that."

He turned back to the window, looking out. "All that hatred down there," he said, "all that hatred and misery and love. It's a wonder it doesn't blow the avenue apart."

We went to the only nightclub on a short, dark street, downtown. We squeezed through the narrow, chattering, jam-packed bar to the entrance of the big room, where the bandstand was. And we stood there for a moment, for the lights were very dim in this room and we couldn't see. Then, "Hello, boy," said a voice and an enormous black man, much older than Sonny or myself, erupted out of all that atmospheric lighting and put an arm around Sonny's shoulder. "I been sitting right here," he said, "waiting for you."

He had a big voice, too, and heads in the darkness turned toward us.

Sonny grinned and pulled a little away, and said, "Creole, this is my brother. I   225
told you about him."

Creole shook my hand. "I'm glad to meet you, son," he said, and it was clear that he was glad to meet me *there*, for Sonny's sake. And he smiled, "You got a real musician in *your* family," and he took his arm from Sonny's shoulder and slapped him, lightly, affectionately, with the back of his hand.

"Well. Now I've heard it all," said a voice behind us. This was another musician, and a friend of Sonny's, a coal-black, cheerful-looking man, built close to the ground. He immediately began confiding to me, at the top of his lungs, the most terrible things about Sonny, his teeth gleaming like a lighthouse and his laugh coming up out of him like the beginning of an earthquake. And it turned out that everyone at the bar knew Sonny, or almost everyone; some were musicians, working there, or nearby, or not working, some were simply hangers-on, and some were there to hear Sonny play. I was introduced to all of them and they were all very polite to me. Yet, it was clear that, for them, I was only Sonny's brother. Here, I was in Sonny's world. Or, rather: his kingdom. Here, it was not even a question that his veins bore royal blood.

They were going to play soon and Creole installed me, by myself, at a table in a dark corner. Then I watched them, Creole, and the little black man, and Sonny, and the others, while they horsed around, standing just below the bandstand. The light from the bandstand spilled just a little short of them and, watching them laughing and gesturing and moving about, I had the feeling that they, nevertheless, were being most careful not to step into that circle of light too suddenly: that if they moved into the light too suddenly, without thinking, they would perish in flame. Then, while I watched, one of them, the small, black man, moved into the light and crossed the bandstand and started fooling around with his drums. Then—being funny and being, also, extremely ceremonious—Creole took Sonny by the arm and led him to the piano. A woman's voice called Sonny's name and a few hands started clapping. And Sonny, also being funny and being ceremonious, and so touched, I think, that he could have cried, but neither hiding it nor showing it, riding it like a man, grinned, and put both hands to his heart and bowed from the waist.

Creole then went to the bass fiddle and a lean, very bright-skinned brown man jumped up on the bandstand and picked up his horn. So there they were, and the atmosphere on the bandstand and in the room began to change and tighten. Someone stepped up to the microphone and announced them. Then there were all kinds of murmurs. Some people at the bar shushed others. The waitress ran around, frantically getting in the last orders, guys and chicks got closer to each other, and the lights on the bandstand, on the quartet, turned to a kind of indigo. Then they all looked different there. Creole looked about him for the last time, as though he were making certain that all his chickens were in the coop, and then he—jumped and struck the fiddle. And there they were.

All I know about music is that not many people ever really hear it. And even   230
then, on the rare occasions when something opens within, and the music enters, what we mainly hear, or hear corroborated, are personal, private, vanishing evocations. But the man who creates the music is hearing something else, is dealing with the roar rising from the void and imposing order on it as it hits the air. What is evoked in him, then, is of another order, more terrible because it has no words, and triumphant, too, for that same reason. And his triumph, when he triumphs, is ours. I just watched Sonny's face. His face was troubled, he was working hard, but he wasn't with it. And I had the feeling that, in a way, everyone on the bandstand was waiting for him, both waiting for him and pushing him along. But as I began to watch Creole, I realized that it was Creole

who held them all back. He had them on a short rein. Up there, keeping the beat with his whole body, wailing on the fiddle, with his eyes half closed, he was listening to everything, but he was listening to Sonny. He was having a dialogue with Sonny. He wanted Sonny to leave the shoreline and strike out for the deep water. He was Sonny's witness that deep water and drowning were not the same thing—he had been there, and he knew. And he wanted Sonny to know. He was waiting for Sonny to do the things on the keys which would let Creole know that Sonny was in the water.

And, while Creole listened, Sonny moved, deep within, exactly like someone in torment. I had never before thought of how awful the relationship must be between the musician and his instrument. He has to fill it, this instrument, with the breath of life, his own. He has to make it do what he wants it to do. And a piano is just a piano. It's made out of so much wood and wires and little hammers and big ones, and ivory. While there's only so much you can do with it, the only way to find this out is to try; to try and make it do everything.

And Sonny hadn't been near a piano for over a year. And he wasn't on much better terms with his life, not the life that stretched before him now. He and the piano stammered, started one way, got scared, stopped; started another way, panicked, marked time, started again; then seemed to have found a direction, panicked again, got stuck. And the face I saw on Sonny I'd never seen before. Everything had been burned out of it, and, at the same time, things usually hidden were being burned in, by the fire and fury of the battle which was occurring in him up there.

Yet, watching Creole's face as they neared the end of the first set, I had the feeling that something had happened, something I hadn't heard. Then they finished, there was scattered applause, and then, without an instant's warning, Creole started into something else, it was almost sardonic, it was *Am I Blue*. And, as though he commanded, Sonny began to play. Something began to happen. And Creole let out the reins. The dry, low, black man said something awful on the drums, Creole answered, and the drums talked back. Then the horn insisted, sweet and high, slightly detached perhaps, and Creole listened, commenting now and then, dry, and driving, beautiful and calm and old. Then they all came together again, and Sonny was part of the family again. I could tell this from his face. He seemed to have found, right there beneath his fingers, a damn brand-new piano. It seemed that he couldn't get over it. Then, for awhile, just being happy with Sonny, they seemed to be agreeing with him that brand-new pianos certainly were a gas.

Then Creole stepped forward to remind them that what they were playing was the blues. He hit something in all of them, he hit something in me, myself, and the music tightened and deepened, apprehension began to beat the air. Creole began to tell us what the blues were all about. They were not about anything very new. He and his boys up there were keeping it new, at the risk of ruin, destruction, madness, and death, in order to find new ways to make us listen. For, while the tale of how we suffer, and how we are delighted, and how we may triumph is never new, it always must be heard. There isn't any other tale to tell, it's the only light we've got in all this darkness.

And this tale, according to that face, that body, those strong hands on those strings,   235
has another aspect in every country, and a new depth in every generation. Listen, Creole seemed to be saying, listen. Now these are Sonny's blues. He made the little black man on the drums know it, and the bright, brown man on the horn. Creole wasn't trying any longer to get Sonny in the water. He was wishing him Godspeed. Then he stepped back, very slowly, filling the air with the immense suggestion that Sonny speak for himself.

Then they all gathered around Sonny and Sonny played. Every now and again one of them seemed to say, amen. Sonny's fingers filled the air with life, his life. But that life contained so many others. And Sonny went all the way back, he really began with the spare, flat statement of the opening phrase of the song. Then he began to make it his. It was very beautiful because it wasn't hurried and it was no longer a lament. I seemed to hear with what burning he had made it his, with what burning we had yet to make it ours, how we could cease lamenting. Freedom lurked around us and I understood, at last, that he could help us to be free if we would listen, that he would never be free until we did. Yet, there was no battle in his face now. I heard what he had gone through, and would continue to go through until he came to rest in earth. He had made it his: that long line, of which we knew only Mama and Daddy. And he was giving it back, as everything must be given back, so that, passing through death, it can live forever. I saw my mother's face again, and felt, for the first time, how the stones of the road she had walked on must have bruised her feet. I saw the moonlit road where my father's brother died. And it brought something else back to me, and carried me past it. I saw my little girl again and felt Isabel's tears again, and I felt my own tears begin to rise. And I was yet aware that this was only a moment, that the world waited outside, as hungry as a tiger, and that trouble stretched above us, longer than the sky.

Then it was over. Creole and Sonny let out their breath, both soaking wet, and grinning. There was a lot of applause and some of it was real. In the dark, the girl came by and I asked her to take drinks to the bandstand. There was a long pause, while they talked up there in the indigo light and after awhile I saw the girl put a Scotch and milk on top of the piano for Sonny. He didn't seem to notice it, but just before they started playing again, he sipped from it and looked toward me, and nodded. Then he put it back on top of the piano. For me, then, as they began to play again, it glowed and shook above my brother's head like the very cup of trembling.

ANALYZING "SONNY'S BLUES"

The primary tools in understanding this powerful short story, written by an African American writer, lay in coming to grips with its basic elements: plot, character, tone, theme, and metaphor/imagery. Let's look at some of these elements in "Sonny's Blues."

Plot

The plot of this story is not overly complicated. A relatively young teacher (and family man) narrates the story of his encounters with his brother Sonny and other characters in Harlem, which is a part of New York and has a significant African American population. The narrator, unnamed, tells the story of his brother's development as a young man. As the story is narrated, we learn more about the narrator, his wife, parents, and deceased daughter. Indeed, "Sonny's Blues" is a story rich in family and personal relationships.

The plot of any narrative contains at least two dimensions: (1) change over time and (2) cause and effect relationships. "Sonny's Blues" begins with the narrator's emotional description of learning that his brother has been arrested for using heroin. This cause leads to certain effects. The narrative ends with the narrator listening to his brother playing blues music in a nightclub. Sonny has clearly changed in the narrator's eyes, from a misguided youth to a professional musician pursuing a career in something he loves. The cause of this change in Sonny is complex, but part of the change is the result of Sonny's encounters with his teacher-brother. The narrator has changed too, from a suspicious, cynical, distanced, and overprotective brother to an admiring older sibling, quite proud of his younger brother and the changes he has made by story's end. The last few paragraphs, in particular, illustrate the significant changes that have come over Sonny and his brother, both of whom have clearly grown in self-knowledge and understanding of others.

Character

"Sonny's Blues" has long been recognized as a narrative with finely developed characters, who are described by Baldwin in a near poetic style. Although the story is named after the younger of two brothers, the narrator is obviously a major character and his growth and changes are surely as important as Sonny's. The larger family unit includes important characters, as well. The deaths of the narrator's uncle and daughter have clearly shaped the way he looks at life, and his good relationship with his wife Isabel also plays a role in the decisions he makes.

At the beginning of the story, the narrator is shocked (and disgusted) when he learns of Sonny's drug use. By the end of the narrative, the narrator is comfortable in the knowledge that his brother has begun a career as a musician. In observing Sonny play the piano, the narrator comes to realize the importance of music in his brother's life, not just as a career but as a way of thinking and living. This realization prompts the narrator to think about his own life. Indeed, the narrator's encounter with his brother's new life at the end of the story signals a rebirth in their relationship. The narrator now understands that Sonny has taken responsibility for himself, he is acting in "good faith." The narrator, too, accepts a new kind of responsibility as a result of this encounter, and clearly comes to see his brother (and himself) in a new light. Other encounters, such as the narrator's vowing to his mother to watch over Sonny, reveal ethical commitments.

Tone and Point of View

"Sonny's Blues" is written from the first-person point of view, and the narrator participates in as well as narrates the story. Although the narrative is about changes in Sonny's life, the narrator tells us much about himself and his past life. Indeed, it would not be unreasonable to say that there are two protagonists in this story—the narrator and Sonny. The portraits of the narrator and Sonny are sympathetic, yet are also objective (insofar as this is possible in a first-person narration). The narrator criticizes both himself and Sonny when it is appropriate, and this creates an atmosphere of fairness in point of view. The tone of this story is complex, sometimes revealing deep frustration, and at other times expressing a sense of tranquillity and peacefulness. James Baldwin creates powerful interior monologues, which occur when narrators "think out loud" in describing events and their responses to them. Throughout "Sonny's Blues," the narrator tells us what he is thinking as he judges himself, Sonny, and other characters as well as events. As both major characters change (and grow), so too does the narrator's attitude and tone.

Theme

This narrative is a rich, powerful story about the struggles of African Americans growing up in Harlem, New York. "Sonny's Blues" is both a personal story (about the narrator and his family) and a broader story about the difficulty of growing up as an African American in the first half of the twentieth century. The narrator depicts himself as an individual who has achieved some success in life as a teacher and happily married husband and father, yet there are pangs of misfortune that haunt the narrator. He is troubled by the tragic and racist death of his uncle. He is deeply bothered by Sonny's irresponsible behavior as a troubled youth, which includes serious drug use. Yet "Sonny's Blues" is also about redemption and regeneration, which are as much a part of life as struggle and failure. Surely a major theme of the story is Sonny's rebirth as an engaged member of his community and, just as important, his rebirth as someone who has confidence in himself and takes responsibility for his actions. The narrator experiences growth as well; in fact, it may be because of Sonny's growth that the narrator is able to learn from him and grow too. There are many important themes woven into "Sonny's Blues," and several of them are illustrated through the narrator's encounters with individuals who played major roles in shaping his life, beginning with his mother and her stories of family experiences.

Metaphor and Imagery

"Sonny's Blues" is rich in symbolism, metaphor, and imagery. The image of Sonny's troubled (unnamed) friend whom the narrator describes at the beginning of the story is powerful in illustrating elements of hopelessness in the community. Indeed, the "unnamed" status of the drug-using friend may suggest his anonymity in the culture of the city. The narrator's retelling of his mother's description of the death of his uncle is tragic and poignant in illustrating an image of racism in America in the early part of the twentieth century. The encounter with his mother teaches the narrator much about the history of his family and explains, in part, his protective attitude toward Sonny.

The story emphasizes the narrator's memory of past events, especially his relationship with Sonny during his formative years. These extended memories dramatize the narrator's search for explanation and identity (both his own and Sonny's). Perhaps the most striking symbol/metaphor illustrating the narrator's search for meaning is the glass of milk and scotch, sitting on the top of the piano as it "glowed and shook above my brother's head like the very cup of trembling." This biblical symbol comes from thousands of years ago when a Jewish prophet recounted, "Thus saith thy Lord the Lord, and thy God that pleadeth the cause of his people, Behold, I have taken out of thine hand the cup of trembling, even the dregs of the cup of my fury; though shalt no more drink it again" (Isaiah 51:22 *King James Version*). This powerful symbol summarizes the narrator's attitude toward Sonny and the world they inhabit.

Questions for Your Analysis of "Sonny's Blues"

1) What are some of your early impressions of the story?
2) What are your observations on the narrator's attitude toward his brother? How does the narrator's attitude change, not only toward Sonny but also toward other things?
3) There are several encounters in the story, including the narrator's encounters with his brother's friend at the beginning of the story, with his mother, with Creole, and of course with Sonny. What are three significant encounters? Does the narrator grow as a result of these encounters? In what other ways do these encounters affect the narrator as well as other characters? How do these encounters affect you?
4) How do you see yourself "fitting into the story" in terms of encounters?
5) What judgments do you make about Sonny's new life in the world of music?
6) What do you see as the guiding principle in the narrator's life as he evolves in the course of the narrative? What are the guiding principles of other characters, such as Sonny and his mother?
7) What is it that the narrator and Sonny learn from their experience?
8) What is there in your personal experience that resonates with some of the themes in this story?
9) What personal moral values are presented in the narrative?
10) In what ways does the narrator foreshadow the evolution of the two major characters?
11) How do you interpret the concluding statement of the narrator: "it [the drink] glowed and shook above my brother's head like the very cup of trembling"?

The textual issues suggested in this chapter can be appropriated to ethical criticism, as well as to other interpretive approaches. Please read the following sample essay on "Sonny's Blues" as an illustration of one form that ethical criticism might take. This essay, as you will see, focuses on encounters between characters and their ethical implications. Other ethical approaches to the story might focus more heavily on the ways in which elements in the story (plot, theme, character) encounter the reader's system of ethical values.

Sample Essay on "Sonny's Blues"

"Sonny's Blues" is a story that takes place in Harlem, New York in the 1950s, and chronicles the developing relationship between two brothers approximately seven years apart in age. The older brother, a teacher, is the unnamed, first-person narrator of the story. The younger brother is Sonny, a developing jazz musician. The tightly written narrative begins with the narrator's reading in the newspaper about his brother's arrest for using and selling heroin. The teacher/brother/narrator is stunned by what he has read: "It was not to be believed and I kept telling myself that." The narrator's encounter with the truth about his brother leads him to conclude that Sonny is well on the way to ruining his life and leads to a series of encounters which reveal much about the narrator's sense of duty and responsibility (as well as that of other characters). These encounters play a significant role in illustrating the narrative's theme of personal responsibility and ethical choice.

The narrator suffers deeply as he agonizes over what he takes to be the certain fate of his brother Sonny after the drug arrest. The incident changes both of their lives in significant ways. Sonny's arrest sparks intense emotions for the narrator, as he recalls growing up in the ghetto and learning about his father's brother's death, as a teenager, at the hands of southern racists. Shortly after reading of Sonny's arrest, the narrator encounters a friend of Sonny's from the past, a drug-using, shiftless, "ne'er-do-well" for whom the narrator has little respect. The meeting turns somewhat nasty when the narrator says, "Don't tell me your sad story." The narrator is clearly seething with frustration because the friend reminds the narrator of his younger brother.

Yet from this bitter encounter, something positive emerges. Indeed, *because* of the encounter, the narrator suddenly recognizes the despair and frustration of growing up in the ghetto and expresses sympathy for the ragged friend. The teacher has spent his rage and now looks more sympathetically upon the friend as representative of Sonny, as someone who desperately needs help, not condemnation: "Then I felt guilty—guilty, probably, for never having supposed that the poor bastard *had* a story of his own, much less a sad one." The narrator clearly recognizes the humanity of the friend, who is no longer a "junkie" but a fellow human in need of help. The older brother sees his younger brother in the troubled friend. The encounter has humanized the narrator, and he now seeks advice from the youth he had despised shortly before. When the narrator faces the friend, he comes away from the encounter declaring his empathy for the friend (as well as for Sonny).

The friend reminds the narrator of Sonny (the narrator even thinks that he is Sonny at first glance) and the encounter starts him thinking and worrying about his brother. The narrator's encounter with the news of his brother's arrest triggers his encounter with the old neighborhood friend, which triggers the narrator's sense of empathy for not only the friend and Sonny, but other characters too, such as the barmaid, about whom the narrator comments "one saw the little girl, one sensed the doomed, still-struggling woman beneath the battered face of the semiwhore." The narrator has clearly faced and empathized with the downtrodden characters of his neighborhood, and this recognition of human suffering is illustrative of the narrator's sense of responsibility for others. It is not an abstract sensitivity to general human suffering, but a very personal reaction to actual individuals. The narrator's ethical understanding is intensely personal and he concludes his meeting with the friend by giving him five dollars, although he was asked for only one dollar.

The narrator's sympathetic attitude is but a brief experience. He tells us that he ignored Sonny after his arrest and did not write him for a long time, and only then because his daughter, Grace, had died. Sonny encounters his brother by writing a very moving letter, telling his older brother "how much I needed to hear from you." Sonny's gesture of reconciliation prompts the narrator to stay in touch with his brother and worry about the kind of life Sonny was leading. When the brothers face one another once again, they take a long drive through the city, which prompts a deep conversation and an attempt to understand one another. Sonny's letter had awakened in his older brother a sense of duty, not only to maintain contact, but also to maintain vigil over his younger sibling. The narrator embraces his new sense of responsibility. Their long conversation evokes their mother's moving story of the death of his uncle, followed by their mother's plea that the narrator "hold on to your brother . . . and don't let him fall." Once again, the narrator promises to remember his brother, yet soon forgets his promise to his mother as he marries and embarks on a new life, without much thought of Sonny.

The subsequent encounter between the brothers, after the narrator returns home from his mother's funeral, sets the stage for yet another test of the narrator's sense of responsibility. Earlier we saw that he had made gestures toward accepting responsibility for being a good brother, but he has not made much of a good faith effort in matching his deeds to his words. The narrator has another opportunity as he and Sonny engage in a long, penetrating conversation in which the narrator learns that Sonny has matured, even though still in high school, and has acquired tastes and interests that are new to the narrator (Sonny's interest in Charlie Parker, for example). The narrator confronts Sonny and insists that he live with his wife Isabel's family until Sonny finishes school. Sonny reluctantly agrees, but only because of his brother's forceful pleas. This encounter illustrates the narrator's acceptance of his responsibility to look after his younger brother in whatever way he can.

Other encounters in the story generate ethical moments, but perhaps the most compelling "face off" between the brothers occurs in the nightclub of the closing scene, where the narrator witnesses the maturation of his brother, now widely respected among his fellow musicians as well as the audience. The narrator comes to understand that life is about suffering, to live is to suffer, but true personal responsibility is to accept suffering, yet not "drown in it," as Sonny says to him. The narrator and Sonny are reunited as members of a family once again, but this time the family includes the community of blues-loving people like Creole, who are brought together by a common love of music. There is a developing sense of identity, not only for Sonny and his community of musicians, but for the narrator too.

The narrator has clearly changed as a result of this last encounter with Sonny and the musical culture. What he once disapproved of, the narrator now firmly embraces, and this includes both his brother and his music. Indeed, it is through music that the narrator is able to understand his brother and accept his choices in life. The reconciliation is complete and is symbolized by the glass of scotch and milk that the narrator sends to Sonny. This symbol, growing out of a powerful ethical moment, reveals how the narrator is able to transcend all of his earlier beliefs and prejudices in unconditionally accepting, finally, his brother. As the narrator gazes at the beverage, he observes that it "glowed and shook above my brother's head like the very cup of trembling." This passage, taken from the Old Testament in which the Jewish community was given hope for its survival, represents the narrator's hope for Sonny (and for himself). The narrator's moment of unconditional love for his brother is the basis for such hope and optimism.

WRITING YOUR ESSAY FROM AN ETHICAL PERSPECTIVE

The following short story, "Cathedral," is by Raymond Carver. This narrative, like "Sonny's Blues," depicts the experiences of a man who encounters someone he takes to be quite different from him, a blind teacher who is a friend of the narrator's wife. This story is also told in the first-person voice of a narrator who is very set in his ways, much like the narrator of "Sonny's Blues." What is striking about this story is the author's attempt to capture the changes that come about in a narrator exposed to someone whom he takes to be so different. The series of encounters with the blind man change the narrator in some important ways. In that respect, the narrator of "Cathedral" and the narrator of "Sonny's Blues" share something in common. Following "Cathedral" is a series of questions to assist you in the analysis of the work, as well as in writing an essay from an ethical perspective.

A SAMPLE READING

"Cathedral" by Raymond Carver (1938–1988)

This blind man, an old friend of my wife's, he was on his way to spend the night. His wife had died. So he was visiting the dead wife's relatives in Connecticut. He called my wife from his in-laws'. Arrangements were made. He would come by train, a five-hour trip, and my wife would meet him at the station. She hadn't seen him since she worked for him one summer in Seattle ten years ago. But she and the blind man had kept in touch. They made tapes and mailed them back and forth. I wasn't enthusiastic about his visit. He was no one I knew. And his being blind bothered me. My idea of blindness came from the movies. In the movies, the blind moved slowly and never laughed. Sometimes they were led by seeing-eye dogs. A blind man in my house was not something I looked forward to.

That summer in Seattle she had needed a job. She didn't have any money. The man she was going to marry at the end of the summer was in officers' training school. He didn't have any money, either. But she was in love with the guy, and he was in love with her, etc. She'd seen something in the paper: HELP WANTED—*Reading to Blind Man*, and a telephone number. She phoned and went over, was hired on the spot. She'd worked with this blind man all summer. She read stuff to him, case studies, reports, that sort of thing. She helped him organize his little office in the county social-service department. They'd become good friends, my wife and the blind man. How do I know these things? She told me. And she told me something else. On her last day in the office, the blind man asked if he could touch her face. She agreed to this. She told me he touched his fingers to every part of her face, her nose—even her neck! She never forgot it. She even tried to write a poem about it. She was always trying to write a poem. She wrote a poem or two every year, usually after something really important had happened to her.

When we first started going out together, she showed me the poem. In the poem, she recalled his fingers and the way they had moved around over her face. In the poem, she talked about what she had felt at the time, about what went through her mind when the blind man touched her nose and lips. I can remember I didn't think much of the poem. Of course, I didn't tell her that. Maybe I just don't understand poetry. I admit it's not the first thing I reach for when I pick up something to read.

Anyway, this man who'd first enjoyed her favors, the officer-to-be, he'd been her childhood sweetheart. So okay. I'm saying that at the end of the summer she let the blind man run his hands over her face, said good-bye to him, married her childhood etc., who was now a commissioned officer, and she moved away from Seattle. But they'd kept in touch, she and the blind man. She made the first contact after a year or so. She called him up one night from an Air Force base in Alabama. She wanted to talk. They talked. He asked her to send a tape and tell him about her life. She did this. She sent the tape. On the tape, she told the blind man about her husband and about their life together in the military. She told the blind man she loved her husband but she didn't like it where they lived and she didn't like it that he was part of the military-industrial thing. She told the blind man she'd written a poem and he was in it. She told him that she was writing a poem about what it was like to be an Air Force officer's wife. The poem wasn't finished yet. She was still writing it. The blind man made a tape. He sent her the tape. She made a tape. This went on for years. My wife's officer was posted to one base and then another. She sent tapes from Moody AFB, McGuire, McConnell, and finally Travis, near Sacramento, where one night she got to feeling lonely and cut off from people she kept losing in that moving-around life. She got to feeling she couldn't go it another step. She went in and swallowed all the pills and capsules in the medicine chest and washed them down with a bottle of gin. Then she got into a hot bath and passed out.

But instead of dying, she got sick. She threw up. Her officer—why should he have   5
a name? he was the childhood sweetheart, and what more does he want?—came home from somewhere, found her, and called the ambulance. In time, she put it all on a tape and sent the tape to the blind man. Over the years, she put all kinds of stuff on tapes and sent the tapes off lickety-split. Next to writing a poem every year, I think it was her chief means of recreation. On one tape, she told the blind man she'd decided to live away from her officer for a time. On another tape, she told him about her divorce. She and I began going out, and of course she told her blind man about it. She told him everything, or so it seemed to me. Once she asked me if I'd like to hear the latest tape from the blind man. This was a year ago. I was on the tape, she said. So I said okay, I'd listen to it. I got us drinks and we settled down in the living room. We made ready to listen. First she inserted the tape into the player and adjusted a couple of dials. Then she pushed a lever. The tape squeaked and someone began to talk in this loud voice.

She lowered the volume. After a few minutes of harmless chitchat, I heard my own name in the mouth of this stranger, this blind man I didn't even know! And then this: "From all you've said about him, I can only conclude—" But we were interrupted, a knock at the door, something, and we didn't ever get back to the tape. Maybe it was just as well. I'd heard all I wanted to.

Now this same blind man was coming to sleep in my house.

"Maybe I could take him bowling," I said to my wife. She was at the draining board doing scalloped potatoes. She put down the knife she was using and turned around.

"If you love me," she said, "you can do this for me. If you don't love me, okay. But if you had a friend, any friend, and the friend came to visit, I'd make him feel comfortable." She wiped her hands with the dish towel.

"I don't have any blind friends," I said.

"You don't have *any* friends," she said. "Period. Besides," she said, "goddamn it, his wife's just died! Don't you understand that? The man's lost his wife!"   10

I didn't answer. She'd told me a little about the blind man's wife. Her name was Beulah. Beulah! That's a name for a colored woman.

"Was his wife a Negro?" I asked.

"Are you crazy?" my wife said. "Have you just flipped or something?" She picked up a potato. I saw it hit the floor, then roll under the stove. "What's wrong with you?" she said. "Are you drunk?"

"I'm just asking," I said.

Right then my wife filled me in with more detail then I cared to know. I made a drink and sat at the kitchen table to listen. Pieces of the story began to fall into place.   15

Beulah had gone to work for the blind man the summer after my wife had stopped working for him. Pretty soon Beulah and the blind man had themselves a church wedding. It was a little wedding—who'd want to go to such a wedding in the first place?—just the two of them, plus the minister and the minister's wife. But it was a church wedding just the same. It was what Beulah had wanted, he'd said. But even then Beulah must have been carrying the cancer in her glands. After they had been inseparable for eight years—my wife's word, *inseparable*—Beulah's health went into a rapid decline. She died in a Seattle hospital room, the blind man sitting beside the bed and holding on to her hand. They'd married, lived and worked together, slept together—had sex, sure—and then the blind man had to bury her. All this without his having ever seen what the goddamned woman looked like. It was beyond my understanding. Hearing this, I felt sorry for the blind man for a little bit. And then I found myself thinking what a pitiful life this woman must have led. Imagine a woman who could never see herself as she was seen in the eyes of her loved one. A woman who could go on day after day and never receive the smallest compliment from her beloved. A woman whose husband could never read the expression on her face, be it misery or something better. Someone who could wear makeup or not—what difference to him? She could, if she wanted, wear green eye-shadow around one eye, a straight pin in her nostril, yellow slacks, and purple shoes, no matter. And then to slip off into death, the blind man's hand on her hand, his blind eyes streaming tears—I'm imagining now—her last thought maybe this: that he never even knew what she looked like, and she on an express to the grave. Robert was left with a small insurance policy and a half of a twenty-peso Mexican coin. The other half of the coin went into the box with her. Pathetic.

So when the time rolled around, my wife went to the depot to pick him up. With nothing to do but wait—sure, I blamed him for that—I was having a drink and watching the TV when I heard the car pull into the drive. I got up from the sofa with my drink and went to the window to have a look.

I saw my wife laughing as she parked the car. I saw her get out of the car and shut the door. She was still wearing a smile. Just amazing. She went around to the other side of the car to where the blind man was already starting to get out. This blind man, feature this, he was wearing a full beard! A beard on a blind man! Too much, I say. The blind man reached into the backseat and dragged out a suitcase. My wife took his arm, shut the car door, and, talking all the way, moved him down the drive and then up the steps to the front porch. I turned off the TV. I finished my drink, rinsed the glass, dried my hands. Then I went to the door.

My wife said, "I want you to meet Robert. Robert, this is my husband. I've told you all about him." She was beaming. She had this blind man by his coat sleeve.

The blind man let go of his suitcase and up came his hand.   20

I took it. He squeezed hard, held my hand, and then he let it go.

"I feel like we've already met," he boomed.

"Likewise," I said. I didn't know what else to say. Then I said, "Welcome. I've heard a lot about you." We began to move then, a little group, from the porch into the living room, my wife guiding him by the arm. The blind man was carrying his suitcase in his other hand. My wife said things like, "To your left here, Robert. That's right. Now watch it, there's a chair. That's it. Sit down right here. This is the sofa. We just bought this sofa two weeks ago."

I started to say something about the old sofa. I'd liked that old sofa. But I didn't say anything. Then I wanted to say something else, small-talk, about the scenic ride along the Hudson. How going *to* New York, you should sit on the right-hand side of the train, and coming *from* New York, the left-hand side.

"Did you have a good train ride?" I said. "Which side of the train did you sit on,   25
by the way?"

"What a question, which side!" my wife said. "What's it matter which side?" she said.

"I just asked," I said.

"Right side," the blind man said. "I hadn't been on a train in nearly forty years. Not since I was a kid. With my folks. That's been a long time. I'd nearly forgotten the sensation. I have winter in my beard now," he said. "So I've been told, anyway. Do I look distinguished, my dear?" the blind man said to my wife.

"You look distinguished, Robert," she said. "Robert," she said. "Robert, it's just so good to see you."

My wife finally took her eyes off the blind man and looked at me. I had the feel-   30
ing she didn't like what she saw. I shrugged.

I've never met, or personally known, anyone who was blind. This blind man was late forties, a heavy-set, balding man with stooped shoulders, as if he carried a great weight there. He wore brown slacks, brown shoes, a light-brown shirt, a tie, a sports coat. Spiffy. He also had this full beard. But he didn't use a cane and he didn't wear dark glasses. I'd always thought dark glasses were a must for the blind. Fact was, I wished he had a pair. At first glance, his eyes looked like anyone else's eyes. But if you looked close, there was something different about them. Too much white in the iris, for one thing, and the pupils seemed to move around in the sockets without his knowing it or being able to stop it. Creepy. As I stared at his face, I saw the left pupil turn in toward his nose while the other made an effort to keep in one place. But it was only an effort, for that eye was on the roam without his knowing it or wanting it to be.

I said, "Let me get you a drink. What's your pleasure? We have a little of everything. It's one of our pastimes."

"Bub, I'm a Scotch man myself," he said fast enough in this big voice.

"Right," I said. Bub! "Sure you are. I knew it."

He let his fingers touch his suitcase, which was sitting alongside the sofa. He was taking his bearings. I didn't blame him for that.

"I'll move that up to your room," my wife said.

"No, that's fine," the blind man said loudly. "It can go up when I go up."

"A little water with the Scotch?" I said.

"Very little," he said.

"I knew it," I said.

He said, "Just a tad. The Irish actor, Barry Fitzgerald? I'm like that fellow. When I drink water, Fitzgerald said, I drink water. When I drink whiskey, I drink whiskey." My wife laughed. The blind man brought his hand up under his beard. He lifted his beard slowly and let it drop.

I did the drinks, three big glasses of Scotch with a splash of water in each. Then we made ourselves comfortable and talked about Robert's travels. First the long flight from the West Coast to Connecticut, we covered that. Then from Connecticut up here by train. We had another drink concerning that leg of the trip.

I remembered having read somewhere that the blind didn't smoke because, as speculation had it, they couldn't see the smoke they exhaled. I thought I knew that much and that much only about blind people. But this blind man smoked his cigarette down to the nubbin and then lit another one. This blind man filled his ashtray and my wife emptied it.

When we sat down at the table for dinner, we had another drink. My wife heaped Robert's plate with cube steak, scalloped potatoes, green beans. I buttered him up two slices of bread. I said, "Here's bread and butter for you." I swallowed some of my drink. "Now let us pray," I said, and the blind man lowered his head. My wife looked at me, her mouth agape. "Pray the phone won't ring and the food doesn't get cold," I said.

We dug in. We ate everything there was to eat on the table. We ate like there was no tomorrow. We didn't talk. We ate. We scarfed. We grazed that table. We were into serious eating. The blind man had right away located his foods, he knew just where everything was on his plate. I watched with admiration as he used his knife and fork on the meat. He'd cut two pieces of meat, fork the meat into his mouth, and then go all out for the scalloped potatoes, the beans next, and then he'd tear off a hunk of buttered bread and eat that. He'd follow this up with a big drink of milk. It didn't seem to bother him to use his fingers once in a while, either.

We finished everything, including half a strawberry pie. For a few moments, we sat as if stunned. Sweat beaded on our faces. Finally, we got up from the table and left the dirty plates. We didn't look back. We took ourselves into the living room and sank into our places again. Robert and my wife sat on the sofa. I took the big chair. We had us two or three more drinks while they talked about the major things that had come to pass for them in the past ten years. For the most part, I just listened. Now and then I joined in. I didn't want him to think I'd left the room, and I didn't want her to think I was feeling left out. They talked of things that had happened to them—to them!—

35
40
45

these past ten years. I waited in vain to hear my name on my wife's sweet lips: "And then my dear husband came into my life"—something like that. But I heard nothing of the sort. More talk of Robert. Robert had done a little of everything, it seemed, a regular blind jack-of-all-trades. But most recently he and his wife had had an Amway distributorship, from which, I gathered, they'd earned their living, such as it was. The blind man was also a ham radio operator. He talked in his loud voice about conversations he'd had with fellow operators in Guam, in the Philippines, in Alaska, and even in Tahiti. He said he'd have a lot of friends there if he ever wanted to go visit those places. From time to time, he'd turn his blind face toward me, put his hand under his beard, ask me something. How long had I been in my present position? (Three years). Did I like my work? (I didn't.) Was I going to stay with it? (What were the options?) Finally, when I thought he was beginning to run down, I got up and turned on the TV.

My wife looked at me with irritation. She was heading toward a boil. Then she looked at the blind man and said, "Robert, do you have a TV?"

The blind man said, "My dear, I have two TVs. I have a color set and a black-and-white thing, an old relic. It's funny, but if I turn the TV on, and I'm always turning it on, I turn on the color set. It's funny, don't you think?"

I didn't know what to say to that. I had absolutely nothing to say to that. No opinion. So I watched the news program and tried to listen to what the announcer was saying.

"This is a color TV," the blind man said. "Don't ask me how, but I can tell."   50

"We traded up a while ago," I said.

The blind man had another taste of his drink. He lifted his beard, sniffed it, and let it fall. He leaned forward on the sofa. He positioned his ashtray on the coffee table, then put the lighter to his cigarette. He leaned back on the sofa and crossed his legs at the ankles.

My wife covered her mouth, and then she yawned. She stretched. She said, "I think I'll go upstairs and put on my robe. I think I'll change into something else. Robert, you make yourself comfortable," she said.

"I'm comfortable," the blind man said.

"I want you to feel comfortable in this house," she said.   55

"I am comfortable," the blind man said.

After she'd left the room, he and I listened to the weather report and then to the sports roundup. By that time, she'd been gone so long I didn't know if she was going to come back. I thought she might have gone to bed. I wished she'd come back downstairs. I didn't want to be left alone with a blind man. I asked him if he wanted another drink, and he said sure. Then I asked if he wanted to smoke some dope with me. I said I'd just rolled a number. I hadn't, but I planned to do so in about two shakes.

"I'll try some with you," he said.

"Damn right," I said. "That's the stuff."

I got our drinks and sat down on the sofa with him. Then I rolled us two fat num-   60
bers. I lit one and passed it. I brought it to his fingers. He took it and inhaled.

"Hold it as long as you can," I said. I could tell he didn't know the first thing.

My wife came back downstairs wearing her pink robe and her pink slippers.

"What do I smell?" she said.

"We thought we'd have us some cannabis," I said.

My wife gave me a savage look. Then she looked at the blind man and said,   65
"Robert, I didn't know you smoked."

He said, "I do now, my dear. There's a first time for everything. But I don't feel anything yet."

"This stuff is pretty mellow," I said. "This stuff is mild. It's dope you can reason with," I said. "It doesn't mess you up."

"Not much it doesn't, bub," he said, and laughed.

My wife sat on the sofa between the blind man and me. I passed her the number. She took it and toked and then passed it back to me. "Which way is this going?" she said. Then she said, "I shouldn't be smoking this. I can hardly keep my eyes open as it is. That dinner did me in. I shouldn't have eaten so much."

"It was the strawberry pie," the blind man said. "That's what did it," he said, and   70
he laughed his big laugh. Then he shook his head.

"There's more strawberry pie," I said.

"Do you want some more, Robert?" my wife said.

"Maybe in a little while," he said.

We gave our attention to the TV. My wife yawned again. She said, "Your bed is made up when you feel like going to bed, Robert. I know you must have had a long day. When you're ready to go to bed, say so." She pulled his arm. "Robert?"

He came to and said, "I've had a real nice time. This beats tapes, doesn't it?"   75

I said, "Coming at you," and I put the number between his fingers. He inhaled, held the smoke, and then let it go. It was like he'd been doing it since he was nine years old.

"Thanks, bub," he said. "But I think this is all for me. I think I'm beginning to feel it," he said. He held the burning roach out for my wife.

"Same here," she said. "Ditto. Me, too." She took the roach and passed it to me. "I may just sit here for a while between you two guys with my eyes closed. But don't let me bother you, okay? Either one of you. If it bothers you, say so. Otherwise, I may just sit here with my eyes closed until you're ready to go to bed," she said. "Your bed's made up, Robert, when you're ready. It's right next to our room at the top of the stairs. We'll show you up when you're ready. You wake me up now, you guys, if I fall asleep." She said that and then she closed her eyes and went to sleep.

The news program ended. I got up and changed the channel. I sat back down on the sofa. I wished my wife hadn't pooped out. Her head lay across the back of the sofa, her mouth open. She'd turned so that her robe slipped away from her legs, exposing a juicy thigh. I reached to draw her robe back over her, and it was then that I glanced at the blind man. What the hell! I flipped the robe open again.

"You say when you want some strawberry pie," I said.   80

"I will," he said.

I said, "Are you tired? Do you want me to take you up to your bed? Are you ready to hit the hay?"

"Not yet," he said. "No, I'll stay up with you, bub. If that's all right. I'll stay up until you're ready to turn in. We haven't had a chance to talk. Know what I mean? I feel like me and her monopolized the evening." He lifted his beard and he let it fall. He picked up his cigarettes and his lighter.

"That's all right," I said. Then I said, "I'm glad for the company."

And I guess I was. Every night I smoked dope and stayed up as long as I could be-   85
fore I fell asleep. My wife and I hardly ever went to bed at the same time. When I did go to sleep, I had these dreams. Sometimes I'd wake up from one of them, my heart going crazy.

Something about the church and the Middle Ages was on the TV. Not your run-of-the-mill TV fare. I wanted to watch something else. I turned to the other channels. But there was nothing on them, either. So I turned back to the first channel and apologized.

"Bub, it's all right," the blind man said. "It's fine with me. Whatever you want to watch is okay. I'm always learning something. Learning never ends. It won't hurt me to learn something tonight. I got ears," he said.

We didn't say anything for a time. He was leaning forward with his head turned at me, his right ear aimed in the direction of the set. Very disconcerting. Now and then his eyelids drooped and then they snapped open again. Now and then he put his fingers into his beard and tugged, like he was thinking about something he was hearing on the television.

On the screen, a group of men wearing cowls was being set upon and tormented by men dressed in skeleton costumes and men dressed as devils. The men dressed as devils wore devil masks, horns, and long tails. This pageant was part of a procession. The Englishman who was narrating the thing said it took place in Spain once a year. I tried to explain to the blind man what was happening.

"Skeletons," he said. "I know about skeletons," he said, and he nodded.   90

The TV showed this one cathedral. Then there was a long, slow look at another one. Finally, the picture switched to the famous one in Paris, with its flying buttresses and its spires reaching up to the clouds. The camera pulled away to show the whole of the cathedral rising above the skyline.

There were times when the Englishman who was telling the thing would shut up, would simply let the camera move around the cathedrals. Or else the camera would tour the countryside, men in fields walking behind oxen. I waited as long as I could. Then I felt I had to say something. I said, "They're showing the outside of this cathedral now. Gargoyles. Little statues carved to look like monsters. Now I guess they're in Italy. Yeah, they're in Italy. There's paintings on the walls of this one church."

"Are those fresco paintings, bub?" he asked, and he sipped from his drink.

I reached for my glass. But it was empty. I tried to remember what I could remember. "You're asking me are those frescoes?" I said. "That's a good question. I don't know."

The camera moved to a cathedral outside Lisbon. The differences in the Por-   95
tuguese cathedral compared with the French and Italian were not that great. But they were there. Mostly the interior stuff. Then something occurred to me, and I said, "Something has occurred to me. Do you have any idea what a cathedral is? What they look like, that is? Do you follow me? If somebody says cathedral to you, do you have any notion what they're talking about? Do you know the difference between that and a Baptist church, say?"

He let the smoke dribble from his mouth. "I know they took hundreds of workers fifty or a hundred years to build," he said. "I just heard the man say that, of course. I know generations of the same families worked on a cathedral. I heard him say that, too. The men who began their life's work on them, they never lived to see the completion of their work. In that wise, bub, they're no different from the rest of us, right?" He laughed. Then his eyelids drooped again. His head nodded. He seemed to be snoozing. Maybe he was imagining himself in Portugal. The TV was showing another cathedral now. This one was in Germany. The Englishman's voice droned on. "Cathedrals," the blind man said. He sat up and rolled his head back and forth. "If you want the truth, bub, that's about all I know. What I just said. What I heard him say. But maybe you could describe one to me? I wish you'd do it. I'd like that. If you want to know, I really don't have a good idea."

I stared hard at the shot of the cathedral on the TV. How could I even begin to describe it? But say my life depended on it. Say my life was being threatened by an insane guy who said I had to do it or else.

I stared some more at the cathedral before the picture flipped off into the countryside. There was no use. I turned to the blind man and said, "To begin with, they're very tall." I was looking around the room for clues. "They reach way up. Up and up. Toward the sky. They're so big, some of them, they have to have these supports. To help hold them up, so to speak. These supports are called buttresses. They remind me of viaducts, for some reason. But maybe you don't know viaducts, either? Sometimes the cathedrals have devils and such carved into the front. Sometimes lords and ladies. Don't ask me why this is," I said.

He was nodding. The whole upper part of his body seemed to be moving back and forth.

"I'm not doing so good, am I?" I said.   100

He stopped nodding and leaned forward on the edge of the sofa. As he listened to me, he was running his fingers through his beard. I wasn't getting through to him, I could see that. But he waited for me to go on just the same. He nodded, like he was trying to encourage me. I tried to think what else to say. "They're really big," I said. "They're massive. They're built of stone. Marble, too, sometimes. In those olden days, when they built cathedrals, men wanted to be close to God. In those olden days, God was an important part of everyone's life. You could tell this from their cathedral-building. I'm sorry," I said, "but it looks like that's the best I can do for you. I'm just no good at it."

"That's all right, bub," the blind man said. "Hey, listen. I hope you don't mind my asking you. Can I ask you something? Let me ask you a simple question, yes or no. I'm just curious and there's no offense. You're my host. But let me ask if you are in any way religious? You don't mind my asking?"

I shook my head. He couldn't see that, though. A wink is the same as a nod to a blind man. "I guess I don't believe in it. In anything. Sometimes it's hard. You know what I'm saying?"

"Sure, I do," he said.

"Right," I said.   105

The Englishman was still holding forth. My wife sighed in her sleep. She drew a long breath and went on with her sleeping.

"You'll have to forgive me," I said. "But I can't tell you what a cathedral looks like. It just isn't in me to do it. I can't do any more than I've done."

The blind man sat very still, his head down, as he listened to me.

I said, "The truth is, cathedrals don't mean anything special to me. Nothing. Cathedrals. They're something to look at on late-night TV. That's all they are."

It was then that the blind man cleared his throat. He brought something up. He took a handkerchief from his back pocket. Then he said, "I get it, bub. It's okay. It happens. Don't worry about it," he said. "Hey, listen to me. Will you do me a favor? I got an idea. Why don't you find us some heavy paper? And a pen. We'll do something. We'll draw one together. Get us a pen and some heavy paper. Go on, bub, get the stuff," he said.   110

So I went upstairs. My legs felt like they didn't have any strength in them. They felt like they did after I'd done some running. In my wife's room, I looked around. I found some ballpoints in a little basket on her table. And then I tried to think where to look for the kind of paper he was talking about.

Downstairs, in the kitchen, I found a shopping bag with onion skins in the bottom of the bag. I emptied the bag and shook it. I brought it into the living room and sat down with it near his legs. I moved some things, smoothed the wrinkles from the bag, spread it out on the coffee table.

The blind man got down from the sofa and sat next to me on the carpet.

He ran his fingers over the paper. He went up and down the sides of the paper. The edges, even the edges. He fingered the corners.

"All right," he said. "All right, let's do her."   115

He found my hand, the hand with the pen. He closed his hand over my hand. "Go ahead, bub, draw," he said. "Draw. You'll see. I'll follow along with you. It'll be okay. Just begin now like I'm telling you. You'll see. Draw," the blind man said.

So I began. First I drew a box that looked like a house. It could have been the house I lived in. Then I put a roof on it. At either end of the roof, I drew spires. Crazy.

"Swell," he said. "Terrific. You're doing fine," he said. "Never thought anything like this could happen in your lifetime, did you, bub? Well, it's a strange life, we all know that. Go on now. Keep it up."

I put in windows with arches. I drew flying buttresses. I hung great doors. I couldn't stop. The TV station went off the air. I put down the pen and closed and opened my fingers. The blind man felt around over the paper. He moved the tips of his fingers over the paper, all over what I had drawn, and he nodded.

"Doing fine," the blind man said.   120

I took up the pen again, and he found my hand. I kept at it. I'm no artist. But I kept drawing just the same.

My wife opened up her eyes and gazed at us. She sat up on the sofa, her robe hanging open. She said, "What are you doing? Tell me, I want to know."

I didn't answer her.

The blind man said, "We're drawing cathedral. Me and him are working on it. Press hard," he said to me. "That's right. That's good," he said. "Sure. You got it, bub, I can tell. You didn't think you could. But you can, can't you? You're cooking with gas now. You know what I'm saying? We're going to really have us something here in a minute. How's the old arm?" he said. "Put some people in there now. What's a cathedral without people?"

My wife said, "What's going on? Robert, what are you doing? What's going on?"   125

"It's all right," he said to her. "Close your eyes now," the blind man said to me.

I did it. I closed them just like he said.

"Are they closed?" he said. "Don't fudge."

"They're closed," I said.

"Keep them that way," he said. He said, "Don't stop now. Draw."   130

So we kept on with it. His fingers rode my fingers as my hand went over the paper. It was like nothing else in my life up to now.

Then he said, "I think that's it. I think you got it," he said. "Take a look. What do you think?"

But I had my eyes closed. I thought I'd keep them that way for a little longer. I thought it was something I ought to do.

"Well?" he said. "Are you looking?"

My eyes were still closed. I was in my house. I knew that. But I didn't feel like I   135
was inside anything.

"It's really something," I said.

Questions for Your Analysis of "Cathedral"

1) What are some of your early impressions of the story? What is the most striking part of the story, something that promotes an instant reaction in you?

2) This story is told in the first-person by an unnamed narrator (referred to as "bub" by the blind man). What is your instinctive response to the narrator? Is he a particularly sympathetic figure to you?

3) What are your observations of the narrator's preoccupation with the blind man?

4) At what point in the narrative does the narrator's attitude toward Robert change?

5) Is there something from your personal experience that assists you in relating to any of the characters in the story?

6) The story describes one long encounter between the narrator and Robert. (There are also encounters between the narrator and his wife, as well as between the narrator and the reader.) What do these encounters reveal about the narrator?

7) What does the story say about stereotypes, and what are some ethical implications to stereotyping?

8) What do the narrator's encounters with his wife say about his sense of duty and responsibility?

9) Do you feel that the narrator prepared you for what happens in the last scene of the story, where the narrator suddenly realizes that he and Robert have much in common, especially as they both "face" one another as identical blind men?

10) By the end of the story, the narrator's attitude toward Robert had clearly changed. What prompted this change, how would you describe it, and what does it say about the narrator's sense of responsibility?

11) In what ways has the narrator demonstrated a sense of ethical responsibility by the end of the story?

STEPS IN WRITING AN ETHICAL ESSAY ABOUT ANY READING

1) Write down your impressions of key moments in the story or poem, events which illustrate significant interactions between characters in a story or personified elements in a poem.

2) Focus on the central characters or elements in the work and identify traits that you do or do not like. Indicate your reasons for sympathy or lack of sympathy.

3) Literary works usually contain elements of conflict. Identify the main forces of conflict in the work.

4) Consider personal experiences you have had that relate to encounters or interactions within the poem or story.

5) Examine the motivations of characters and analyze them from an ethical perspective.
6) Analyze conflicts in the work and then detail the moral implications of those conflicts. Indicate what the conflicts say about the characters directly or indirectly involved.
7) Detail events in the story, especially interactions among characters, which lead you to draw moral conclusions about the work as a whole.
8) A good general electronic source to investigate the context of any literary reading is google.com. By typing in the title of the work, especially if it is a well-known literary work, you will locate several sources that provide background information.

STEPS IN WRITING AN ESSAY ABOUT "CATHEDRAL"

Brainstorming Your Topic

1) Identify those elements in the text (character, plot, theme, metaphor) that prompt an immediate response from you. Write down whatever impressions you have.
2) Focus on the main character, the narrator. What is it about him that you do or do not like? Identify his initial personality traits and then compare them to his behavior after his encounter with Robert.
3) The narrator's initial reaction to Robert is one of disdain, perhaps even contempt. What is your reaction to the narrator's experience?
4) What personal experiences have you had that connect to parts of "Cathedral"? Have you ever encountered someone significantly different from yourself who has lead you to new insights about yourself as a result of your encounter?
5) Why is the narrator so intrigued by the blind man that the narrator agrees to pretend that he is blind in order to draw a cathedral with the help of Robert?
6) The story contains many references to the past lives of all of the characters, including Robert's deceased wife. Write down what effect(s) these references to the past have on you.
7) Personal responsibility plays a role in the story. How does this emphasis affect your interpretive reaction?
8) Are you satisfied with the ending? Why or why not?
9) What does the narrator do or say that suggests a change in ethical perspective?
10) Unless your instructor insists that you not consult outside sources in brainstorming your topic, refer to the electronic sources for Raymond Carver listed at the end of this chapter. There are many good links that will connect you to biographical sources and detailed criticism. Any ideas and words drawn directly from outside sources should be properly cited, of course. Consult the appendix for documentation procedures.

Creating an Outline

1) Collect your answers to the questions above in short two-word or three-word categories and use them as preliminary "writing points."

2) Think about the points and consider whether they add up to a central idea (for example, ethical changes in the narrator of "Cathedral").

3) Identify five or six main writing points that support your central idea. These points should come from the main literary elements in the story (character, plot, theme, point of view, metaphor). All of the points should provide support for your controlling idea. A good starting place is to examine the story's encounters and then look for ways in which characters change as a result of the encounters.

4) If you have more than five or six points, try to combine one or more of them. If you have fewer than five or six points, see if some of them can be used to generate additional points. You may have some large points that include smaller issues that can stand alone as paragraph topic sentences.

5) Look for transitional devices that connect your main points of support, particularly as they connect various encounters in the story.

Preparing a Rough Draft

1) Now that you have created a working outline, you have already completed your major organizational work. Each major point is the topic of a paragraph, and your essay will have between five and ten paragraphs, depending on development. These paragraphs need not be of equal length, but each one should sufficiently develop the topic sentence.

2) Now that you have your major writing points, assemble a preliminary draft by developing each topic idea with two or three sentences that discuss evidence from the text.

3) Focus on developing transitions between your paragraphs. Professional writers often begin a new paragraph with a direct reference to an idea expressed at the end of the preceding paragraph.

4) It is not too early to begin writing your concluding paragraph. Conclusions often summarize the main points of a central idea (but do not repeat word for word what has already been said). A conclusion may also refer to implications of what has been said (but what cannot be developed because of space limits). Your conclusion must examine ethical issues in the story.

5) Don't be afraid to include questions in your writing. No reader of literature can ever be absolutely certain of every observation that he or she makes, and perceptive observations often generate excellent questions, many of which are useful even if unanswerable.

Editing Your Draft

1) At this stage, you should have a draft of a few hundred words. You have already done the most difficult work in thinking out your ideas, organizing them into an outline, and preparing a rough version of the final product. Look for ways to edit your paper that will strengthen the essay.

2) Search for repetitious wording (and ideas). Do not repeat ideas, however important, throughout the essay. Use a thesaurus to locate synonyms for terms and ideas that reappear. Attempt to emphasize variety in your language.

3) If your instructor encourages peer editing, choose someone in your class, or perhaps a roommate, and solicit advice about how your essay reads. Is it articulate, compelling, insightful, and interesting? (All of these qualities are important.) Although your peer editor may not be taking a literature class, he or she may be a very good source of feedback on how effective your writing is. Professional writers often seek feedback from peers, not only from professional colleagues.

4) Be open to make changes in your writing, both conceptually and in specific language. Professional writers know that writing is recursive (which means that the act of writing constantly generates new ways of looking at the topic), and student writers should also take advantage of changes in thinking *as they write*. Don't be afraid to make efficient and effective changes, especially in terms of cutting out words, phrases, and sections that may not be working very well in supporting your overall idea.

5) Proofread carefully for spelling errors, punctuation problems, run-on sentences, and ambiguous or awkward constructions. You should use a solid grammar handbook to assist you in these areas.

Final Checklist

1) Make sure that your central idea (sometimes called a thesis statement) appears in the first paragraph. It is important that your reader know what major points(s) you are attempting to make.

2) Because this essay is an ethical investigation, check to see that the essay represents your analysis of ethical issues in the story. Your major points should be understandable, of course, to the community of readers to which you are writing.

3) Examine your essay for sufficient evidence. Each one of your major ideas will need illustration that comes from the text.

4) Review your conclusion to see if you have ended the essay in an effective manner, either summarizing what you have said (in different language) or suggesting some important implications of your reading.

5) Proofread one last time for errors, repetitious language, and awkward phrasing.

ELECTRONIC RESOURCES FOR JAMES BALDWIN

http://www.public.aus.edu/~metro/aflit/baldwin.   An introduction to Baldwin and his life, which contains biographical, bibliographic, and criticism links.

http://www.bookwire.com/bbr/interviews/baldwin.html.   An article about the life of James Baldwin.

http://www.bobbyseale.com/baldwin/htm.   A foreword written by Baldwin for *A Lonely Rage*, the autobiography of Bobby Seale.

http://www.encyclopedia.com/articles/01042.html.   Encyclopedia entry on James Baldwin.

http://encarta.msn.com/index/conciseindex/4D/04D67000.htm?z=1&pg=2&br=1. Concise encyclopedia link.

ELECTRONIC RESOURCES FOR RAYMOND CARVER

http://world.std.com/~ptc/. Raymond Carver home page.
http://people.whitman.edu/~lucetb/carver/. Raymond Carver Web site.
http://www.encyclopedia.com/articles/02368.html. Encyclopedia entry on Raymond Carver.
http://www.vega.net/wendy.htm. Essay on the literary style of Raymond Carver.

Further Readings in Ethical Criticism

Edie, James M., ed. *New Essays in Phenomenology: Studies in the Philosophy of Experience*. Chicago: Quadrangle Books, 1969.

Embree, Lester, ed. et al. *Encyclopedia of Phenomenology*. Boston: Kluwer Academic Publishers, 1997.

Gordon, Haim, ed. *Dictionary of Existentialism*. Westport, CT: Greenwood Press, 1999.

Grossmann, Reinhardt. *Phenomenology and Existentialism: An Introduction*. London: Routledge & K. Paul, 1984.

Levinas, Emmanuel. *Ethics and Infinity*. Trans. by Richard A. Cohen. Pittsburgh: Duquesne University Press, 1985.

Sallis, John. *Phenomenology and the Return to Beginnings*. Pittsburgh: Duquesne University Press, 1973.

chapter 5

Civic Criticism

This chapter is thematically related to the previous chapter, "Ethical Criticism," in that both chapters deal with issues of morality and ethics. This chapter could just as easily be called "Public Ethical Criticism" because it approaches literature for moral values that have significance for individuals as members of communities. Reading literature for many reasons, including lessons on morality, has long been a tradition in western civilization (and in eastern civilizations also).

Reading literature as "civic argument" grows out of a western tradition that dates back to the ancient Greeks (and possibly much earlier than that to Egyptian civilization). The Greeks of two millennia ago, particularly in Athens, strongly believed in the power of literature to transmit moral values to discerning readers. The principal instrument of teaching morality was Homer in his epic poems, the *Iliad* and the *Odyssey* (written between 850 and 750 BCE). The poems are about the moral ethics of a culture, what might be called an "ethical ideal." It would not be an exaggeration to say that reading Homer provided the Greeks with a moral education.

Educators who study ancient Greece have an expression, "Homer was the teacher of Greece." What they mean by this is that Homer's epics taught Greeks, young and old, how to live. Lessons of right and wrong, courage in battle, empathy for others, loyalty to community, and so forth are all part of the Homeric legacy, represented in characters like Odysseus and Achilles. The most important value represented by Greek heroes was a moral virtue called *arête*, which means honor and duty to everything one cherishes. *Arête* includes bravery, honor, courage, and obligation, but it always implies a sense of moral duty. There is a sense of grandeur and nobility in the concept of *arête*, and it is a virtue to which many Greeks aspired to embody in their own actions. Homer was able to teach Greek students about morality through his literature because the Greeks could relate to figures in literature, whether they were humans, demigods, or gods.

These heroic figures were read as immortal literary heroes, and their deeds of valor and kindness were meant for all time. The immortality of literary protagonists is important because it means that the values and ideas they represent are timeless and provide valuable lessons of civic behavior for generation after generation. One of Homer's greatest contributions, perhaps far more important than his aesthetics (the beauty of the work), was his principle of the heroic example. Greek youths studied passages from the epics with great care in order to memorize and explain the heroic behavior of their heroes. The highest point of learning, though, was the ability to make literary judgments (that is, literary criticism) that always resulted in moral instruction. It would not be an exaggeration to say that ancient Greek teachers attempted to teach a complete moral code through Homer. The civic-minded, virtuous, heroic action figures that permeate the popular culture of the early twenty-first century owe their origins to these classical Greek epics and the teachers who taught their moral truths. Ancient Greeks learned their civic responsibilities through Homer's literary arguments.

What does Homer and the ancient tradition of Greek moral education through literature have to do with our contemporary world in which "timeless" values are often called into question, if not openly challenged? There are some literary critics who argue that literature is not about teaching moral values. It is sometimes argued (in deconstructive criticism, for example) that the analysis of literature should focus on the rigorous interrogation on values represented in literary texts (which indeed may be a value itself). The purpose of this chapter is not to enter the debate about the "teachability" of moral values through literature, but to approach literature for its representations of civic responsibility. The moral lessons of literature may or may not affect readers, but there should be little doubt that works of literature often articulate civic moral themes quite openly, as the two sample readings in this chapter illustrate. There is no question that readers are exposed to ethical issues in literature, as characters make public decisions that have moral consequences.

This chapter is called "Civic Criticism" because some works of literature explicitly address the responsibility of an individual to his or her community and its culture (and subcultures). It is assumed that some literary works can be analyzed as civic arguments. There are works of literature (John Steinbeck's *The Grapes of Wrath*, for example, which exposed the inhumane treatment of displaced Oklahomans—"Okies"—who migrated into California in the 1930s) that do cause serious readers to consider the ethical effects and implications of characters' words and actions. And, occasionally, works of literature actually have effects on the "real world." Upton Sinclair's *The Jungle,* published in 1906, was a powerful exposé of abuses in the meat-packing industry, and reform legislation was passed as a direct result of Sinclair's novel. The history of literature is rich in texts that address moral issues quite openly.

What form (or forms) might a "public" ethical analysis that considers the issues of civic responsibility and personal honor take? Unquestionably, there are several approaches. First, you might consider a text's portrait of social injustice, as in the novels of Steinbeck and Sinclair. Second, you might evaluate specific words and actions of characters that have clear ethical effects and implications (for example, Macbeth's murder of King Duncan kills both a man and a head of state). Third, you might examine a text for its treatment of the expectation of civic responsibility. Fourth, civic responsibility obviously involves a sense of community, but there are also personal responsibilities and loyalties, such as responsibility to the family and the self. It is sometimes said that for evil to succeed, it is only necessary that good people do nothing. Literary texts with themes of civic moral responsibility sometimes deal with characters who do nothing in response to the presence of evil.

When we speak of such moral issues as "good" and "doing the right thing," these expressions do not always contain the same meaning for all individuals. Literary passages that horrify and disgust some readers may be read with passivity or equanimity by other readers. No two individuals have the same moral code, sensitivity to injustice, or notions of personal and public responsibility. However, it is a premise of this chapter that there are codes of conduct and ethical values that are reasonable and are shared by most readers. The ancient Greeks built their educational system on the concept of a common culture, and this chapter assumes shared values in the general area of civic responsibility. Although our culture is far more diverse than that of ancient Athens, we do share some common cultural values.

Literary texts such as *The Jungle* and *The Grapes of Wrath* illustrate injustice as part of their essential narrative plot structure. You may not have read these novels, but you can relate to the mistreatment of individuals and groups of individuals because they are in circumstances in which they can be exploited. The exploitation of the weak by the strong is a story as old as cave drawings. Although these narratives may differ significantly in their representations of victims and those who exploit, they all share one common value: They all depict abuses of the human condition, with the implication that evil must be challenged wherever it is found. Whether the writer is John Steinbeck, Upton Sinclair, or Aleksander Solzhenitsyn (whose novels, *The Gulag Archipelago,* I and II, depict human rights abuses in Soviet prison camps), one of the major themes of these writers is that something can and should be done about the conditions of which they write. Although these writers articulate individual situations of immoral action, the circumstances that allow for the perpetuation of evil are what concern them. These writers are concerned with the institutionalization of evil, be it in the valleys of California, the factories of Chicago, or the prison camps of Russia.

Philosophers (sometimes called metaphysicians) who specialize in issues of morality and ethics make useful distinctions in discussing the various grounds for morality. One major category of moral philosophy is the concern for the general, or public, good. The acts of humans are considered good if they contribute to the general well-being of others. The converse is true if an individual or group says or does something that promotes the suffering of others (or creates the conditions for suffering). Creative writers constantly make judgments about the rightness or wrongness of actions, and these judgments appear in the cloak of literary garb: character, plot, metaphor, point of view, and so on. Literary artists usually do not articulate their moral concerns in the form of treatises (a formal written work that usually deals with a subject systematically and extensively) as those kinds of formal argument would normally be out of place in a literary text. When creative writers are too explicit in moral views, as sometimes happens, literary qualities often suffer. Moral values in literature are oftentimes more implicit than explicit.

A literary text often reveals its "arguments" within the fabric of literary conventions. The master metaphor, irony, for example, plays a major role in many literary texts that reveal moral arguments, such as in Shirley Jackson's "The Lottery," one of this chapter's readings. Kurt Vonnegut, Jr., a major contemporary fiction writer, often contextualizes his concerns for immoral behavior in dark comedy, as you will see in "Harrison Bergeron." In order for moral arguments to be effective in literature, however, they must appear within the context of literary conventions.

What are the ways in which you might approach literature from the perspective of civic argument? The first and most important step is to follow the analytical process outlined in every chapter in this book. You should examine each of the major elements of the literary text in terms of what each one contributes to the articulation of the work's moral issues. In particular, you will want to look closely at tone and metaphor. Moral argument is often cloaked in ironic and sarcastic language, which often results in penetrating satire (Jonathan Swift's "A Modest Proposal" is a good example, in which he sarcastically proposes the eating of babies as a British solution to Ireland's famine). A second important step is to examine the major themes of the work for ethical implications, particularly as they apply to the public good. A strategic dimension of civic argument is the advocacy of personal and public responsibility to the community at large. Literature as civic argument often exposes explicit irresponsibility, callousness, and self-centeredness that results in public immoral behavior. Pay particular attention to characters' words and actions that reveal their insensitivity or outright rejection of any notion of civic responsibility.

Any analysis of literary civic responsibility depends upon your sense of right and wrong. Some literary texts reveal complex and ambiguous moral dilemmas that have public implications. Other works of literature are less than ambiguous in articulating the moral positions of the narrator, speaker, dramatic characters, and/or author. (Kurt Vonnegut, Jr. and Joseph Heller, for example, are well known as social critics of government behavior, particularly during wartime.) What is important in your analysis is the articulation of the elements of civic argument that *you* find in the text, according to your experience and informed judgment of personal and civic responsibility. No two readers will agree entirely on the elements of civic interpretation, but it is not uncommon for individuals to arrive at common interpretations of works in which civic responsibility is a major issue.

This chapter, like all the others, emphasizes the tools of your analysis more than the interpretation(s) they generate. Perceptive and articulate readers and writers can, and often do, arrive at interpretations that vary, sometimes considerably, from one another. The primary concern of this chapter is to introduce you to the elements that will enable you to perform a probing analysis of literature as civic argument. Following "The Lottery" is a series of reading and writing strategies to assist you in sharpening your reading and writing skills.

A SAMPLE READING

"The Lottery" by Shirley Jackson (1919–1965)

The morning of June 27th was clear and sunny, with the fresh warmth of a full-summer day; the flowers were blossoming profusely and the grass was richly green. The people of the village began to gather in the square, between the post office and the bank, around ten o'clock; in some towns there were so many people that the lottery took two days and had to be started on June 26th, but in this village, where there were only about three hundred people, the whole lottery took less than two hours, so it could begin at ten o'clock in the morning and still be through in time to allow the villagers to get home for noon dinner.

The children assembled first, of course. School was recently over for the summer, and the feeling of liberty sat uneasily on most of them; they tended to gather together quietly for a while before they broke into boisterous play, and their talk was still of the classroom and the teacher, of books and reprimands. Bobby Martin had already stuffed his pockets full of stones, and the other boys soon followed his example, selecting the smoothest and roundest stones; Bobby and Harry Jones and Dickie Delacroix—the villagers pronounced his name "Dellacroy"—eventually made a great pile of stones in one corner of the square and guarded it against the raids of the other boys. The girls stood aside, talking among themselves, looking over their shoulders at the boys, and the very small children rolled in the dust or clung to the hands of their older brothers or sisters.

Soon the men began to gather, surveying their own children, speaking of planting and rain, tractors and taxes. They stood together, away from the pile of stones in the corner, and their jokes were quiet and they smiled rather than laughed. The women, wearing faded house dresses and sweaters, came shortly after their menfolk. They greeted one another and exchanged bits of gossip as they went to join their husbands. Soon the women, standing by their husbands, began to call to their children, and the children came reluctantly, having to be called four or five times. Bobby Martin ducked under his mother's grasping hand and ran, laughingly, back to the pile of stones. His father spoke up sharply, and Bobby came quickly and took his place, between his father and his oldest brother.

The lottery was conducted—as were the square dances, the teenage club, the Halloween program—by Mr. Summers, who had time and energy to devote to civic activities. He was a round-faced, jovial man and he ran the coal business, and people were sorry for him, because he had no children and his wife was a scold. When he arrived in the square, carrying the black wooden box, there was a murmur of conversation among the villagers, and he waved and called "Little late today, folks." The postmaster, Mr. Graves, followed him, carrying a three-legged stool, and the stool was put in the center of the square and Mr. Summers set the black box down on it. The villagers kept their distance, leaving a space between themselves and the stool, and when Mr. Summers said, "Some of you fellows want to give me a hand?" there was a hesitation before two men, Mr. Martin and his oldest son, Baxter, came forward to hold the box steady on the stool while Mr. Summers stirred up the papers inside it.

The original paraphernalia for the lottery had been lost long ago, and the black box now resting on the stool had been put into use even before Old Man Warner, the oldest man in town, was born. Mr. Summers spoke frequently to the villagers about making a new box, but no one liked to upset even as much tradition as was represented by the black box. There was a story that the present box had been made with some pieces of the box that had preceded it, the one that had been constructed when the first people settled down to make a village here. Every year, after the lottery, Mr. Summers began talking about a new box, but every year the subject was allowed to fade off without anything's being done. The black box grew shabbier each year; by now it was no longer completely black but splintered badly along one side to show the original wood color, and in some places faded and stained.

Mr. Martin and his oldest son, Baxter, held the black box securely on the stool until Mr. Summers had stirred the papers thoroughly with his hand. Because so much of the ritual had been forgotten or discarded, Mr. Summers had been successful in having slips of paper substituted for the chips of wood that had been used for generations. Chips of wood, Mr. Summers had argued, had been all very well when the village was tiny, but now that the population was more than three hundred and likely to keep on growing, it was necessary to use something that would fit more easily into the black box. The night before the lottery, Mr. Summers and Mr. Graves made up the slips of paper and put them in the box, and it was then taken to the safe of Mr. Summers' coal company and locked up until Mr. Summers was ready to take it to the square the next morning. The rest of the year, the box was put away, sometimes one place, sometimes another; it had spent one year in Mr. Graves' barn and another year underfoot in the post office, and sometimes it was set on a shelf in the Martin grocery and left there.

5

There was a great deal of fussing to be done before Mr. Summers declared the lottery open. There were the lists to make up—of heads of families, heads of households in each family, members of each household in each family. There was the proper swearing-in of Mr. Summers by the postmaster, as the official of the lottery: at one time, some people remembered, there had been a recital of some sort, performed by the official of the lottery, a perfunctory, tuneless chant that had been rattled off duly each year; some people believed that the official of the lottery used to stand just so when he said or sang it, others believed that he was supposed to walk among the people, but years and years ago this part of the ritual had been allowed to lapse. There had been, also, a ritual salute, which the official of the lottery had had to use in addressing each person who came up to draw from the box, but this also had changed with time, until now it was felt necessary only for the official to speak to each person approaching. Mr. Summers was very good at all this; in his clean white shirt and blue jeans, with one hand resting carelessly on the black box, he seemed very proper and important as he talked interminably to Mr. Graves and the Martins.

Just as Mr. Summers finally left off talking and turned to the assembled villagers, Mrs. Hutchinson came hurriedly along the path to the square, her sweater thrown over her shoulders, and slid into place in the back of the crowd. "Clean forgot what day it was," she said to Mrs. Delacroix, who stood next to her, and they both laughed softly. "Thought my old man was out back stacking wood," Mrs. Hutchinson went on, "and then I looked out the window and the kids were gone, and then I remembered it was the twenty-seventh and came a-running." She dried her hands on her apron, and Mrs. Delacroix said, "You're in time, though. They're still taking away up there."

Mrs. Hutchinson craned her neck to see through the crowd and found her husband and children standing near the front. She tapped Mrs. Delacroix on the arm as a farewell and began to make her way through the crowd. The people separated good-humoredly to let her through; two or three people said, in voices just loud enough to be heard across the crowd, "Here comes your Missus, Hutchinson," and "Bill, she made it after all." Mrs. Hutchinson reached her husband, and Mr. Summers, who had been waiting, said cheerfully, "Thought we were going to have to get on without you, Tessie." Mrs. Hutchinson said, grinning. "Wouldn't have me leave m'dishes in the sink, now, would you, Joe?" and soft laughter ran through the crowd as the people stirred back into position after Mrs. Hutchinson's arrival.

"Well, now," Mr. Summers said soberly, "guess we better get started, get this over   10
with, so's we can go back to work. Anybody ain't here?"

"Dunbar," several people said. "Dunbar, Dunbar."

Mr. Summers consulted his list. "Clyde Dunbar," he said. "That's right. He's broke his leg, hasn't he? Who's drawing for him?"

"Me, I guess," a woman said, and Mr. Summers turned to look at her. "Wife draws for her husband," Mr. Summers said. "Don't you have a grown boy to do it for you, Janey?" Although Mr. Summers and everyone else in the village knew the answer perfectly well, it was the business of the official of the lottery to ask such questions formally. Mr. Summers waited with an expression of polite interest while Mrs. Dunbar answered.

"Horace's not but sixteen yet," Mrs. Dunbar said regretfully. "Guess I gotta fill in for the old man this year."

"Right," Mr. Summers said. He made a note on the list he was holding. Then the   15
asked, "Watson boy drawing this year?"

A tall boy in the crowd raised his hand. "Here," he said. "I'm drawing for m'mother and me." He blinked his eyes nervously and ducked his head as several voices in the crowd said things like "Good fellow, Jack," and "Glad to see your mother's got a man to do it."

"Well," Mr. Summers said, "guess that's everyone. Old Man Warner make it?"

"Here," a voice said, and Mr. Summers nodded.

A sudden hush fell on the crowd as Mr. Summers cleared his throat and looked at the list. "All ready?" he called. "Now, I'll read the names—heads of families first—and the men come up and take a paper out of the box. Keep the paper folded in your hand without looking at it until everyone has had a turn. Everything clear?"

The people had done it so many times they only half listened to the directions; 20 most of them were quiet, wetting their lips, not looking around. Then Mr. Summers raised one hand high and said, "Adams." A man disengaged himself from the crowd and came forward. "Hi, Steve," Mr. Summers said, and Mr. Adams said, "Hi, Joe." They grinned at one another humorlessly and nervously. Then Mr. Adams reached into the black box and took out a folded paper. He held it firmly by one corner as he turned and went hastily back to his place in the crowd, where he stood a little apart from his family, not looking down at his hand.

"Allen," Mr. Summers said. "Anderson . . . Betham."

"Seems like there's no time at all between lotteries any more," Mrs. Delacroix said to Mrs. Graves in the back row. "Seems like we got through the last one only last week."

"Time sure goes fast," Mrs. Graves said.

"Clark . . . Delacroix."

"There goes my old man." Mrs. Delacroix said. She held her breath while her 25 husband went forward.

"Dunbar," Mr. Summers said, and Mrs. Dunbar went steadily to the box while one of the women said, "Go on, Janey," and another said, "There she goes."

"We're next," Mrs. Graves said. She watched while Mr. Graves came around from the side of the box, greeted Mr. Summers gravely, and selected a slip of paper from the box. By now, all through the crowd there were men holding the small folded papers in their large hands, turning them over and over nervously. Mrs. Dunbar and her two sons stood together, Mrs. Dunbar holding the slip of paper.

"Harburt . . . Hutchinson."

"Get up there, Bill," Mrs. Hutchinson said, and the people near her laughed.

"Jones."   30

"They do say," Mr. Adams said to Old Man Warner, who stood next to him, "that over in the north village they're talking of giving up the lottery."

Old Man Warner snorted. "Pack of crazy fools," he said. "Listening to the young folks, nothing's good enough for *them*. Next thing you know, they'll be wanting to go back to living in caves, nobody work any more, live *that* way for a while. Used to be a saying about 'Lottery in June, corn be heavy soon.' First thing you know, we'd all be eating stewed chickweed and acorns. There's *always* been a lottery," he added petulantly. "Bad enough to see young Joe Summers up there joking with everybody."

"Some places have already quit lotteries," Mrs. Adams said.

"Nothing but trouble in *that*," Old Man Warner said stoutly. "Pack of young fools."

"Martin." And Bobby Martin watched his father go forward. "Overdyke . . . Percy."   35
"I wish they'd hurry," Mrs. Dunbar said to her older son. "I wish they'd hurry."
"They're almost through," her son said.
"You get ready to run tell Dad," Mrs. Dunbar said.
Mr. Summers called his own name and then stepped forward precisely and se-
lected a slip from the box. Then he called, "Warner."
"Seventy-seventh year I been in the lottery," Old Man Warner said as he went   40
through the crowd. "Seventy-seventh time."
"Watson." The tall boy came awkwardly through the crowd. Someone said,
"Don't be nervous, Jack," and Mr. Summers said, "Take your time, son."
"Zanini."

After that, there was a long pause, a breathless pause, until Mr. Summers, holding
his slip of paper in the air, said, "All right fellows." For a minute, no one moved, and
then all the slips of paper were opened. Suddenly, all the women began to speak at
once, saying, "Who is it," "Who's got it?," "Is it the Dunbars?," "Is it the Watsons?"
Then the voices began to say, "It's Hutchinson. It's Bill," "Bill Hutchinson's got it."
"Go tell your father," Mrs. Dunbar said to her older son.
People began to look around to see the Hutchinsons. Bill Hutchinson was stand-   45
ing quiet, staring down at the paper in his hand. Suddenly, Tessie Hutchinson shouted
to Mr. Summers, "You didn't give him time enough to take any paper he wanted. I saw
you. It wasn't fair!"
"Be a good sport, Tessie," Mrs. Delacroix called, and Mrs. Graves said, "All of us
took the same chance."
"Shut up, Tessie," Bill Hutchinson said.
"Well, everyone," Mr. Summers said, "that was done pretty fast, and now we've
got to be hurrying a little more to get it done in time." He consulted his next list. "Bill,"
he said, "you draw for the Hutchinson family. You got any other households in the
Hutchinsons?"
"There's Don and Eva," Mrs. Hutchinson yelled. "Make *them* take their chance!"
"Daughters draw with their husbands' families, Tessie," Mr. Summers said gently.   50
"You know that as well as anyone else."
"It wasn't *fair*," Tessie said.
"I guess not, Joe," Bill Hutchinson said regretfully. "My daughter draws with her
husband's family, that's only fair. And I've got no other family except the kids."
"Then, as far as drawing for families is concerned, it's you," Mr. Summers said in
explanation, "and as far as drawing for households is concerned, that's you, too. Right?"
"Right," Bill Hutchinson said.
"How many kids, Bill?" Mr. Summers asked formally.   55
"Three," Bill Hutchinson said. "There's Bill, Jr., and Nancy, and little Dave. And
Tessie and me."
"All right then," Mr. Summers said. "Harry, you got their tickets back?"
Mr. Graves nodded and held up the slips of paper. "Put them in the box, then,"
Mr. Summers directed. "Take Bill's and put it in."
"I think we ought to start over," Mrs. Hutchinson said, as quietly as she could. "I
tell you it wasn't *fair*. You didn't give him time enough to choose. *Everybody* saw that."
Mr. Graves had selected the five slips and put them in the box, and he dropped all   60
the papers but those onto the ground, where the breeze caught them and lifted them off.

"Listen, everybody," Mrs. Hutchinson was saying to the people around her.

"Ready, Bill?" Mr. Summers asked, and Bill Hutchinson, with one quick glance around at his wife and children, nodded.

"Remember," Mr. Summers said, "take the slips and keep them folded until each person has taken one. Harry, you help little Dave." Mr. Graves took the hand of the little boy, who came willingly with him up to the box. "Take a paper out of the box, Davy," Mr. Summers said. Davy put his hand into the box and laughed. "Take just *one* paper," Mr. Summers said. "Harry, you hold it for him." Mr. Graves took the child's hand and removed the folded paper from the tight fist and held it while little Dave stood next to him and looked up at him wonderingly.

"Nancy next," Mr. Summers said. Nancy was twelve, and her school friends breathed heavily as she went forward, switching her skirt, and took a slip daintily from the box. "Bill, Jr.," Mr. Summers said, and Billy, his face red and his feet over-large, nearly knocked the box over as he got a paper out. "Tessie," Mr. Summers said. She hesitated for a minute, looking around defiantly, and then set her lips and went up to the box. She snatched a paper out and held it behind her.

"Bill," Mr. Summers said, and Bill Hutchinson reached into the box and felt   65
around, bringing his hand out at last with the slip of paper in it.

The crowd was quiet. A girl whispered, "I hope it's not Nancy," and the sound of the whisper reached the edges of the crowd.

"It's not the way it used to be," Old Man Warner said clearly. "People ain't the way they used to be."

"All right," Mr. Summers said. "Open the papers. Harry, you open little Dave's."

Mr. Graves opened the slip of paper and there was a general sigh through the crowd as he held it up and everyone could see that it was blank. Nancy and Bill, Jr., opened theirs at the same time, and both beamed and laughed, turning around to the crowd and holding their slips of paper above their heads.

"Tessie," Mr. Summers said. There was a pause, and then Mr. Summers looked at   70
Bill Hutchinson, and Bill unfolded his paper and showed it. It was blank.

"It's Tessie," Mr. Summers said, and his voice was hushed. "Show us her paper, Bill."

Bill Hutchinson went over to his wife and forced the slip of paper out of her hand. It had a black spot on it, the black spot Mr. Summers had made the night before with the heavy pencil in the coal-company office. Bill Hutchinson held it up, and there was a stir in the crowd.

"All right, folks," Mr. Summers said. "Let's finish quickly."

Although the villagers had forgotten the ritual and lost the original black box, they still remembered to use stones. The pile of stones the boys had made earlier was ready; there were stones on the ground with the blowing scraps of paper that had come out of the box. Mrs. Delacroix selected a stone so large she had to pick it up with both hands and turned to Mrs. Dunbar. "Come on," she said. "Hurry up."

Mrs. Dunbar had small stones in both hands, and she said, gasping for breath, "I   75
can't run at all. You'll have to go ahead and I'll catch up with you."

The children had stones already, and someone gave little Davy Hutchinson a few pebbles.

Tessie Hutchinson was in the center of a cleared space by now, and she held her hands out desperately as the villagers moved in on her. "It isn't fair," she said. A stone hit her on the side of the head.

Old Man Warner was saying, "Come on, come on, everyone." Steven Adams was in the front of the crowd of villagers, with Mrs. Graves beside him.

"It isn't fair, it isn't right," Mrs. Hutchinson screamed, and then they were upon her.

ANALYZING "THE LOTTERY"

An important issue in understanding this compelling story is to consider the descriptions of the town's citizens and their behavior. Let us begin by examining the main literary elements of "The Lottery."

Plot

The plot of this story reads almost like a fairy tale in its simplicity. The story is narrated from the objective, third-person perspective, with great attention to the rituals of small town living, including lively, friendly banter among the 300 plus townspeople. Early in the story we know that the town is holding its annual lottery, always on June 27th, and there is little hint of the real meaning of the lottery except for references to the piling of stones, which requires astute reading to anticipate the ultimate use of the stones.

There are at least two distinct movements in the plot. First, the townspeople are festively preparing for the annual ritual of drawing by lots, and most readers assume that this ritual is something quite benign, judging by the lighthearted conversation among the citizens. Second, there is a dark, parallel plot, in which events are taking place that will result in the murder of one of the citizens. No one knows who that person will be, but they all know that it will be one of them, and everyone knows everyone else in the tiny town with no anonymous citizens. The two plots are carefully constructed and intertwined, and there is no sense of terror or fear among the townspeople until the very end, and that is only the dread and horror of Tessie, the victim. The story's final paragraphs reveal the frightening terror that exists for the victim and the reader, once the truth is known of what it means to "win" the lottery.

Character

Shirley Jackson's depictions of characters are particularly effective. The townspeople are identified by name and some even by occupation, which makes them personal and even likeable. What is obvious early on is the narrator's emphasis on the citizens as ordinary, good, and "normal." There are schoolchildren, a postmaster, and a coal company operator, nattily dressed in his "clean white shirt and blue jeans." Other respectable occupations are represented, too, along with a rich cast of typical children. Everything about the town and its people is essentially hometown, middle America, except that the citizens murder, arbitrarily, one of their own every June. Until the very end of the story, there is no hint that the town's characters are any different from those of neighboring towns, except that they refuse to abandon their lottery, as other communities have done. Indeed, the citizens of the unnamed town are "perfectly respectable" to most readers until the very end of the story.

Part of the shocking attraction of "The Lottery" is that this is a story about universal evil, with no honorable or ethical characters to offset the evil ethic of the community at large. This lack of goodness in a town populated by such "apparently" respectable citizens is one of the powerful ironies of the narrative. Whereas much fiction that emphasizes public moral issues sets off good and evil characters against one another, this story is about an absence of good characters. Indeed, one of the most puzzling aspects of the narrative is its stunning lack of conflict between the forces of good and the forces of evil.

Tone and Point of View

It would not be an exaggeration to say that "The Lottery" is intensely ironic in tone. The trope of irony always involves evaluation, and there is no question that the ironic tone of "The Lottery" implicitly condemns the townspeople (without explicit condemnation of them, which suggests another layer of irony). It would be surprising if a conscientious reader does not arrive at this conclusion. "The Lottery" concludes ironically with Tessie's final words, "It isn't fair," which is inaccurate, as the lottery is conducted with absolute fairness to each family of the town. The story is narrated from the third-person, objective point of view. There is no obvious sympathy or empathy for any of the characters, as we sometimes find in third-person narratives (which is called the Uncle Charles Principle, as you observed in Chapter 1). The narrative carefully weaves a tale of barbarity cloaked in language of temperance, gentility, and civility. The contrast between the tone of the story and the plot are striking in impact.

Theme

This narrative is a compelling depiction of a barbaric community garbed in civility, gentility, and social decorum. The narrator describes with precision the exemplary qualities of the citizens of the unnamed town. The adults are considerate and polite to one another. The children are well-mannered and respectful of their elders, and the people as a whole are not troubled by their murderous ritual. Indeed, they refer to other towns that have outlawed the lottery as "crazy." One of the important themes in "The Lottery" is a warning against civil irresponsibility. Vigilant citizens are a primary defense against evil in any community. The townspeople of this story are presented as unthinking and sheep-like in their adherence to an ancient ritual, one whose origins no one can even recall. The villagers commit murder once each year and they do not know why they do it, other than that they have done it in the past.

Metaphor and Imagery

"The Lottery" is rich in symbolism, metaphor, and imagery. The box that contains the lottery tickets is black, a traditional color symbolic of evil. The winner of the lottery receives a prize of death, an illustration of the story's rich irony. The villagers are exceptionally polite and cordial to one another, another trope of satiric irony. The village is unnamed, making it representative of all communities whose citizens are unthinking and blindly committed to mindlessly and uncritically following the traditions of the past. The lottery winner, Tessie Hutchinson, complains of unfairness to her dying breath, although the lottery officials take painstaking efforts to ensure that every villager has an equal chance of winning his or her death by stoning. Tessie's complaint has a metaphoric resonance to it in that it is indeed unfair, but as a general practice, and not unfair only to her, as she proclaims. The image of the actual stoning is a subtle one revealed in the story's concluding words, "and then they were upon her."

Questions for Your Analysis of "The Lottery"

1) What are some of your early impressions of the story, especially of the way the villagers treat one another as they prepare for the lottery?
2) What are your observations on the narrative's attitude toward the villagers? Does the narrator's attitude change as the story develops?
3) There are several illustrations of civic civility and responsibility as the story unfolds. Villagers are polite to one another and the lottery is conducted fairly. How would you compare these superficial civilities with the story's underlying gross incivility of the ritual of death?
4) What are the civic responsibilities of the villagers?
5) "The Lottery" is obviously making an argument beyond the position that civic murder is wrong. What are some other examples of civic irresponsibility in the story?
6) How do you see yourself "fitting into the story" as a resident of a town like the one in this story?
7) Identify some basic civic arguments that you find in the story.
8) Can you describe the theme, or themes, of this story specifically in terms of the narrative as argument? Cite specific argumentative elements.

9) What do you learn from this narrative about civic responsibility that goes beyond the obvious condemnation of community murder?

10) Is there anything in your personal experience that resonates with some of the themes in this story? If so, describe.

11) In what ways does the narrator foreshadow the end of the story?

The textual issues suggested in this chapter can be appropriated to civic criticism, as well as to other interpretive approaches. Please read the following sample essay on "The Lottery" as an illustration of one form that civic criticism might take. This essay, as you will see, focuses on the reader's encounter with amoral behavior and its social and civic implications. A significant issue in this story is the reader's reaction to the portrait of the villagers and local government as representations of moral bankruptcy.

Sample Essay on "The Lottery"

"The Lottery" is one of the most popular American short stories ever written, having horrified readers since its publication in 1948 in the New Yorker magazine, causing hundreds of irate readers to cancel their subscriptions. Readers' moral outrage at the story's cold description of ritual murder was too much for them to take. Indeed, the narrative is so powerful that it has been banned in certain parts of the world.

The narrative takes place in a small, unnamed village of slightly more than 300 residents. The relatively small size of the town is important because it means that the citizens all know one another. Anonymity is impossible in a community of 300 people. The fact that the town is unnamed is significant, also, because it suggests universality. Indeed, this town may be thought of as "Everytown," with one stunning exception: This town commits ritual murder once a year. Not only is one villager randomly selected as the "winner" of a lottery, the ritual has been part of the town's culture for so long that no one remembers, or even knows, how it began so long ago. And the death ritual will continue into the future, as the town's children are taught to participate as soon as they are big enough to pick up and hurl a killing stone. Indeed, little Davy Hutchinson actively takes part in the stoning murder of his mother. He may be too young to know that he is participating in her murder, but he does understand that he is doing what is expected of him. He is learning the cultural codes of the village.

The townspeople are introduced as common, good-natured, upstanding citizens. Summer has just begun, flowers are blossoming, the grass is green, and the children are happily finished with school for the year. A spirit of camaraderie fills the air, punctuated by lighthearted banter among the friendly villagers. The town itself is quite average, with a school, post office, bank, and coal-supply company; in short, all of the institutions of an average town. Indeed, as its mayor and leading citizen, Mr. Summers conducts the lottery as well as the town's other major business. Mr. Graves, another high-ranking citizen and the town's postmaster, lends legitimacy to the ritual of murder (he, like Mr. Summers, is a government official, no less!). Even Mr. Martin, the town's grocer, plays a major role in the ritual. All three leading citizens play active roles in maintaining the efficient running of the lottery. These town leaders are the civic custodians of ritual murder.

"The Lottery" abounds in irony, which serves to reinforce the dark message of the story: The reality of evil lurks beneath the appearance of good. The "winner" of each year's lottery receives the prize of death by stoning. The lottery is conducted with absolute fairness, as all citizens are required to draw lots by way of the heads of families. The year's winner is Tessie Hutchinson, and there is particular irony in her repeated assertion that the lottery "isn't fair." What she means, of course, is that it is not fair that she was selected. There is no reason to believe that she would have complained if someone else had been selected. The lottery is brutal but fair.

Why do the "good" citizens of Everytown maintain the tradition of ritual murder? Perhaps one reason that nearly every citizen supports the lottery (with the possible exception of the Adams family) is because he or she feels that if anyone opposes it, that person may be selected for punishment for going against the civic values of the community. The barbaric system of randomly murdering one of its citizens provides predictability and order, something sustained over many generations. Indeed, Mr. Warner boasts that he has witnessed 77 lotteries, and he rejects any suggestion that the ritual be outlawed. The only rationale for the lottery, ironically, is that it does offer some continuity to the lives of the citizens and to the life of the community. It provides the community with a victim (sometimes called a scapegoat), almost like the sacrifices of primitive cultures in order to appease the gods and cleanse the community. There seems to be a necessity in the village to sacrifice something, an ancient ritual that no one understands, or even remembers. This practice produces citizens that are unthinking sheep, following customs without thinking about their brutality and implications, which is another moral outrage of the story. The town considers itself progressive, another striking illustration of irony.

What does civic responsibility mean in interpreting "The Lottery"? It must surely involve a critique of the villagers for unthinkingly following a ritual without thoughtful reflection and debate (unlike some neighboring villages). Only one family, the Adams, refer to towns that have outlawed the lottery (implying that their village ought to consider doing the same). The Adams are belittled as rejecting the cultural traditions of their town. "A pack of crazy fools," Mr. Warner snorts, in reference to the mention of outlawing the lottery.

In a newspaper interview, Shirley Jackson once said that she wanted to "shock the story's readers with a graphic dramatization of the pointless violence and general inhumanity in their own lives."[1] In other words, it is critical that the reader be drawn into the story. We become, in a sense, citizens of Everytown. The townspeople's public, "democratic" actions are illustrations of public evil. (The Salem witch trials would be another example, so poignantly described by Nathaniel Hawthorne.) We as readers are encouraged to participate by reacting in horror against the inhumane and arbitrary violence that takes place annually.

One of the major themes in "The Lottery" is a warning about the danger of an unthinking citizenry. The collective mentality of a mob, even one democratically organized, can and does inflict public evil on its own citizens. "The Lottery" is a warning to the reader to maintain vigilance against civic or public tyranny. The story is shocking in its depiction of murder by gentle and civil townspeople, but the implications of the ritual serve as a cautionary signal to be aware of civic responsibility, even when the issues are lesser evils. The greatest danger to any society, suggests "The Lottery," lies in the apathy of its citizens.

[1]Friedman, Lenemaja. *Shirley Jackson*. Boston: Twayne Publishers, 1975, 64.

WRITING YOUR ESSAY
FROM A CIVIC PERSPECTIVE

The following short story, "Harrison Bergeron," is by Kurt Vonnegut, Jr. This narrative, like "The Lottery," depicts a government that is deeply immoral. Like "The Lottery," this story depicts the abuse (including murder) of some citizens by other citizens, who derive their power and authority as agents of the national government. The immoral behavior of the government is a direct effect of the nonparticipation of ordinary citizens. A government run amok can thrive only when average citizens do nothing. This story, like Jackson's narrative, attempts to shock the reader with descriptions of government abuse. Following "Harrison Bergeron," is a series of questions to assist you in the analysis of the work, as well as in writing an essay from the perspective of literature as civic argument.

A SAMPLE READING

"Harrison Bergeron" by Kurt Vonnegut, Jr. (1922–)

The year was 2081, and everybody was finally equal. They weren't only equal before God and the law. They were equal every which way. Nobody was smarter than anybody else. Nobody was better looking than anybody else. Nobody was stronger or quicker than anybody else. All this equality was due to the 211th, 212th, and 213th Amendments to the Constitution, and to the unceasing vigilance of agents of the United States Handicapper General.

Some things about living still weren't quite right, though. April, for instance, still drove people crazy by not being springtime. And it was in that clammy month that the H-G men took George and Hazel Bergeron's fourteen-year-old son, Harrison, away.

It was tragic, all right, but George and Hazel couldn't think about it very hard. Hazel had a perfectly average intelligence, which meant she couldn't think about anything except in short bursts. And George, while his intelligence was way above normal, had a little mental handicap radio in his ear. He was required by law to wear it at all times. It was tuned to a government transmitter. Every twenty seconds or so, the transmitter would send out some sharp noise to keep people like George from taking unfair advantage of their brains.

George and Hazel were watching television. There were tears on Hazel's cheeks, but she'd forgotten for the moment what they were about.

On the television screen were ballerinas.

A buzzer sounded in George's head. His thoughts fled in panic, like bandits from a burglar alarm.

"That was a real pretty dance, that dance they just did," said Hazel.

"Huh?" said George.

"That dance—it was nice," said Hazel.

"Yup," said George. He tried to think a little about the ballerinas. They weren't really very good—no better than anybody else would have been, anyway. They were burdened with sashweights and bags of birdshot, and their faces were masked, so that no one, seeing a free and graceful gesture or a pretty face, would feel like something the cat drug in. George was toying with the vague notion that maybe dancers shouldn't be handicapped. But he didn't get very far with it before another noise in his ear radio scattered his thoughts.

George winced. So did two out of the eight ballerinas.

Hazel saw him wince. Having no mental handicap herself, she had to ask George what the latest sound had been.

"Sounded like somebody hitting a milk bottle with a ball peen hammer," said George.

"I'd think it would be real interesting, hearing all the different sounds," said Hazel, a little envious. "All the things they think up."

"Um," said George.   15

"Only, if I was Handicapper General, you know what I would do?" said Hazel. Hazel, as a matter of fact, bore a strong resemblance to the Handicapper General, a woman named Diana Moon Glampers. "If I was Diana Moon Glampers," said Hazel, "I'd have chimes on Sunday—just chimes. Kind of in honor of religion."

"I could think, if it was just chimes," said George.

"Well—maybe make 'em real loud," said Hazel. "I think I'd make a good Handicapper General."

"Good as anybody else," said George.

"Who knows better'n I do what normal is?" said Hazel.   20

"Right," said George. He began to think glimmeringly about his abnormal son who was now in jail, about Harrison, but a twenty-one-gun salute in his head stopped that.

"Boy!" said Hazel, "that was a doozy, wasn't it?"

It was such a doozy that George was white and trembling, and tears stood on the rims of his red eyes. Two of the eight ballerinas had collapsed to the studio floor, and were holding their temples.

"All of a sudden you look so tired," said Hazel. "Why don't you stretch out on the sofa, so's you can rest your handicap bag on the pillows, honeybunch." She was referring to the forty-seven pounds of birdshot in a canvas bag, which was padlocked around George's neck. "Go on and rest the bag for a little while," she said. "I don't care if you're not equal to me for a while."

George weighed the bag with his hands. "I don't mind it," he said. "I don't notice   25
it any more. It's just a part of me."

"You been so tired lately—kind of wore out," said Hazel. "If there was just some way we could make a little hole in the bottom of the bag, and just take out a few of them lead balls. Just a few."

"Two years in prison and two thousand dollars fine for every ball I took out," said George. "I don't call that a bargain."

"If you could just take a few out when you came home from work," said Hazel. "I mean—you don't compete with anybody around here. You just set around."

"If I tried to get away with it," said George, "then other people'd get away with it—and pretty soon we'd be right back to the dark ages again, with everybody competing against everybody else. You wouldn't like that, would you?"

"I'd hate it," said Hazel.   30

"There you are," said George. "The minute people start cheating on laws, what do you think happens to society?"

If Hazel hadn't been able to come up with an answer to this question, George couldn't have supplied one. A siren was going off in his head.

"Reckon it'd fall all apart," said Hazel.

"What would?" said George blankly.

"Society," said Hazel uncertainly. "Wasn't that what you just said?"   35

"Who knows?" said George.

The television program was suddenly interrupted for a news bulletin. It wasn't clear at first as to what the bulletin was about, since the announcer, like all announcers, had a serious speech impediment. For about half a minute, and in a state of high excite-ment, the announcer tried to say, "Ladies and gentlemen—"

He finally gave up, handed the bulletin to a ballerina to read.

"That's all right—" Hazel said of the announcer, "he tried. That's the big thing. He tried to do the best he could with what God gave him. He should get a nice raise for trying so hard."

"Ladies and gentlemen—" said the ballerina, reading the bulletin. She must have   40
been extraordinarily beautiful, because the mask she wore was hideous. And it was easy to see that she was the strongest and most graceful of all the dancers, for her handicap bags were as big as those worn by two-hundred-pound men.

And she had to apologize at once for her voice, which was a very unfair voice for a woman to use. Her voice was a warm, luminous, timeless melody. "Excuse me—" she said, and she began again, making her voice absolutely uncompetitive.

"Harrison Bergeron, age fourteen," she said in a grackle squawk, "has just escaped from jail, where he was held on suspicion of plotting to overthrow the government. He is a genius and an athlete, is under-handicapped, and should be regarded as extremely dangerous."

A police photograph of Harrison Bergeron was flashed on the screen upside down, then sideways, upside down again, then right side up. The picture showed the full length of Harrison against a background calibrated in feet and inches. He was exactly seven feet tall.

The rest of Harrison's appearance was Halloween and hardware. Nobody had ever born heavier handicaps. He had outgrown hindrances faster than the H-G men could think them up. Instead of a little ear radio for a mental handicap, he wore a tremendous pair of earphones, and spectacles with thick wavy lenses. The spectacles were intended to make him not only half blind, but to give him whanging headaches besides.

Scrap metal was hung all over him. Ordinarily, there was a certain symmetry, a   45
military neatness to the handicaps issued to strong people, but Harrison looked like a walking junkyard. In the race of life, Harrison carried three hundred pounds.

And to offset his good looks, the H-G men required that he wear at all times a red rubber ball for a nose, keep his eyebrows shaved off, and cover his even white teeth with black caps at snaggle-tooth random.

"If you see this boy," said the ballerina, "do not—I repeat, do not—try to reason with him."

There was the shriek of a door being torn from its hinges.

Screams and barking cries of consternation came from the television set. The photograph of Harrison Bergeron on the screen jumped again and again, as though dancing to the tune of an earthquake.

George Bergeron correctly identified the earthquake, and well he might have—   50
for many was the time his own home had danced to the same crashing tune. "My God—" said George, "that must be Harrison!"

The realization was blasted from his mind instantly by the sound of an automobile collision in his head.

When George could open his eyes again, the photograph of Harrison was gone. A living, breathing Harrison filled the screen.

Clanking, clownish, and huge, Harrison stood in the center of the studio. The knob of the uprooted studio door was still in his hand. Ballerinas, technicians, musicians, and announcers cowered on their knees before him, expecting to die.

"I am the Emperor!" cried Harrison. "Do you hear? I am the Emperor! Everybody must do what I say at once!" He stamped his foot and the studio shook.

"Even as I stand here—" he bellowed, "crippled, hobbled, sickened—I am a   55
greater ruler than any man who ever lived! Now watch me become what I *can* become!"

Harrison tore the straps of his handicap harness like wet tissue paper, tore straps guaranteed to support five thousand pounds.

Harrison's scrap-iron handicaps crashed to the floor.

Harrison thrust his thumbs under the bar of the padlock that secured his head harness. The bar snapped like celery. Harrison smashed his headphones and spectacles against the wall.

He flung away his rubber-ball nose, revealed a man that would have awed Thor, the god of thunder.

"I shall now select my Empress!" he said, looking down on the cowering people.   60
"Let the first woman who dares rise to her feet claim her mate and her throne!"

A moment passed, and then a ballerina arose, swaying like a willow.

Harrison plucked the mental handicap from her ear, snapped off her physical handicaps with marvelous delicacy. Last of all, he removed her mask.

She was blindingly beautiful.

"Now—" said Harrison, taking her hand, "shall we show the people the meaning of the word dance? Music!" he commanded.

The musicians scrambled back into their chairs, and Harrison stripped them of   65
their handicaps, too. "Play your best," he told them, "and I'll make you barons and dukes and earls."

The music began. It was normal at first—cheap, silly, false. But Harrison snatched two musicians from their chairs, waved them like batons as he sang the music as he wanted it played. He slammed them back into their chairs.

The music began again and was much improved.

Harrison and his Empress merely listened to the music for a while—listened gravely, as though synchronizing their heartbeats with it.

They shifted their weights to their toes.

Harrison placed his big hands on the girl's tiny waist, letting her sense the   70
weightlessness that would soon be hers.

And then, in an explosion of joy and grace, into the air they sprang!

Not only were the laws of the land abandoned, but the law of gravity and the laws of motion as well.

They reeled, whirled, swiveled, flounced, capered, gamboled, and spun.

They leaped like deer on the moon.

The studio ceiling was thirty feet high, but each leap brought the dancers nearer   75
to it.

It became their obvious intention to kiss the ceiling.

They kissed it.

And then, neutralizing gravity with love and pure will, they remained suspended in air inches below the ceiling, and they kissed each other for a long, long time.

It was then that Diana Moon Glampers, the Handicapper General, came into the studio with a double-barreled ten-gauge shotgun. She fired twice, and the Emperor and the Empress were dead before they hit the floor.

Diane Moon Glampers loaded the gun again. She aimed it at the musicians and   80
told them they had ten seconds to get their handicaps back on.

It was then that the Bergerons' television tube burned out.

Hazel turned to comment about the blackout to George. But George had gone out into the kitchen for a can of beer.

George came back in with the beer, paused while a handicap signal shook him up. And then he sat down again. "You been crying?" he said to Hazel.

"Yup," she said.

"What about?" he said.   85

"I forget," she said. "Something real sad on television."

"What was it?" he said.

"It's all kind of mixed up in my mind," said Hazel.

"Forget sad things," said George.

"I always do," said Hazel.   90

"That's my girl," said George. He winced. There was the sound of a riveting gun in his head.

"Gee—I could tell that one was a doozy," said Hazel.

"You can say that again," said George.

"Gee—" said Hazel, "I could tell that one was a doozy."

Questions for Your Analysis of "Harrison Bergeron"

1) What are some of your early impressions of the story? What is the most striking feature of the story, something that promotes an instant reaction in you?

2) This story is narrated in the third-person. What is your instinctive response to the narrator's satire and sarcasm? What are the responsibilities to the community of the citizens of 2081?

3) What are your reactions to the descriptions of the government's actions, particularly in the ways they restrict citizens, making everyone "equal"?

4) The story is set in 2081, 120 years after it was written. What effect does the future setting have on you? Does it suggest that governmental abuse could not happen in the near future?

5) Is there something from your personal experience that assists you in relating to any of the characters in the story?

6) The story describes a series of encounters between the characters and the government. What do these encounters reveal about the characters and the government?

7) What does the story say about stereotypes, and what are some ethical implications to stereotyping?

8) "Harrison Bergeron" is obviously making an argument beyond the position that excessive civic intrusion into the life of the citizens is wrong. What are some other examples of civic irresponsibility in the story?

9) How do you see yourself "fitting into the story" as a 2081 resident under a repressive government?
10) Identify some basic civic arguments that you find in the story.
11) In what ways has George Bergeron demonstrated a sense of ethical responsibility by the end of the story?
12) Can you describe the theme, or themes, of this story specifically in terms of the narrative as civic argument? Cite specific argumentative elements.

STEPS IN WRITING YOUR ESSAY

Brainstorming Your Topic

1) Identify those elements in the text (character, plot, theme, metaphor) that prompt an immediate response from you. Write down whatever impressions you have.
2) Focus on the main characters: George, Hazel, and Harrison Bergeron. What is it about their situations that strike you as most important? The government's treatment of them may appear to be grossly exaggerated, but how true does it ring in principle?
3) The narrator's reaction to the government is one of disdain, perhaps even contempt. What is your reaction to the narrator's experience?
4) What personal experiences have you had that connect to parts of "Harrison Bergeron"? Have you ever encountered government treatment and/or regulations that give new meaning to this story?
5) What effects do the grotesquely comic depictions of the characters and their plights have on you?
6) Why does the narrator have so much anger against the government, and how do you respond to that anger?
7) List points of civic abuse. Does the story suggest moral imperatives, specific or otherwise?
8) What might citizens do to counteract governmental abuse?
9) Are you satisfied with the ending? Why or why not?
10) Unless your instructor insists that you not consult outside sources in brainstorming your topic, refer to the electronic sources listed at the end of this chapter for Kurt Vonnegut, Jr. There are many good links that will connect you to biographical sources and detailed criticism. Any ideas and words drawn directly from outside sources should be properly cited, of course. Consult Chapter 10 for documentation procedures.

Creating an Outline

1) Collect your answers to the questions above in short two-word categories, and use them as preliminary "writing points."
2) Think about the points and consider whether they add up to a central idea (for example, government gone wild in "Harrison Bergeron").
3) Identify five or six main writing points that support your central idea. These points should come from the main literary elements in the story (character, plot,

theme, point of view, metaphor). All of the points should provide support for your controlling idea. A good starting place is to examine the story's encounters and then look for ways in which characters change as a result of the encounters.

4) If you have more than five or six points, try to combine one or more of them. If you have fewer than five or six points, see if some of them can be used to generate additional points. You may have some large points that include smaller issues that can stand alone as paragraph topic sentences.

5) Look for transitional devices that connect your main points of support, particularly as they connect various encounters in the story.

Preparing a Rough Draft

1) Now that you have created a working outline, you have already completed your major organizational work. Each major point is the topic of a paragraph, and your essay will have between 5 and 10 paragraphs, depending on development. These paragraphs need not be of equal length, but each one should sufficiently develop the topic sentence.

2) Now that you have your major writing points, assemble a preliminary draft by developing each topic idea with two or three sentences that discuss evidence from the text.

3) Focus on developing transitions between your paragraphs. Professional writers often begin a new paragraph with a direct reference to an idea expressed at the end of the preceding paragraph.

4) It is not too early to begin writing your concluding paragraph. Conclusions often summarize the main points of a central idea (but do not repeat word for word what has already been said). A conclusion may also refer to implications of what has been said (but what cannot be developed because of space limits). Your conclusion must examine ethical issues in the story.

5) Don't be afraid to include questions in your writing. No reader of literature can ever be absolutely certain of every observation that he or she makes, and perceptive observations often generate excellent questions, many of which are useful, even though unanswerable.

Editing Your Draft

1) At this stage, you should have a draft of a few hundred words. You have already done the most difficult work in thinking out your ideas, organizing them into an outline, and preparing a rough version of the final product. Look for ways to edit your paper that will strengthen the essay.

2) Search for repetitious wording (and ideas). Do not repeat ideas, however important, throughout the essay. Use a thesaurus to locate synonyms for terms and ideas that reappear. Attempt to emphasize variety in your language.

3) If your instructor encourages peer editing, choose someone in your class, or perhaps a roommate, and solicit advice about how your essay reads. Is it articulate, compelling, insightful, and interesting? (All of these qualities are important.) Although your peer editor may not be taking a literature class, he or she may be a

very good source of feedback on how effective your writing is. Professional writers often seek feedback from peers, and not only from professional colleagues.

4) Be open to make changes in your writing, both conceptually and in specific language. Professional writers know that writing is recursive (which means that the act of writing constantly generates new ways of looking at the topic), and student writers should also take advantage of changes in thinking *as they write*. Don't be afraid to make efficient and effective changes, especially in terms of cutting out words, phases, and sections that may not be working very well in supporting your overall idea.

5) Proofread carefully for spelling errors, punctuation problems, run-on sentences, and ambiguous or awkward constructions. You should use a solid grammar handbook to assist you in these areas.

Final Checklist

1) Make sure that your central idea (sometimes called a thesis statement) appears in the first paragraph. It is important that your reader know what major point(s) you are attempting to make.

2) Because this essay is an investigation of civic responsibility, check to see that the essay represents your analysis of civic issues in the story. Your major points should be understandable, of course, to the community of readers to which you are writing.

3) Examine your essay for sufficient evidence. Each one of your major ideas will need illustration that comes from the text.

4) Review your conclusion to see if you have ended the essay in an effective manner, either summarizing what you have said (in different language) or suggesting some important implications of your reading.

5) Proofread one last time for errors, repetitious language, and awkward phrasing.

A SAMPLE READING

"The X in My Name" by Francisco X. Alarcón

the poor
signature
of my illiterate
and peasant
self
giving away
all rights
in a deceiving
contract for life

Questions for Analyzing "The X in My Name"

1) Write down key terms, being careful to define them and write down possible connotations. (You might begin with some of these words: "poor," "signature," "illiterate," "peasant," "self," "rights," "deceiving," "contract," "life.")

2) Consider key moments in the poem. (For example: What is the effect of the speaker's relating the present to the past?)

3) Describe your impressions of the tone of the poem and how the tone changes, if it does. (For example: Consider the speaker's attitude toward the state.)

4) Indicate possible themes in the poem. (For example: "The X in a name signifies illiteracy.")

5) Examine key metaphors and images that appear, noting how they relate to one or more themes. (For example: Analyze the relationship between a peasant's life and a legal contract.)

6) Focus on the narrating persona. Write down your impressions of what he says about himself and his community.

7) The speaker implies anger and frustration by what the X in his name suggests. What inferences do you draw about the responsibility of the community to the speaker?

8) The speaker suggests that he is a common figure in his culture. What are the implications of his stereotype?

9) What personal experiences have you had, if any, that connect you to "The X in My Name"?

10) Are you satisfied with the conclusion of the poem, which raises the issue of deceit? Why or why not? What are the civic implications?

ELECTRONIC RESOURCES FOR SHIRLEY JACKSON

http://www.underthesun.cc/Classics/Jackson.   A biographical site for details on the life of Shirley Jackson.

http://www.bcsd.org/BHS/english/mag97/papers/jackson/htm.   An essay on the life and work of Jackson.

http://www.courses.vcu.edu/ENG-jkh/PW/Criticism.htm.   This site contains information on biography, bibliography, criticism, and resources (with links to other sites).

ELECTRONIC RESOURCES FOR KURT VONNEGUT, JR.

http://www.vonnegut.com/.   The Kurt Vonnegut, Jr. homepage.

http://www.duke.edu/~crh4/kv/.   Index to the major works of Kurt Vonnegut, Jr.

http://www.duke.edu/~crh4/vonnegut/.   A comprehensive Vonnegut resource with numerous links.

http://www.salon.com/books/int/1999/10/08/vonnegut_interview/.   Salon interview with Kurt Vonnegut, Jr.

http://www.nytimes.com/books/97/09/28/lifetimes/vonnegut.html.   Contains links to reviews of Vonnegut's works.

http://www.geocites.com/Hollywood/4953/vonn.html.   A general Vonnegut guide to resources and links.

chapter 6

Cultural Criticism

Cultural criticism is an approach to interpretation that has been prominent over the past two decades, although some earlier expressions of cultural criticism, such as traditional historical criticism, have been around for a very long time. Indeed, in the nineteenth century, historical criticism, which included investigations into the life of the author (biographical criticism) as well as studies of the historical background of the work, was the dominant mode of literary criticism in America and Europe. An educated person was expected to be able to interpret a work based upon a familiarity with the author and the historical context of the work, including specific sources for the literary work (called source studies criticism). For example, readers of Henry James' novel *The Portrait of a Lady* studied real English mansions that may have served as the model of the main house in the narrative (the Touchett manor) and interpreters of Edgar Allan Poe dug deeply into the author's life and times for explanations of his works.

Other chapters in this book emphasize the reader, the structure of the text itself, the psychological dimensions of literature, and assumptions about gender. Cultural criticism seeks to explain a text by examining situations and contexts (small and large) that reflect the conditions that give birth to a literary work. Cultural criticism often focuses on (1) the life of the author, (2) the context (social, economic, and political) of the time the work was written, and (3) the various cultural representations contained within the work. All three of these areas are important, although an emphasis on one or more of them may depend upon the work of literature and the particular interests of the cultural reader.

Cultural interpretations look at a work of literature as *connecting* the life of the author, the historical contexts, and the literary cultural representations as revealed in the work. In other words, no cultural interpretation can be considered rigorous unless it takes into consideration these three strategic elements. The author's life experiences are critical because he or she could not have produced the literary work without incorporating or reflecting something of his or her life in the creation of a literary text. It would be naïve to interpret a text from a cultural perspective without considering the social, cultural, and economic dimensions of the times in which the author wrote the story, poem, or play. No work is produced in a vacuum, either personal or social. Further, the work itself always says something about the culture of the characters and the times. There is no question that the cultural reader brings together elements of the past, present, and future in reading a text. If you have assumed that the literary work always contains and reveals at least these three contexts, you are correct (at least from the perspective of a cultural reader). Cultural criticism assumes that no reader can ever know the "whole truth" about any of these elements, but by exploring them together, we may achieve a level of knowledge that contributes significantly to an understanding of the work.

As you have seen in other chapters, each critical perspective teaches us to be aware of our own backgrounds in interpreting literature. As we read and interpret from a cultural perspective, we should think about the culture in which we live, as well as our personal history. Just as we question and investigate cultural assumptions in literature, we should always be aware of the importance of questioning (and sometimes challenging) the cultural assumptions that make up who and what we are. Literary interpretation, after all, is as much about reading a text and making sense out of it as it is about getting to know ourselves better. Literature can be a great mirror, offering self-insight into the careful and thoughtful reader.

When you read about an author's life and times, you will necessarily have to select certain experiences and historical contexts that seem to have particular relevance, just as you will have to select certain literary passages to illustrate your interpretive points. Just as you cannot "cite" an entire work, you cannot examine all of an author's life or all of the major historical events surrounding the production of a literary text. It is very important to be cautiously selective in choosing events in the life of the author and his or her times. And it is important to remember that it is always risky to equate events in an author's life exactly with events in his or her literary text, but knowing personal information about an author can shed some insight into our reading of a text. The more we know about an author's personal experiences before writing, the better informed we are to make assumptions about the creation of a literary work.

Readers have always been interested in the biographies of the writers they enjoy. It is only natural to want to know about the kind of person (and mind) that has created powerful literature. Readers of "Babylon Revisited" enrich their understanding of this story when they learn that F. Scott Fitzgerald lived an alcoholic life of wild excess in Paris in the 1920s, with his wife Zelda (and their daughter Scottie). Although Fitzgerald did not lose custody of his daughter, he was part of the international "party scene" and later came to regret many of his excesses, as did Charlie Wales. Readers of Emily Dickinson's poetry may be interested to know that the Massachusetts poet lived a life of quiet seclusion, never married, and left the world her poems in neatly tied bundles, to be published after her death. Unlike F. Scott Fitzgerald, who was an internationally recognized writer while still in his mid-twenties, Emily Dickinson went to her grave with almost no reputation as a writer, yet is now regarded as perhaps America's finest poet. Elizabeth Bishop was born in Worcester, Massachusetts but spent part of her childhood with her Canadian grandparents after her father's death and her mother's permanent hospitalization in a sanitarium in Nova Scotia. James Baldwin was born in Harlem, New York, where he experienced racial prejudice, which prompted him to live out most of his life as an expatriate writer in France.

Some readers may not have quite the same natural curiosity about the historical context of a work as about the biographical history of the author, but historical context is an important component of cultural interpretation. Creative writers, like everyone else, live with political events (including changes in government), social activities (including unrest), and economic movements (including volatile financial ups and downs). At certain times of crisis, during war for example, all of these elements become highly charged and provide an explosive atmosphere for many writers. America has experienced deep and significant changes over the past two centuries, and many creative writers have chronicled some of these important changes and their effects in their stories, poems, and plays.

The works you have already read reflect the historical contexts of their times. "Babylon Revisited" is set against the background of financial exuberance in the mid 1920s, followed by worldwide depression in the late 1920s and early 1930s. Emily Dickinson's poems reflect the culture of America in the mid-nineteenth century, including America's attitude toward women, religion, and roles in society. James Baldwin's narrative reflects Harlem in the 1950s, a time connected closely to two major wars (World War II and the Korean War) and, of course, to racial prejudice and stereotyping. While still a young man, Baldwin left America for France, where he felt that there was significantly less prejudice against Africans and African Americans. The background of war and the racial tension of the times are reflected in "Sonny's Blues."

When we consider the historical context of a work, we think of major events such as war, depression, social unrest, and so forth, but we should also consider smaller, more "mundane" events that reflect the culture of the times. Some critics call this approach *new historicism*, in order to contrast it with a more traditional historical approach that focuses on "big" events. New historicism looks at cultural history as a complex weave of major and minor events, public and private, that come together to give us "textual material" to articulate the history and culture of the times. In other words, the history and culture of the times are fluid. They are always in a process of "restatement" based on new evidence that constantly surfaces, especially those minor events in the life of the author and his or her social milieu.

Personal and cultural events in the lives and times of Fitzgerald, Dickinson, and Baldwin clearly played a role in shaping their literature. In the wild and ecstatic Paris days of the 1920s, F. Scott Fitzgerald and many of his fellow expatriate writers lavishly spent money in search of a good time. Charley Wales talks of giving a musician a thousand-franc note ($100 at that time) to play a single song, and in this example Fitzgerald is drawing upon his own experiences in reckless spending. In several of Dickinson's poems, the speaker reveals a fascination with death, loneliness, and distant travel. We know that Dickinson led a sheltered, secluded life and let her imagination roam freely to explore the experiences that she was not allowed to experience in the mid-nineteenth century because of the restricted lives many women were expected to live. Dickinson was raised in the puritanical Massachusetts of the 1800s, the product of a strict Christian tradition. Her father served in powerful positions on the General Court of Massachusetts and his daughter was expected to take up her parents' religious beliefs and values. In her poetry, Dickinson would come to challenge these conventional religious viewpoints of her parents, her church, and her community.

James Baldwin, the eldest of nine children, was born in Harlem, New York City, the son of a domestic worker. Born illegitimately, he never knew his own father and was brought up in great poverty. When he was very young, his mother married a factory worker and street preacher. Baldwin adopted the surname from his stepfather, who died eventually in a mental hospital. At the age of 17, Baldwin left his home. As a result of his strained relations with his stepfather, growing conflict over his sexual identity, the suicide of a close friend, and racism in his work in Newark, Baldwin left America in 1948. Baldwin lived in Europe for 10 years, mainly in Paris and Istanbul, and later spent long, troubled periods in New York. In 1957 he returned to America in order to become involved in the Southern school desegregation struggle. The 1950s and 1960s were intense decades in the struggle for social justice for black Americans, and Baldwin's personal experience in these conflicts clearly shaped his fiction. After the assassination of Martin Luther King in 1968, Baldwin felt, bitterly, that violence may be the only route to racial justice. This period of time was a critical juncture in his life and in his writing.

The cultural experiences, private and public, of a writer tell us something about his or her work, but the writer's work also tells us about his or her life and times. Charlie Wales' rehabilitation of himself from his earlier life of debauchery makes a statement about living through times of excess, suffering as a result of personal weakness, and then rebuilding one's life through hard work and dedication to positive new principles. Dickinson's speaker's probing inquiry into life and death tells us about her insight into her times and culture. On a larger scale, we know that in the nineteenth century many people, including Dickinson, were interested in experiences that "transcended" the physical limitations of life. (This philosophy is called *transcendentalism*.)

On a smaller scale, we know from biographical critics that Dickinson was an excellent cook (black cake and fruitcake were two of her favorite recipes), she loved to tend her garden, and she often sent baskets with personal messages and flowers to friends and even strangers who were ill. She never married, and after the age of 30, she saw few people outside of the circle of her immediate family. This conscious decision to sequester herself may have been her answer to those who did not want women authors writing about anything other than domestic and sentimental topics. Her poems say much about the suffocating conditions for many female writers of the nineteenth century. Baldwin's story says much about growing up as an African American in Harlem, experiencing hardship and crime in the ghetto. Sonny's mother's poignant story of her brother-in-law articulates the long-term struggle against racism in American history.

Cultural illustrations within a work reveal the cultural fabric of the times. Indeed, we might call this dimension of literature the "cultural text." In many cases, literary events may appear to be trivial: Charlie Wales unthinkingly giving his address to a barman, the speaker in Dickinson's poem observing children at play, the narrator of "Sonny's Blues" thinking about the profound implications of a high-school boy whistling, blending in with the other sounds of the ghetto. These "insignificant" events reveal how closely and carefully connected everything is in a first-rate literary text. These "little" cultural events mirror the larger cultural themes in the respective works. At one time, readers of literature thought that only major historical events were important, but the cultural reader realizes that minor events may be just as important as major ones in the interpretation of a text.

The interpretation of literature from a cultural perspective means that we have to be conscious of the biographical experience of the author, the general historical context of the time, and the "small" details in a text that reveal its larger cultural context. It is important to remember that when we interpret literature, we are pursuing knowledge of the times, author, and text in order to generate our knowledge of the text. These levels of knowledge are deeply interconnected.

In the formalist chapter, you learned how the close reading of a text may serve any kind of critical approach. Cultural readers, like formalist readers, should always be on the lookout for details that stand out as having particular importance (as you will see in the analysis of Jack London's "To Build a Fire").

A SAMPLE READING

"To Build a Fire" by Jack London (1876–1916)

Day had broken cold and gray, exceedingly cold and gray, when the man turned aside from the main Yukon trail and climbed the high earth-bank, where a dim and little-travelled trail led eastward through the fat spruce timberland. It was a steep bank, and he paused for breath at the top, excusing the act to himself by looking at his watch. It was nine o'clock. There was no sun nor hint of sun, though there was not a cloud in the sky. It was a clear day, and yet there seemed an intangible pall over the face of things, a subtle gloom that made the day dark, and that was due to the absence of sun. This fact did not worry the man. He was used to the lack of sun. It had been days since he had seen the sun, and he knew that a few more days must pass before that cheerful orb, due south, would just peep above the sky line and dip immediately from view.

The man flung a look back along the way he had come. The Yukon lay a mile wide and hidden under three feet of ice. On top of this ice were as many feet of snow. It was all pure white, rolling in gentle undulations where the ice jams of the freeze-up had formed. North and south, as far as the eye could see, it was unbroken white, save for a dark hairline that curved and twisted from around the spruce-covered island to the south, and that curved and twisted away into the north, where it disappeared behind another spruce-covered island. This dark hairline was the trail—the main trail—that led south five hundred miles to the Chilcoot Pass, Dyea, and salt water; and that led north seventy miles to Dawson, and still on to the north a thousand miles to Nulato, and finally to St. Michael, on Bering Sea, a thousand miles and half a thousand more.

But all this—the mysterious, far-reaching hairline trail, the absence of sun from the sky, the tremendous cold, and the strangeness and weirdness of it all—made no impression on the man. It was not because he was long used to it. He was a newcomer in the land, a *chechaquo*, and this was his first winter. The trouble with him was that he was without imagination. He was quick and alert in the things of life, but only in the things, and not in the significances. Fifty degrees below zero meant eighty-odd degrees of frost. Such fact impressed him as being cold and uncomfortable, and that was all. It did not lead him to meditate upon his frailty as a creature of temperature, and upon man's frailty in general, able only to live within certain narrow limits of heat and cold; and from there on it did not lead him to the conjectural field of immortality and man's place in the universe. Fifty degrees below zero stood for a bite of frost that hurt and that must be guarded against by the use of mittens, ear flaps, warm moccasins, and thick socks. Fifty degrees below zero was to him just precisely fifty degrees below zero. That there should be anything more to it than that was a thought that never entered his head.

As he turned to go on, he spat speculatively. There was a sharp, explosive crackle that startled him. He spat again. And again, in the air, before it could fall to the snow, the spittle crackled. He knew that at fifty below spittle crackled on the snow, but this spittle had crackled in the air. Undoubtedly it was colder than fifty below—how much colder he did not know. But the temperature did not matter. He was bound for the old claim on the left fork of Henderson Creek, where the boys were already. They had come over across the divide from the Indian Creek country, while he had come the roundabout way to take a look at the possibilities of getting out logs in the spring from the islands in the Yukon. He would be in to camp by six o'clock; a bit after dark, it was true, but the boys would be there, a fire would be going, and a hot supper would be ready. As for lunch, he pressed his hand against the protruding bundle under his jacket. It was also under his shirt, wrapped up in a handkerchief and lying against the naked skin. It was the only way to keep the biscuits from freezing. He smiled agreeably to himself as he thought of those biscuits, each cut open and stopped in bacon grease, and each enclosing a generous slice of fried bacon.

He plunged in among the big spruce trees. The trail was faint. A foot of snow had fallen since the last sled had passed over, and he was glad he was without a sled, travelling light. In fact, he carried nothing but the lunch wrapped in the handkerchief. He was surprised, however, at the cold. It certainly was cold, he concluded, as he rubbed his numb nose and cheekbones with his mittened hand. He was a warm-whiskered man, but the hair on his face did not protect the high cheekbones and the eager nose that thrust itself aggressively into the frosty air.   5

At the man's heels trotted a dog, a big native husky, the proper wolf dog, gray-coated and without any visible or temperamental difference from its brother, the wild wolf. The animal was depressed by the tremendous cold. It knew that it was no time for travelling. Its instinct told it a truer tale than was told to the man by the man's judgment. In reality, it was not merely colder than fifty below zero; it was colder than sixty below, than seventy below. It was seventy-five below zero. Since the freezing point is thirty-two above zero, it meant that one hundred and seven degrees of frost obtained. The dog did not know anything about thermometers. Possibly in its brain there was no sharp consciousness of a condition of very cold such as was in the man's brain. But the brute had its instinct. It experienced a vague but menacing apprehension that subdued it and made it slink along at the man's heels, and that made it question eagerly every unwonted movement of the man as if expecting him to go into camp or to seek shelter somewhere and build a fire. The dog had learned fire, and it wanted fire, or else to burrow under the snow and cuddle its warmth away from the air.

The frozen moisture of its breathing had settled on its fur in a fine powder of frost, and especially were its jowls, muzzle, and eyelashes whitened by its crystalled breath. The man's red beard and mustache were likewise frosted, but more solidly, the deposit taking the form of ice and increasing with every warm, moist breath he exhaled. Also, the man was chewing tobacco, and the muzzle of ice held his lips so rigidly that he was unable to clear his chin when he expelled the juice. The result was that a crystal beard of the color and solidity of amber was increasing its length on his chin. If he fell down it would shatter itself, like glass, into brittle fragments. But he did not mind the appendage. It was the penalty all tobacco chewers paid in that country, and he had been out before in two cold snaps. They had not been so cold as this, he knew, but by the spirit thermometer at Sixty Mile he knew they had been registered at fifty below and at fifty-five.

He held on through the level stretch of woods for several miles, crossed a wide flat, and dropped down a bank to the frozen bed of a small stream. This was Henderson Creek, and he knew he was ten miles from the forks. He looked at his watch. It was ten o'clock. He was making four miles an hour, and he calculated that he would arrive at the forks at half-past twelve. He decided to celebrate that event by eating his lunch there.

The dog dropped in again at his heels, with a tail drooping discouragement, as the man swung along the creek bed. The furrow of the old sled trail was plainly visible, but a dozen inches of snow covered the marks of the last runners. In a month no man had come up or down that silent creek. The man held steadily on. He was not much given to thinking, and just then particularly he had nothing to think about save that he would eat lunch at the forks and that at six o'clock he would be in camp with the boys. There was nobody to talk to; and, had there been, speech would have been impossible because of the ice muzzle on his mouth. So he continued monotonously to chew tobacco and to increase the length of his amber heard.

Once in a while the thought reiterated itself that it was very cold and that he had   10
never experienced such cold. As he walked along he rubbed his cheekbones and nose with the back of his mittened hand. He did this automatically, now and again changing hands. But, rub as he would, the instant he stopped his cheekbones were numb, and the following instant the end of his nose went numb. He was sure to frost his cheeks; he knew that, and experienced a pang of regret that he had not devised a nose strap of the sort Bud wore in cold snaps. Such a strap passed across the cheeks, as well, and saved them. But it didn't matter much, after all. What were frosted cheeks? A bit painful, that was all; they were never serious.

Empty as the man's mind was of thoughts, he was keenly observant, and he noticed the changes in the creek, the curves and bends and timber jams, and always he sharply noted where he placed his feet. Once, coming around a bend, he shied abruptly, like a startled horse, curved away from the place where he had been walking, and retreated several paces back along the trail. The creek he knew was frozen clear to the bottom—no creek could contain water in that arctic winter—but he knew also that there were springs that bubbled out from the hillsides and ran along under the snow and on top of the ice of the creek. He knew that the coldest snaps never froze these springs, and he knew likewise their danger. They were traps. They hid pools of water under the snow that might be three inches deep, or three feet. Sometimes a skin of ice half an inch thick covered them, and in turn was covered by the snow. Sometimes there were alternate layers of water and ice skin, so that when one broke through he kept on breaking through for a while, sometimes wetting himself to the waist.

That was why he had shied in such panic. He had felt the give under his feet and heard the crackle of a snow-hidden ice skin. And to get his feet wet in such a temperature meant trouble and danger. At the very least it meant delay, for he would be forced to stop and build a fire, and under its protection to bare his feet while he dried his socks and moccasins. He stood and studied the creek bed and its banks, and decided that the flow of water came from the right. He reflected awhile, rubbing his nose and cheeks, then skirted to the left, stepping gingerly and testing the footing for each step. Once clear of the danger, he took a fresh chew of tobacco and swung along at his four-mile gait.

In the course of the next two hours he came upon several similar traps. Usually the snow above the hidden pools had a sunken, candied appearance that advertised the danger. Once again, however, he had a close call; and once, suspecting danger, he compelled the dog to go on in front. The dog did not want to go. It hung back until the man shoved it forward, and then it went quickly across the white, unbroken surface. Suddenly it broke through, floundered to one side, and got away to firmer footing. It had wet its forefeet and legs, and almost immediately the water that clung to it turned to ice. It made quick efforts to lick the ice off its legs, then dropped down in the snow and began to bite out the ice that had formed between the toes. This was a matter of instinct. To permit the ice to remain would mean sore feet. It did not know this. It merely obeyed the mysterious prompting that arose from the deep crypts of its being. But the man knew, having achieved a judgment on the subject, and he removed the mitten from his right hand and helped tear out the ice particles. He did not expose his fingers more than a minute, and was astonished at the swift numbness that smote them. It certainly was cold. He pulled on the mitten hastily, and beat the hand savagely across his chest.

At twelve o'clock the day was at its brightest. Yet the sun was too far south on its winter journey to clear the horizon. The bulge of the earth intervened between it and Henderson Creek, where the men walked under a clear sky at noon and cast no shadow. At half-past twelve, to the minute, he arrived at the forks of the creek. He was pleased at the speed he had made. If he kept it up, he would certainly be with the boys by six. He unbuttoned his jacket and shirt and drew forth his lunch. The action consumed no more than a quarter of a minute, yet in that brief moment the numbness laid hold of the exposed fingers. He did not put the mitten on, but, instead, struck the fingers a dozen sharp smashes against his leg. Then he sat down on a snow-covered log to eat. The sting that followed upon the striking of his fingers against his leg ceased so quickly that he was startled. He had had no chance to take a bite of biscuit. He struck the fingers repeatedly and returned them to the mitten, baring the other hand for the purpose of eating. He tried to take a mouthful, but the ice muzzle prevented. He had forgotten to build a fire and thaw out. He chuckled at his foolishness, and as he chuckled he noted the numbness creeping into the exposed fingers. Also, he noted that the stinging which had first come to his toes when he sat down was already passing away. He wondered whether the toes were warm or numb. He moved them inside the moccasins and decided that they were numb.

He pulled the mitten on hurriedly and stood up. He was a bit frightened. He stamped up and down until the stinging returned into the feet. It certainly was cold, was his thought. That man from Sulphur Creek had spoken the truth when telling how cold it sometimes got in the country. And he had laughed at him at the time! That showed one must not be too sure of things. There was no mistake about it, it *was* cold. He strode up and down, stamping his feet and threshing his arms, until reassured by the returning warmth. Then he got out matches and proceeded to make a fire. From the undergrowth, where high water of the previous spring had lodged a supply of seasoned twigs, he got his firewood. Working carefully from a small beginning, he soon had a roaring fire, over which he thawed the ice from his face and in the protection of which he ate his biscuits. For the moment the cold of space was outwitted. The dog took satisfaction in the fire, stretching out close enough for warmth and far enough away to escape being singed.

When the man had finished, he filled his pipe and took his comfortable time over a smoke. Then he pulled on his mittens, settled the ear flaps of his cap firmly about his ears, and took the creek trail up the left fork. The dog was disappointed and yearned back toward the fire. This man did not know cold. Possibly all the generations of his ancestry had been ignorant of cold, of real cold, of cold one hundred and seven degrees below freezing point. But the dog knew; all its ancestry knew, and it had inherited the knowledge. And it knew that it was not good to walk abroad in such fearful cold. It was the time to lie snug in a hole in the snow and wait for a curtain of cloud to be drawn across the face of outer space whence this cold came. On the other hand, there was no keen intimacy between the dog and the man. The one was the toil slave of the other, and the only caresses it had ever received were the caresses of the whip lash and of harsh and menacing throat sounds that threatened the whip lash. So the dog made no effort to communicate its apprehension to the man. It was not concerned in the welfare of the man; it was for its own sake that it yearned back toward the fire. But the man whistled, and spoke to it with the sound of whip lashes, and the dog swung in at the man's heels and followed after.

The man took a chew of tobacco and proceeded to start a new amber beard. Also, his moist breath quickly powdered with white his mustache, eyebrows, and lashes. There did not seem to be so many springs on the left fork of the Henderson, and for half an hour the man saw no signs of any. And then it happened. At a place where there were no signs, where the soft, unbroken snow seemed to advertise solidity beneath, the man broke through. It was not deep. He went himself halfway to the knees before he floundered out to the firm crust.

He was angry, and cursed his luck aloud. He had hoped to get into camp with the boys at six o'clock, and this would delay him an hour, for he would have to build a fire and dry out his footgear. This was imperative at that low temperature—he knew that much; and he turned aside to the bank, which he climbed. On top, tangled in the un-derbrush about the trunks of several small spruce trees, was a high-water deposit of dry firewood—sticks and twigs, principally, but also larger portions of seasoned branches and fine, dry, last year's grasses. He threw down several large pieces on top of the snow. This served for a foundation and prevented the young flame from drowning itself in the snow it otherwise would melt. The flame he got by touching a match to a small shred of birch bark that he took from his pocket. This burned even more readily than paper. Placing it on the foundation, he fed the young flame with wisps of dry grass and with the tiniest dry twigs.

He worked slowly and carefully, keenly aware of his danger. Gradually, as the flame grew stronger, he increased the size of the twigs with which he fed it. He squatted in the snow, pulling the twigs out from their entanglement in the brush and feeding di-rectly to the flame. He knew there must be no failure. When it is seventy-five below zero, a man must not fail in his first attempt to build a fire—that is, if his feet are wet. If his feet are dry, and he fails, he can run along the trail for half a mile and restore his cir-culation. But the circulation of wet and freezing feet cannot be restored by running when it is seventy-five below. No matter how fast he runs, the wet feet will freeze the harder.

All this the man knew. The old-timer on Sulphur Creek had told him about it   20 the previous fall, and now he was appreciating the advice. Already all sensation had gone out of his feet. To build the fire he had been forced to remove his mittens, and the fingers had quickly gone numb. His pace of four miles an hour had kept his heart pump-ing blood to the surface of his body and to all the extremities. But the instant he stopped, the action of the pump eased down. The cold of space smote the unprotected tip of the planet, and he, being on that unprotected tip, received the full force of the blow. The blood of his body recoiled before it. The blood was alive, like the dog, and like the dog it wanted to hide away and cover itself up from the fearful cold. So long as he walked four miles an hour, he pumped that blood, willy-nilly, to the surface; but now it ebbed away and sank down into the recesses of his body. The extremities were the first to feel its absence. His wet feet froze the faster, and his exposed fingers numbed the faster, though they had not yet begun to freeze. Nose and cheeks were already freezing, while the skin of all his body chilled as it lost its blood.

But he was safe. Toes and nose and cheeks would be only touched by the frost, for the fire was beginning to burn with strength. He was feeding it with twigs the size of his finger. In another minute he would be able to feed it with branches the size of his wrist, and then he could remove his wet footgear, and, while it dried, he could keep his naked feet warm by the fire, rubbing them at first, of course, with snow. The fire was a success. He was safe. He remembered the advice of the old-timer on Sulphur Creek, and smiled. The old-timer had been very serious in laying down the law that no man must travel alone in the Klondike after fifty below. Well, here he was; he had had the accident; he was alone; and he had saved himself. Those old-timers were rather womanish, some of them, he thought. All a man had to do was to keep his head, and he was all right. Any man who was a man could travel alone. But it was surprising, the rapidity with which his cheeks and nose were freezing. And he had not thought his fingers could go lifeless in so short a time. Lifeless they were, for he could scarcely make them move together to grip a twig, and they seemed remote from his body and from him. When he touched a twig, he had to look and see whether or not he had hold of it. The wires were pretty well down between him and his finger ends.

All of which counted for little. There was the fire, snapping and crackling and promising life with every dancing flame. He started to untie his moccasins. They were coated with ice; the thick German socks were like sheaths of iron halfway to the knees; and the moccasin strings were like rods of steel all twisted and knotted as by some conflagration. For a moment he tugged with his numb fingers, then, realizing the folly of it, he drew his sheath knife.

But before he could cut the strings, it happened. It was his own fault or, rather, his mistake. He should not have built the fire under the spruce tree. He should have built it in the open. But it had been easier to pull the twigs from the brush and drop them directly on the fire. Now the tree under which he had done this carried a weight of snow on its boughs. No wind had blown for weeks, and each bough was fully freighted. Each time he had pulled a twig he had communicated a slight agitation to the tree—an imperceptible agitation, so far as he was concerned, but an agitation sufficient to bring about the disaster. High up in the tree one bough capsized its load of snow. This fell on the boughs beneath, capsizing them. This process continued, spreading out and involving the whole tree. It grew like an avalanche, and it descended without warning upon the man and the fire, and the fire was blotted out! Where it had burned was a mantle of fresh and disordered snow.

The man was shocked. It was as though he had just heard his own sentence of death. For a moment he sat and stared at the spot where the fire had been. Then he grew very calm. Perhaps the old-timer on Sulphur Creek was right. If he had only had a trail mate he would have been in no danger now. The trail mate could have built the fire. Well, it was up to him to build the fire over again, and this second time there must be no failure. Even if he succeeded, he would most likely lose some toes. His feet must be badly frozen by now, and there would be some time before the second fire was ready.

Such were his thoughts, but he did not sit and think them. He was busy all the time they were passing through his mind. He made a new foundation for a fire, this time in the open, where no treacherous tree could blot it out. Next he gathered dry grasses and tiny twigs from the high-water flotsam. He could not bring his fingers together to pull them out, but he was able to gather them by the handful. In this way he got many rotten twigs and bits of green moss that were undesirable, but it was the best he could do. He worked methodically, even collecting an armful of the larger branches to be used

25

later when the fire gathered strength. And all the while the dog sat and watched him, a certain yearning wistfulness in its eye, for it looked upon him as the fire provider, and the fire was slow in coming.

When all was ready, the man reached in his pocket for a second piece of birch bark. He knew the bark was there, and, though he could not feel it with his fingers, he could hear its crisp rustling as he fumbled for it. Try as he would, he could not clutch hold of it. And all the time, in his consciousness, was the knowledge that each instant his feet were freezing. This thought tended to put him in a panic, but he fought against it and kept calm. He pulled on his mittens with his teeth, and threshed his arms back and forth, beating his hands with all his might against his sides. He did this sitting down, and he stood up to do it; and all the while the dog sat in the snow, its wolf brush of a tail curled around warmly over its forefeet, its sharp wolf ears pricked forward intently as it watched the man. And the man, as he beat and threshed with his arms and hands, felt a great surge of envy as he regarded the creature that was warm and secure in its natural covering.

After a time he was aware of the first faraway signals of sensation in his beaten fingers. The faint tingling grew stronger till it evolved into a stinging ache that was excruciating, but which the man hailed with satisfaction. He stripped the mitten from his right hand and fetched forth the birch bark. The exposed fingers were quickly going numb again. Next he brought out his bunch of sulphur matches. But the tremendous cold had already driven the life out of his fingers. In his effort to separate one match from the others, the whole bunch fell in the snow. He tried to pick it out of the snow, but failed. The dead fingers could neither touch nor clutch. He was very careful. He drove the thought of his freezing feet, and nose, and cheeks, out of his mind, devoting his whole soul to the matches. He watched, using the sense of vision in place of that of touch, and when he saw his fingers on each side the bunch, he closed them—that is, he willed to close them, for the wires were down, and the fingers did not obey. He pulled the mitten on the right hand, and beat it fiercely against his knee. Then, with both mittened hands, he scooped the bunch of matches, along with much snow, into his lap. Yet he was no better off.

After some manipulation he managed to get the bunch between the heels of his mittened hands. In this fashion he carried it to his mouth. The ice crackled and snapped when by a violent effort he opened his mouth. He drew the lower jaw in, curled the upper lip out of the way, and scraped the bunch with his upper teeth in order to separate a match. He succeeded in getting one, which he dropped on his lap. He was no better off. He could not pick it up. Then he devised a way. He picked it up in his teeth and scratched it on his leg. Twenty times he scratched before he succeeded in lighting it. As it flamed he held it with his teeth to the birch bark. But the burning brimstone went up his nostrils and into his lungs, causing him to cough spasmodically. The match fell into the snow and went out.

The old-timer on Sulphur Creek was right, he thought in the moment of controlled despair that ensued: after fifty below, a man should travel with a partner. He beat his hands, but failed in exciting any sensation. Suddenly he bared both hands, removing the mittens with his teeth. He caught the whole bunch between the heels of his hands. His arm muscles not being frozen enabled him to press the hand heels tightly against the matches. Then he scratched the bunch along his leg. It flared into flame, seventy sulphur matches at once! There was no wind to blow them out. He kept his head to one side to escape the strangling fumes, and held the blazing bunch to the birch bark. As he so held it, he became aware of sensation in his hand. His flesh was burning.

He could smell it. Deep down below the surface he could feel it. The sensation developed into pain that grew acute. And still he endured it, holding the flame of the matches clumsily to the bark that would not light readily because his own burning hands were in the way, absorbing most of the flame.

At last, when he could endure no more, he jerked his hands apart. The blazing matches fell sizzling into the snow, but the birch bark was alight. He began laying dry grasses and the tiniest twigs on the flame. He could not pick and choose, for he had to lift the fuel between the heels of his hands. Small pieces of rotten wood and green moss clung to the twigs, and he bit them off as well as he could with his teeth. He cherished the flame carefully and awkwardly. It meant life, and it must not perish. The withdrawal of blood from the surface of his body now made him begin to shiver, and he grew more awkward. A large piece of green moss fell squarely on the little fire. He tried to poke it out with his fingers, but his shivering frame made him poke too far, and he disrupted the nucleus of the little fire, the burning grasses and tiny twigs separating and scattering. He tried to poke them together again, but in spite of the tenseness of the effort, his shivering got away from him, and the twigs were hopelessly scattered. Each twig gushed a puff of smoke and went out. The fire provider had failed. As he looked apathetically about him, his eyes chanced on the dog, sitting across the ruins of the fire from him, in the snow, making restless, hunching movements, slightly lifting one forefoot and then the other, shifting its weight back and forth on them with a wistful eagerness.

The sight of the dog put a wild idea into his head. He remembered the tale of the man, caught in the blizzard, who killed a steer and crawled inside the carcass, and so was saved. He would kill the dog and bury his hands in the warm body until the numbness went out of them. Then he could build another fire. He spoke to the dog, calling it to him; but in his voice was a strange note of fear that frightened the animal, who had never known the man to speak in such a way before. Something was the matter, and its suspicious nature sensed danger—it knew not what danger, but somewhere, somehow, in its brain arose an apprehension of the man. It flattened its ears down at the sound of the man's voice, and its restless, hunching movements and the liftings and shiftings of its forefeet became more pronounced; but it would not come to the man. He got on his hands and knees and crawled toward the dog. This unusual posture again excited suspicion, and the animal sidled mincingly away.

The man sat up in the snow for a moment and struggled for calmness. Then he pulled on his mittens, by means of his teeth, and got upon his feet. He glanced down at first in order to assure himself that he was really standing up, for the absence of sensation in his feet left him unrelated to the earth. His erect position in itself started to drive the webs of suspicion from the dog's mind; and when he spoke peremptorily, with the sound of whip lashes in his voice, the dog rendered its customary allegiance and came to him. As it came within reaching distance, the man lost his control. His arms flashed out to the dog, and he experienced genuine surprise when he discovered that his hands could not clutch, that there was neither bend nor feeling in the fingers. He had forgotten for the moment that they were frozen and that they were freezing more and more. All this happened quickly, and before the animal could get away, he encircled its body with his arms. He sat down in the snow, and in this fashion held the dog, while it snarled and whined and struggled.

But it was all he could do, hold its body encircled in his arms and sit there. He realized that he could not kill the dog. There was no way to do it. With his helpless hands

30

he could neither draw nor hold his sheath knife nor throttle the animal. He released it, and it plunged wildly anyway, with tail between its legs, and still snarling. It halted forty feet away and surveyed him curiously, with ears sharply pricked forward.

The man looked down at his hands in order to locate them, and found them hanging on the ends of his arms. It struck him as curious that one should have to use his eyes in order to find out where his hands were. He began threshing his arms back and forth, beating the mittened hands against his sides. He did this for five minutes, violently, and his heart pumped enough blood up to the surface to put a stop to his shivering. But no sensation was aroused in the hands. He had an impression that they hung like weights on the ends of his arms, but when he tried to run the impression down, he could not find it.

A certain fear of death, full and oppressive, came to him. This fear quickly became poignant as he realized that it was no longer a mere matter of freezing his fingers and toes, or of losing his hands and feet, but that it was a matter of life and death with the chances against him. This threw him into a panic, and he turned and ran up the creek bed along the old, dim trail. The dog joined in behind and kept up with him. He ran blindly, without intention, in fear such as he had never known in his life. Slowly, as he plowed and floundered through the snow, he began to see things again—the banks of the creek, the old timber jams, the leafless aspens, and the sky. The running made him feel better. He did not shiver. Maybe, if he ran on, his feet would thaw out; and anyway, if he ran far enough, he would reach camp and the boys. Without doubt he would lose some fingers and toes and some of his face; but the boys would take care of him, and save the rest of him when he got there. And at the same time there was another thought in his mind that said he would never get to the camp and the boys; that it was too many miles away, that the freezing had too great a start on him, and that he would soon be stiff and dead. This thought he kept in the background and refused to consider. Sometimes it pushed itself forward and demanded to be heard, but he thrust it back and strove to think of other things.

It struck him as curious that he could run at all on feet so frozen that he could not feel them when they struck the earth and took the weight of his body. He seemed to himself to skim along above the surface, and to have no connection with the earth. Somewhere he had once seen a winged Mercury, and he wondered if Mercury felt as he felt when skimming over the earth.

His theory of running until he reached the camp and the boys had one flaw in it: he lacked the endurance. Several times he stumbled, and finally he tottered, crumpled up, and fell. When he tried to rise, he failed. He must sit and rest, he decided, and next time he would merely walk and keep on going. As he sat and regained his breath, he noted that he was feeling quite warm and comfortable. He was not shivering, and it even seemed that a warm glow had come to his chest and trunk. And yet, when he touched his nose and cheeks, there was no sensation. Running would not thaw them out. Nor would it thaw out his hands and feet. Then the thought came to him that the frozen portions of his body must be extending. He tried to keep this thought down, to forget it, to think of something else; he was aware of the panicky feeling that it caused, and he was afraid of the panic. But the thought asserted itself, and persisted, until it produced a vision of his body totally frozen. This was too much, and he made another wild run along the trail. Once he slowed down to a walk, but the thought of the freezing extending itself made him run again.

35

And all the time the dog ran with him, at his heels. When he fell down a second time, it curled its tail over its forefeet and sat in front of him, facing him, curiously eager and intent. The warmth and security of the animal angered him, and he cursed it till it flattened down its ears appeasingly. This time the shivering came more quickly upon the man. He was losing in his battle with the frost. It was creeping into his body from all sides. The thought of it drove him on, but he ran no more than a hundred feet, when he staggered and pitched headlong. It was his last panic. When he had recovered his breath and control, he sat up and entertained in his mind the conception of meeting death with dignity. However, the conception did not come to him in such terms. His idea of it was that he had been making a fool of himself, running around like a chicken with its head cut off—such was the simile that occurred to him. Well, he was bound to freeze anyway, and he might as well take it decently. With this new-found peace of mind came the first glimmerings of drowsiness. A good idea, he thought, to sleep off to death. It was like taking an anesthetic. Freezing was not so bad as people thought. There were lots worse ways to die.

He pictured the boys finding his body next day. Suddenly he found himself with them, coming along the trail and looking for himself. And, still with them, he came around a turn in the trail and found himself lying in the snow. He did not belong with himself any more, for even then he was out of himself, standing with the boys and looking at himself in the snow. It certainly was cold, was his thought. When he got back to the States he could tell the folks what real cold was. He drifted on from this to a vision of the old-timer on Sulphur Creek. He could see him quite clearly, warm and comfortable, and smoking a pipe.

"You were right, old hoss; you were right," the man mumbled to the old-timer of   40
Sulphur Creek.

Then the man drowsed off into what seemed to him the most comfortable and satisfying sleep he had ever known. The dog sat facing him and waiting. The brief day drew to a close in a long, slow twilight. There were no signs of a fire to be made, and, besides, never in the dog's experience had it known a man to sit like that in the snow and make no fire. As the twilight drew on, its eager yearning for the fire mastered it, and with a great lifting and shifting of forefeet, it whined softly, then flattened its ears down in anticipation of being chidden by the man. But the man remained silent. Later the dog whined loudly. And still later it crept close to the man and caught the scent of death. This made the animal bristle and back away. A little longer it delayed, howling under the stars that leaped and danced and shone brightly in the cold sky. Then it turned and trotted up the trail in the direction of the camp it knew, where were the other food providers and fire providers.

ANALYZING "TO BUILD A FIRE"

Understanding this moving story involves examining the basic elements of its historical context as well as considering major literary elements such as plot, character, tone, theme, metaphor and imagery. Let's look at some of these elements in "To Build a Fire," which was published in 1908.

Plot

The plot of this story involves a struggle for survival, one of the oldest plots in human history. The unnamed man, a *chechaquo* (one who searches for gold), with his unnamed dog (a husky) is traveling from one camp to another in the Klondike, a region in the Yukon territory and a site of abundant gold deposits in northwestern Canada. No other characters are present, although the man often thinks of the "boys at camp" and the "old-timer" at Sulphur Creek, who has given the man advice about traveling in the bitter cold, where temperatures often drop under 50 degrees below zero. The story is narrated from the third-person, objective perspective. As the story develops, we come to know a great deal about the man and his ability to survive the bitter cold. The plot line reveals at least three kinds of nature: (1) the natural world, depicted as a dangerous, unforgiving place, (2) human nature, which is depicted in the man's attitude and beliefs as he travels through the Klondike, and (3) the nature of survival, which is represented by the careful logic of the old-timer and the instinctive logic of the dog. The narrative resonates with lessons about all three kinds of nature.

All literary plots reveal change over time and cause-and-effect relationships. "To Build a Fire" begins with a man alone on a short journey to a friendly base camp, seeking protection from the bitter cold. He has a limited amount of time—the light of one day—to reach the camp. He has calculated that he has enough time to make it safely by 6:00 P.M. As the story develops, the man makes several decisions that have critical effects on him and the success of his journey. When the journey begins, the man knows that it is very cold. At first, he thinks that it is 50 degrees below zero, but he soon comes to realize that it is much colder, perhaps as much at 75 degrees below zero. Because of the intense cold, it is critical for survival that the traveler make the right decisions. These judgments involve understanding weather conditions, his personal knowledge and instincts, and the advice given to him by the old-timer. The plot turns on personal qualities and natural events. The conclusion of the story reveals the result of the man's inability to properly understand these two events or histories. In order to survive, he must know the culture of nature and the culture of survival (and his own personal culture). The closing paragraphs illustrate the dire lessons that are learned because of a character's failure to understand nature and, more important, himself.

Character

"To Build a Fire" has long been recognized as a masterful narrative with a spellbinding plot about one man's struggle for survival (and a dog's struggle, too). Although there are only two characters, man and dog, in the present time of the story, both are well developed and illustrate the theme of survival against the forces of nature. Although the man is unnamed, we come to know him very well because of the intensely descriptive illustrations of his actions and qualities. We also learn much about the unnamed dog. Because this story is about a struggle for survival, it depicts the strengths and weaknesses of the main character.

At the beginning of the story, the man is quite confident in, even proud of, his ability to survive the frigid temperatures of the Yukon trail. The narrator tells us that he is inexperienced, yet self-assured. He knows the "facts" of his surroundings, but not the significance (and dangers) of them. He doesn't know how cold it is, but in his mind "it doesn't matter." He carries with him a sense of invincibility, a feeling of immunity against the laws of nature to which all humans are subject. His overconfidence is surely a significant character weakness. The man is quite comfortable in his travel plans, yet his companion dog knows better, and the narrator tells us that the dog realizes "that it was no time for traveling." The animal's instinct tells him what the man should have sensed about the dangers in traveling alone in such inhospitable weather. The dog, as a character, possesses a survivalist, intuitive logic. The narrator tells us "it experienced a vague but menacing apprehension." As the narrative progresses, the man slowly comes to understand what the dog instinctively knows.

Tone and Point of View

"To Build a Fire" is written from the third-person, objective point of view. In some third-person accounts, there is obvious sympathy for the main character, but this does not appear to be the case in this story. Indeed, the portrait of the man and his experiences is ironic in its focus on the polarities of life and death. Although the narrative is about the man's life and death decisions, the narrator tells us much about the nature or "culture" of the Yukon trail and those who traverse it, humans and their trusted dogs. The portrait of the man is actually unsympathetic, as the narrator makes clear that the man has violated important codes of conduct for survival in the Klondike. Further, the man suffers from hubris in disregarding the wise advice from the old-timer. The man believes that he is not quite human, and is above the laws of nature that apply to everyone else. The tone of this story is complex, as the man is portrayed as "one of the boys" he journeys to meet, yet he is not one of the boys in observing the laws of Yukon survival. The narrator's portrait of community is further revealed in the man's strained relationship with the dog, wiser than his master because of the dog's correct instincts, which tell him from the beginning that it is too cold to travel. The man cannot even kill the dog for warmth because the human sends the wrong signals in approaching the animal. Throughout the story, the narrator creates a mood of foreboding and intense loneliness, illustrating the conflict between man and nature (and man and himself). Setting and imagery are carefully selected to create a sense of impending doom, all of which are part of the narrator's attitude and tone.

Theme

The Klondike is a region rich in tales of human struggles and this narrative is a gripping tale of the struggle to survive in the grim conditions of the frozen Yukon trail. It is a story of man versus nature, but within that story is another narrative about a man's pride and unwillingness to accept nature for what it is. When the man disregards the basic laws of nature, the punishment dealt out by nature is severe. It is ironic that the penalty of death comes about as a result of trying to avoid it. The unnamed explorer dies not because it is cold, but because he foolishly travels alone and fails to observe the safety procedures of seasoned travelers like the old-timer. There is a huge difference between the knowledge the man has and the knowledge he should have had.

A major theme in this story is the importance of communities. "To Build a Fire" emphasizes the necessity of community and the interrelationships between the cultures of various communities. The unnamed traveler is symbolic of everyone who travels the trail of life, everyone who needs the companionship and support of others in order to survive life's challenges and crises. Rather than embrace the company and help of others, the man travels alone, except for his dog, and this decision reflects his world view of self-reliance and stoicism. He is a man who does not possess a need for the companionship of others. Even his relationship with his dog reveals a coldness that shows him to be detached from the world of relationships. He sees the dog only as something that might help him, not as a companion, friend, or fellow traveler. Because of his selfish relationship with his dog, we can assume much about his relationships with his fellow humans. The man is completely devoid of any sense of the need for community, whether with others or even with his animal-companion. The narrator makes us see that the lonely, misguided *chechaquo* lacks imagination, empathy, and sympathy for anyone except himself. This self-centeredness is one of the major motifs of this chilling tale.

Metaphor and Imagery

"To Build a Fire" is rich in symbolism, metaphor, and imagery. The story begins with a sense of foreboding: "there seemed to be an intangible pall over the face of things, a subtle gloom that made the day dark." Early on, nature is personified as a hostile force, an ever-present threat to the *chechaquo* traveling alone. The man's companion dog, too, is personified as having a sense of understanding of the conditions around him. The dog understands what the man does not—danger in weather that is too cold. This personification symbolizes the comparative levels of awareness and understanding between man and animal.

Irony is a master metaphor and "To Build a Fire" just drips with irony, from the man's overconfidence in his own abilities in the face of dangerous weather conditions to the futility of his attempts to build a fire in spite of what he has been old by wiser heads. The traveler very carefully calculates the time and distance he must travel, paying no attention to the severity of the weather conditions. He is proud of his analytical abilities and he surmises that it really isn't very cold, far above the −75 degrees that it really is. And it is ironic that the dog survives the ordeal, in spite of its "inferior" intelligence. The man disregards basic laws of nature at will and does not expect to pay a price for his pride and foolishness. As the narrator tells us, "all this—the mysterious, far-reaching hairline trail, the absence of the sun from the sky, the tremendous cold, and the strangeness and weirdness of it all—made no impression on the man." Such imperceptions carry a heavy price.

Other symbols and images play a significant role in this story. Man and nature come together in large and small ways. The man feeds the fire with twigs "twice the size of his finger" and then larger "branches the size of his wrist." After the fire is snuffed out by melting snow falling from branches of the tree, the man runs blindly along the trail, flailing toward nowhere, like a figure out of ancient mythology (a "winged mercury," says the narrator). As his mind freezes, he dreams of being "one of the boys," discovering his own body the following day. Ironically, the man comes to realize his need for community as he enters death's door.

Questions for Your Analysis of "To Build a Fire"

1) What are some of your early impressions of the story?
2) What are your observations on the traveler's assessment of his journey, his minute calculations of time and distance? How does the man's attitude change, once he begins to suspect that he may not have perfect knowledge about traveling in the Klondike?
3) There are several cultures and communities represented, including the natural culture of the Klondike, the culture of the Yukon trail travelers, the personal culture of the *chechaquo*, and the culture of the native husky. How do these cultures interact with one another? Are there other cultures in the story?
4) How might you relate your personal experiences to those of the traveler (especially if you read the story as symbolic of a "journey through life")?
5) What kind of judgments do you make about the traveler's contest with nature (and his contest with himself)?
6) In what way(s) does the story depict the traveler's personal culture in comparison to those other cultures mentioned? What are the principles of each culture and how do they relate to the traveler's culture?
7) Is nature presented as a hostile force, or do you see nature as more of a neutral force? How responsible do you hold the traveler for not observing the laws of nature as he rejects the advice of the old-timer from Sulphur Springs?
8) What is it that we learn from this grim Klondike tale?

9) In what ways does the narrator foreshadow the end of the story?

10) How do you interpret the concluding statement of the narrator: "Then it [the dog] turned and trotted up the trail in the direction of the camp it knew, where were the other food providers and fire providers"?

The textual issues suggested in this chapter can be appropriated to cultural criticism, as well as to other interpretive approaches. Please read the following sample essay on "To Build a Fire" as an illustration of one form that cultural criticism might take. This essay, as you will see, focuses on the culture and history of the Yukon trail, the personal experiences of Jack London, and the cultural facts and implications in the story itself. All insightful cultural criticism takes account of multiple cultural contexts, although there may be more emphasis on some over others. Other cultural approaches to the story might focus more heavily on London's own traveling experiences in the Klondike or on other "true" stories of survival in this frigid part of the world as the basis of "To Build a Fire."

Sample Essay on "To Build a Fire"

"To Build a Fire," one of the most popular adventure stories ever written, is set in the Klondike in the late 1800s and tells the story of a man's struggle against nature and with himself. The main character, an unnamed man traveling across the frozen Yukon terrain, attempts to reach a base camp, with only his "wolf-dog" (also unnamed) as his companion. The chilling narrative is told from an objective, third-person perspective, which informs the reader not only of the context of the inhospitable setting and weather conditions, but also of the psychological processes in the mind of the main character. The companion dog, a native husky, is portrayed as having survival "instincts," and these qualities become an important part of the theme of the narrative, which suggests that humans must understand various communities in the struggle for survival. These cultural communities include nature, other characters (the boys at the camp, including the old-timer), the dog, and perhaps most important, the personal culture of the main character.

This story is very realistic and is based on Jack London's experience as a traveler on the Yukon trail in the Klondike, as well as on his keen ear for stories of adventure told by others. Over his career, London wrote many Klondike tales, some with heroes as protagonists who meet obstacles they overcome, and others with protagonists who fail tests such as the challenge of survival, as did the main character in "To Build a Fire." This character would not be unfamiliar to London because of the wide range of gold hunters who invaded the Klondike in the late 1800s. Indeed, Jack London was intimately familiar with experiences of gruesome adventure in the Yukon Territory, having lived some Klondike adventures of his own in the winter of 1897–98, as chronicled in Franklin Walker's biography of Jack London, *Jack London and the Klondike* (San Marino, CA: Huntington Library, 1966). The men (and some women) who braved the fierce Klondike winter weather conditions have generated fascinating tales of adventure in their struggle for survival.

This chilling tale begins with the context of nature, which can be nurturing and protective or dangerously threatening to man. As the unnamed man (perhaps representing every man) decides to undertake a one-day trip to a base camp, he has concluded, naïvely, that he can safely make the journey, even though he has been advised by the old wise man from Sulphur Creek never to travel alone. The main character brims with self-confidence and dismisses the old-timer's counsel, recalling that the man had laughed at him when he warned the *chechaquo* (a newcomer searching for gold) how cold it could get in the Klondike. The man foolishly believes that the only kind of knowledge or understanding that he needs is what he already knows. He fails to recognize that there are at least two other kinds of understanding that are necessary for survival: (1) an acquired knowledge of nature as understood by well-experienced residents of the Yukon like the old-timer, and (2) an instinctive knowledge of nature, as represented by the dog's intuitive understanding of what is necessary for survival. (A good example of instinctive knowledge is when the dog immediately bites off the icicles that form on his fur after getting wet. The dog knows that failing to do so would mean his death.) This tale repeatedly compares what the man does not know to what the dog instinctively does know. The world of the Klondike is a constant struggle for survival and only the strong (meaning intelligent and able to adapt) do survive.

The old-timer has warned the man never to travel alone. This principle is a guiding rule of life in the Klondike. Yet the traveler believes that his predicament, falling through the snow into water underneath, is a matter of luck, rather than the direct result of his poor judgment and failure to heed the advice of those wiser and more experienced than he. Indeed, he "cursed his luck" after falling through the surface ice. After managing to successfully build a fire and dry himself out, he develops a false sense of confidence in his abilities to cope with nature. For much of the story, the main character maintains a sense of denial of the challenges he faces.

The moral of this story is "never travel alone," but there are several important lessons to be learned from the experiences of the unnamed traveler. The old-timer's warning to never travel alone is based on his understanding and fear of the power of nature. Anything can happen on the open trail in the frozen tundra, and a traveler must always be prepared. The old man's warning also underscores the importance of another community, the community of humankind. The traveler rejects the warnings of his fellow human beings, but he also fails to bond in any meaningful way with his companion dog. The man sees the dog not as a true companion, but rather as a servant to him, there only to provide the essential services of a sled dog (in spite of the fact that the man is not traveling by dogsled this time). In other words, the dog is something to be used, not a true companion. Indeed, the man attempts to kill the dog to save himself, which is understandable, yet also reflects the man's disdain for others, human or animal. The dog serves as a constant reminder that its instinctive knowledge is superior to the man's knowledge of the forces of nature.

The man dies because he fails to heed the advice to never travel alone, but the larger moral of the story is the importance of community. If the traveler had listened to others, he would have traveled safely, in the company of others. There are grim lessons to be learned from "To Build a Fire," including the lesson that the world is a dangerous and hostile place. Only by living and learning within a community can one survive. Instinctive knowledge, such as the dog possesses, is significant, but for humans, knowledge gained from cultural communities is especially important. And the only way that humans can acquire this kind of knowledge is to interact, in a positive way, with those more knowledgeable, such as the old-timer.

The protagonist is a deeply flawed character and there is (grim) poetic justice to his end. He, and he alone, is responsible for the decision he has made that leads to his death. His personal culture, or character, is sadly deficient. He is guilty of excessive pride in believing that he knows all there is to know about nature. He expresses no desire for real friendship; he just wants the safe haven of the campfire, where he hopes to join the "boys." Further, the traveler possesses little common sense or practical wisdom. For example, he builds a fire under a tree, not anticipating that falling snow might snuff out the life-saving fire. He also underestimates the time it will take him to travel certain distances. Indeed, his miscalculations are part of his basic personal culture. He adjusts his actions to his perception of "reality," rather than realistically adapting to the forces of nature. Perhaps it is not too strong to suggest that he is totally ego-driven, with little regard for others or for the dangers of the natural world.

It is clear that the protagonist fails to understand the cultures in which he finds himself, whether the culture of the natural world or the culture of the community of Klondike explorers. Perhaps most important, however, is the traveler's failure to understand his own personal culture; that is, his overpowering ego and pride that cost him his life. Failing to recognize the laws of nature, the rules of the community, or the importance of self-knowledge leave the main character completely subject to the awesome power of the natural world. Without understanding any of the three cultures, he cannot survive. This failure to understand and respond to cultures and their laws is an important lesson to be learned, both for the reader and the ill-fated traveler.

WRITING YOUR ESSAY
FROM A CULTURAL PERSPECTIVE

The following short story, "The Horse Dealer's Daughter," is by D. H. Lawrence. This narrative, like other readings such as "To Build a Fire," "Sonny's Blues," and "Babylon Revisited," depicts the struggles of individuals trapped in frustrating and lonely experiences. This story, like London's narrative, is told in the third-person voice of a narrator who is somewhat sympathetic to the characters, but who establishes a point of view that is coldly objective in tone.

What is engaging about this story is the author's attempt to capture the experiences of characters desperately in need of love, to counteract the lonely, dreadful existences they lead. In that respect, the narrator of "The Horse Dealer's Daughter" and the narrator of "To Build a Fire" share something in common—telling a story about individuals trapped in a hostile universe. The traveler faces a hostile nature. Mabel Pervin faces a loveless life of loneliness and poverty. Following "The Horse Dealer's Daughter," is a series of questions to assist you in the analysis of the work, as well as in writing an essay from a cultural perspective.

A SAMPLE READING

"The Horse Dealer's Daughter" by D. H. Lawrence (1885–1930)

"Well, Mabel, and what are you going to do with yourself?" asked Joe, with foolish flippancy. He felt quite safe himself. Without listening for an answer, he turned aside, worked a grain of tobacco to the tip of his tongue, and spat it out. He did not care about anything, since he felt safe himself.

The three brothers and the sister sat round the desolate breakfast-table, attempting some sort of desultory consultation. The morning's post had given the final tap to the family fortunes, and all was over. The dreary dining-room itself, with its heavy mahogany furniture, looked as if it were waiting to be done away with.

But the consultation amounted to nothing. There was a strange air of ineffectuality about the three men, as they sprawled at table, smoking and reflecting vaguely on their own condition. The girl was alone, a rather short, sullen-looking young woman of twenty-seven. She did not share the same life as her brothers. She would have been good-looking, save for the impressive fixity of her face, 'bulldog,' as her brothers called it.

There was a confused tramping of horses' feet outside. The three men all sprawled round in their chairs to watch. Beyond the dark holly bushes that separated the strip of lawn from the high-road, they could see a cavalcade of shire horses swinging out of their own yard, being taken for exercise. This was the last time. These were the last horses that would go through their hands. The young men watched with critical, callous look. They were all frightened at the collapse of their lives, and the sense of disaster in which they were involved left them no inner freedom.

Yet they were three fine, well-set fellows enough. Joe, the eldest, was a man of   5
thirty-three, broad and handsome in a hot, flushed way. His face was red, he twisted his black moustache over a thick finger, his eyes were shallow and restless. He had a sensual way of uncovering his teeth when he laughed, and his bearing was stupid. Now he watched the horses with a glazed look of helplessness in his eyes, a certain stupor of downfall.

The great draught-horses swung past. They were tied head to tail, four of them, and they heaved along to where a lane branched off from the high-road, planting their great hoofs floutingly in the fine black mud, swinging their great rounded haunches sumptuously, and trotting a few sudden steps as they were led into the lane, round the corner. Every movement showed a massive, slumberous strength, and a stupidity which held them in subjection. The groom at the head looked back, jerking the leading rope. And the cavalcade moved out of sight up the lane, the tail of the last horse, bobbed up tight and stiff, held out taut from the swinging great haunches as they rocked behind the hedges in a motion-like sleep.

Joe watched with glazed hopeless eyes. The horses were almost like his own body to him. He felt he was done for now. Luckily he was engaged to a woman as old as himself, and therefore her father, who was steward of a neighbouring estate, would provide him with a job. He would marry and go into harness. His life was over, he would be a subject animal now.

He turned uneasily aside, the retreating steps of the horses echoing in his ears. Then, with foolish restlessness, he reached for the scraps of bacon-rind from the plates,

and making a faint whistling sound, flung them to the terrier that lay against the
fender. He watched the dog swallow them, and waited till the creature looked into his
eyes. Then a faint grin came on his face, and in a high, foolish voice he said:

"You won't get much more bacon, shall you, you little b——?"

The dog faintly and dismally wagged its tail, then lowered its haunches, circled   10
round, and lay down again.

There was another helpless silence at the table. Joe sprawled uneasily in his seat,
not willing to go till the family conclave was dissolved. Fred Henry, the second brother,
was erect, clean-limbed, alert. He had watched the passing of the horses with more
sang-froid. If he was an animal, like Joe, he was an animal which controls, not one
which is controlled. He was master of any horse, and he carried himself with a well-
tempered air of mastery. But he was not master of the situations of life. He pushed his
coarse brown moustache upwards, off his lip, and glanced irritably at his sister, who was
impassive and inscrutable.

"You'll go and stop with Lucy for a bit, shan't you?" he asked. The girl did not
answer.

"I don't see what else you can do," persisted Fred Henry.

"Go as a skivvy," Joe interpolated laconically.

The girl did not move a muscle.   15

"If I was her, I should go in for training for a nurse," said Malcolm, the youngest
of them all. He was the baby of the family, a young man of twenty-two, with a fresh,
jaunty *museau*.

But Mabel did not take any notice of him. They had talked at her and round her
for so many years, that she hardly heard them at all.

The marble clock on the mantelpiece softly chimed the half-hour, the dog rose
uneasily from the hearth-rug and looked at the party at the breakfast-table. But still
they sat on in ineffectual conclave.

"Oh, all right," said Joe suddenly, apropos of nothing. "I'll get a move on."

He pushed back his chair, straddled his knees with a downward jerk, to get them   20
free, in horsey fashion, and went to the fire. Still he did not go out of the room; he was
curious to know what the others would do or say. He began to charge his pipe, looking
down at the dog and saying in a high, affected voice:

"Going wi' me? Going wi' me are ter? Tha'rt goin' further than tha counts on just
now, dost hear?"

The dog faintly wagged its tail, the man stuck out his jaw and covered his pipe
with his hands, and puffed intently, losing himself in the tobacco, looking down all the
while at the dog with an absent brown eye. The dog looked up at him in mournful distrust. Joe stood with his knees stuck out, in real horsey fashion.

"Have you had a letter from Lucy?" Fred Henry asked of his sister.

"Last week," came the neutral reply.

"And what does she say?"   25

There was no answer.

"Does she *ask* you to go and stop there?" persisted Fred Henry.

"She says I can if I like."

"Well, then, you'd better. Tell her you'll come on Monday."

This was received in silence.   30

"That's what you'll do then, is it?" said Fred Henry, in some exasperation.

But she made no answer. There was a silence of futility and irritation in the room. Malcolm grinned fatuously.

"You'll have to make up your mind between now and next Wednesday," said Joe loudly, "or else find yourself lodgings on the kerbstone."

The face of the young woman darkened, but she sat on immutable.

"Here's Jack Fergusson!" exclaimed Malcolm, who was looking aimlessly out of   35
the window.

"Where?" exclaimed Joe loudly.

"Just gone past."

"Coming in?"

Malcolm craned his neck to see the gate.

"Yes," he said.   40

There was a silence. Mabel sat on like one condemned, at the head of the table. Then a whistle was heard from the kitchen. The dog got up and barked sharply. Joe opened the door and shouted:

"Come on."

After a moment a young man entered. He was muffled up in overcoat and a purple woollen scarf, and his tweed cap, which he did not remove, was pulled down on his head. He was of medium height, his face was rather long and pale, his eyes looked tired.

"Hello, Jack! Well, Jack!" exclaimed Malcolm and Joe. Fred Henry merely said: "Jack."

"What's doing?" asked the newcomer, evidently addressing Fred Henry.   45

"Same. We've got to be out by Wednesday. Got a cold?"

"I have—got it bad, too."

"Why don't you stop in?"

"*Me* stop in? When I can't stand on my legs, perhaps I shall have a chance." The young man spoke huskily. He had a slight Scotch accent.

"It's a knock-out, isn't it," said Joe, boisterously, "if a doctor goes round croaking   50
with a cold. Looks bad for the patients, doesn't it?"

The young doctor looked at him slowly.

"Anything the matter with *you*, then?" he asked sarcastically.

"Not as I know of. Damn your eyes, I hope not. Why?"

"I thought you were very concerned about the patients, wondered if you might be one yourself."

"Damn it, no, I've never been patient to no flaming doctor, and hope I never   55
shall be," returned Joe.

At this point Mabel rose from the table, and they all seemed to become aware of her existence. She began putting the dishes together. The young doctor looked at her, but did not address her. He had not greeted her. She went out of the room with the tray, her face impassive and unchanged.

"When are you off then, all of you?" asked the doctor.

"I'm catching the eleven-forty," replied Malcolm. "Are you goin' down wi' th' trap, Joe?"

"Yes, I've told you I'm going down wi' th' trap, haven't I?"

"We'd better be getting her in then. So long, Jack, if I don't see you before I go,"   60
said Malcolm, shaking hands.

He went out, followed by Joe, who seemed to have his tail between his legs.

"Well, this is the devil's own," exclaimed the doctor, when he was left alone with Fred Henry. "Going before Wednesday, are you?"

"That's the orders," replied the other.

"Where, to Northampton?"

"That's it." 65

"The devil!" exclaimed Fergusson, with quiet chagrin.

And there was silence between the two.

"All settled up, are you?" asked Fergusson.

"About."

There was another pause. 70

"Well, I shall miss yer, Freddy, boy," said the young doctor.

"And I shall miss thee, Jack," returned the other.

"Miss you like hell," mused the doctor.

Fred Henry turned aside. There was nothing to say. Mabel came in again, to finish clearing the table.

"What are *you* going to do, then, Miss Pervin?" asked Fergusson. "Going to your 75 sister's, are you?"

Mabel looked at him with her steady, dangerous eyes, that always made him uncomfortable, unsettling his superficial ease.

"No," she said.

"Well, what in the name of fortune *are* you going to do? Say what you mean to do," cried Fred Henry, with futile intensity.

But she only averted her head, and continued her work. She folded the white table-cloth, and put on the chenille cloth.

"The sulkiest bitch that ever trod!" muttered her brother. 80

But she finished her task with perfectly impassive face, the young doctor watching her interestedly all the while. Then she went out.

Fred Henry stared after her, clenching his lips, his blue eyes fixing in sharp antagonism, as he made a grimace of sour exasperation.

"You could bray her into bits, and that's all you'd get out of her," he said, in a small, narrowed tone.

The doctor smiled faintly.

"What's she *going* to do, then?" he asked. 85

"Strike me if I know!" returned the other.

There was a pause. Then the doctor stirred.

"I'll be seeing you to-night, shall I?" he said to his friend.

"Ay—where's it to be? Are we going over to Jessdale?"

"I don't know. I've got such a cold on me. I'll come round to the 'Moon and 90 Stars,' anyway."

"Let Lizzie and May miss their night for once, eh?"

"That's it—if I feel as I do now."

"All's one——"

The two young men went through the passage and down to the back door together. The house was large, but it was servant-less now, and desolate. At the back was a small bricked houseyard and beyond that a big square, gravelled fine and red, and having stables on two sides. Sloping, dank, winter-dark fields stretched away on the open sides.

But the stables were empty. Joseph Pervin, the father of the family, had been a   95
man of no education, who had become a fairly large horse dealer. The stables had been
full of horses, there was a great turmoil and come-and-go of horses and of dealers and
grooms. Then the kitchen was full of servants. But of late things had declined. The old
man had married a second time, to retrieve his fortunes. Now he was dead and everything was gone to the dogs, there was nothing but debt and threatening.

For months, Mabel had been servant-less in the big house, keeping the home together in penury for her ineffectual brothers. She had kept house for ten years. But previously it was with unstinted means. Then, however brutal and coarse everything was,
the sense of money had kept her proud, confident. The men might be foul-mouthed,
the women in the kitchen might have bad reputations, her brothers might have illegiti-
mate children. But so long as there was money, the girl felt herself established, and brutally proud, reserved.

No company came to the house, save dealers and coarse men. Mabel had no associates of her own sex, after her sister went away. But she did not mind. She went regularly to church, she attended to her father. And she lived in the memory of her mother,
who had died when she was fourteen, and whom she had loved. She had loved her father, too, in a different way, depending upon him, and feeling secure in him, until at
the age of fifty-four he married again. And then she had set hard against him. Now he
had died and left them all hopelessly in debt.

She had suffered badly during the period of poverty. Nothing, however, could
shake the curious, sullen, animal pride that dominated each member of the family.
Now, for Mabel, the end had come. Still she would not cast about her. She would
follow her own way just the same. She would always hold the keys of her own situation. Mindless and persistent, she endured from day to day. Why should she think?
Why should she answer anybody? It was enough that this was the end, and there was
no way out. She need not pass any more darkly along the main street of the small
town, avoiding every eye. She need not demean herself any more, going into the shops
and buying the cheapest food. This was at an end. She thought of nobody, not even
of herself. Mindless and persistent, she seemed in a sort of ecstasy to be coming nearer
to her fulfillment, her own glorification, approaching her dead mother, who was
glorified.

In the afternoon she took a little bag, with shears and sponge and a small
scrubbing-brush, and went out. It was a grey, wintry day, with saddened, dark green fields
and an atmosphere blackened by the smoke of foundries not far off. She went quickly,
darkly along the causeway, heeding nobody, through the town to the churchyard.

There she always felt secure, as if no one could see her, although as a matter of   100
fact she was exposed to the stare of everyone who passed along under the churchyard
wall. Nevertheless, once under the shadow of the great looming church, among the
graves, she felt immune from the world, reserved within the thick churchyard wall as in
another country.

Carefully she clipped the grass from the grave, and arranged the pinky white,
small chrysanthemums in the tin cross. When this was done, she took an empty jar
from a neighbouring grave, brought water, and carefully, most scrupulously sponged the
marble headstone and the coping-stone.

It gave her sincere satisfaction to do this. She felt in immediate contact with the
world of her mother. She took minute pains, went through the park in a state bordering
on pure happiness, as if in performing this task she came into a subtle, intimate connec-

tion with her mother. For the life she followed here in the world was far less real than the world of death she inherited from her mother.

The doctor's house was just by the church. Fergusson, being a mere hired assistant, was slave to the country-side. As he hurried now to attend to the out-patients in the surgery, glancing across the graveyard with his quick eye, he saw the girl at her task at the grave. She seemed so intent and remote, it was like looking into another world. Some mystical element was touched in him. He slowed down as he walked, watching her as if spellbound.

She lifted her eyes, feeling him looking. Their eyes met. And each looked again at once, each feeling, in some way, found out by the other. He lifted his cap and passed on down the road. There remained distinct in his consciousness, like a vision, the memory of her face, lifted from the tombstone in the churchyard, and looking at him with slow, large, portentous eyes. It *was* portentous, her face. It seemed to mesmerise him. There was a heavy power in her eyes which laid hold of his whole being, as if he had drunk some powerful drug. He had been feeling weak and done before. Now the life came back into him, he felt delivered from his own fretted, daily self.

He finished his duties at the surgery as quickly as might be, hastily filling up the   105 bottles of the waiting people with cheap drugs. Then, in perpetual haste, he set off again to visit several cases in another part of his round, before tea-time. At all times he preferred to walk if he could, but particularly when he was not well. He fancied the motion restored him.

The afternoon was falling. It was grey, deadened, and wintry, with a slow, moist, heavy coldness sinking in and deadening all the faculties. But why should he think or notice? He hastily climbed the hill and turned across the dark green fields, following the black cinder-track. In the distance, across a shallow dip in the country, the small town was clustered like smouldering ash, a tower, a spire, a head of low, raw, extinct houses. And on the nearest fringe of the town, sloping into the dip, was Oldmeadow, the Pervins' house. He could see the stables and the outbuildings distinctly, as they lay towards him on the slope. Well, he would not go there many more times! Another resource would be lost to him, another place gone: the only company he cared for in the alien, ugly little town he was losing. Nothing but work, drudgery, constant hastening from dwelling to dwelling among the colliers and the iron-workers. It wore him out, but at the same time he had a craving for it. It was a stimulant to him to be in the homes of the working people, moving, as it were, through the innermost body of their life. His nerves were excited and gratified. He could come so near, into the very lives of the rough, inarticulate, powerfully emotional men and women. He grumbled, he said he hated the hellish hole. But as a matter of fact it excited him, the contact with the rough, strongly-feeling people was a stimulant applied direct to his nerves.

Below Oldmeadow, in the green, shallow, soddened hollow of field, lay a square, deep pond. Roving across the landscape, the doctor's quick eye detected a figure in black passing through the gate of the field, down towards the pond. He looked again. It would be Mabel Pervin. His mind suddenly became alive and attentive.

Why was she going down there? He pulled up on the path on the slope above, and stood staring. He could just make sure of the small black figure moving in the hollow of the failing day. He seemed to see her in the midst of such obscurity, that he was like a clairvoyant, seeing rather with the mind's eye than with ordinary sight. Yet he could see her positively enough, whilst he kept his eye attentive. He felt, if he looked away from her, in the thick, ugly falling dusk, he would lose her altogether.

He followed her minutely as she moved, direct and intent, like something transmitted rather than stirring in voluntary activity, straight down the field towards the pond. There she stood on the bank for a moment. She never raised her head. Then she waded slowly into the water.

He stood motionless as the small black figure walked slowly and deliberately towards the centre of the pond, very slowly, gradually moving deeper into the motionless water, and still moving forward as the water got up to her breast. Then he could see her no more in the dusk of the dead afternoon.   110

"There!" he exclaimed. "Would you believe it?"

And he hastened straight down, running over the wet, soddened fields, pushing through the hedges, down into the depression of callous wintry obscurity. It took him several minutes to come to the pond. He stood on the bank, breathing heavily. He could see nothing. His eyes seemed to penetrate the dead water. Yes, perhaps that was the dark shadow of her black clothing beneath the surface of the water.

He slowly ventured into the pond. The bottom was deep, soft clay, he sank in, and the water clasped dead cold round his legs. As he stirred he could smell the cold, rotten clay that fouled up into the water. It was objectionable in his lungs. Still, repelled and yet not heeding, he moved deeper into the pond. The cold water rose over his thighs, over his loins, upon his abdomen. The lower part of his body was all sunk in the hideous cold element. And the bottom was so deeply soft and uncertain, he was afraid of pitching with his mouth underneath. He could not swim, and was afraid.

He crouched a little, spreading his hands under the water and moving them round, trying to feel for her. The dead cold pond swayed upon his chest. He moved again, a little deeper, and again, with his hands underneath, he felt all around under the water. And he touched her clothing. But it evaded his fingers. He made a desperate effort to grasp it.

And so doing he lost his balance and went under, horribly, suffocating in the foul   115
earthy water, struggling madly for a few moments. At last, after what seemed an eternity, he got his footing, rose again into the air and looked around. He gasped, and knew he was in the world. Then he looked at the water. She had risen near him. He grasped her clothing, and drawing her nearer, turned to take his way to land again.

He went very slowly, carefully, absorbed in the slow progress. He rose higher, climbing out of the pond. The water was now only about his legs; he was thankful, full of relief to be out of the clutches of the pond. He lifted her and staggered on to the bank, out of the horror of wet, grey clay.

He laid her down on the bank. She was quite unconscious and running with water. He made the water come from her mouth, he worked to restore her. He did not have to work very long before he could feel the breathing begin again in her; she was breathing naturally. He worked a little longer. He could feel her live beneath his hands; she was coming back. He wiped her face, wrapped her in his overcoat, looked around into the dim, dark grey world, then lifted her and staggered down the bank and across the fields.

It seemed an unthinkably long way, and his burden, so heavy he felt he would never get to the house. But at last he was in the stable-yard, and then in the house-yard. He opened the door and went into the house. In the kitchen he laid her down on the hearth-rug and called. The house was empty. But the fire was burning in the grate.

Then again he kneeled to attend to her. She was breathing regularly, her eyes were wide open and as if conscious, but there seemed something missing in her look. She was conscious in herself, but unconscious of her surroundings.

He ran upstairs, took blankets from a bed, and put them before the fire to warm. 120
Then he removed her saturated, earthy-smelling clothing, rubbed her dry with a towel,
and wrapped her naked in the blankets. Then he went into the dining-room, to look for
spirits. There was a little whisky. He drank a gulp himself, and put some into her
mouth.

The effect was instantaneous. She looked full into his face, as if she had been seeing him for some time, and yet had only just become conscious of him.

"Dr. Fergusson?" she said.

"What?" he answered.

He was divesting himself of his coat, intending to find some dry clothing upstairs.
He could not bear the smell of the dead, clayey water, and he was mortally afraid for his
own health.

"What did I do?" she asked. 125

"Walked into the pond," he replied. He had begun to shudder like one sick, and
could hardly attend to her. Her eyes remained full on him, he seemed to be going dark
in his mind, looking back at her helplessly. The shuddering became quieter in him, his
life came back to him, dark and unknowing, but strong again.

"Was I out of my mind?" she asked, while her eyes were fixed on him all the time.

"Maybe, for the moment," he replied. He felt quiet, because his strength had
come back. The strange fretful strain had left him.

"Am I out of my mind now?" she asked.

"Are you?" he reflected a moment. "No," he answered truthfully, "I don't see that 130
you are." He turned his face aside. He was afraid now, because he felt dazed, and felt
dimly that her power was stronger than his, in this issue. And she continued to look at
him fixedly all the time. "Can you tell me where I shall find some dry things to put on?"
he asked.

"Did you dive into the pond for me?" she asked.

"No," he answered. "I walked in. But I went in overhead as well."

There was silence for a moment. He hesitated. He very much wanted to go upstairs to get into dry clothing. But there was another desire in him. And she seemed to
hold him. His will seemed to have gone to sleep, and left him, standing there slack before her. But he felt warm inside himself. He did not shudder at all, though his clothes
were sodden on him.

"Why did you?" she asked.

"Because I didn't want you to do such a foolish thing," he said. 135

"It wasn't foolish," she said, still gazing at him as she lay on the floor, with a sofa
cushion under her head. "It was the right thing to do. I knew best, then."

"I'll go and shift these wet things," he said. But still he had not the power to
move out of her presence, until she sent him. It was as if she had the life of his body in
her hands, and he could not extricate himself. Or perhaps he did not want to.

Suddenly she sat up. Then she became aware of her own immediate condition.
She felt the blankets about her, she knew her own limbs. For a moment it seemed as if
her reason were going. She looked round, with wild eye, as if seeking something. He
stood still with fear. She saw her clothing lying scattered.

"Who undressed me?" she asked, her eyes resting full and inevitable on his face.

"I did," he replied, "to bring you round." 140

For some moments she sat and gazed at him awfully, her lips parted.

"Do you love me, then?" she asked.

He only stood and stared at her, fascinated. His soul seemed to melt.

She shuffled forward on her knees, and put her arms round him, round his legs, as he stood there, pressing her breasts against his knees and thighs, clutching him with strange, convulsive certainty, pressing his thighs against her, drawing him to her face, her throat, as she looked up at him with flaring, humble eyes of transfiguration, triumphant in first possession.

"You love me," she murmured, in strange transport, yearning and triumphant and   145
confident. "You love me. I know you love me, I know."

And she was passionately kissing his knees, through the wet clothing, passionately and indiscriminately kissing his knees, his legs, as if unaware of everything.

He looked down at the tangled wet hair, the wild, bare, animal shoulders. He was amazed, bewildered, and afraid. He had never thought of loving her. He had never wanted to love her. When he rescued her and restored her, he was a doctor, and she was a patient. He had had no single personal thought of her. Nay, this introduction of the personal element was very distasteful to him, a violation of his professional honour. It was horrible to have her there embracing his knees. It was horrible. He revolted from it, violently. And yet—and yet—he had not the power to break away.

She looked at him again, with the same supplication of powerful love, and that same transcendent, frightening light of triumph. In view of the delicate flame which seemed to come from her face like a light, he was powerless. And yet he had never intended to love her. He had never intended. And something stubborn in him could not give way.

"You love me," she repeated, in a murmur of deep, rhapsodic assurance. "You love me."

Her hands were drawing him, drawing him down to her. He was afraid, even a lit-   150
tle horrified. For he had, really, no intention of loving her. Yet her hands were drawing him towards her. He put out his hand quickly to steady himself, and grasped her bare shoulder. A flame seemed to burn the hand that grasped her soft shoulder. He had no intention of loving her: his whole will was against his yielding. It was horrible. And yet wonderful was the touch of her shoulders, beautiful the shining of her face. Was she perhaps mad? He had a horror of yielding to her. Yet something in him ached also.

He had been staring away at the door, away from her. But his hand remained on her shoulder. She had gone suddenly very still. He looked down at her. Her eyes were now wide with fear, with doubt, the light was dying from her face, a shadow of terrible greyness was returning. He could not bear the touch of her eyes' question upon him, and the look of death behind the question.

With an inward groan he gave way, and let his heart yield towards her. A sudden gentle smile came on his face. And her eyes, which never left his face, slowly, slowly filled with tears. He watched the strange water rise in her eyes, like some slow fountain coming up. And his heart seemed to burn and melt away in his breast.

He could not bear to look at her any more. He dropped on his knees and caught her head with his arms and pressed her face against his throat. She was very still. His heart, which seemed to have broken, was burning with a kind of agony in his breast. And he felt her slow, hot tears wetting his throat. But he could not move.

He felt the hot tears wet his neck and the hollows of his neck, and he remained motionless, suspended through one of man's eternities. Only now it had become indispensable to him to have her face pressed close to him; he could never let her go again. He could never let her head go away from the close clutch of his arm. He wanted to remain like that for ever, with his heart hurting him in a pain that was also life to him. Without knowing, he was looking down on her damp, soft brown hair.

Then, as it were suddenly, he smelt the horrid stagnant smell of that water. And at the same moment she drew away from him and looked at him. Her eyes were wistful and unfathomable. He was afraid of them, and he fell to kissing her, not knowing what he was doing. He wanted her eyes not to have that terrible, wistful, unfathomable look.

When she turned her face to him again, a faint delicate flush was glowing, and there was again dawning that terrible shining of joy in her eyes, which really terrified him, and yet which he now wanted to see, because he feared the look of doubt still more.

"You love me?" she said, rather faltering.

"Yes." The word cost him a painful effort. Not because it wasn't true. But because it was too newly true, the *saying* seemed to tear open again his newly-torn heart. And he hardly wanted it to be true, even now.

She lifted her face to him, and he bent forward and kissed her on the mouth, gently, with the one kiss that is an eternal pledge. And as he kissed her his heart strained again in his breast. He never intended to love her. But now it was over. He had crossed over the gulf to her, and all that he had left behind had shrivelled and became void.

After the kiss, her eyes again slowly filled with tears. She sat still, away from him, with her face drooped aside, and her hands folded in her lap. The tears fell very slowly. There was complete silence. He too sat there motionless and silent on the hearth-rug. The strange pain of his heart that was broken seemed to consume him. That he should love her? That this was love! That he should be ripped open in this way! Him, a doctor! How they would all jeer if they knew! It was agony to him to think they might know.

In the curious naked pain of the thought he looked again to her. She was sitting there drooped into a muse. He saw a tear fall, and his heart flared hot. He saw for the first time that one of her shoulders was quite uncovered, one arm bare, he could see one of her small breasts; dimly, because it had become almost dark in the room.

"Why are you crying?" he asked, in an altered voice.

She looked up at him, and behind her tears the consciousness of her situation for the first time brought a dark look of shame to her eyes.

"I'm not crying, really," she said, watching him, half frightened.

He reached his hand, and softly closed it on her bare arm.

"I love you! I love you!" he said in a soft, low vibrating voice, unlike himself.

She shrank, and dropped her head. The soft, penetrating grip of his hand on her arm distressed her. She looked up at him.

"I want to go," she said. "I want to go and get you some dry things."

"Why?" he said. "I'm all right."

"But I want to go," she said. "And I want you to change your things."

He released her arm, and she wrapped herself in the blanket, looking at him rather frightened. And still she did not rise.

"Kiss me," she said wistfully.

He kissed her, but briefly, half in anger.

Then, after a second, she rose nervously, all mixed up in the blanket. He watched her in her confusion as she tried to extricate herself and wrap herself up so that she could walk. He watched her relentlessly, as she knew. And as she went, the blanket trailing, and as he saw a glimpse of her feet and her white leg, he tried to remember her as she was when he had wrapped her in the blanket. But then he didn't want to remember, because she had been nothing to him then, and his nature revolted from remembering her as she was when she was nothing to him.

A tumbling, muffled noise from within the dark house startled him. Then he   175
heard her voice: "There are clothes." He rose and went to the foot of the stairs, and gathered up the garments she had thrown down. Then he came back to the fire, to rub himself down and dress. He grinned at his own appearance when he had finished.

The fire was sinking, so he put on coal. The house was now quite dark, save for the light of a street-lamp that shone in faintly from beyond the holly trees. He lit the gas with matches he found on the mantelpiece. Then he emptied the pockets of his own clothes, and threw all his wet things in a heap in the scullery. After which he gathered up her sodden clothes, gently, and put them in a separate heap on the coppertop in the scullery.

It was six o'clock on the clock. His own watch had stopped. He ought to go back to the surgery. He waited, and still she did not come down. So he went to the foot of the stairs and called:

"I shall have to go."

Almost immediately he heard her coming down. She had on her best dress of black voile, and her hair was tidy, but still damp. She looked at him—and in spite of herself, smiled.

"I don't like you in those clothes," she said.   180

"Do I look a sight?" he answered.

They were shy of one another.

"I'll make you some tea," she said.

"No, I must go."

"Must you?" And she looked at him again with the wide, strained, doubtful eyes.   185
And again, from the pain of his breast, he knew how he loved her. He went and bent to kiss her, gently, passionately, with his heart's painful kiss.

"And my hair smells so horrible," she murmured in distraction. "And I'm so awful, I'm so awful! Oh no, I'm too awful." And she broke into bitter, heartbroken sobbing. "You can't want to love me, I'm horrible."

"Don't be silly, don't be silly," he said, trying to comfort her, kissing her, holding her in his arms. "I want you, I want to marry you, we're going to be married, quickly, quickly—to-morrow if I can."

But she only sobbed terribly, and cried:

"I feel awful. I feel awful. I feel I'm horrible to you."

"No, I want you, I want you," was all he answered, blindly, with that terrible in-   190
tonation which frightened her almost more than her horror lest he should *not* want her.

Questions for Your Analysis of "The Horse Dealer's Daughter"

1) What are some of your early impressions of the story? What is the most striking incident of the story, something that promotes an instant reaction in you?

2) This story is told in the third-person. What is your instinctive response to the form of the narration? Do you find the narrator very sympathetic to the major characters?

3) What are your observations of the narrator's preoccupation with the fate of the Pervin family?

4) At what point in the narrative does the narrator's focus on Mabel become apparent?

5) Is there something from your personal experience that assists you in relating to any of the characters in the story?

6) Much of the story is concerned with the encounter between the Mabel and Dr. Jack Fergusson. (There are also encounters among the Pervin brothers and other characters.) What do these encounters reveal about the characters, especially about Mabel and Jack?

7) What does the story say about English family life in the 1920s?

8) What experiences has the author had that may have shaped this story? (This narrative is not the only story that D. H. Lawrence has written about struggling families.)

9) Why have economic conditions changed for the Pervin family? What are some of the personal effects of their economic experiences?

10) Mabel Pervin is clearly a suffering character before she encounters Dr. Fergusson. Her life changes dramatically when they experience love for each other. What is it about his personal character (or culture) that inspires changes in Mabel?

11) By the end of the story, "love" has become a major issue. What does Mabel's hesitation to accept Jack's proposal say about her feelings toward herself?

12) In what ways has the story examined the personal cultures of the characters as a result of the culture (economic and social) of the time?

STEPS IN WRITING A CULTURAL ESSAY ABOUT ANY READING

1) Write down your impressions of key moments or settings in the story or poem that illustrate cultural contexts.

2) Identify central characters and examine the contexts within which they exist. These contexts would include their background, their relations with others, and the historical setting of the story.

3) Consider events in the author's life that may have influenced elements in the work.

4) Examine cultural representations in the work. These would include values that are held by characters, social customs, and economic contexts.

5) Detail any cultural changes that take place in the work.

6) Compare your cultural values with those in the work. Identify areas in which your cultural experiences are significantly different from the work's perspectives.

7) A good general electronic source to investigate the context of any literary reading is google.com. By typing in the title of the work, especially if it is a well-known literary work, you will locate several sources that provide background information.

STEPS IN WRITING AN ESSAY ABOUT "THE HORSE-DEALER'S DAUGHTER"

Brainstorming Your Topic

1) Identify those elements in the text (character, plot, theme, metaphor) that prompt an immediate response from you. Write down whatever impressions you have.
2) Focus on the main characters, Mabel Pervin and Jack Fergusson. What is it about them that you do or do not like? Identify their personal traits before and after their encounter.
3) The narrator's portrait of the Pervin family is one of deterioration, as the family falls into ruin and literally dissolves. What is your reaction to the disintegration of the Pervins?
4) What personal experiences have you had that connect to parts of "The Horse Dealer's Daughter"? Have you ever encountered someone who led you to new insights about yourself as a result of one encounter?
5) Why is the narrator so emphatic on the importance of love and how Mabel responds to it?
6) The story contains references to the past lives of all of the characters, with particular emphasis on the fact that the family's fortunes have fallen. Write down what effect(s) these references to the past have on you.
7) Love plays a role in the story. How does this emphasis affect your interpretive reaction?
8) Are you satisfied with the ending? Why or why not?
9) What does the narrative show that suggests a change in cultural perspectives, especially in Mabel and Jack?
10) Unless your instructor insists that you not consult outside sources in brainstorming your topic, refer to the electronic sources listed for D. H. Lawrence. There are many good links that will connect you to biographical sources and detailed criticism. Any ideas and words drawn directly from outside sources should be properly cited, of course. Consult the appendix for documentation procedures.

Creating an Outline

1) Collect your answers to the questions above in short two-word or three-word categories and use them as preliminary "writing points."
2) Think about the points and consider whether they add up to a central idea (for example, cultural representations in "The Horse Dealer's Daughter").
3) Identify five or six main writing points that support your central idea. These points should come from the main literary elements in the story (character, plot, theme, point of view, metaphor). All of the points should provide support for your controlling idea. A good stating place is to examine the story's cultural context, the personal experiences of the author, and the cultural representations of the main characters.
4) If you have more than five or six points, try to combine one or more of them. If you have fewer than five or six points, see if some of them can be used to generate

additional points. You may have some large points that include smaller issues that can stand alone as paragraph topic sentences.

5) Look for transitional devices that connect your main points of support, particularly as they connect various encounters in the story.

Preparing a Rough Draft

1) Now that you have created a working outline, you have already completed your major organizational work. Each major point is the topic of a paragraph and your essay will have between 5 and 10 paragraphs, depending on development. These paragraphs need not be of equal length, but each one should sufficiently develop the topic sentence.

2) Now that you have your major writing points, assemble a preliminary draft by developing each topic idea with two or three sentences that discuss evidence from the text.

3) Focus on developing transitions between your paragraphs. Professional writers often begin a new paragraph with a direct reference to an idea expressed at the end of the preceding paragraph.

4) It is not too early to begin writing your concluding paragraph. Conclusions often summarize the main points of a central idea (but do not repeat word for word what has already been said). A conclusion may also refer to implications of what has been said (but what cannot be developed because of space limits). Your conclusion must examine cultural issues in the story.

5) Don't be afraid to include questions in your writing. No reader of literature can ever be absolutely certain of every observation that he or she makes, and perceptive observations often generate excellent questions, many of which are useful, even if unanswerable.

Editing Your Draft

1) At this stage, you should have a draft of a few hundred words. You have already done the most difficult work in thinking out your ideas, organizing them into an outline, and preparing a rough version of the final product. Look for ways to edit your paper that will strengthen the essay.

2) Search for repetitious wording (and ideas). Do not repeat ideas, however important, throughout the essay. Use a thesaurus to locate synonyms for terms and ideas that reappear. Attempt to emphasize variety in your language.

3) If your instructor encourages peer editing, choose someone in your class, or perhaps a roommate, and solicit advice about how your essay reads. Is it articulate, compelling, insightful, and interesting? (All of these qualities are important.) Although your peer editor may not be taking a literature class, he or she may be a very good source of feedback on how effective your writing is. Professional writers often seek feedback from peers, not only from professional colleagues.

4) Be open to make changes in your writing, both conceptually and in specific language. Professional writers know that writing is recursive (which means that the act of writing constantly generates new ways of looking at the topic), and student writers should also take advantage of changes in thinking *as they write*. Don't be

afraid to make efficient and effective changes, especially in terms of cutting out words, phrases, and sections that may not be working very well in supporting your overall idea.

5) Proofread carefully for spelling errors, punctuation problems, run-on sentences, and ambiguous or awkward constructions. You should use a solid grammar hand-book to assist you in these areas.

Final Checklist

1) Make sure that your central idea (sometimes called a thesis statement) appears in the first paragraph. It is important that your reader know what major point(s) you are attempting to make.

2) Because this essay is a cultural investigation, check to see that the essay represents your analysis of ethical issues in the story. Your major points should be understandable, of course, to the community of readers to which you are writing.

3) Examine your essay for sufficient evidence. Each one of your major ideas will need illustration that comes from the text.

4) Review your conclusion to see if you have ended the essay in an effective manner, either summarizing what you have said (in different language) or suggesting some important implications of your reading.

5) Proofread one last time for errors, repetitious language, and awkward phrasing.

A SAMPLE READING

"Helen" by Hilda Doolittle (HD) (1886–1961)

All Greece hates
the still eyes in the white face,
the lustre as of olives
where she stands,
and the white hands.   5

All Greece reviles
the wan face when she smiles,
hating it deeper still
when it grows wan and white,
remembering past enchantments   10
and past ills.

Greece sees unmoved,
God's daughter, born of love,
the beauty of cool feet
and slenderest knees,   15
could love indeed the maid,
only if she were laid,
white ash amid funereal cypresses.

Questions for Analyzing "Helen"

1) Write down key terms, being careful to define them and write down possible connotations. (You might begin with some of these words: "lustre," "reviles," "wan," "enchantments," "cypresses.")
2) Consider key moments in the poem. (For example: Your reaction to the speaker's personification of Greece and what the people feel about Helen.)
3) Describe your impressions of the tone of the poem and how the poem changes, if it does. (For example: Consider the effect of strong verbs such as "hates" and "reviles.")
4) Examine possible themes in the poem. (For example: What are the effects of Helen's enchantment and past ills?)
5) Indicate key metaphors and images that appear, noting how they relate to one or more themes. (For example: "God's daughter," "white face," "cool feet," "maid," "funeral cypresses.")
6) Focus on the main character, Helen. Write down your impressions of what she meant to the Greeks.
7) The speaker describes the deep emotion generated by a real historical figure. Why was Helen so important to Greek culture?
8) What personal experiences have you had that connect you to "Helen"?
9) Are you satisfied with the ending, which contains a complex "only if" construction? Why or why not? What are the cultural implications?

ELECTRONIC RESOURCES FOR JACK LONDON

http://www.jack-london.org/. This Web site is maintained and developed by a group of German Jack London afficionados and experts, along with direct descendants of Jack London and other members of Jack London's family.
http://www.jacklondon.com/. General information on Jack London.
http://london.centenary.edu/. Contains a bibliography on works about Jack London.
http://www.getyourwordsworth.com/WORDSWORTH-JackLondon.html. An overview of the life of Jack London.
http://edwcb.sdsu.edu/courses/EDTEC572/final_projects/JL_Pages/Jack_London.html. Jack London's philosophy and stories.

ELECTRONIC RESOURCES FOR D. H. LAWRENCE

http://www.utexas.edu/research/dhlr/. The home page for the official review devoted to D. H. Lawrence.
http://www.utexas.edu/research/dhlr/. Contains many useful links to information about D. H. Lawrence.
http://mss.library.nottingham.ac.uk/dhlbiog-contents.html. Biographical information on D. H. Lawrence.
http://www.eastwood.co.uk/frontier/dhl/dhl_home.htm. The D. H. Lawrence home page.

Further Readings in Cultural Criticism

Brook, Thomas. "The Historical Necessity for—and Difficulties with—New Historical Analysis in Introductory Literature Courses." *College English* 49 (1987): 509–22.

Foucault, Michel. *The Foucault Reader*. Paul Rabinow, ed. New York: Pantheon, 1984.

Greenblatt, Stephen. "The Politics of Culture." In *Falling Into Theory: Conflicting Views of Reading Literature*. Ed. David Richter. Boston: St. Martin's Press, 1994: 288–90.

Jauss, Hans Robert. *Aesthetic Experience and Literary Hermeneutics*. Minneapolis: U of Minnesota, 1982.

Patterson, Annabel. "Historical Scholarship." In *An Introduction to Scholarship in Modern Languages and Literatures*. Ed. Joseph Gibaldi. 2nd ed. New York: MLA, 1992: 183–200.

Rosenblatt, Louise M. "Towards a Transactional Theory of Reading." *Journal of Reading Behavior* 1 (1969): 31–47.

chapter 7

Feminist Criticism

Joyce Y. Karpay

Feminist literary criticism differs from other theoretical approaches to literature in that it springs from a feminist social movement with a significant political history. Although feminism has developed into a field of thought encompassing varied and even contradictory concerns, most feminists believe that we live in a patriarchal society—a place where men have historically controlled cultural, social, and economic institutions. Many feminists argue that the rigid gender separations that result from patriarchal institutions oppress both men and women and require all of us to fulfill restrictive cultural expectations. Feminist literary critics look at how patriarchal structures are reflected in literature and analyze how structures based on dominance and submission affect all aspects of our lives: our economic situations, our psychological and physical well-being, and our interpersonal relationships. A feminist critic will look carefully at a text and critique social institutions and traditions such as marriage, motherhood, and the beauty culture. A feminist critic may also question the effects public institutions (such as the educational system, the corporate world, and the medical profession) have on both men and women.

Recent literary critics look at how even our system of language provides advantages for men and disadvantages for women, and some feminists investigate the importance of this sexual difference. These feminist scholars examine to what extent the style of women's writing (as well as the topics women choose to write about) differs from the writing of men and strive to determine ways in which women can (1) become aware of these discrepancies, (2) discover a distinctively feminine voice, and (3) find ways to articulate a specifically feminine voice.

In the second half of the twentieth century, feminist literary critics recovered texts written by women and provided new readings of the male-authored texts that were already being studied on college campuses. Feminist scholars' insistence on the importance of women writers such as Jane Austen, Emily and Charlotte Brontë, Kate Chopin, and others had an enormous effect on what was considered the "canon" of literature—that body of work viewed as the "best" and the most influential in our literary tradition. This increased interest in women's writing coincided with a growing recognition among cultural critics and historians that the public and the private spheres are not two distinct areas within any culture. In fact, feminists increasingly declare that "the personal is political." Historical critics, emphasizing a "new" way of reading history, became interested not only in public history—war, politics, the society of the dominant class—but in the historical significance of private lives. The personal lives of women (and other social groups previously neglected by historians) are now more actively investigated. Women's personal lives are recognized as not only vibrant and interesting, but important in understanding our cultural tradition. While the addition of women writers to university studies was certainly an important step in recovering women's cultural heritage, minority feminists have noted that racial, class, and sexual exclusions remain and that the selection of texts by scholars too often replicates the cultural prejudices of our society. Fortunately, feminist critical practice on most college campuses has acknowledged its deficiencies and expanded to become an even richer cultural critique that includes a vast collection of writers—minority writers, heterosexual and homosexual writers, and writers representing a diversity of class positions.

Feminist critics look at the images of women in culture and evaluate cultural expectations as they relate to gender—the effect that living in a system of dominance and submission has on both men and women—and ask questions such as: Where do we find evidence of subversion within these patriarchal systems? What outdated stereotypes remain in our society regarding women? In literature, are male characters allowed complexity and humanity while female characters are faced with limited options, trapped within stereotypic notions of what it means to be a woman? Are women still restricted to a virgin/whore dichotomy—still defined as either "good" or "bad" girls? Do certain texts perpetuate notions that women must live up to unattainable ideals, oversimplified representations that do not accurately reflect the complexity of most women? Do these inadequate representations perpetuate women's oppression? Do certain texts, or specific characters within a text, subvert cultural expectations as well as patriarchal structures, where women remain secondary?

In looking at literature we can ask, in what ways are feminine cultural stereotypes repeated by the author? In the powerful nineteenth-century novel *Jane Eyre*, does Charlotte Brontë merely provide the image of a passive, obedient governess? Or, does Jane demonstrate a courage and independence rarely associated with young women of the time? In the character of Emma (recently reinterpreted by Amy Heckerling as Cher in *Clueless*), does Jane Austen present a dutiful daughter or a fully developed, even flawed, heroine unusual to eighteenth-century literature? In what ways are traditional stereotypes subverted? Moreover, since all texts written by women are not feminist texts, gender subversion can be located in many texts authored by men. Numerous scholars have noted that Shakespeare's heroines are often vibrant, opinionated, and outspoken. In Shakespeare's *The Merchant of Venice*, critics have noted that it is Portia who "controls" the action of the play, and in *Antony and Cleopatra*, it is Cleopatra who is shown most magnificently on stage. In presenting characters that subvert a social system based on hierarchy, is Shakespeare commenting on gender politics between fathers and daughters, husbands and wives? Is he critiquing traditional gender roles? Does his critique broaden and include political commentary?

Equality and the material conditions of women also remain a focus of feminist thought. Mary Wollstonecraft and John Stuart Mill, in the eighteenth and nineteenth centuries respectively, both discussed the connection between women's economic reality and their personal well-being. In the early part of the twentieth century, Virginia Woolf showed concern not only for modern narrative style but for the economic conditions of women. In *A Room of One's Own*, Woolf points out that the intellectual freedom necessary to create art depends on the material conditions of women. Artistry does not depend on brilliance alone but, as Woolf emphasizes, requires an adequate work environment. A woman must have decent food, a decent education, access to some financial means, and a room of her own (elements of professional life that many men have taken for granted) in order to produce art. Within this tradition, feminist literary critics ask themselves: In what ways do economics effect the various characters in a text? To what extent are characters' choices in a story determined by their economic situation? A feminist critic working within the Marxist tradition may approach a text as a product of a specific culture and determine in what ways the text reproduces and/or resists the religious or cultural beliefs of a specific society. For example, "The Short Happy Life of Francis Macomber" by Ernest Hemingway is the story of rich Americans on safari in Africa. Is Hemingway commenting on the effect Western culture, a culture driven by capitalism, has on other cultures? Does the "moneyed lifestyle" of people like Francis and Margaret Macomber impact life in Africa? Is this a negative or a positive impact? What impact does American culture and its expectations have on gender relations or marital relations?

Feminist interpreters of literature also locate structures of dominance and oppression within society in less obvious places. Leslie Marmon Silko's "Yellow Woman" is both a story about the tradition of storytelling *and* an examination of the profound effects of government policy on individual lives. While Ernest Hemingway's "Indian Camp" (a story in this collection) chronicles a young man's observations of the medical profession and his father's practice of medicine, it also exposes a world troubled with racial and sexual bigotry. Kate Chopin's "The Story of an Hour" certainly provides insight into the Mallard marriage, but it also reveals how easily our cultural expectations lead us to misinterpret the actions of others.

Feminists who work within the tradition of French feminist theory view equality, although a worthwhile goal, as unattainable given that the very language we use is a structure embedded with assumptions that exclude women. French feminists argue that—whether culturally created or not—women experience the world differently from men. Thus, women must learn to speak and write from this difference. French feminists attempt to recognize and perpetuate a practice of women's writing (a practice that has become known as *écriture feminine*) that relates more closely to feminine sexuality and women's cultural experience than to masculine sexuality and patriarchal definitions of society. French feminists note a difference in the writing style of women—"feminine" writing is more fluid and often lacks the formal mastery and structure of male texts. Other critics have noted that within women's writings, a different culture is revealed—a culture with a different sense of community, a different approach to emotion, and a different relationship with language. Women's writing may reveal interruptions, a lack of closure, and at times, characters that have difficulty articulating meaning. A French feminist critic of literature may be attracted to obscure rather than traditionally straightforward texts and will investigate the fluid nature of the prose, omissions that exist in the text, and/or the difficulties that characters have accessing language (and any critical limitations that result from such difficulties). A feminist critic working within this tradition looks beyond the exclusionary nature of sexist language (mankind, chairman, and so forth) and looks at how female characters in literature are unable to complete their thoughts or find the words to explain their situation. These critics may also look at how the language used by female characters in the text differs from the language used by male characters. A critic concerned with language may look closely at the narrator's sensual observations in "Yellow Woman" and her unwillingness or inability to provide concrete assessments of her situation.

Feminism has developed into a vibrant, varied, and rich critique—a critique that frequently overlaps with other critical approaches such as New Historicism, Marxism, psychoanalytic criticism, and African American studies. Feminist criticism has also expanded its critique of men in our culture. Feminists ask questions such as: What does it mean to be a man or a woman in our society? Do inherently feminine or masculine traits even exist? If what it means to be a woman or to be a man shifts through time—and from one society to another—are these traits culturally constructed? Feminists and feminist thought are often divided into categories: liberal, cultural, or radical feminism; Anglo-American feminism; or French feminism. Although these categories are used in an effort to understand shifts in thought and political alliances, they never remain distinct or unalterable. The tradition of feminist literary criticism offers a variety of critical and theoretical approaches that help critics analyze gender expectations, gender relations, and gender constructions in our society. Because feminist criticism is so diverse, no definitive feminist approach to literature exists. Feminist criticism remains open to individual interpretation; however, here are a few suggestions for developing a feminist approach to literature:

1. Read the work at least twice and consider the context of the story. In what culture do the characters find themselves? In what ways do they adhere to traditional notions of masculine or feminine behavior? In what ways do they subvert these traditional modes of behavior?

2. Do any of the characters appear stifled or oppressed because of society's expectations? Are these expectations specific to one gender?

3. Is this a story about gender relations? Does tension seem to exist between the characters based on gender?

4. How are the characters economically, psychologically, or physically situated?

5. Does their economic situation, mental well-being, or health relate in any way to their gender?

6. Is there an apparent (or subtle) difference in the language used by female characters? Do they demonstrate a different access to language?

As a feminist reader, you can develop your own approach to gender issues within a text. Following "Yellow Woman" is a series of strategies designed to assist you in sharpening your reading and writing skills.

A SAMPLE READING

"Yellow Woman" by Leslie Marmon Silko (1948–)

I

My thigh clung to his with dampness, and I watched the sun rising up through the tamaracks and willows. The small brown water birds came to the river and hopped across the mud, leaving brown scratches in the alkali-white crust. They bathed in the river silently. I could hear the water, almost at our feet where the narrow fast channel bubbled and washed green ragged moss and fern leaves. I looked at him beside me, rolled in the red blanket on the white river sand. I cleaned the sand out of the cracks between my toes, squinting because the sun was above the willow trees. I looked at him for the last time, sleeping on the white river sand.

I felt hungry and followed the river south the way we had come the afternoon before, following our footprints that were already blurred by lizard tracks and bug trails. The horses were still lying down, and the black one whinnied when he saw me but he did not get up—maybe it was because the corral was made out of thick cedar branches and the horses had not yet felt the sun like I had. I tried to look beyond the pale red mesas to the pueblo. I knew it was there, even if I could not see it, on the sandrock hill above the river, the same river that moved past me now and had reflected the moon last night.

The horse felt warm underneath me. He shook his head and pawed the sand. The bay whinnied and leaned against the gate trying to follow, and I remembered him asleep in the red blanket beside the river. I slid off the horse and tied him close to the other horse. I walked north with the river again, and the white sand broke loose in footprints over footprints.

"Wake up."

He moved in the blanket and turned his face to me with his eyes still closed. I   5
knelt down to touch him.

"I'm leaving."

He smiled now, eyes still closed. "You are coming with me, remember?" He sat up now with his bare dark chest and belly in the sun.

"Where?"

"To my place."

"And will I come back?"   10

He pulled his pants on. I walked away from him, feeling him behind me and smelling the willows.

"Yellow Woman," he said.

I turned to face him. "Who are you?" I asked.

He laughed and knelt on the low, sandy bank, washing his face in the river. "Last night you guessed my name, and you knew why I had come."

I stared past him at the shallow moving water and tried to remember the night,   15
but I could only see the moon in the water and remember his warmth around me.

"But I only said that you were him and that I was Yellow Woman—I'm not really her—I have my own name and I come from the pueblo on the other side of the mesa. Your name is Silva and you are a stranger I met by the river yesterday afternoon."

He laughed softly. "What happened yesterday has nothing to do with what you will do today, Yellow Woman."

"I know—that's what I'm saying—the old stories about the ka'tsina spirit and Yellow Woman can't mean us."

My old grandpa liked to tell those stories best. There is one about Badger and Coyote who went hunting and were gone all day, and when the sun was going down they found a house. There was a girl living there alone, and she had light hair and eyes and she told them that they could sleep with her. Coyote wanted to be with her all night so he sent Badger into a prairie-dog hole, telling him he thought he saw something in it. As soon as Badger crawled in, Coyote blocked up the entrance with rocks and hurried back to Yellow Woman.

"Come here," he said gently.   20

He touched my neck and I moved close to him to feel his breathing and to hear his heart. I was wondering if Yellow Woman had known who she was—if she knew that she would become part of the stories. Maybe she'd had another name that her husband and relatives called her so that only the ka'tsina from the north and the storytellers would know her as Yellow Woman. But I didn't go on; I felt him all around me, pushing me down into the white river sand.

Yellow Woman went away with the spirit from the north and lived with him and his relatives. She was gone for a long time, but then one day she came back and she brought twin boys.

"Do you know the story?"

"What story?" He smiled and pulled me close to him as he said this. I was afraid lying there on the red blanket. All I could know was the way he felt, warm, damp, his body beside me. This is the way it happens in the stories. I was thinking, with no thought beyond the moment she meets the ka'tsina spirit and they go.

"I don't have to go. What they tell in stories was real only then, back in time immemorial, like they say."   25

He stood up and pointed at my clothes tangled in the blanket. "Let's go," he said.

I walked beside him, breathing hard because he walked fast, his hand around my wrist. I had stopped trying to pull away from him, because his hand felt cool and the sun was high, drying the river bed into alkali. I will see someone, eventually I will see someone, and then I will be certain that he is only a man—some man from nearby—and I will be sure that I am not Yellow Woman. Because she is from out of time past and I live now and I've been to school and there are highways and pickup trucks that Yellow Woman never saw.

It was an easy ride north on horseback. I watched the change from the cottonwood trees along the river to the junipers that brushed past us in the foothills, and finally there were only pinons, and when I looked up at the rim of the mountain plateau I could see pine trees growing on the edge. Once I stopped to look down, but the pale sandstone had disappeared and the river was gone and the dark lava hills were all around. He touched my hand, not speaking, but always singing softly a mountain song and looking into my eyes.

I felt hungry and wondered what they were doing at home now—my mother, my grandmother, my husband, and the baby. Cooking breakfast, saying, "Where did she go?—maybe kidnapped," and Al going to the tribal police with the details: "She went walking along the river."

The house was made with black lava rock and red mud. It was high above the spreading miles of arroyos and long mesas. I smelled a mountain smell of pitch and buck brush. I stood there beside the black horse, looking down on the small, dim country we had passed, and I shivered.   30

"Yellow Woman, come inside where it's warm."

II

He lit a fire in the stove. It was an old stove with a round belly and an enamel coffeepot on top. There was only the stove, some faded Navajo blankets, and a bedroll and cardboard box. The floor was made of smooth adobe plaster, and there was one small window facing east. He pointed at the box.

"There's some potatoes and the frying pan." He sat on the floor with his arms around his knees pulling them close to his chest and he watched me fry the potatoes. I didn't mind him watching me because he was always watching me—he had been watching me since I came upon him sitting on the river bank trimming leaves from a willow twig with his knife. We ate from the pan and he wiped the grease from his fingers on his Levis.

"Have you brought women here before?" He smiled and kept chewing, so I said, "Do you always use the same tricks?"

"What tricks?" He looked at me like he didn't understand.   35

"The story about being a ka'tsina from the mountains. The story about Yellow Woman."

Silva was silent; his face was clam.

"I don't believe it. Those stories couldn't happen now," I said.

He shook his head and said softly, "But someday they will talk about us, and they will say, '"Those two lived long ago when things like that happened."'"

He stood up and went out. I ate the rest of the potatoes and thought about things—about the noise the stove was making and the sound of the mountain wind outside. I remembered yesterday and the day before, and then I went outside.   40

I walked past the corral to the edge where the narrow trail cut through the black rim rock. I was standing in the sky with nothing around me but the wind that came down from the blue mountain peak behind me. I could see faint mountain images in the distance miles across the vast spread of mesas and valleys and plains. I wondered who was over there to feel the mountain wind on those sheer blue edges—who walks on the pine needles in those blue mountains.

"Can you see the pueblo?" Silva was standing behind me.

I shook my head. "We're too far away."

"From here I can see the world." He stepped out on the edge. "The Navajo reservation begins over there." He pointed to the east. "The Pueblo boundaries are over here." He looked below us to the south, where the narrow trail seemed to come from. "The Texans have their ranches over there, starting with that valley, the Concho Valley. The Mexicans run some cattle over there too."

"Do you ever work for them?"   45

"I steal from them," Silva answered. The sun was dropping behind us and the shadows were filling the land below. I turned away from the edge that dropped forever into the valleys below.

"I'm cold," I said; "I'm going inside." I started wondering about this man who could speak the Pueblo language so well but who lived on a mountain and rustled cattle. I decided that this man Silva must be Navajo, because Pueblo men didn't do things like that.

"You must be a Navajo."

Silva shook his head gently. "Little Yellow Woman," he said, "you never give up, do you? I have told you who I am. The Navajo people know me, too." He knelt down and unrolled the bedroll and spread the extra blankets out on a piece of canvas. The sun was down, and the only light in the house came from outside—the dim orange light from sundown.

I stood there and waited for him to crawl under the blankets.   50

"What are you waiting for?" he said, and I lay down beside him. He undressed me slowly like the night before beside the river—kissing my face gently and running his hands up and down my belly and legs. He took off my pants and then he laughed.

"Why are you laughing?"

"You are breathing so hard."

I pulled away from him and turned my back to him.

He pulled me around and pinned me down with his arms and chest. "You don't   55
understand, do you, little Yellow Woman? You will do what I want."

And again he was all around me with his skin slippery against mine, and I was afraid because I understood that his strength could hurt me. I lay underneath him and I knew that he could destroy me. But later, while he slept beside me, I touched his face and I had a feeling—the kind of feeling for him that overcame me that morning along the river. I kissed him on the forehead and he reached out for me.

When I woke up in the morning he was gone. It gave me a strange feeling because for a long time I sat there on the blankets and looked around the little house for some object of his—some proof that he had been there or maybe that he was coming back. Only the blankets and the cardboard box remained. The .30-30 that had been leaning in the corner was gone, and so was the knife I had used the night before. He was gone, and I had my chance to go now. But first I had to eat, because I knew it would be a long walk home.

I found some dried apricots in the cardboard box, and I sat down on a rock at the edge of the plateau rim. There was no wind and the sun warmed me. I was surrounded by silence. I drowsed with apricots in my mouth, and I didn't believe that there were highways or railroads or cattle to steal.

When I woke up, I stared down at my feet in the black mountain dirt. Little black ants were swarming over the pine needles around my foot. They must have smelled the apricots. I thought about my family far below me. They would be wondering about me, because this had never happened to me before. The tribal police would file a report. But if old Grandpa weren't dead he would tell them what happened—he would laugh and say, "Stolen by a ka'tsina, a mountain spirit. She'll come home—they usually do." There are enough of them to handle things. My mother and grandmother will raise the baby like they raised me. Al will find someone else, and they will go on like before, except that there will be a story about the day I disappeared while I was walking along the river. Silva had come for me; he said he had. I did not decide to go. I just went. Moonflowers blossom in the sand hills before dawn, just as I followed him. That's what I was thinking as I wandered along the trail through the pine trees.

It was noon when I got back. When I saw the stone house I remembered that I   60
had meant to go home. But that didn't seem important any more, maybe because there were little blue flowers growing in the meadow behind the stone house and the gray squirrels were playing in the pines next to the house. The horses were standing in the corral, and there was a beef carcass hanging on the shady side of a big pine in front of the house. Flies buzzed around the clotted blood that hung from the carcass. Silva was washing his hands in a bucket full of water. He must have heard me coming because he spoke to me without turning to face me.

"I've been waiting for you."

"I went walking in the big pine trees."

I looked into the bucket full of bloody water with brown-and-white animal hairs floating in it. Silva stood there letting his hand drip, examining me intently.

"Are you coming with me?"

"Where?" I asked him.   65

"To sell the meat in Marquez."

"If you're sure it's O.K."

"I wouldn't ask you if it wasn't," he answered.

He sloshed the water around in the bucket before he dumped it out and set the bucket upside down near the door. I followed him to the corral and watched him saddle the horses. Even beside the horses he looked tall, and I asked him again if he wasn't Navajo. He didn't say anything; he just shook his head and kept cinching up the saddle.

"But Navajos are tall." 70
"Get on the horse," he said, "and let's go."

The last thing he did before we started down the steep trail was to grab the .30-30 from the corner. He slid the rifle into the scabbard that hung from his saddle.

"Do they ever try to catch you?" I asked.

"They don't know who I am."

"Then why did you bring the rifle?" 75

"Because we are going to Marquez where the Mexicans live."

III

The trail leveled out on a narrow ridge that was steep on both sides like an animal spine. On one side I could see where the trail went around the rocky gray hills and disappeared into the southeast where the pale sandrock mesas stood in the distance near my home. On the other side was a trail that went west, and as I looked far into the distance I thought I saw the little town. But Silva said no, that I was looking in the wrong place, that I just thought I saw houses. After that I quit looking off into the distance; it was hot and the wildflowers were closing up their deep-yellow petals. Only the waxy cactus flowers bloomed in the bright sun, and I saw every color that a cactus blossom can be; the white ones and the red ones were still buds, but the purple and the yellow were blossoms, open full and the most beautiful of all.

Silva saw him before I did. The white man was riding a big gray horse, coming up the trail toward us. He was traveling fast and the gray horse's feet sent rocks rolling off the trail into the dry tumbleweeds. Silva motioned for me to stop and we watched the white man. He didn't see us right away, but finally his horse whinnied at our horses and he stopped. He looked at us briefly before he loped the gray horse across the three hundred yards that separated us. He stopped his horse in front of Silva, and his young fat face was shadowed by the brim of his hat. He didn't look mad, but his small, pale eyes moved from the blood-soaked gunny sacks hanging from my saddle to Silva's face and then back to my face.

"Where did you get the fresh meat?" the white man asked.

"I've been hunting" Silva said, and when he shifted his weight in the saddle the 80 leather creaked.

"The hell you have, Indian. You've been rustling cattle. We've been looking for the thief for a long time."

The rancher was fat, and sweat began to soak through his white cowboy shirt and the wet cloth stuck to the thick rolls of belly fat. He almost seemed to be panting from the exertion of talking, and he smelled rancid, maybe because Silva scared him.

Silva turned to me and smiled. "Go back up the mountain, Yellow Woman."

The white man got angry when he heard Silva speak in a language he couldn't understand. "Don't try anything, Indian. Just keep riding to Marquez. We'll call the state police from there."

The rancher must have been unarmed because he was very frightened and if he 85 had a gun he would have pulled it out then. I turned my horse around and the rancher yelled, "Stop!" I looked at Silva for an instant and there was something ancient and dark—something I could feel in my stomach—in his eyes, and when I glanced at his hand I saw his finger on the trigger of the .30-30 that was still in the saddle scabbard. I slapped my horse across the flank and the sacks of raw meat swung against my knees as the horse leaped up the trail. It was hard to keep my balance, and once I thought I felt the saddle slipping backward; it was because of this that I could not look back.

I didn't stop until I reached the ridge where the trail forked. The horse was breathing deep gasps and there was a dark film of sweat on its neck. I looked down in the direction I had come from, but I couldn't see the place. I waited. The wind came up and pushed warm air past me. I looked up at the sky, pale blue and full of thin clouds and fading vapor trails left by jets.

I think four shots were fired—I remember hearing four hollow explosions that reminded me of deer hunting. There could have been more shots after that, but I couldn't have heard them because my horse was running again and the loose rocks were making too much noise as they scattered around his feet.

Horses have a hard time running downhill, but I went that way instead of uphill to the mountain because I thought it was safer. I felt better with the horse running southeast past the round gray hills that were covered with cedar trees and black lava rock. When I got to the plain in the distance I could see the dark green patches of tamaracks that grew along the river; and beyond the river I could see the beginning of the pale sandrock mesas. I stopped the horse and looked back to see if anyone was coming; then I got off the horse and turned the horse around, wondering if it would go back to its corral under the pines on the mountain. It looked back at me for a moment and then plucked a mouthful of green tumbleweeds before it trotted back up the trail with its ears pointed forward, carrying its head daintily to one side to avoid stepping on the dragging reins. When the horse disappeared over the last hill, the gunny sacks full of meat were still swinging and bouncing.

IV

I walked toward the river on a wood-hauler's road that I knew would eventually lead to the paved road. I was thinking about waiting beside the road for someone to drive by, but by the time I got to the pavement I had decided it wasn't very far to walk if I followed the river back the way Silva and I had come.

The river water tasted good, and I sat in the shade under a cluster of silvery willows. I thought about Silva, and I felt sad at leaving him; still, there was something strange about him, and I tried to figure it out all the way back home.

I came back to the place on the river bank where he had been sitting the first time I saw him. The green willow leaves that he had trimmed from the branch were still lying there, wilted in the sand. I saw the leaves and I wanted to go back to him— to kiss him and to touch him—but the mountains were too far away now. And I told myself, because I believe it, he will come back sometime and be waiting again by the river.

I followed the path up from the river into the village. The sun was getting low, and I could smell supper cooking when I got to the screen door of my house. I could hear their voices inside—my mother was telling my grandmother how to fix the Jell-O and my husband, Al, was playing with the baby. I decided to tell them that some Navajo had kidnaped me, but I was sorry that old Grandpa wasn't alive to hear my story because it was the Yellow Woman stories he liked to tell best.

[1974]

ANALYZING "YELLOW WOMAN"

Although a feminist approach to literature may focus on gender issues in its analysis, feminists often incorporate many critical methods associated with other types of criticism. In order to provide an interesting interpretation, it is important to look closely at the characters, the plot, the metaphors or images, the point of view, and the themes of any work. Also, pay attention to any conflicts and the cultural context of the story. If anything is not immediately obvious or seems confusing, take the time to read the story again. Often the best readers of literature are those who reread confusing or unclear passages.

Plot

The plot of "Yellow Woman" is quite simple—a brief sexual encounter with a stranger produces a moment of self-reflection. The narrator reflects on her cultural heritage, her current roles and responsibilities as wife and mother, her deep connection to her dead grandfather, and her distinctly personal desires. Her confusion and her vacillation—more than once during the story, she starts to leave then chooses to remain—provide evidence that she is deeply conflicted. Although we sense that the narrator experiences a significant moment of insight, it is impossible to determine exactly how she is changed. The issues that emerge during the course of the story are too varied and psychologically complex to fully articulate, and we are left to make our own assumptions.

Theme

The narrative of "Yellow Woman" examines a multitude of issues. A list of themes that are woven through this short story include myth, heritage, storytelling, desire, the importance of maintaining an individual identity, and the divisions that result from cultural and gender expectations. The narrator's cultural heritage is certainly important to her, but she seems to have difficulty reconciling the ancient myths of her grandfather with her place in the modern world. She is also faced with a conflict between her desire for an enigmatic man and her ties to a community and its laws. The Western laws and conventions that may not have applied to the lives of the previous Yellow Women play an integral part in her life. Although she feels a connection to these ancient stories, she must deal with the inevitability of change.

Metaphor

Like all the literature in this collection, "Yellow Woman" is rich with images and metaphors. The rising and setting of the sun and the movement of the river figure prominently from the beginning of the story. The sun rises above the trees and exposes the earth and all its colors below, as well as Silva's bare belly. The river both reflects the moon above and blurs the footprints on the bank. Neither the sun nor the river allow stagnation or inactivity; both indicate constant movement and alteration. The warmth and dampness that results from the sun and the constant movement of the river also evoke the sensual aspects of the story. We are reminded of how the sun feels on our skin and how water leaves us feeling damp. Silko also evokes the strangeness of this brief encounter. Although at first the setting appears to be a balanced, peaceful portrait of nature, the image of the horses lying down (rather than in the more typical position of standing) could indicate that something is askew. Of course, by the end of the story, the narrator acknowledges that there is "something strange" about her lover.

The Cultural Context of the Story

When you read "Yellow Woman," determine the cultural context of the story. What information have you gleaned from reading the story? At one point in the story, Silva and the narrator look out over the Navajo reservation and the Pueblo boundaries. They also meet a white rancher while they are traveling to a city. From which culture does our narrator spring? What details in the story provide that information? What is the historical context of the story? Is this a story from the past or a story about contemporary society? Are there tensions that exist between multiple cultures? How do you know? Why are the stories of the past important to the narrator and to Silva? Do these common stories bind these characters in some significant way?

Point of View

The first-person narration of Silko's "Yellow Woman," and the intimate nature of the story, immediately draw us into a familiar relationship with the narrator. The narrator shares her sensual observations of the natural surroundings of the riverbank—details of her wooded surroundings are carefully drawn—and a picture develops of this moment in her life. The narration alternates between her sensual observations, her immediate conversations with Silva, her thoughts of the past, and her confusion in the present moment. What develops from this kind of close, personal narration is that our confusion often mirrors the confused state of the narrator. The very personal nature of Silko's narration invites readers to look closely at this sexual interlude between strangers and at the traditions that define us, while reminding us that storytelling is always about perspective, that the meaning of a story will shift with each teller and each reader.

Gender Perspectives

In producing a feminist critique, it is important to pay attention to sexual differences among the characters. This may be a story about both men and women, but because of the title we know it is a story of a woman. What we learn through the references to Yellow Woman stories is that Silko is presenting a cultural archetype. Ask yourself: What traits are associated with the Yellow Women of the story? Are these characteristics you usually associate with women? Can the narrator of the story be viewed within the Yellow Woman tradition? Is this a positive or negative association? Is tension created between characters because of their gender? Do the men in the story, and the men referred to in the story, differ from the women? In what ways? Does anyone in the story share the narrator's confusion about her situation? What does her confusion imply? Does your opinion of the narrator shift when you learn she is a wife and mother? Are her actions in conflict with cultural expectations you might have? What do you think of Silva? Do we judge him differently because he is a man?

In analyzing "Yellow Woman" pay attention to the structure and style of the story as well as to any thematic issues you see developing. Also, pay close attention to images that are evoked throughout the story.

Questions for Your Analysis of "Yellow Woman"

1) What are your initial impressions of the story?
2) What actually happens in the story? What is the basic plot or action of the story?
3) What do you think about the way the story is narrated? Is it confusing? Straight-forward? Why do you think the author chooses to tell the story in this way?
4) What images are evoked? Are there any repetitions? For example, images of movement and color appear throughout the story. Do these images add meaning to the story?
5) What is your initial reaction to the characters in the story? Do you respond emotionally to any of the characters? Do all of their actions make sense? Why or why not?
6) What culture or cultures are described in the story? Do any cultural conflicts seem apparent?
7) What is the mood of the story? Is it light-hearted? Tense? Does it shift? If so, why?
8) How do you respond to the narrator once you learn she is a wife and mother? Does that information alter your interpretation of the story? How? How would your interpretation change if she were a single woman? If she were a man?
9) What is the significance of the narrator's grandfather to the story? Does his version of the Yellow Woman differ from Silva's version?
10) Although not central to the action of the story, there are several references to violence—thoughts or instances of violence that may or may not have occurred. Thematically, does violence have a significant place in the text?

The issues raised above may facilitate a feminist reading of the text, as well as a different critical approach. Please read the following sample essay on "Yellow Woman" as just one example of feminist criticism. This essay focuses on Silko's narrator and how she simultaneously subverts cultural expectations and perpetuates cultural traditions.

Sample Essay on "Yellow Woman"

Leslie Marmon Silko's short story "Yellow Woman" opens with the warmth of the sun, birds bathing in the river, a woman's hunger, and the vision of a man asleep on the riverbank. We realize immediately that this is a story of sensuality, a story of sexual experience. In fact, the first sentence is overtly sexual. Here, the unnamed narrator says, "My thigh clung to his with dampness," and within a few paragraphs, Silva (her lover) reveals his bare chest and belly as he pulls on his pants. What do we think about a woman—a mother and a wife—who abandons her family for sex with a stranger? Who returns home only after violence erupts and she is faced with the possibility that her lover may be a murderer?

In "Yellow Woman" Silko creates a female character who both confronts Western assumptions about women and expands the Pueblo storytelling tradition by altering its abduction myth. What Silko offers us is a woman outside of Western stereotypes, a narrator whose responsibilities (within the context of the story) as wife, mother, and daughter remain secondary. Here, she is a sexual being; however, she is not the adulteress of American fiction—shunned from her society. In fact, the sexually active Yellow Woman is admired rather than judged by the men in the story. She is even made credible by the family patriarch—the grandfather who "liked to tell those [the Yellow Woman] stories best." Her lover, Silva, addresses her with the same humor and acceptance—their conversation about Yellow Woman and the ka'tsina spirit (the male spirit who traditionally abducts a woman from the outskirts of the pueblo) is filled with laughter and warmth. Silva insists that she *is* Yellow Woman; however, the narrator argues against any connection between herself and the women of Pueblo myth who engage in sexual activities with the ka'tsina spirit. She argues that Yellow Woman "is from out of time past and I live now and I've been to school and there are highways and pickup trucks that Yellow Woman never saw." The narrator continues the "Laguna tradition of spinning personal identity from communal stories."[1] The Yellow Woman of the past differs greatly from the Yellow Woman of the present; she is necessarily altered with each transformation. In Pueblo myth, the Yellow Women who encounter the ka'tsina spirit meet with varying degrees of violence but often escape and return to their communities altered, even renewed, by their experience outside the pueblo.[2] The narrator in Silko's story may be deeply connected to the Yellow Woman of Pueblo myth, but she is also unique to her own historical moment. Although the narrator's experience resembles the Yellow Woman narrative, she chooses to remember specifically the Yellow Woman of her grandfather's stories (a woman in tremendous control who chooses her mate and controls not one, but two, men sexually). The Yellow Woman of her memory

[1]Hertha Dawn Wong, *Sending My Heart Back Across the Years: Tradition and Innovation in Native American Autobiography*, (New York: Oxford UP, 1992) 188.
[2]A. La Vonne Ruoff, "Ritual and Renewal: Keres Traditions in the Short Fiction of Leslie Silko," *MELUS* 5:4 (1978): 2–17.

does not evoke associations with cowardice or "being mellow," but implies fertility, sexuality, boldness, power, and control—traits in conflict with her position in society. Silko's narrator mimics that sense of control, and it is Silva who becomes her sexual object; she provides intimate descriptions of Silva's body. In contrast, no physical description is offered of the narrator at all.

As critics have commented, the woman in Silko's story exists in a state of confusion not only toward Silva but toward her culture and her roles within that culture. In the opening paragraph, she looks at her lover sleeping in the sand "for the last time" and travels south on the river; yet she remembers him and returns before he wakes—returns "with no thought beyond the moment [as] she meets the ka'tsina spirit." By allowing her narrator freedom, Silko's "Yellow Woman" does not mimic either the Western myth of a woman seduced by her captor or the abduction stories of Pueblo tradition. Here, the woman is held captive only by her own unwillingness to leave. Although the depiction of a lone cattle rustler, living outside of the law and speaking of mythic connections, strikes a romantic figure in the Western sense (as well as maintaining the tradition of the violent ka'tsina spirit who lures women away from their community), Silva does not display violence toward his "captor." When he holds her wrist, *she* stops trying to pull away from him. In another scene, while he is gently kissing her face, she pulls away and becomes frightened of a strength that could destroy her; however, there is no indication that this fear is based on his actions. In fact, because he does not act violently toward her or imprison her, her constant vacillation is laced with humor. On the second morning, when she awakes and Silva is gone, she acknowledges that she could go now but remains, eats some apricots, and takes a nap. Thus, Silva never holds her in any real way. Her vacillation (which becomes almost irritating) is the result of her own personal conflicts; her sexual desires as a woman and her need for experience outside of her culture exist in direct conflict with her mundane life and the cultural expectations of her as wife, mother, and daughter. Yet, her desire and her heritage allow a temporary escape, and a context for this momentary escape is made valid by the traditions of her people and her grandfather's repetition of Yellow Woman stories. Although she lives now and has "been to school and there are highways and pickup trucks that Yellow Woman never saw," she remains deeply connected to her cultural tradition.

Her flight illustrates this tradition. As she escapes from Silva, realizing that he is certainly a cattle thief and possibly a murderer (saying "there was something strange about him" seems an understatement at this point), she takes the path that leads her to her village. Although she returns to her family, her home, and the prepackaged sterility of Jell-O mix, she wishes she could tell her grandfather that some Navajo had kidnapped her. Of course, she can't; her grandfather is dead, but she realizes that the "old ways" are not totally lost. She has reclaimed not only her grandfather's tradition, but the soul of Yellow Woman within her.

STEPS IN WRITING AN ESSAY FROM A FEMINIST PERSPECTIVE

"The Story of an Hour," written by Kate Chopin, describes Louise Mallard's emotional response to the news that her husband has been killed in a railroad disaster. Louise's feelings regarding her husband's death (as they are ultimately revealed to us) exist in sharp contrast to the expectations of her sister and friend. Chopin explores the disparity often existing between women's public and private lives and illuminates the fact that cultural traditions and expectations often conflict with women's personal desires. If Brently Mallard was depicted as a difficult or terrible man, interpreting the story would be easier; however, both Louise and Brently Mallard are presented sympathetically, and it is the institution of marriage and its effect on gender relations that Chopin asks us to critique.

A SAMPLE READING

"The Story of an Hour" by Kate Chopin (1851–1904)

Knowing that Mrs. Mallard was afflicted with a heart trouble, great care was taken to break to her as gently as possible the news of her husband's death.

It was her sister Josephine who told her, in broken sentences; veiled hints that revealed in half concealing. Her husband's friend Richards was there, too, near her. It was he who had been in the newspaper office when intelligence of the railroad disaster was received, with Brently Mallard's name leading the list of "killed." He had only taken the time to assure himself of its truth by a second telegram, and had hastened to forestall any less careful, less tender friend in bearing the sad message.

She did not hear the story as many women have heard the same, with a paralyzed inability to accept its significance. She wept at once, with sudden, wild abandonment, in her sister's arms. When the storm of grief had spent itself she went away to her room alone. She would have no one follow her.

There stood, facing the open window, a comfortable, roomy armchair. Into this she sank, pressed down by a physical exhaustion that haunted her body and seemed to reach into her soul.

She could see in the open square before her house the tops of trees that were all aquiver with the new spring life. The delicious breath of rain was in the air. In the street below a peddler was crying his wares. The notes of a distant song which some one was singing reached her faintly, and countless sparrows were twittering in the eaves.   5

There were patches of blue sky showing here and there through the clouds that had met and piled one above the other in the west facing her window.

She sat with her head thrown back upon the cushion of the chair, quite motionless, except when a sob came up into her throat and shook her, as a child who has cried itself to sleep continues to sob in its dreams.

She was young, with a fair, calm face, whose lines bespoke repression and even a certain strength. But now there was a dull stare in her eyes, whose gaze was fixed away off yonder on one of those patches of blue sky. It was not a glance of reflection, but rather indicated a suspension of intelligent thought.

There was something coming to her and she was waiting for it, fearfully. What was it? She did not know; it was too subtle and elusive to name. But she felt it, creeping out of the sky, reaching toward her through the sounds, the scents, the color that filled the air.

Now her bosom rose and fell tumultuously. She was beginning to recognize this   10
thing that was approaching to possess her, and she was striving to beat it back with her
will—as powerless as her two white slender hands would have been.

When she abandoned herself a little whispered word escaped her slightly parted
lips. She said it over and over under her breath: "free, free, free!" The vacant stare
and the look of terror that had followed it went from her eyes. They stayed keen and
bright. Her pulses beat fast, and the coursing blood warmed and relaxed every inch of
her body.

She did not stop to ask if it were or were not a monstrous joy that held her. A
clear and exalted perception enabled her to dismiss the suggestion as trivial.

She knew that she would weep again when she saw the kind, tender hands folded
in death; the face that had never looked save with love upon her, fixed and gray and
dead. But she saw beyond that bitter moment a long procession of years to come that
would belong to her absolutely. And she opened and spread her arms out to them in
welcome.

There would be no one to live for her during those coming years; she would live
for herself. There would be no powerful will bending hers in that blind persistence with
which men and women believe they have a right to impose a private will upon a fellow-
creature. A kind intention or a cruel intention made the act seem no less a crime as she
looked upon it in that brief moment of illumination.

And yet she had loved him—sometimes. Often she had not. What did it matter!   15
What could love, the unsolved mystery, count for in face of this possession of self-
assertion which she suddenly recognized as the strongest impulse of her being!

"Free! Body and soul free!" she kept whispering.

Josephine was kneeling before the closed door with her lips to the keyhole, im-
ploring for admission. "Louise, open the door! I beg; open the door—you will make
yourself ill. What are you doing, Louise? For heaven's sake open the door."

"Go away. I am not making myself ill." No; she was drinking in a very elixir of life
through that open window.

Her fancy was running riot along those days ahead of her. Spring days, and summer days, and all sorts of days that would be her own. She breathed a quick prayer that
life might be long. It was only yesterday she had thought with a shudder that life might
be long.

She arose at length and opened the door to her sister's importunities. There was a   20
feverish triumph in her eyes, and she carried herself unwittingly like a goddess of Victory. She clasped her sister's waist, and together they descended the stairs. Richards
stood waiting for them at the bottom.

Some one was opening the front door with a latchkey. It was Brently Mallard
who entered, a little travel-stained, composedly carrying his grip-sack and umbrella. He
had been far from the scene of accident, and did not even know there had been one. He
stood amazed at Josephine's piercing cry; at Richards' quick motion to screen him from
the view of his wife.

But Richards was too late.

When the doctors came they said she had died of heart disease—of joy that
kills.

Questions for Your Analysis of "The Story of an Hour"

1) What is your initial reaction to the story? Were your surprised, shocked, or initially confused?

2) Chopin presents us literally with a "story of an hour." What is revealed in this very brief story?

3) What are the cultural contexts of the story? Chopin was an American woman writing in the late nineteenth century. Is there any significance to this historical moment?

4) What do we know about the characters in the story? What information do we have to evaluate Louise, Brently, Josephine, or Richards?

5) Because we have greater knowledge of Louise Mallard's emotional life than of the other characters in the story, our response to her death is different from theirs. What does this narrative tactic accomplish?

6) Does this story address specific codes of behavior or cultural expectations based on gender?

7) How would you describe the Mallards' marriage? Do they have a "happy" marriage? If not, discuss the irony of the last sentence.

8) Neither Louise's sister Josephine nor the Mallard's "tender" friend Richards has any grasp of Louise's feelings about her marriage. What does this emotional isolation indicate about Louise? What does it indicate about the society she lives in?

9) The narrator of the story does disclose some information to the reader, but much remains concealed. Why doesn't Chopin provide us with more details of the Mallard's life? Is this an effective narrative technique?

10) Finally, how did you initially respond to the story's ending? On reflection, does your response change?

STEPS IN WRITING A FEMINIST ESSAY ABOUT ANY READING

1) Write down your impressions of key moments or settings in the story or poem that illustrate feminist issues.

2) Identify central characters and examine the gender contexts within which they exist. These contexts might include their background, their relations with others, and the historical setting of the story.

3) Describe portraits of women and men in the text.

4) Examine characters' characteristics and behavior that suggests gender stereotypes and assumptions.

5) Detail any changes in gender representation that take place in the work.

6) Compare your gender values with those in the work. Identify areas in which your gender experiences are significantly different from the work's representation.

7) Analyze and explore tensions in the work that might be gender specific. Examine those tensions for underlying assumptions and stereotypes about gender roles.

8) A good general electronic source to investigate the context of any literary reading is google.com. By typing in the title of the work, especially if it is a

well-known literary work, you will locate several sources that provide background information.

STEPS IN WRITING AN ESSAY ABOUT "THE STORY OF AN HOUR"

Brainstorming Your Topic

1) Identify those elements of the text (character, plot, theme) that prompt an immediate response from you. Write down whatever impressions you have.
2) Focus on the three main characters. What do you know about each of the characters? How do you view each character? Positively or negatively?
3) Look at the title of the story. What expectations did you have from the beginning? Were they met?
4) Do these characters remind you of anyone you know?
5) In what ways are the personal traits specific to each character's gender? Would you expect only a woman to act in a certain way?
6) How do the other characters in the story act? Can you gather additional information about the main characters from the responses of secondary characters?
7) Do any tensions exist that are specifically related to the gender of the characters? What are they?
8) This story appears to be about marriage. What else is the story about?
9) Unless your instructor insists that you not consult outside sources in brainstorming your topic, refer to the electronic sources listed for Kate Chopin. There are many good links that will connect you to biographical sources and detailed criticism. Any ideas and words drawn directly from outside sources should be properly cited, of course. Consult Chapter 10 for documentation procedures.

Creating an Outline

1) Collect your answers to the questions above in short two-word or three-word categories and use them as preliminary "writing points."
2) Think about the points and consider whether they add up to a central idea (for example, freedom and confinement in "The Story of an Hour").
3) Identify five or six main writing points that support your central idea. These points should come from the main literary elements in the story (character, plot, theme, point of view, metaphor). All of the points should provide support for your controlling idea. A good starting place is to examine the story's encounters and then look for ways in which characters react to these encounters.
4) If you have more than five or six points, try to combine one or more of them. If you have fewer than five or six points, see if some of them can be used to generate additional points. You may have some large points that include smaller issues that can stand alone as paragraph topic sentences.
5) Look for transitional devices that connect your main points of support, particularly as they connect various encounters in the story.

Preparing a Rough Draft

1) Now that you have created a working outline, you have already completed your major organizational work. Each major point is the topic of a paragraph, and your essay will have between 5 and 10 paragraphs, depending on development. These paragraphs need not be of equal length, but each one should sufficiently develop the topic sentence.

2) Now that you have your major writing points, assemble a preliminary draft by developing each topic idea with two or three sentences that discuss evidence from the text.

3) Focus on developing transitions between your paragraphs. Professional writers often begin a new paragraph with a direct reference to an idea expressed at the end of the preceding paragraph.

4) It is not too early to begin writing your concluding paragraph. Conclusions often summarize the main points of a central idea (but do not repeat word for word what has already been said). A conclusion may also refer to implications of what has been said (but what cannot be developed because of space limits). Your conclusions should examine feminist issues in the story.

5) Don't be afraid to include questions in your writing. No reader of literature can ever be absolutely certain of every observation that he or she makes, and perceptive observations often generate excellent questions, many of which are useful, even if unaswerable.

Editing Your Draft

1) At this stage, you should have a draft of a few hundred words. You have already done the most difficult work in thinking out your ideas, organizing them into an outline, and preparing a rough version of the final product. Look for ways to edit your paper that will strengthen the essay.

2) Search for repetitious wording (and ideas). Do not repeat ideas, however important, throughout the essay. Use a thesaurus to locate synonyms for terms and ideas that reappear. Attempt to emphasize variety in your language.

3) If your instructor encourages peer editing, choose someone in your class, or perhaps a roommate, and solicit advice about how your essay reads. Is it articulate, compelling, insightful, and interesting? (All of these qualities are important.) Although your peer editor may not be taking a literature class, he or she may be a very good source of feedback on how effective your writing is. Professional writers often seek feedback from peers, and not only from professional colleagues.

4) Be open to make changes in your writing, both conceptually and in specific language. Professional writers know that writing is recursive (which means that the act of writing constantly generates new ways of looking at the topic), and student writers should also take advantage of changes in thinking *as they write*. Don't be afraid to make efficient and effective changes, especially in terms of cutting out words, phrases, and sections that may not be working very well in supporting your overall idea.

5) Proofread carefully for spelling errors, punctuation problems, run-on sentences, and ambiguous or awkward constructions. You should use a solid grammar handbook to assist you in these areas.

Final Checklist

1) Make sure that your central idea (sometimes called a thesis statement) appears in the first paragraph. It is important that your reader know what major point(s) you are attempting to make.
2) Because this essay is a feminist critique, check to see that the essay addresses gender issues in the story. Look at how characters' actions relate to cultural expectations.
3) Examine your essay for sufficient evidence. Each one of your major ideas will need illustration that comes from the text.
4) Review your conclusion to see if you have ended the essay in an effective manner, either summarizing what you have said (in different language) or suggesting some important implications of your reading.
5) Proofread one last time for errors, repetitious language, and awkward phrasing.

ELECTRONIC RESOURCES FOR LESLIE MARMON SILKO

http://www.ipl.org/cgi-bin/ref/litcrit/litcrit.out.pl?au=sil-306. IPL online literary criticism of Leslie Marmon Silko.
http://voices.cla.umn.edu/authors/lesliemarmonsilko.html. Voices from the Gaps: Women Writers of Color—University of Minnesota.
http://web.nmsu.edu/~tomlynch/swlit.silko.html. A brief biography and student responses to Silko's work.

ELECTRONIC RESOURCES FOR KATE CHOPIN

http://encarta.msn.com/find/Concise.asp?z=1&pg=2&ti=761579519. Concise encyclopedia link.
http://docsouth.unc.edu/chopinawak/menu.html. A brief biography and links to other Web sites.

Further Readings in Feminist Criticism

Fuss, Diana. *Essentially Speaking: Feminism, Nature & Difference*. New York: Routledge, 1989.
Gilbert, Sandra M., and Susan Gubar. *The Madwoman in the Attic: The Woman Writer and the Nineteenth-Century Imagination*. New Haven: Yale UP, 1979.

Gubar, Susan. *Critical Condition: Feminism at the Turn of the Century*. New York: Columbia UP, 2000

Hooks, Bell. *Yearning: Race, Gender, and Cultural Politics*. Boston: South End Press, 1990.

Irigaray, Luce. *je, tu, nous: Toward a Culture of Difference*. Trans. Alison Martin. New York: Routledge, 1993.

Jehlen, Myra. "Gender." In *Critical Terms for Literary Study*. Eds. Frank Lentricchia and Thomas McLaughlin. Chicago: U of Chicago P, 1990.

Moi, Toril. *Sexual/Textual Politics: Feminist Literary Theory*. New York: Routledge, 1985.

Nicholson, Linda J., ed. *Feminism/Postmodernism*. New York: Routledge, 1990.

Nye, Andrea. *Feminist Theory and the Philosophies of Man*. New York: Routledge, 1988.

Ruthven, K. K. *Feminist Literary Studies: An Introduction*. Cambridge, England: Cambridge UP, 1984.

Showalter, Elaine. *A Literature of Their Own: British Women Novelists from Brontë to Lessing*. Princeton: Princeton UP, 1977.

Warhol, Robyn R., and Diane Price Herndl, eds. *Feminisms: An Anthology of Literary Theory and Criticism*. New Brunswick, NJ: Rutgers UP, 1997.

Woolf, Virginia. *A Room of One's Own*. New York: Harcourt, 1981.

chapter 8

Psychological Criticism

Psychological criticism (or psychoanalytical criticism, as it is sometimes called) is an approach to literature that emphasizes psychological processes and issues in relation to a literary text. Interest in exploring the psychological terrain in literature is not a new practice. Indeed, in the days of ancient Greece, Plato and Aristotle both wrote about the psychological dimensions of literature. It was not until the nineteenth century, however, when prominent theories of psychology became common among educated people, that the field of psychology would become part of the world of literary interpretation.

It would be inaccurate to suggest that there is one mainstream psychological method of reading literature. On the contrary, psychological criticism refers to a vast array of theories and concepts that offer the possibility of insights into understanding human behavior. Psychological criticism may focus on the intent of the author (conscious or subconscious), characters, plot, and other dimensions of literary content; it may focus on readers' reactions to texts (which explore the psychological terrain of the reader); and it may focus on the psychological dimensions of textual issues (for example, ideological forces in literature that represent psychological stages of development). Emerging theories of psychology add new relevance to literary interpretation as well.

The range of psychological approaches to criticism is so vast that any attempt to survey, however superficially, major psychological approaches is an impossible task. As a practical matter, most professional psychological critics choose one approach with which they are comfortable, and employ that approach to analyze works of literature. Much psychological criticism derives from the theoretical work of Sigmund Freud (1856–1939) and Jacques Lacan (1901–1981). The theoretical work of these pioneering psychoanalysts fills many volumes. Indeed, the psychological concepts and methods they have introduced to the intellectual community are far too numerous to list. The most one can do is select strategic concepts and employ them as vehicles of literary interpretation. The use of psychological insights to examine literary texts can be an exciting and rewarding process, not because psychological criticism has a special window into the "truth" of what a literary text means, but because psychological principles are such a critical part of human experience that they naturally lend themselves to literary interpretation.

All psychological criticism begins with the work of Sigmund Freud, who was one of the early psychoanalysts to trace patients' problems to psychological rather than physical origins. Freud shocked the world in the late nineteenth century and early twentieth century with his theory of psychoanalysis. There are many components of his theories, but in particular we are interested in his portrait of the human psyche, a complex structure that is the result of the interaction of the unconscious mind with the conscious mind. The subconscious terrain, according to Freud, is a landscape where our desires, urges, passions, fears, irrational impulses, and dreams reside. The conscious mind, on the contrary, houses rational processes and attempts to process information and experience with reason. Freud believed that individuals process information and react to circumstances using *both* the conscious and unconscious parts of the mind. Prior to Freud, most psychologists believed that the conscious mind controlled human behavior. One of Freud's greatest achievements was to show the significant role the subconscious mind plays in human behavior.

There are three competing forces in the human psyche, according to Freud: the id, ego, and superego. The id may be defined as uncontrolled appetite or basic desire and this part of the psyche is primarily interested in satisfying itself or seeking pleasure. The ego is a moderating dimension of the personality, the conscious, rational part of our personalities, the center of consciousness. It is the ego that controls and regulates various impulses bubbling up in the other parts of the unconscious mind, especially the id. The ego might be seen as a police officer in the mind, controlling the irrational impulses of the id. The superego is the conscience of the mind, the area of the psyche in which moral judgments are made and individuals punish themselves in the form of guilt, fear, or regret. Many Freudians see the ego as in constant tension with the desires of the id, balanced or moderated by the temperance and self-control of the superego, or center of morality. Sometimes individuals surrender their behavior to the drives of the id. At other times, the superego becomes a dominant force in human thought and action. For the purposes of literary interpretation, the presence of the three parts of human personality plays a role in explaining human behavior in fictional contexts.

Jacques Lacan, a disciple of Freud, learned much from him. Lacan once told his followers, "As far as I am concerned, I'm a Freudian." Lacan has also made a significant number of original contributions, developing Freudian theory in interesting and compelling directions. Lacan drew upon Freud's work on the terrain of the unconscious, subscribing to Freud's model of the id, ego and superego, and developed a theory of human development, which emphasizes interaction with others. One of the basic differences between Lacan and Freud, however, is that Lacan asserts that language plays a significant role in structuring the terrain of both the conscious and unconscious mind.

There are three stages to Lacanian theory: (1) the *mirror stage*, in which a child discovers his or her image (and comes to understand his or her function or agency); (2) the *imaginary stage*, in which children consciously and unconsciously interact with their perceptions of the self-image; and (3) the *symbolic order stage*, in which individuals, both children and adults, come to order or organize their lives through language. Each of these stages interacts with the other periods of development. The symbolic order is the developed, interrelated construction of life and language. Individuals become "speaking subjects" through which they project themselves to the outer world. These subjects encounter the "Other" in their daily experiences, and life is a series of encounters between the subject and the Other. An important part of this project is the way individuals see themselves; hence the importance of the mirror (or specular) image.

The symbolic order stage is particularly important for literary interpretation. It is in this stage that individuals learn to make sexual differentiations between male and female. According to Lacan, the symbolic order stage is when children come to recognize fathers (and other adult males) as figures of authority, representing and enforcing the rules, codes, and customs of society. Boys and girls react differently, of course, as they experience the symbolic order stage. It is in the symbolic order stage that boys learn to do things that are expected of boys (playing with cars, for example) and girls learn to do things that are expected of girls (playing with dolls, for example). These kinds of gender behavior, Lacan emphasizes, are culturally rather than biologically determined. Boys and girls learn what to do by way of what they should not do (boys do not play with dolls and girls do not play with cars). Both sexes learn codes of behavior by observing what they should not do. As a consequence, girls identify with their mothers and boys with their fathers. For girls, according to Lacan, this results in their deference to their fathers (and other males) as authority figures, symbolic representations of power in society. Entering the symbolic order results in significant frustration for members of both sexes, with both yearning for a return to the more comforting mirror and imaginary stages. Children and adults become fragmented and divided as a result of the symbolic stage. Approaching literature from a psychological perspective, readers are able to analyze characters and their behavior as a reflection of these psychological processes.

If these psychological theories sound complex and confusing, they are to most people, and this brief sketch has outlined only a small portion of the work of Freud and Lacan. The importance of the unconscious, which Freud and Lacan agreed upon, is the starting point for our treatment of psychological criticism. This chapter is also concerned with the ways in which individuals see themselves as speaking subjects. A subject or agent says things in order to maintain some kind of order and stability with his or her perception of himself or herself and of others. As some philosophers (called phenomenologists) remind us, the world is a complex environment, and one of the major tasks in anyone's life is to learn how to live in the world, how to interact with others, and how to maintain some sense of self-identification. Language always exists in us in a pre-state, waiting for us to use it according to the needs of circumstances and contexts. The catalyst for igniting these reserves of language is our encounters with the Other—friend, family member, stranger, coworker, or whatever the case may be. We, as speaking subjects, use our language reserves to survive the best we can in a complex, challenging, and confusing world.

Literary characters, as subjects, say and do things (which can be reported to us only through language) that come from the conscious and unconscious spheres of their minds. Like us, literary characters are presented as always in the process of shaping and reshaping their images of themselves and the relationship between those images and the outside world. Think of Charlie Wales of "Babylon Revisited," for example, as a character who interprets and reinterprets himself throughout the story according to his interaction with other characters. His world is one of constant reinterpretation, and his mirror image is under constant change. He thinks quite differently of himself between the story's beginning and its end. The specular (mirror) image, whether in real life or literature, is never completely stable. All of life itself, according to this psychological perspective, involves an intense, ongoing effort to organize our experiences through language (the symbolic order).

The focus of this chapter is to explore ways in which the conscious mind continually interacts with the unconscious, in order to find expression in the subjectivity (or agency) of character, particularly major characters. According to Lacan, the realm of the unconscious mind understands language, particularly the structure of language and the ways in which language organizes our lives. This way of interpretation is necessarily speculative, perhaps even more so than other approaches, because it involves hypothetical incursions into the unconscious terrain of characters. We, like the characters, can never "really know" what is going on deep in the recesses of human minds, but we can speculate about the impulses that generate language and behavior. For Lacan, the ego is only an expression or extension of the unconscious itself. Indeed, the unconscious is the basis of all human experience. The unconscious elements of our psychological being come forward to form the "I," or the speaking subject. According to Lacanian theory, the words we utter to make sense out of our lives are always in reference to other elements of our mind/language system. There is no "true reality" or stable reference behind the language we use. Our words refer to other words, infinitely. (The technical language is that signifiers—words that show something—relate not to reality, or signifieds—but only to other signifiers.) In theory this may sound very confusing, even nonsensical, but in the analysis of "Bartleby, the Scrivener," I hope to show how the narrator struggles with his language to explain reality, only to find that his language refers strategically to other language. Indeed, the narrator's frustration with the limitations of language is one of the major motifs in the story, if read from a psychological/linguistic point of view. The narrator tries desperately to make sense out of the signs, symbols, images, and signifiers that come from other characters, especially Bartleby.

This chapter, like every other chapter in this book, does not pretend to show you how to explain or "solve" literary texts. A major underlying assumption of this book is that various theoretical approaches allow us to explore literary works for insight into those works, as well as insight into ourselves. The modes of investigation are always speculative and hypothetical. Indeed, if there were one "true" method of literary interpretation, there would not be so many interesting, compelling, and articulate schools of literary criticism.

"Bartleby, the Scrivener" is an intense, psychological profile that has generated a wide range of interpretations since its publication nearly 150 years ago. Much of that criticism has focused on Bartleby, the strange, robotic, almost inhuman character who confounds his boss (the unnamed narrator) and everyone else with whom he interacts. There is no question that Bartleby's character is a major focus in the narrative, but it might be argued that the narrator is also a significant force to be reckoned with, particularly since whatever we know necessarily comes to us through his perceptions and perspectives. Further, much of the narrative involves the narrator's commentary about himself. Indeed, the narrator continually struggles with himself as a speaking subject. Throughout the story, he refines the image of himself that he considers so stable at the beginning of the narrative. His encounter with Bartleby changes his life, his methods of ordering his language, and his perceptions of himself and his world. There are numerous forces at work as he attempts to narrate his surreal story. The narrator's conscious mind (ego) and unconscious mind (id and superego) come together to form the basis for his storytelling. "Bartleby, the Scrivener" has much to say about the narrator's struggles with himself in attempting to tell a story about Bartleby—and himself. And this narrative also says something about readers' conscious and unconscious impulses in arriving at an interpretation of this story.

SAMPLE READING

"Bartleby, the Scrivener" by Herman Melville (1819–1891)

I am a rather elderly man. The nature of my avocations, for the last thirty years, has brought me into more than ordinary contact with what would seem an interesting and somewhat singular set of men, of whom, as yet, nothing, that I know of, has ever been written—I mean, the law-copyists, or scriveners. I have known very many of them, professionally and privately, and, if I pleased, could relate divers histories, at which good-natured gentlemen might smile, and sentimental souls might weep. But I waive the biographies of all other scriveners, for a few passages in the life of Bartleby, who was a scrivener, the strangest I ever saw, or heard of. While, of other law-copyists, I might write the complete life, of Bartleby nothing of that sort can be done. I believe that no materials exist, for a full and satisfactory biography of this man. It is an irreparable loss to literature. Bartleby was one of those beings of whom nothing is ascertainable, except from the original sources, and, in his case, those are very small. What my own astonished eyes saw of Bartleby, *that* is all I know of him, except, indeed, one vague report, which will appear in the sequel.

Ere introducing the scrivener, as he first appeared to me, it is fit I make some mention of myself, my *employés*, my business, my chambers, and general surroundings, because some such description is indispensable to an adequate understanding of the chief character about to be presented. Imprimis: I am a man who, from his youth upwards, has been filled with a profound conviction that the easiest way of life is the best. Hence, though I belong to a profession proverbially energetic and nervous, even to turbulence, at times, yet nothing of that sort have I ever suffered to invade my peace. I am one of those unambitious lawyers who never address a jury, or in any way draw down public applause; but, in the cool tranquility of a snug retreat, do a snug business among rich men's bonds, and mortgages, and title-deeds. All who know me, consider me an eminently *safe* man. The late John Jacob Astor, a personage little given to poetic enthusiasm, had no hesitation in pronouncing my first grand point to be prudence; my next, method. I do not speak it in vanity, but simply record the fact, that I was not unemployed in my profession by the late John Jacob Astor; a name which, I admit, I love to repeat; for it hath a rounded and orbicular sound to it, and rings like unto bullion. I will freely add, that I was not insensible to the late John Jacob Astor's good opinion.

Some time prior to the period at which this little history begins, my avocations had been largely increased. The good old office, now extinct in the State of New York, of a Master in Chancery, had been conferred upon me. It was not a very arduous office, but very pleasantly remunerative. I seldom lose my temper; much more seldom indulge in dangerous indignation at wrongs and outrages; but I must be permitted to be rash here and declare, that I consider the sudden and violent abrogation of the office of Master in Chancery, by the new Constitution, as a—premature act; inasmuch as I had counted upon a life-lease of the profits, whereas I only received those of a few short years. But this is by the way.

My chambers were up stairs, at No.—Wall Street. At one end, they looked upon the white wall of the interior of a spacious skylight shaft, penetrating the building from top to bottom.

This view might have been considered rather tame than otherwise, deficient in   5
what landscape painters call "life." But, if so, the view from the other end of my chambers offered, at least, a contrast, if nothing more. In that direction, my windows commanded an unobstructed view of a lofty brick wall, black by age and everlasting shade;
which wall require no spy-glass to bring out its lurking beauties, but, for the benefit of
all near-sighted spectators, was pushed up to within ten feet of my window-panes.
Owing to the great height of the surrounding buildings, and my chambers being on the
second floor, the interval between this wall and mine not a little resembled a huge
square cistern.

At the period just preceding the advent of Bartleby, I had two persons as copyists
in my employment, and a promising lad as an office-boy. First, Turkey; second, Nippers;
third, Ginger Nut. These may seem names, the like of which are not usually found in
the Directory. In truth, they were nicknames, mutually conferred upon each other by
my three clerks, and were deemed expressive of their respective persons or characters.
Turkey was a short, pursy Englishman, of about my own age—that is, somewhere not far
from sixty. In the morning, one might say, his face was of a fine florid hue, but after
twelve o'clock, meridian—his dinner hour—it blazed like a grate full of Christmas
coals; and continued blazing—but, as it were, with a gradual wane—till six o'clock,
P.M., or thereabouts; after which, I saw no more of the proprietor of the face, which,
gaining its meridian with the sun, seemed to set with it, to rise, culminate, and decline
the following day, with the like regularity and undiminished glory. There are many singular coincidences I have known in the course of my life, not the least among which
was the fact, that, exactly when Turkey displayed his fullest beams from his red and radiant countenance, just then, too, at that critical moment, began the daily period when
I considered his business capacities as seriously disturbed for the remainder of the
twenty-four hours. Not that he was absolutely idle, or averse to business then; far from
it. The difficulty was, he was apt to be altogether too energetic. There was a strange, inflamed, flurried, flighty recklessness of activity about him. He would be incautious in
dipping his pen into his inkstand. All his blots upon my documents were dropped there
after twelve o'clock, meridian. Indeed, not only would he be reckless, and sadly given to
making blots in the afternoon, but, some days, he went further, and was rather noisy. At
such times, too, his face flamed with augmented blazonry, as if cannel coal had been
heaped on anthracite. He made an unpleasant racket with his chair; spilled his sand-
box; in mending his pens, impatiently split them all to pieces, and threw them on the
floor in a sudden passion; stood up, and leaned over his table, boxing his papers about
in a most indecorous manner, very sad to behold in an elderly man like him. Nevertheless, as he was in many ways a most valuable person to me, and all the time before
twelve o'clock, meridian, was the quickest, steadiest creature, too, accomplishing a
great deal of work in a style not easily to be matched—for these reasons, I was willing to
overlook his eccentricities, though, indeed, occasionally, I remonstrated with him. I did
this very gently, however, because, though the civilest, nay, the blandest and most rev-
erential of men in the morning, yet, in the afternoon, he was disposed, upon provoca-
tion, to be slightly rash with his tongue—in fact, insolent. Now, valuing his morning
services as I did, and resolved not to lose them—yet, at the same time, made uncomfortable by his inflamed ways after twelve o'clock—and being a man of peace, unwilling
by my admonitions to call forth unseemly retorts from him, I took upon me, one Saturday noon (he was always worse on Saturdays) to hint to him, very kindly, that, perhaps,
now that he was growing old, it might be well to abridge his labors; in short, he need

not come to my chambers after twelve o'clock, but, dinner over, had best go home to his lodgings, and rest himself till tea-time. But no; he insisted upon his afternoon devotions. His countenance became intolerably fervid, as he oratorically assured me—gesticulating with a long ruler at the other end of the room—that if his services in the morning were useful, how indispensable, then, in the afternoon?

"With submission, sir," said Turkey, on this occasion, "I consider myself your right-hand man. In the morning I but marshal and deploy my columns; but in the afternoon I put myself at their head, and gallantly charge the foe, thus"—and he made a violent thrust with the ruler.

"But the blots, Turkey," intimated I.

"True; but, with submission, sir, behold these hairs! I am getting old. Surely, sir, a blot or two of a warm afternoon is not to be severely urged against gray hairs. Old age— even if it blot the page—is honorable. With submission, sir, we *both* are getting old."

This appeal to my fellow-feeling was hardly to be resisted. At all events, I saw   10
that go he would not. So, I made up my mind to let him stay, resolving, nevertheless, to see to it that, during the afternoon, he had to do with my less important papers.

Nippers, the second on my list, was a whiskered, sallow, and, upon the whole, rather piratical-looking young man, of about five-and-twenty. I always deemed him the victim of two evil powers—ambition and indigestion. The ambition was evinced by a certain impatience of the duties of a mere copyist, an unwarrantable usurpation of strictly professional affairs such as the original drawing up of legal documents. The indigestion seemed betokened in an occasional nervous testiness and grinning irritability, causing the teeth to audibly grind together over mistakes committed in copying; unnecessary maledictions, hissed, rather than spoken, in the heat of business; and especially by a continual discontent with the height of the table where he worked. Though of a very ingenious mechanical turn, Nippers could never get this table to suit him. He put chips under it, blocks of various sorts, bits of pasteboard, and at last went so far as to attempt an exquisite adjustment, by final pieces of folded blotting paper. But no invention would answer. If, for the sake of easing his back, he brought the table-lid at a sharp angle well up towards his chin, and wrote there like a man using the steep roof of a Dutch house for his desk, then he declared that it stopped the circulation in his arms. If now he lowered the table to his waistbands, and stooped over it in writing, then there was a sore aching in his back. In short, the truth of the matter was, Nippers knew not what he wanted. Or, if he wanted anything, it was to be rid of a scrivener's table altogether. Among the manifestations of his diseased ambition was a fondness he had for receiving visits from certain ambiguous-looking fellows in seedy coats, whom he called his clients. Indeed, I was aware that not only was he, at times, considerable of a ward-politician, but he occasionally did a little business at the justices' courts, and was not unknown on the steps of the Tombs. I have good reason to believe, however, that one individual who called upon him at my chambers, and who, with a grand air, he insisted was his client, was no other than a dun, and the alleged title-deed, a bill. But, with all his failings, and the annoyances he caused me, Nippers, like his compatriot Turkey, was a very useful man to me; wrote a neat, swift hand; and, when he chose, was not deficient in a gentlemanly sort of deportment. Added to this, he always dressed in a gentlemanly sort of way; and so, incidentally, reflected credit upon my chambers. Whereas, with respect to Turkey, I had much ado to keep him from being a reproach to me. His clothes were apt to look oily, and smell of eating-houses. He wore his pantaloons very loose and baggy in summer. His coats were execrable, his hat not to be handled. But while the hat was a thing of indifference to me, inasmuch as his natural civility and deference, as a dependent Englishman, always led him to doff it the moment he entered the room, yet his coat was another matter. Concerning his coats, I reasoned with him; but with no effect. The truth was, I suppose, that a man with so small an income could not afford to sport such a lustrous face and a lustrous coat at one and the same time. As Nippers once observed, Turkey's money went chiefly for red ink. One winter day, I presented Turkey with a highly respectable-looking coat of my own—a padded gray coat, of a most comfortable warmth, and which buttoned straight up from the knee to the neck. I thought Turkey would appreciate the favor, and abate his rashness and obstreperousness of afternoons. But no; I verily believe that buttoning himself up in so downy and blanket-like a coat had a pernicious effect upon him upon the same principle that too much oats are bad for horses. In fact, precisely as a rash, restive horse is said to feel his oats, so Turkey felt his coat. It made him insolent. He was a man whom prosperity harmed.

Though, concerning the self-indulgent habits of Turkey, I had my own private surmises, yet, touching Nippers, I was well persuaded that, whatever might be his faults in other respects, he was, at least, a temperate young man. But, indeed, nature herself seemed to have been his vintner, and, at his birth, charged him so thoroughly with an irritable, brandy-like disposition, that all subsequent potations were needless. When I consider how, amid the stillness of my chambers, Nippers would sometimes impatiently rise from his seat, and stooping over his table, spread his arms wide apart, seize the whole desk, and move it, and jerk it, with a grim, grinding motion on the floor, as if the table were a perverse voluntary agent, intent on thwarting and vexing him, I plainly perceive that, for Nippers, brandy-and-water were altogether superfluous.

It was fortunate for me that, owing to its peculiar cause—indigestion—the irritability and consequent nervousness of Nippers were mainly observable in the morning, while in the afternoon he was comparatively mild. So that, Turkey's paroxysms only coming on about twelve o'clock, I never had to do with their eccentricities at one time. Their fits relieved each other, like guards. When Nippers' was on, Turkey's was off; and *vice versa*. This was a good natural arrangement, under the circumstances.

Ginger Nut, the third on my list, was a lad, some twelve years old. His father was a carman, ambitious of seeing his son on the bench instead of a cart, before he died. So he sent him to my office, as student at law, errand-boy, cleaner, and sweeper, at the rate of one dollar a week. He had a little desk to himself, but he did not use it much. Upon inspection, the drawer exhibited a great array of the shells of various sorts of nuts. Indeed, to this quick-witted youth, the whole noble science of the law was contained in a nutshell. Not the least among the employments of Ginger Nut, as well as one which he discharged with the most alacrity, was his duty as cake and apple purveyor for Turkey and Nippers. Copying lawpapers being proverbially a dry, husky sort of business, my two scriveners were fain to moisten their mouths very often with Spitzenbergs, to be had at the numerous stalls nigh the Custom House and Post Office. Also, they sent Ginger Nut very frequently for that peculiar cake—small, flat, round, and very spicy—after which he had been named by them. Of a cold morning, when business was but dull, Turkey would gobble up scores of these cakes, as if they were mere wafers—indeed, they sell them at the rate of six or eight for a penny—the scrape of his pen blending with the crunching of the crisp particles in his mouth. Of all the fiery afternoon blunders and flurried rashness of Turkey, was his once moistening a ginger-cake between his lips, and clapping it on to a mortgage, for a seal. I came within an ace of dismissing him then. But he mollified me by making an oriental bow, and saying—

"With submission, sir, it was generous of me to find you in stationery on my own account." 15

Now my original business—that of a conveyancer and title hunter, and drawer-up of recondite documents of all sorts—was considerably increased by receiving the Master's office. There was now great work for scriveners. Not only must I push the clerks already with me, but I must have additional help.

In answer to my advertisement, a motionless young man one morning stood upon my office threshold, the door being open, for it was summer. I can see that figure now—pallidly neat, pitiably respectable, incurably forlorn! It was Bartleby.

After a few words touching his qualifications, I engaged him, glad to have among my corps of copyists a man of so singularly sedate an aspect, which I thought might operate beneficially upon the flighty temper of Turkey, and the fiery one of Nippers.

I should have stated before that ground-glass folding-doors divided my premises into two parts, one of which was occupied by my scriveners, the other by myself. According to my humor, I threw open these doors, or closed them. I resolved to assign Bartleby a corner by the folding-doors, but on my side of them, so as to have this quiet man within easy call, in case any trifling thing was to be done. I placed his desk close up to a small side-window in that part of the room, a window which originally had afforded a lateral view of certain grimy brickyards and bricks, but which, owing to subsequent erections, commanded at present no view at all, though it gave some light. Within three feet of the panes was a wall, and the light came down from far above, between two lofty buildings, as from a very small opening in a dome. Still further to a satisfactory arrangement, I procured a high green folding screen, which might entirely isolate Bartleby from my sight, though not remove him from my voice. And thus, in a manner, privacy and society were conjoined.

At first, Bartleby did an extraordinary quantity of writing. As if long famishing 20 for something to copy, he seemed to gorge himself on my documents. There was no pause for digestion. He ran a day and night line, copying by sunlight and by candlelight. I should have been quite delighted with his application, had he been cheerfully industrious. But he wrote on silently, palely, mechanically.

It is, of course, an indispensable part of a scrivener's business to verify the accuracy of his copy, word by word. Where there are two or more scriveners in an office, they assist each other in this examination, one reading from the copy, the other holding the original. It is a very dull, wearisome, and lethargic affair. I can readily imagine that, to some sanguine temperaments, it would be altogether intolerable. For example, I cannot credit that the mettlesome poet, Byron, would have contentedly sat down with Bartleby to examine a law document of, say five hundred pages, closely written in a crimpy hand.

Now and then, in the haste of business, it had been my habit to assist in comparing some brief document myself, calling Turkey or Nippers for this purpose. One object I had, in placing Bartleby so handy to me behind the screen, was, to avail myself of his services on such trivial occasions. It was on the third day, I think, of his being with me, and before any necessity had arisen for having his own writing examined, that, being much hurried to complete a small affair I had in hand, I abruptly called to Bartleby. In my haste and natural expectancy of instant compliance, I sat with my head bent over the original on my desk, and my right hand sideways, and somewhat nervously extended with the copy, so that, immediately upon emerging from his retreat, Bartleby might snatch it and proceed to business without the least delay.

In this very attitude did I sit when I called to him, rapidly stating what it was I wanted him to do—namely, to examine a small paper with me. Imagine my surprise, nay, my consternation, when, without moving from his privacy, Bartleby, in a singularly mild, firm voice, replied, "I would prefer not to."

I sat awhile in perfect silence, rallying my stunned faculties. Immediately it occurred to me that my ears had deceived me, or Bartleby had entirely misunderstood my meaning. I repeated my request in the clearest tone I could assume; but in quite as clear a one came the previous reply, "I would prefer not to."

"Prefer not to," echoed I, rising in high excitement, and crossing the room with a   25
stride. "What do you mean? Are you moonstruck? I want you to help me compare this sheet here—take it," and I thrust it towards him.

"I would prefer not to," said he.

I looked at him steadfastly. His face was leanly composed; his gray eye dimly calm. Not a wrinkle of agitation rippled him. Had there been the least uneasiness, anger, impatience, or impertinence in his manner; in other words, had there been anything ordinarily human about him, doubtless I should have violently dismissed him from the premises. But as it was, I should have as soon thought of turning my pale plaster-of-paris bust of Cicero out of doors. I stood gazing at him awhile, as he went on with his own writing, and then reseated myself at my desk. This is very strange, thought I. What had one best do? But my business hurried me. I concluded to forget the matter for the present, reserving it for my future leisure. So, calling Nippers from the other room, the paper was speedily examined.

A few days after this, Bartleby concluded four lengthy documents, being quadruplicates of a week's testimony taken before me in my High Court of Chancery. It became necessary to examine them. It was an important suit, and great accuracy was imperative. Having all things arranged, I called Turkey, Nippers, and Ginger Nut, from the next room, meaning to place the four copies in the hands of my four clerks, while I should read from the original. Accordingly, Turkey, Nippers, and Ginger Nut had taken their seats in a row, each with his document in his hand, when I called to Bartleby to join this interesting group.

"Bartleby! quick, I am waiting."

I heard a slow scrape of his chair legs on the uncarpeted floor, and soon he ap-   30
peared standing at the entrance of his hermitage.

"What is wanted?" said he, mildly.

"The copies, the copies," said I, hurriedly. "We are going to examine them. There"—and I held towards him the fourth quadruplicate.

"I would prefer not to," he said, and gently disappeared behind the screen.

For a few moments I was turned into a pillar of salt, standing at the head of my seated column of clerks. Recovering myself, I advanced towards the screen, and demanded the reason for such extraordinary conduct.

"Why do you refuse?"   35

"I would prefer not to."

With any other man I should have flown outright into a dreadful passion, scorned all further words, and thrust him ignominiously from my presence. But there was something about Bartleby that not only strangely disarmed me, but, in a wonderful manner, touched and disconcerted me. I began to reason with him.

"These are your own copies we are about to examine. It is labor saving to you, because one examination will answer for your four papers. It is common usage. Every copyist is bound to help examine his copy. Is it not so? Will you not speak? Answer!"

"I prefer not to," he replied in a flute-like tone. It seemed to me that, while I had been addressing him, he carefully revolved every statement that I made; fully comprehended the meaning; could not gainsay the irresistible conclusion; but, at the same time, some paramount consideration prevailed with him to reply as he did.

"You are decided, then, not to comply with my request—a request made accord-   40
ing to common usage and common sense?"

He briefly gave me to understand, that on that point my judgment was sound. Yes: his decision was irreversible.

It is not seldom the case that, when a man is browbeaten in some unprecedented and violently unreasonable way, he begins to stagger in his own plainest faith. He begins, as it were, vaguely to surmise that, wonderful as it may be, all the justice and all the reason is on the other side. Accordingly, if any disinterested persons are present, he turns to them for some reinforcement for his own faltering mind.

"Turkey," said I, "what do you think of this? Am I not right?"

"With submission, sir," said Turkey, in his blandest tone, "I think that you are."

"Nippers," said I, "what do *you* think of it?"   45

"I think I should kick him out of the office."

(The reader of nice perceptions will have perceived that, it being morning, Turkey's answer is couched in polite and tranquil terms, but Nippers replies in ill-tempered ones. Or, to repeat a previous sentence, Nippers' ugly mood was on duty, and Turkey's off.)

"Ginger Nut," said I, willing to enlist the smallest suffrage in my behalf, "what do *you* think of it?"

"I think, sir, he's a little *luny*," replied Ginger Nut, with a grin.

"You hear what they say," said I, turning towards the screen, "come forth and do   50
your duty."

But he vouchsafed no reply. I pondered a moment in sore perplexity. But once more business hurried me. I determined again to postpone the consideration of this dilemma to my future leisure. With a little trouble we made out to examine the papers without Bartleby, though at every page or two Turkey deferentially dropped his opinion, that this proceeding was quite out of the common; while Nippers, twitching in his chair with a dyspeptic nervousness, ground out, between his set teeth, occasional hissing maledictions against the stubborn oaf behind the screen. And for his (Nippers') part, this was the first and the last time he would do another man's business without pay.

Meanwhile Bartleby sat in his hermitage, oblivious to everything but his own peculiar business there.

Some days passed, the scrivener being employed upon another lengthy work. His late remarkable conduct led me to regard his ways narrowly. I observed that he never went to dinner; indeed, that he never went anywhere. As yet I had never, of my personal knowledge, known him to be outside of my office. He was a perpetual sentry in the corner. At about eleven o'clock though, in the morning, I noticed that Ginger Nut would advance towards the opening in Bartleby's screen, as if silently beckoned thither by a gesture invisible to me where I sat. The boy would then leave the office, jingling a few pence, and reappear with a handful of ginger-nuts, which he delivered in the hermitage, receiving two of the cakes for his trouble.

He lives, then, on ginger-nuts, thought I; never eats a dinner, properly speaking; he must be a vegetarian, then, but no; he never eats even vegetables, he eats nothing but ginger-nuts. My mind then ran on in reveries concerning the probable effects upon the human constitution of living entirely on ginger-nuts. Ginger-nuts are so called, because they contain ginger as one of their peculiar constituents, and the final flavoring one. Now, what was ginger? A hot, spicy thing. Was Bartleby hot and spicy? Not at all. Ginger, then, had no effect upon Bartleby. Probably he preferred it should have none.

Nothing so aggravates an earnest person as a passive resistance. If the individual so resisted be of a not inhumane temper, and the resisting one perfectly harmless in his passivity, then, in the better moods of the former, he will endeavor charitably to construe to his imagination what proves impossible to be solved by his judgment. Even so, for the most part, I regarded Bartleby and his ways. Poor fellow! thought I, he means no mischief; it is plain he intends no insolence; his aspect sufficiently evinces that his eccentricities are involuntary. He is useful to me. I can get along with him. If I turn him away, the chances are he will fall in with some less indulgent employer, and then he will be rudely treated, and perhaps driven forth miserably to starve. Yes. Here I can cheaply purchase a delicious self-approval. To befriend Bartleby; to humor him in his strange wilfulness, will cost me little or nothing, while I lay up in my soul what will eventually prove a sweet morsel for my conscience. But this mood was not invariable with me. The passiveness of Bartleby sometimes irritated me. I felt strangely goaded on to encounter him in new opposition—to elicit some angry spark from him answerable to my own. But, indeed, I might as well have essayed to strike fire with my knuckles against a bit of Windsor soap. But one afternoon the evil impulse in me mastered me, and the following little scene ensued:

"Bartleby," said I, "when those papers are all copied, I will compare them with you."

"I would prefer not to."

"How? Surely you do not mean to persist in that mulish vagary?"

No answer.

I threw open the folding-doors nearby, and turning upon Turkey and Nippers, exclaimed:

"Bartleby a second time says, he won't examine his papers. What do you think of it, Turkey?"

It was afternoon, be it remembered. Turkey sat glowing like a brass boiler; his bald head steaming; his hands reeling among his blotted papers.

"Think of it?" roared Turkey. "I think I'll just step behind his screen, and black his eyes for him!"

So saying, Turkey rose to his feet and threw his arms into a pugilistic position. He was hurrying away to make good his promise, when I detained him, alarmed at the effect of incautiously rousing Turkey's combativeness after dinner.

"Sit down, Turkey," said I, "and hear what Nippers has to say. What do you think of it, Nippers? Would I not be justified in immediately dismissing Bartleby?"

"Excuse me, that is for you to decide, sir. I think his conduct quite unusual, and, indeed, unjust, as regards Turkey and myself. But it may only be a passing whim."

"Ah," exclaimed I, "you have strangely changed your mind, then—you speak very gently of him now."

"All beer," cried Turkey; "gentleness is effects of beer—Nippers and I dined together to-day. You see how gentle I am, sir. Shall I go and black his eyes?"

"You refer to Bartleby, I suppose. No, not to-day, Turkey," I replied; "pray, put up your fists."

I closed the doors, and again advanced towards Bartleby. I felt additional incen-   70
tives tempting me to my fate. I burned to be rebelled against again. I remembered that
Bartleby never left the office.

"Bartleby," said I, "Ginger Nut is away; just step around to the Post Office, won't
you?" (it was but a three minutes' walk) "and see if there is anything for me."

"I would prefer not to."

"You *will* not?"

"I *prefer* not."

I staggered to my desk, and sat there in a deep study. My blind inveteracy re-   75
turned. Was there any other thing in which I could procure myself to be ignominiously
repulsed by this lean, penniless wight? my hired clerk? What added thing is there, perfectly reasonable, that he will be sure to refuse to do?

"Bartleby!"

No answer.

"Bartleby," in a louder tone.

No answer.

"Bartleby," I roared.   80

Like a very ghost, agreeably to the laws of magical invocation, at the third summons, he appeared at the entrance of his hermitage.

"Go to the next room, and tell Nippers to come to me."

"I would prefer not to," he respectfully and slowly said, and mildly disappeared.

"Very good, Bartleby," said I, in a quiet sort of serenely-severe self-possessed tone,
intimating the unalterable purpose of some terrible retribution very close at hand. At
the moment I half intended something of the kind. But upon the whole, as it was drawing towards my dinner-hour, I thought it best to put on my hat and walk home for the
day, suffering much from perplexity and distress of mind.

Shall I acknowledge it? The conclusion of this whole business was, that it soon   85
became a fixed fact of my chambers, that a pale young scrivener, by the name of
Bartleby, had a desk there; that he copied for me at the usual rate of four cents a folio
(one hundred words); but he was permanently exempt from examining the work done
by him, that duty being transferred to Turkey and Nippers, out of compliment, doubtless, to their superior acuteness; moreover, said Bartleby was never, on any account, to
be dispatched on the most trivial errand of any sort; and that even if entreated to take
upon him such a matter, it was generally understood that he would "prefer not to"—in
other words, that he would refuse point blank.

As days passed on, I became considerably reconciled to Bartleby. His steadiness,
his freedom from all dissipation, his incessant industry (except when he chose to throw
himself into a standing revery behind his screen), his great stillness, his unalterableness
of demeanor under all circumstances, made him a valuable acquisition. One prime
thing was this—*he was always there*—first in the morning, continually through the day,
and the last at night. I had a singular confidence in his honesty. I felt my most precious
papers perfectly safe in his hands. Sometimes, to be sure, I could not, for the very soul of
me, avoid falling into sudden spasmodic passions with him. For it was exceeding difficult to bear in mind all the time those strange peculiarities, privileges, and unheard-of
exemptions, forming the tacit stipulations on Bartleby's part under which he remained
in my office. Now and then, in the eagerness of dispatching pressing business, I would
inadvertently summon Bartleby, in a short, rapid tone, to put his finger, say, on the

incipient tie of a bit of red tape with which I was about compressing some papers. Of course, from behind the screen the usual answer, "I prefer not to," was sure to come; and then, how could a human creature, with the common infirmities of our nature, refrain from bitterly exclaiming upon such perverseness—such unreasonableness? However, every added repulse of this sort which I received only tended to lessen the probability of my repeating the inadvertence.

Here it must be said, that, according to the custom of most legal gentlemen occupying chambers in densely populated law buildings, there were several keys to my door. One was kept by a woman residing in the attic, which person weekly scrubbed and daily swept and dusted my apartments. Another was kept by Turkey for convenience sake. The third I sometimes carried in my own pocket. The fourth I knew not who had.

Now, one Sunday morning I happened to go to Trinity Church, to hear a celebrated preacher, and finding myself rather early on the ground I thought I would walk round to my chambers for a while. Luckily I had my key with me; but upon applying it to the lock, I found it resisted by something inserted from the inside. Quite surprised, I called out; when to my consternation a key was turned from within; and thrusting his lean visage at me, and holding the door ajar, the apparition of Bartleby appeared, in his shirt-sleeves, and otherwise in a strangely tattered *deshabille*, saying quietly that he was sorry, but he was deeply engaged just then, and preferred not admitting me at present. In a brief word or two, he moreover added, that perhaps I had better walk round the block two or three times, and by that time he would probably have concluded his affairs.

Now, the utterly unsurmised appearance of Bartleby, tenanting my law-chambers of a Sunday morning, with his cadaverously gentlemanly *nonchalance*, yet withal firm and self-possessed, had such a strange effect upon me, that incontinently I slunk away from my own door, and did as desired. But not without sundry twinges of impotent rebellion against the mild effrontery of this unaccountable scrivener. Indeed, it was his wonderful mildness chiefly, which not only disarmed me, but unmanned me, as it were. For I consider that one, for the time, is sort of unmanned when he tranquilly permits his hired clerk to dictate to him, and order him away from his own premises. Furthermore, I was full of uneasiness as to what Bartleby could possibly be doing in my office in his shirt sleeves, and in an otherwise dismantled condition on a Sunday morning. Was anything amiss going on? Nay, that was out of the question. It was not to be thought of for a moment that Bartleby was an immoral person. But what could he be doing there?—copying? Nay again, whatever might be his eccentricities, Bartleby was an eminently decorous person. He would be the last man to sit down to his desk in any state approaching to nudity. Besides, it was Sunday; and there was something about Bartleby that forbade the supposition that he would by any secular occupation violate the proprieties of the day.

Nevertheless, my mind was not pacified; and full of a restless curiosity, at last I returned to the door. Without hindrance I inserted my key, opened it, and entered. Bartleby was not to be seen. I looked round anxiously, peeped behind his screen; but it was very plain that he was gone. Upon more closely examining the place, I surmised that for an indefinite period Bartleby must have ate, dressed, and slept in my office, and that too without plate, mirror, or bed. The cushioned seat of a rickety old sofa in one corner bore the faint impress of a lean, reclining form. Rolled away under his desk, I found a blanket; under the empty grate, a blacking box and brush; on a chair, a tin

90

basin, with soap and a ragged towel; in a newspaper a few crumbs of ginger-nuts and a morsel of cheese. Yes, thought I, it is evident enough that Bartleby has been making his home here, keeping bachelor's hall all by himself. Immediately then the thought came sweeping across me, what miserable friendliness and loneliness are here revealed! His poverty is great; but his solitude, how horrible! Think of it. Of a Sunday, Wall Street is deserted as Petra; and every night of every day it is an emptiness. This building, too, which of week-days hums with industry and life, at nightfall echoes with sheer vacancy, and all through Sunday is forlorn. And here Bartleby makes his home; sole spectator of a solitude which he has seen all populous—a sort of innocent and transformed Marius brooding among the ruins of Carthage!

For the first time in my life a feeling of overpowering stinging melancholy seized me. Before, I had never experienced aught but a not unpleasing sadness. The bond of a common humanity now drew me irresistibly to gloom. A fraternal melancholy! For both I and Bartleby were sons of Adam. I remembered the bright silks and sparkling faces I had seen that day, in gala trim, swan-like sailing down the Mississippi of Broadway; and I contrasted them with the pallid copyist, and thought to myself, Ah, happiness courts the light, so we deem the world is gay; but misery hides aloof, so we deem that misery there is none. These sad fancyings—chimeras, doubtless, of a sick and silly brain—led on to other and more special thoughts, concerning the eccentricities of Bartleby. Presentiments of strange discoveries hovered round me. The scrivener's pale form appeared to me laid out, among uncaring strangers, in its shivering winding-sheet.

Suddenly I was attracted by Bartleby's closed desk, the key in open sight left in the lock.

I mean no mischief, seek the gratification of no heartless curiosity, thought I; besides, the desk is mine, and its contents, too, so I will make bold to look within. Everything was methodically arranged, the papers smoothly placed. The pigeonholes were deep, and removing the files of documents, I groped into their recesses. Presently I felt something there, and dragged it out. It was an old bandanna handkerchief, heavy and knotted. I opened it, and saw it was a saving's bank.

I now recalled all the quiet mysteries which I had noted in the man. I remembered that he never spoke but to answer; that, though at intervals he had considerable time to himself, yet I had never seen him reading—no, not even a newspaper; that for long periods he would stand looking out, at his pale window behind the screen, upon the dead brick wall; I was quite sure he never visited any refectory or eating-house; while his pale face clearly indicated that he never drank beer like Turkey; or tea and coffee even, like other men; that he never went anywhere in particular that I could learn; never went out for a walk, unless, indeed, that was the case at present; that he had declined telling who he was, or whence he came, or whether he had any relatives in the world; that though so thin and pale, he never complained of ill-health. And more than all, I remembered a certain unconscious air of pallid—how shall I call it?—of pallid haughtiness, say, or rather an austere reserve about him, which has positively awed me into my tame compliance with his eccentricities, when I had feared to ask him to do the slightest incidental thing for me, even though I might know, from his long-continued motionlessness, that behind his screen he must be standing in one of those dead-wall reveries of his.

Revolving all these things, and coupling them with the recently discovered fact, 95 that he made my office his constant abiding place and home, and not forgetful of his morbid moodiness; revolving all these things, a prudential feeling began to steal over me. My first emotions had been those of pure melancholy and sincerest pity; but just in proportion as the forlornness of Bartleby grew and grew to my imagination, did that same melancholy merge into fear, that pity into repulsion. So true it is, and so terrible, too, that up to a certain point the thought or sight of misery enlists our best affections; but, in certain special cases, beyond that point it does not. They err who would assert that invariably this is owing to the inherent selfishness of the human heart. It rather proceeds from a certain hopelessness of remedying excessive and organic ill. To a sensitive being, pity is not seldom pain. And when at last it is perceived that such pity cannot lead to effectual succor, common sense bids the soul be rid of it. What I saw that morning persuaded me that the scrivener was the victim of innate and incurable disorder. I might give alms to his body; but his body did not pain him; it was his soul that suffered, and his soul I could not reach.

I did not accomplish the purpose of going to Trinity Church that morning. Somehow, the things I had seen disqualified me for the item from church-going. I walked homeward, thinking what I would do with Bartleby. Finally, I resolved upon this—I would put certain calm questions to him the next morning, touching his history, etc., and if he declined to answer them openly and unreservedly (and I supposed he would prefer not), then to give him a twenty dollar bill over and above whatever I might owe him, and tell him his services were no longer required; but that if in any other way I could assist him, I would be happy to do so, especially if he desired to return to his native place, wherever that might be, I would willingly help to defray the expenses. Moreover, if, after reaching home, he found himself at any time in want of aid, a letter from him would be sure of a reply.

The next morning came.

"Bartleby," said I, gently calling to him behind his screen.

No reply.

"Bartleby," said I, in a still gentler tone, "come here; I am not going to ask you to   100
do anything you would prefer not to do—I simply wish to speak to you."

Upon this he noiselessly slid into view.

"Will you tell me, Bartleby, where you were born?"

"I would prefer not to."

"Will you tell me *anything* about yourself?"

"I would prefer not to."   105

"But what reasonable objection can you have to speak to me? I feel friendly towards you."

He did not look at me while I spoke, but kept his glance fixed upon my bust of Cicero, which, as I then sat, was directly behind me, some six inches above my head.

"What is your answer, Bartleby?" said I, after waiting a considerable time for a reply, during which his countenance remained immovable, only there was the faintest conceivable tremor of the white attenuated mouth.

"At present I prefer to give no answer," he said, and retired into his hermitage.

It was rather weak in me I confess, but his manner, on this occasion, nettled me.   110
Not only did there seem to lurk in it a certain calm disdain, but his perverseness seemed ungrateful, considering the undeniable good usage and indulgence he had received from me.

Again I sat ruminating what I should do. Mortified as I was at his behavior, and resolved as I had been to dismiss him when I entered my office, nevertheless I strangely felt something superstitious knocking at my heart, and forbidding me to carry out my purpose, and denouncing me for a villain if I dared to breathe one bitter word against this forlornest of mankind. At last, familiarly drawing my chair behind his screen, I sat down and said: "Bartleby, never mind, then, about revealing your history; but let me entreat you, as a friend, to comply as far as may be with the usages of this office. Say now, you will help to examine papers tomorrow or next day: in short, say now, that in a day or two you will begin to be a little reasonable:—say so, Bartleby."

"At present I would prefer not to be a little reasonable," was his mildly cadaverous reply.

Just then the folding-doors opened, and Nippers approached. He seemed suffering from an unusually bad night's rest, induced by severer indigestion than common. He overheard those final words of Bartleby.

"*Prefer not, eh?*" gritted Nippers—"I'd *prefer* him, if I were you, sir," addressing me—"I'd *prefer* him; I'd give him preferences, the stubborn mule! What is it, sir, pray, that he *prefers* not to do now?"

Bartleby moved not a limb.   115

"Mr. Nippers," said I, "I'd prefer that you would withdraw for the present."

Somehow, of late, I had got into the way of involuntarily using this word "prefer" upon all sorts of not exactly suitable occasions. And I trembled to think that my contact with the scrivener had already and seriously affected me in a mental way. And what further and deeper aberration might it not yet produce? This apprehension had not been without efficacy in determining me to summary measures.

As Nippers, looking very sour and sulky, was departing, Turkey blandly and deferentially approached.

"With submission, sir," said he, "yesterday I was thinking about Bartleby here, and I think that if he would but prefer to take a quart of good ale every day, it would do much towards mending him, and enabling him to assist in examining his papers."

"So you have got the word, too," said I, slightly excited.   120

"With submission, what word, sir?" asked Turkey, respectfully crowding himself into the contracted space behind the screen, and by so doing, making me jostle the scrivener. "What word, sir?"

"I would prefer to be left alone here," said Bartleby, as if offended at being mobbed in his privacy.

"*That's* the word, Turkey," said I—"*that's* it."

"Oh, *prefer?* oh yes—queer word. I never use it myself. But, sir, as I was saying, if he would but prefer—"

"Turkey," interrupted I, "you will please withdraw."   125

"Oh certainly, sir, if you prefer that I should."

As he opened the folding-door to retire, Nippers at his desk caught a glimpse of me, and asked whether I would prefer to have a certain paper copied on blue paper or white. He did not in the least roguishly accent the word "prefer." It was plain that it involuntarily rolled from his tongue. I thought to myself, surely I must get rid of a demented man, who already has in some degree turned the tongues, if not the heads of myself and clerks. But I thought it prudent not to break the dismission at once.

The next day I noticed that Bartleby did nothing but stand at his window in his dead-wall revery. Upon asking him why he did not write, he said that he had decided upon doing no more writing.

"Why, how now? what next?" exclaimed I, "do no more writing?"

"No more."   130

"And what is the reason?"

"Do you not see the reason for yourself?" he indifferently replied.

I looked steadfastly at him, and perceived that his eyes looked dull and glazed. Instantly it occurred to me, that his unexampled diligence in copying by his dim window for the first few weeks of his stay with me might have temporarily impaired his vision.

I was touched. I said something in condolence with him. I hinted that of course he did wisely in abstaining from writing for a while; and urged him to embrace that opportunity of taking wholesome exercise in the open air. This, however, he did not do. A few days after this, my other clerks being absent, and being in a great hurry to dispatch certain letters by the mail, I thought that, having nothing else earthly to do, Bartleby would surely be less inflexible than usual, and carry these letters to the Post Office. But he blankly declined. So, much to my inconvenience, I went myself.

Still added days went by. Whether Bartleby's eyes improved or not, I could not   135
say. To all appearance, I thought they did. But when I asked him if they did he vouch-safed no answer. At all events, he would do no copying. At last, in replying to my urgings, he informed me that he had permanently given up copying.

"What!" exclaimed I; "suppose your eyes should get entirely well—better than ever before—would you not copy then?"

"I have given up copying," he answered, and slid aside.

He remained as ever, a fixture in my chamber. Nay—if that were possible—he became still more of a fixture than before. What was to be done? He would do nothing in the office; why should he stay there? In plain fact, he had now become a millstone to me, not only useless as a necklace, but afflictive to bear. Yet I was sorry for him. I speak less than truth when I say that, on his own account, he occasioned me uneasiness. If he would but have named a single relative or friend, I would instantly have written, and urged their taking the poor fellow away to some convenient retreat. But he seemed alone, absolutely alone in the universe. A bit of wreck in the mid-Atlantic. At length, necessities connected with my business tyrannized over all other considerations. Decently as I could, I told Bartleby that in six days' time he must unconditionally leave the office. I warned him to take measures, in the interval, for procuring some other abode. I offered to assist him in this endeavor, if he himself would but take the first step towards a removal. "And when you finally quit me, Bartleby," added I, "I shall see that you go not away entirely unprovided. Six days from this hour, remember."

At the expiration of that period, I peeped behind the screen, and lo! Bartleby was there.

I buttoned up my coat, balanced myself; advanced slowly towards him, touched   140
his shoulder, and said, "The time has come; you must quit this place; I am sorry for you; here is money; but you must go."

"I would prefer not," he replied, with his back still towards me.

"You *must*."

He remained silent.

Now I had an unbounded confidence in this man's common honesty. He had frequently restored to me sixpences and shillings carelessly dropped upon the floor, for I am apt to be very reckless in such shirt-button affairs. The proceeding, then, which followed will not be deemed extraordinary.

"Bartleby," said I, "I owe you twelve dollars on account; here are thirty-two; the   145
odd twenty are yours—Will you take it?" and I handed the bills towards him.

But he made no motion.

"I will leave them here, then," putting them under a weight on the table. Then
taking my hat and cane and going to the door, I tranquilly turned and added—"After
you have removed your things from these offices, Bartleby, you will of course lock the
door—since every one is now gone for the day but you—and if you please, slip your key
underneath the mat, so that I may have it in the morning. I shall not see you again; so
good-bye to you. If, hereafter, in your new place of abode, I can be of any service to you,
do not fail to advise me by letter. Good-bye, Bartleby, and fare you well."

But he answered not a word; like the last column of some ruined temple, he remained standing mute and solitary in the middle of the otherwise deserted room.

As I walked home in a pensive mood, my vanity got the better of my pity. I could
not but highly plume myself on my masterly management in getting rid of Bartleby.
Masterly I call it, and such it must appear to any dispassionate thinker. The beauty of
my procedure seemed to consist in its perfect quietness. There was no vulgar bullying,
no bravado of any sort, no choleric hectoring, and striding to and fro across the apartment, jerking out vehement commands for Bartleby to bundle himself off with his beg-
garly traps. Nothing of the kind. Without loudly bidding Bartleby depart—as an
inferior genius might have done—I *assumed* the ground that depart he must; and upon
that assumption built all I had to say. The more I thought over my procedure, the more
I was charmed with it. Nevertheless, next morning, upon awakening, I had my
doubts—I had somehow slept off the fumes of vanity. One of the coolest and wisest
hours a man has, is just after he awakes in the morning. My procedure seemed as saga-
cious as ever—but only in theory. How it would prove in practice—there was the rub.
It was truly a beautiful thought to have assumed Bartleby's departure; but, after all, that
assumption was simply my own, and none of Bartleby's. The great point was, not
whether I had assumed that he would quit me, but whether he would prefer to do so. He
was more a man of preferences than assumptions.

After breakfast, I walked down town, arguing the probabilities *pro* and *con*. One   150
moment I thought it would prove a miserable failure, and Bartleby would be found all
alive at my office as usual; the next moment it seemed certain that I should find his
chair empty. And so I kept veering about. At the corner of Broadway and Canal Street,
I saw quite an excited group of people standing in earnest conversation.

"I'll take odds he doesn't," said a voice as I passed.

"Doesn't go?—done!" said I, "put up your money."

I was instinctively putting my hand in my pocket to produce my own, when I remembered that this was an election day. The words I had overheard bore no reference
to Bartleby, but to the success or non-success of some candidate for the mayoralty. In
my intent frame of mind, I had, as it were, imagined that all Broadway shared in my excitement, and were debating the same question with me. I passed on, very thankful that
the uproar of the street screened my momentary absent-mindedness.

As I had intended, I was earlier than usual at my office door. I stood listening for
a moment. All was still. He must be gone. I tried the knob. The door was locked. Yes,
my procedure had worked to a charm; he indeed must be vanished. Yet a certain melancholy mixed with this: I was almost sorry for my brilliant success. I was fumbling under
the door mat for the key, which Bartleby was to have left there for me, when

accidentally my knee knocked against a panel, producing a summoning sound, and in response a voice came to me from within—"Not yet; I am occupied."

It was Bartleby.   155

I was thunderstruck. For an instant I stood like the man who, pipe in mouth, was killed one cloudless afternoon long ago in Virginia, by summer lightning; at his own warm open window he was killed, and remained leaning out there upon the dreamy afternoon, till someone touched him, when he fell.

"Not gone!" I murmured at last. But again obeying that wondrous ascendancy which the inscrutable scrivener had over me, and from which ascendancy, for all my chafing, I could not completely escape, I slowly went down stairs and out into the street, and while walking round the block, considered what I should next do in this unheard-of perplexity. Turn the man out by an actual thrusting I could not; to drive him away by calling him hard names would not do; calling in the police was an unpleasant idea; and yet, permit him to enjoy his cadaverous triumph over me—this, too, I could not think of. What was to be done? or, if nothing could be done, was there anything further that I could *assume* in the matter? Yes, as before I had prospectively assumed that Bartleby would depart, so now I might retrospectively assume that departed he was. In the legitimate carrying out of this assumption, I might enter my office in a great hurry, and pretending not to see Bartleby at all, walk straight against him as if he were air. Such a proceeding would in a singular degree have the appearance of a home-thrust. It was hardly possible that Bartleby could withstand such an application of the doctrine of assumption. But upon second thoughts the success of the plan seemed rather dubious. I resolved to argue the matter over with him again.

"Bartleby," said I, entering the office, with a quietly severe expression, "I am seriously displeased. I am pained, Bartleby. I had thought better of you. I had imagined you of such a gentlemanly organization, that in any delicate dilemma a slight hint would suffice—in short, an assumption. But it appears I am deceived. Why," I added, unaffectedly starting, "you have not even touched that money yet," pointing to it, just where I had left it the evening previous.

He answered nothing.

"Will you, or will you not, quit me?" I now demanded in a sudden passion, advancing close to him.   160

"I would prefer *not* to quit you," he replied, gently emphasizing the *not*.

"What earthly right have you to stay here? Do you pay any rent? Do you pay my taxes? Or is this property yours?"

He answered nothing.

"Are you ready to go on and write now? Are your eyes recovered? Could you copy a small paper for me this morning? or help examine a few lines? or step round to the Post Office? In a word, will you do anything at all, to give a coloring to your refusal to depart the premises?"

He silently retired into his hermitage.   165

I was now in such a state of nervous resentment that I thought it but prudent to check myself at present from further demonstrations. Bartleby and I were alone. I remembered the tragedy of the unfortunate Adams and the still more unfortunate Colt in the solitary office of the latter; and how poor Colt, being dreadfully incensed by Adams, and imprudently permitting himself to get wildly excited, was at unawares hurried into his fatal act—an act which certainly no man could possibly deplore more than the actor himself. Often it had occurred to me in my ponderings upon the subject that had that altercation taken place in the public street, or at a private residence, it would not have terminated as it did. It was the circumstance of being alone in a solitary office, up stairs, of a building entirely unhallowed by humanizing domestic associations—an uncarpeted office, doubtless, of a dusty, haggard sort of appearance—this it must have been, which greatly helped to enhance the irritable desperation of the hapless Colt.

But when this old Adam of resentment rose in me and tempted me concerning Bartleby, I grappled him and threw him. How? Why, simply by recalling the divine injunction: "A new commandment give I unto you, that ye love one another." Yes, this it was that saved me. Aside from higher considerations, charity often operates as a vastly wise and prudent principle—a great safeguard to its possessor. Men have committed murder for jealousy's sake, and anger's sake, and hatred's sake, and selfishness' sake, and spiritual pride's sake; but no man, that ever I heard of, ever committed a diabolical murder for sweet charity's sake. Mere self-interest, then, if no better motive can be enlisted, should, especially with high-tempered men, prompt all beings to charity and philanthropy. At any rate, upon the occasion in question, I strove to drown my exasperated feelings towards the scrivener by benevolently construing his conduct. Poor fellow, poor fellow! thought I, he don't mean anything; and besides, he has seen hard times, and ought to be indulged.

I endeavored, also, immediately to occupy myself, and at the same time to comfort my despondency. I tried to fancy, that in the course of the morning, at such time as might prove agreeable to him, Bartleby, of his own free accord, would emerge from his hermitage and take up some decided line of march in the direction of the door. But no. Half-past twelve o'clock came; Turkey began to glow in the face, overturn his inkstand, and become generally obstreperous; Nippers abated down into quietude and courtesy; Ginger Nut munched his noon apple; and Bartleby remained standing at his window in one of his profoundest dead-wall reveries. Will it be credited? Ought I to acknowledge it? That afternoon I left the office without saying one further word to him.

Some days now passed, during which, at leisure intervals I looked a little into "Edwards on the Will," and "Priestley on Necessity." Under the circumstances, those books induced a salutary feeling. Gradually I slid into the persuasion that these troubles of mine, touching the scrivener, had been all predestined from eternity, and Bartleby was billeted upon me for some mysterious purpose of an all-wise Providence, which it was not for a mere mortal like me to fathom. Yes, Bartleby, stay there behind your screen, thought I; I shall persecute you no more; you are harmless and noiseless as any of these old chairs; in short, I never feel so private as when I know you are here. At last I see it, I feel it; I penetrate to the predestined purpose of my life. I am content. Others may have loftier parts to enact; but my mission in this world, Bartleby, is to furnish you with the office-room for such period as you may see fit to remain.

I believe that this wise and blessed frame of mind would have continued with me, 170 had it not been for the unsolicited and uncharitable remarks obtruded upon me by my professional friends who visisted the rooms. But thus it often is, that the constant friction of illiberal minds wears out at last the best resolves of the more generous. Though to be sure, when I reflected upon it, it was not strange that people entering my office should be struck by the peculiar aspect of the unaccountable Bartleby, and so be tempted to throw out some sinister observations concerning him. Sometimes an attorney, having business with me, and calling at my office, and finding no one but the scrivener there, would undertake to obtain some sort of precise information from him touching my whereabouts; but without heeding his idle talk, Bartleby would remain standing immovable in the middle of the room. So after contemplating him in that position for a time, the attorney would depart, no wiser than he came.

Also, when a reference was going on, and the room full of lawyers and witnesses, and business driving fast, some deeply-occupied legal gentleman present, seeing Bartleby wholly unemployed, would request him to run round to his (the legal gentleman's) office and fetch some papers for him. Thereupon, Bartleby would tranquilly decline, and yet remain idle as before. Then the lawyer would give a great stare, and turn to me. And what could I say? At last I was made aware that all through the circle of my professional acquaintance, a whisper of wonder was running round, having reference to the strange creature I kept at my office. This worried me very much. And as the idea came upon me of his possibly turning out a long-lived man, and keeping occupying my chambers, and denying my authority; and perplexing my visitors; and scandalizing my professional reputation; and casting a general gloom over the premises; keeping soul and body together to the last upon his savings (for doubtless he spent but half a dime a day), and in the end perhaps outlive me, and claim possession of my office by right of his perpetual occupancy: as all these dark anticipations crowded upon me more and more, and my friends continually intruded their relentless remarks upon the apparition in my room; a great change was wrought in me. I resolved to gather all my faculties together, and forever rid me of this intolerable incubus.

Ere revolving any complicated project, however, adapted to this end, I first simply suggested to Bartleby the propriety of his permanent departure. In a calm and serious tone, I commended the idea to his careful and mature consideration. But, having taken three days to meditate upon it, he apprised me, that his original determination remained the same; in short, that he still preferred to abide with me.

What shall I do? I now said to myself, buttoning up my coat to the last button. What shall I do? what ought I to do? what does conscience say I *should* do with this man, or, rather, ghost. Rid myself of him, I must; go, he shall. But how? You will not thrust him, the poor, pale, passive mortal you will not thrust such a helpless creature out of your door? you will not dishonor yourself by such cruelty? No, I will not, I cannot do that. Rather would I let him live and die here, and then mason up his remains in the wall. What, then, will you do? For all your coaxing, he will not budge. Bribes he leaves under your own paper-weight on your table; in short, it is quite plain that he prefers to cling to you.

Then something severe, something unusual must be done. What! surely you will not have him collared by a constable, and commit his innocent pallor to the common jail? And upon what ground could you procure such a thing to be done?—a vagrant, is he? What! he a vagrant, a wanderer, who refuses to budge? It is because he will not be a vagrant, then, that you seek to count him *as* a vagrant. That is too absurd. No visible means of support: there I have him. Wrong again: for indubitably he *does* support himself, and that is the only unanswerable proof that any man can show of his possessing the means so to do. No more, then. Since he will not quit me, I must quit him. I will change my offices; I will move elsewhere, and give him fair notice, that if I find him on my new premises I will then proceed against him as a common trespasser.

Acting accordingly, next day I thus addressed him: "I find these chambers too far 175
from the City Hall; the air is unwholesome. In a word, I propose to remove my offices next week, and shall no longer require your services. I tell you this now, in order that you may seek another place."

He made no reply, and nothing more was said.

On the appointed day I engaged carts and men, proceeded to my chambers, and, having but little furniture, everything was removed in a few hours. Throughout, the scrivener remained standing behind the screen, which I directed to be removed the last thing. It was withdrawn; and, being folded up like a huge folio, left him the motionless occupant of a naked room. I stood in the entry watching him a moment, while something from within me upbraided me.

I re-entered, with my hand in pocket—and—and my heart in my mouth.

"Good-bye, Bartleby; I am going—good-bye, and God some way bless you; and take that," slipping something in his hand. But it dropped upon the floor, and then—strange to say—I tore myself from him whom I had so longed to be rid of.

Established in my new quarters, for a day or two I kept the door locked, started at every footfall in the passages. When I returned to my rooms, after any little absence, I would pause at the threshold for an instant, and attentively listen, ere applying my key. But these fears were needless. Bartleby never came nigh me.

I thought all was going well, when a perturbed-looking stranger visited me, inquiring whether I was the person who had recently occupied rooms at No.—Wall Street.

Full of forebodings, I replied that I was.

"Then, sir," said the stranger, who proved a lawyer, "you are responsible for the man you left there. He refuses to do any copying; he refuses to do anything; he says he prefers not to; and he refuses to quit the premises."

"I am very sorry, sir," said I, with assumed tranquillity, but an inward tremor, "but, really, the man you allude to is nothing to me—he is no relation or apprentice of mine, that you should hold me responsible for him."

"In mercy's name, who is he?"

"I certainly cannot inform you. I know nothing about him. Formerly I employed him as a copyist; but he has done nothing for me now for some time past."

"I shall settle him, then—good morning, sir."

Several days passed, and I heard nothing more; and, though I often felt a charitable prompting to call at the place and see poor Bartleby, yet a certain squeamishness, of I know not what, withheld me.

All is over with him, by this time, thought I, at last, when, through another week, no further intelligence reached me. But, coming to my room the day after, I found several persons waiting at my door in a high state of nervous excitement.

"That's the man here—he comes," cried the foremost one, whom I recognized as the lawyer who had previously called upon me alone.

"You must take him away, sir, at once," cried a portly person among them, advancing upon me, and whom I knew to be the landlord of No.—Wall Street. "These gentlemen, my tenants, cannot stand it any longer; Mr. B——" pointing to the lawyer, "has turned him out of his room, and he now persists in haunting the building generally, sitting upon the banisters of the stairs by day, and sleeping in the entry by night. Everybody is concerned; clients are leaving the offices; some fears are entertained of a mob; something you must do, and that without delay."

Aghast at this torrent, I fell back before it, and would fain have locked myself in my new quarters. In vain I persisted that Bartleby was nothing to me—no more than to any one else. In vain—I was the last person known to have anything to do with him, and they held me to the terrible account. Fearful, then, of being exposed in the papers

180

185

190

(as one person present obscurely threatened), I considered the matter, and, at length, said, that if the lawyer would give me a confidential interview with the scrivener, in his (the lawyer's) own room, I would, that afternoon, strive my best to rid them of the nuisance they complained of.

Going up stairs to my old haunt, there was Bartleby silently sitting upon the banister at the landing.

"What are you doing here, Bartleby?" said I.

"Sitting upon the banister," he mildly replied.   195

I motioned him into the lawyer's room, who then left us.

"Bartleby," said I, "are you aware that you are the cause of great tribulation to me, by persisting in occupying the entry after being dismissed from the office?"

No answer.

"Now one of two things must take place. Either you must do something, or something must be done to you. Now what sort of business would you like to engage in? Would you like to re-engage in copying for some one?"

"No; I would prefer not to make any change."   200

"Would you like a clerkship in a dry-goods store?"

"There is too much confinement about that. No, I would not like a clerkship; but I am not particular."

"Too much confinement," I cried, "why, you keep yourself confined all the time!"

"I would prefer not to take a clerkship," he rejoined, as if to settle that little item at once.

"How would a bartender's business suit you? There is no trying of the eyesight in   205
that."

"I would not like it at all; though, as I said before, I am not particular."

His unwonted wordiness inspirited me. I returned to the charge.

"Well, then, would you like to travel through the country collecting bills for the merchants? That would improve your health."

"No, I would prefer to be doing something else."

"How, then, would going as a companion to Europe, to entertain some young   210
gentleman with your conversation—how would that suit you?"

"Not at all. It does not strike me that there is anything definite about that. I like to be stationary. But I am not particular."

"Stationary you shall be, then," I cried, now losing all patience, and, for the first time in all my exasperating connections with him, fairly flying into a passion. "If you do not go away from these premises before night, I shall feel bound—indeed, I *am* bound—to—to—to quit the premises myself!" I rather absurdly concluded, knowing not with what possible threat to try to frighten his immobility into compliance. Despairing of all further efforts, I was precipitately leaving him, when a final thought occurred to me—one which had not been wholly unindulged before.

"Bartleby," said I, in the kindest tone I could assume under such exciting circumstances, "will you go home with me now not to my office, but my dwelling—and remain there till we can conclude upon some convenient arrangement for you at our leisure? Come, let us start now, right away."

"No: at present I would prefer not to make any change at all."

I answered nothing; but, effectually dodging every one by the suddenness and ra-   215
pidity of my flight, rushed from the building, ran up Wall Street towards Broadway, and, jumping into the first omnibus, was soon removed from pursuit. As soon as tranquillity

returned, I distinctly perceived that I had now done all that I possibly could, both in respect to the demands of the landlord and his tenants, and with regard to my own desire and sense of duty, to benefit Bartleby, and shield him from rude persecution. I now strove to be entirely care-free and quiescent; and my conscience justified me in the attempt; though, indeed, it was not so successful as I could have wished. So fearful was I of being again hunted out by the incensed landlord and his exasperated tenants, that, surrendering my business to Nippers, for a few days, I drove about the upper part of the town and through the suburbs, in my rockaway; crossed over to Jersey City and Hoboken, and paid fugitive visits to Manhattanville and Astoria. In fact, I almost lived in my rockaway for the time.

When again I entered my office, lo, a note from the landlord lay upon the desk. I opened it with trembling hands. It informed me that the writer had sent to the police, and had Bartleby removed to the Tombs as a vagrant. Moreover, since I knew more about him than any one else, he wished me to appear at that place, and make a suitable statement of the facts. These tidings had a conflicting effect upon me. At first I was indignant; but, at last, almost approved. The landlord's energetic, summary disposition, had led him to adopt a procedure which I do not think I would have decided upon myself; and yet, as a last resort, under such peculiar circumstances, it seemed the only plan.

As I afterwards learned, the poor scrivener, when told that he must be conducted to the Tombs, offered not the slightest obstacle, but, in his pale, unmoving way, silently acquiesced.

Some of the compassionate and curious by-standers joined the party; and headed by one of the constables arm-in-arm with Bartleby, the silent procession filed its way through all the noise, and heat, and joy of the roaring thoroughfares at noon.

The same day I received the note, I went to the Tombs, or, to speak more properly, the Halls of Justice. Seeking the right officer, I stated the purpose of my call, and was informed that the individual I described was, indeed, within. I then assured the functionary that Bartleby was a perfectly honest man, and greatly to be compassionated, however unaccountably eccentric. I narrated all I knew, and closed by suggesting the idea of letting him remain in as indulgent confinement as possible, till something less harsh might be done—though, indeed, I hardly knew what. At all events, if nothing else could be decided upon, the alms-house must receive him. I then begged to have an interview.

Being under no disgraceful charge, and quite serene and harmless in all his ways,   220
they had permitted him freely to wander about the prison, and, especially, in the inclosed grass-platted yards thereof. And so I found him there, standing all alone in the quietest of the yards, his face towards a high wall, while all around, from the narrow slits of the jail windows, I thought I saw peering out upon him the eyes of murderers and thieves.

"Bartleby!"

"I know you," he said, without looking round—"and I want nothing to say to you."

"It was not I that brought you here, Bartleby," said I, keenly pained at his implied suspicion. "And to you, this should not be so vile a place. Nothing reproachful attaches to you by being here. And see, it is not so sad a place as one might think. Look, there is the sky, and here is the grass."

"I know where I am," he replied, but would say nothing more, and so I left him.

As I entered the corridor again, a broad meat-like man, in an apron, accosted me,   225
and, jerking his thumb over my shoulder, said "Is that your friend?"

"Yes."

"Does he want to starve? If he does, let him live on the prison fare, that's all."

"Who are you?" asked I, not knowing what to make of such an unofficially speaking person in such a place.

"I am the grub-man. Such gentlemen as have friends here, hire me to provide them with something good to eat."

"Is this so?" said I, turning to the turnkey.   230

He said it was.

"Well, then," said I, slipping some silver into the grub-man's hands (for so they called him), "I want you to give particular attention to my friend there; let him have the best dinner you can get. And you must be as polite to him as possible."

"Introduce me, will you?" said the grub-man, looking at me with an expression which seemed to say he was all impatience for an opportunity to give a specimen of his breeding.

Thinking it would prove of benefit to the scrivener, I acquiesced; and, asking the grub-man his name, went up with him to Bartley.

"Bartleby, this is a friend; you will find him very useful to you."   235

"Your sarvant, sir, your sarvant," said the grub-man, making a low salutation behind his apron. "Hope you find it pleasant here, sir; nice grounds—cool apartments—hope you'll stay with us some time—try to make it agreeable. What will you have for dinner to-day?"

"I prefer not to dine to-day," said Bartleby, turning away. "It would disagree with me; I am unused to dinners." So saying, he slowly moved to the other side of the inclosure, and took up a position fronting the dead-wall.

"How's this?" said the grub-man, addressing me with a stare of astonishment. "He's odd, ain't he?"

"I think he is a little deranged," said I, sadly.

"Deranged? deranged is it? Well, now, upon my word, I thought that friend of   240
yourn was a gentleman forger; they are always pale and genteel-like, them forgers. I can't help pity 'em—can't help it, sir. Did you know Monroe Edwards?" he added, touchingly, and paused. Then, laying his hand piteously on my shoulder, sighed, "he died of consumption at Sing-Sing. So you weren't acquainted with Monroe?"

"No, I was never socially acquainted with any forgers. But I cannot stop longer. Look to my friend yonder. You will not lose by it. I will see you again."

Some few days after this, I again obtained admission to the Tombs, and went through the corridors in quest of Bartleby; but without finding him.

"I saw him coming from his cell not long ago," said a turnkey, "maybe he's gone to loiter in the yards."

So I went in that direction.

"Are you looking for the silent man?" said another turnkey, passing me. "Yonder   245
he lies—sleeping in the yard there. 'Tis not twenty minutes since I saw him lie down."

The yard was entirely quiet. It was not accessible to the common prisoners. The surrounding walls, of amazing thickness, kept off all sounds behind them. The Egyptian character of the masonry weighted upon me with its gloom. But a soft imprisoned turf grew under foot. The heart of the eternal pyramids, it seemed, wherein, by some strange magic, through the clefts, grass-seed, dropped by birds, had sprung.

Strangely huddled at the base of the wall, his knees drawn up, and lying on his side, his head touching the cold stones, I saw the wasted Bartleby. But nothing stirred. I paused; then went close up to him; stooped over, and saw that his dim eyes were open;

otherwise he seemed profoundly sleeping. Something prompted me to touch him. I felt his hand, when a tingling shiver ran up my arm and down my spine to my feet.

The round face of the grub-man peered upon me now. "His dinner is ready. Won't he dine to-day, either? Or does he live without dining?"

"Lives without dining," said I, and closed the eyes.

"Eh!—He's asleep, ain't he?"   250

"With kings and counselors," murmured I.

There would seem little need for proceeding further in this history. Imagination will readily supply the meagre recital of poor Bartleby's interment. But, ere parting with the reader, let me say, that if this little narrative has sufficiently interested him, to awaken curiosity as to who Bartleby was, and what manner of life he led prior to the present narrator's making his acquaintance, I can only reply, that in such curiosity I fully share, but am wholly unable to gratify it. Yet here I hardly know whether I should divulge one little item of rumor, which came to my ear a few months after the scrivener's decease. Upon what basis it rested, I could never ascertain; and hence, how true it is I cannot now tell. But, inasmuch as this vague report has not been without a certain suggestive interest to me, however sad, it may prove the same with some others; and so I will briefly mention it. The report was this: that Bartleby had been a subordinate clerk in the Dead Letter Officer at Washington, from which he had been suddenly removed by a change in the administration. When I think over this rumor, hardly can I express the emotions which seize me. Dead letters! does it not sound like dead men? Conceive a man by nature and misfortune prone to a pallid hopelessness, can any business seem more fitted to heighten it than that of continually handling these dead letters, and assorting them for the flames? For by the cart-load they are annually burned. Sometimes from out the folded paper the pale clerk takes a ring—the finger it was meant for, perhaps, moulders in the grave; a bank-note sent in swiftest charity he whom it would relieve, nor eats nor hungers any more; pardon for those who died despairing; hope for those who died unhoping; good tidings for those who died stifled by unrelieved calamities. On errands of life, these letters speed to death.

Ah, Bartleby! Ah, humanity!

[1853]

ANALYZING "BARTLEBY, THE SCRIVENER"

Interpreting this moving story involves understanding the basic elements of its historical context as well as considering major literary elements, such as plot, character, tone, theme, and metaphor/imagery. Let's look at some of these elements in "Bartleby," which was published in 1853.

Plot

The plot of this story is one of the oldest in the annals of literature: the story of an individual (the narrator) attempting to understand another person and, in so doing, coming to learn about himself. The narrator is unnamed, which gives him a sense of universality. The plot is fairly simple: An elderly, father-figure businessman runs an office of law-copyists (scriveners), a very mundane job. The firm is small and employs three other scriveners, all with unusual eccentric personalities and nicknames to match—Turkey, Nippers, and Ginger Nut. And then there is Bartleby, the man who will not work, represented by his famous phrase, "I would prefer not to." From the beginning of the narrative, it is clear that the narrator is a father figure to his eccentric copyists, each of whom has his idiosyncrasies and each of whom requires special handling by the benevolent boss. As the plot unfurls, the copyists, except for Bartleby, remain basically the same characters, but it is the narrator who changes significantly as he confronts himself as a result of his interactions with Bartleby.

"Bartleby," like any narrative, chronicles change over time and cause and effect. The story begins with the 60-year-old narrator telling us that he is a relatively easygoing man whose motto is, "the easiest way is the best." He neither seeks nor relishes conflict, especially in the workplace. Indeed, he does his best to accommodate his eccentric scriveners, particularly Bartleby. As the plot develops, the narrator's relationship with Bartleby becomes more complex, and the narrator looks deeply into himself as he seeks to muster the language and action that will address the Bartleby problem. The plot turns, significantly, on the narrator's struggles with himself as he balances the forces of his conscious mind with the unconscious. The closing paragraphs reveal the narrator's final struggle to find an explanation for Bartleby's behavior, and in so doing, he comes to learn more about his own impulses, desires, and values.

Character

"Bartleby" has long been recognized as a story about a fascinating character—a man who refuses, politely, to work for a very accommodating employer. Although the story includes several characters, Bartleby and the unnamed narrator are clearly the two most important figures in the story. Much criticism has focused on Bartley and his elusive nature. Does he have any friends or relatives? Why does he refuse to work? What does he do after hours in the building where he spends 24 hours a day? What does his former occupation as a clerk in the Dead Letter Office have to do with his eccentric behavior? There have been numerous answers to these questions, ranging from ideological analyses to economic explanations to issues of literary form and the story's surprise ending. Treatments of the narrator-lawyer have also been mixed. Some critics find him to be an endearing, sympathetic figure, whereas other readers take him to be deliberately obscure and misleading, giving readers ground to doubt his truthfulness and full disclosure, as if it were possible to posit a stable and fully understandable mind-set, especially in a complex character.

At the beginning of the story, the narrator reveals a genial and avuncular persona. He portrays himself as a friendly, father figure to Bartleby and the other scriveners. We are told that he seldom loses his temper, implying that he is a man of patience, compassion, and understanding. He describes himself as viewed by others as an "eminently safe man," and no less than John Jacob Astor has pronounced his "first grand point to be prudence." The narrator tells us that he agrees with this opinion, a statement that might give us pause before readily accepting his laudatory self-descriptions. The important point is that the narrator is a dominant figure in the story and just as worthy of detailed analysis as Bartleby. His continual struggles with his basic instincts, his business sense, and his conscience provide material for a rich analysis of a character perhaps just as enigmatic as Bartleby. As the narrative develops, we come to learn increasingly more about the psychological struggles of the teller of the tale.

Tone and Point of View

Since "Bartleby" is told from the first-person perspective, it is important to analyze carefully everything that the narrator says about himself. There is no emphasis on objectivity with a first-person narrator, and the subjectivity of the speaking persona becomes a significant point-of-view issue. The tone of the narration is one of gentle and sympathetic detachment. The narrator works to establish a tone of kindly, paternal description. He clearly attempts to present himself and his characters emphathetically, especially Bartleby, although he describes Turkey, Nippers, and Ginger Nut in endearing terms also. They all have eccentricities, which he accepts because he views himself as a compassionate man, comfortable with humanity. Throughout the story, the narrator creates a mood of reconciliation, as he attempts to resolve his conflicts with Bartleby and, equally important, his conflicts within himself.

Theme

New York's Wall Street was a bustling center of business activity in the 1850s, just as it is today. This area is rich in tales of eccentric personalities and ambiguous personal histories of its inhabitants. There are many themes imbedded inside this seductive narrative, but one of the story's motifs is the narrator's attempt to fully understand Bartleby. The narrator-lawyer is fascinated by Bartleby's stubborn resistance to authority, in sharp contrast to the narrator's orderly, well-disciplined life. One of the ways in which the narrator comes to grips with explaining Bartleby's life is through his own psychological impulses. In short, these impulses are linguistic expressions of the narrator's id, ego, and superego. At times, the narrator rages about his scrivener's personality. At other times, he is quite sympathetic, even compassionate. And the rest of the time, he attempts to rationalize and explain, in coldly logical language, Bartleby's behavior. Each of these explanatory attempts is in some way an expression of the narrator's psychological makeup. The "mind state" of the narrator is one of the more fascinating movements in the narrative, right up to the very end, when he bemoans Bartleby's fate and the fate of humanity.

Metaphor and Imagery

"Bartleby" is rich in symbolism, metaphor, and imagery. The story begins with a sense of quiet frustration, as the narrator introduces himself in positively glowing terms, emphasizing his prudence and self-control (which he loses periodically in spite of his self-proclamations). His gesture of immodest modesty—his compliments of himself—sets the tone of the story, one of rich irony. Eccentricity is a major metaphor in this story. Indeed, all four scriveners are described as being well out of the ordinary. Each one of them possesses character flaws that require special understanding from the narrator. And, of course, no one is more eccentric than Bartleby, a metaphor for resistance to authority. Yet, the lawyer-narrator is rather eccentric himself. His excessive compassion (by most standards) for Bartleby reveals an atypical individual, particularly when the narrator vacates his own building rather than force Bartleby to move out. The image of the narrator is one of gentility and civility, friendly to Bartleby and his fellow copyists. Yet beneath that image, the narrator is a moving and complex figure himself, and just as interesting and eccentric as Bartleby.

Questions for Your Analysis of "Bartleby, the Scrivener"

1) What are some of your early impressions of the story?
2) What are your observations of the narrator's assessment of himself, especially as he describes his personal and business traits? Do you trust the narrator to be sincere? Do you accept what he says about himself and the other characters, without hesitation or qualification?
3) The scriveners are all described as eccentric, beginning with their nicknames. What do these copyists tell us about the workplace and its head, the narrator-lawyer?
4) What are some examples of situations when the narrator's id seems to be the driving force behind his utterances?
5) What are some examples of situations when the narrator's ego seems to be the driving force behind his utterances?
6) What are some examples of situations when the narrator's superego seems to be the driving force behind his utterances?
7) The narrator can reconcile his conflicts only through language. What are examples of his statements that attempt to achieve some kind of reconciliation in his own mind, some balance among the three psychological impulses introduced above?
8) What is it that we learn from this bizarre Wall Street tale?
9) In what ways does the narrator foreshadow the end of the story?
10) How do you interpret the concluding statement of the story: "Ah, Bartleby! Ah, humanity!"?

The textual issues suggested in this chapter can be appropriated to psychological criticism, as well as to other interpretive approaches. Please read the following sample essay on "Bartleby" as an illustration of one form that psychological criticism might take. This essay, as you will see, focuses on the developing character of the narrator, particularly as he attempts to comprehend "reality" (Bartleby's bizarre behavior), his reactions to Bartleby's behavior, and his sense of himself. The narrator, as a speaking subject bewildered by the Other (Bartleby), expresses himself the only way he can—through language (the symbolic order)—which is under the influence of his conscious and unconscious drives, desires, and experiences. All insightful psychological criticism is well served to bear in mind the limitations and complexities of any particular psychological theory or combination of theories. Other psychological approaches to the story, for example, might focus more on Freudian elements, such as repression, displacement, dream theory, or Oedipal interpretations. Indeed, there are many, many possible psychological readings of "Bartleby."

Sample Essay on "Bartleby, the Scrivener"

Herman Melville has entertained readers for 150 years with his fascinating tale of the clerk who wouldn't clerk. The name Bartleby, in some circles, has come to stand for someone who "prefers not to." He is the epitome of the immovable object, an employee who refuses to take any directives from his superior. Readers have long been intrigued, and frustrated, by how little we really know about Bartleby, his background, and his motivations. We do know much more about Bartleby's boss, the narrator-lawyer, however, and what the narrator tells us about Bartleby reveals a great deal about himself. What is particularly important, from a psychological perspective, is the narrator's struggle to articulate the forces that are at work deep within his own mind, forces that are both conscious and subconscious. The narrator, as a speaking subject, strives to explain himself in terms of his encounters with others, especially with Bartleby.

In order to read "Bartleby" from a psychological perspective, I will approach the story using Sigmund Freud's views on the conscious and subconscious mind, comprised of the id, ego, and superego. The id represents raw, unchecked human emotions, fears, and passions. The ego is a control center, enforcing rules of good conduct and keeping the emotions in check. It is the ego that regulates irrational impulses lurking in the human psyche. The superego is the moral judge of the psyche. Freudian critics often see the ego as regulating the desires of the id, counter balanced by the moral and authority of the superego.

Jacques Lacan is another theorist who builds upon Freud's theory of the unconscious mind. Lacan speaks of the symbolic order stage, in which children and adults come to structure and explain their lives through language. This stage of development illustrates the importance to express, through language, that which was thought to be inexpressible. Individuals are understood, psychologically, by their statements to and about others. Indeed, life becomes a sequence of exchanges between the self and other individuals. The speaking subject reveals much about his or her psychological makeup through the language they use. Lacan's theory of the speaking subject, coupled with Freud's theory of the id, ego, and superego, offers a conceptual framework from which we might read "Bartleby" in order to explore the language of the narrator and thereby gain insight into this complex narrative.

At the beginning of the story, the unnamed narrator adopts a genial and avuncular persona. He clearly attempts to present himself as a friendly father figure to Bartleby and the other scriveners (and even to us readers). We are told that he seldom loses his temper, implying that he is a man of patience, compassion, and understanding. He describes himself as viewed by others as an "eminently safe man," and John Jacob Astor has pronounced the lawyer's "first grand point to be prudence." The narrator tells us that he agrees with this opinion, a statement that might give us pause before readily accepting his positive self-descriptions. His continual struggles with his basic instincts, his business sense, and his conscience provide material for a rich analysis of a character perhaps equally enigmatic as Bartleby. As the narrative develops, we learn increasingly more about the psychological struggles of the teller of the tale.

We learn from the narrator that he is compassionate, putting up with the eccentricities of all four scriveners. Indeed, he chaperons his four charges, three of whom have childrens' nicknames: Turkey, Nippers, and Ginger Nut. The narrator's fourth "offspring," Bartleby, cannot be defined by the narrator with the same precision that he describes the other three copyists. We learn that Bartleby has only recently been hired and, for the first two days, performs quite well. As the narrator says, "he seemed to gorge himself on my documents." Bartleby works day and night, "copying by sunlight and by candle-light." These characteristics suggest that Bartleby is robotic and mechanical, perhaps not fully human in his mechanical devotion to copying. On the third day, Bartleby utters for the first time his famous reply, "I would prefer not to," in response to the lawyer's request for assistance in comparing legal documents. The lawyer responds instinctively, perhaps subconsciously allowing his id to control his language: "Are you moonstruck? . . . I want you to help me compare this sheet here—take it," as the narrator thrusts it at Bartleby. The scrivener refuses again, of course, and the lawyer is taken aback, like a befuddled father whose child has shown disobedience and insubordination. This time, the narrator chooses a far more temperate response, as if his ego were controlling his language of caution and concern.

Bartleby, at this point, has not totally abandoned work; he just refuses to work with anyone else in comparing documents that he has generated. After Bartleby's second, "I would prefer not to," the narrator responds not with anger and passion, but with understanding, reason, and compassion. The lawyer's ego is firmly in control: "There was something in Bartleby that not only strangely disarmed me, but, in a wonderful manner, touched and disconcerted me. I began to reason with him." The narrator is moved by his encounter with his "son," and, perhaps, sees an image of himself. The narrator has told us that he is a hard-working, "safe" man, who is well disciplined. Bartleby represents rebellion and disorder (perhaps pure id), something we do not see in the narrator, but these may be characteristics he has repressed in himself, or maybe Bartleby is the rebellious son the lawyer never had. There is no question that he is kindly and sympathetic to Bartleby, and there must be some basis for his compassion.

The narrator periodically defers to his conscience in dealing with Bartleby, which suggests that his superego plays an important role in his dealings with Bartleby. The lawyer explains his compassion in clear terms: "To befriend Bartleby, to humor him in his strange willfulness, will cost me little or nothing, which I lay up in my soul what will eventually prove a sweet morsel for my conscience." Like an infant, Bartleby is always there to haunt the narrator. Even on weekends, Bartleby remains in the office, like some lost soul, afraid to go out into the world, displaying infantile characteristics. The narrator surmises that Bartleby is almost supernatural in his lifestyle: "for an indefinite period Bartleby must have ate, dressed, and slept in my office, and that too without plate, mirror, or bed." The narrator begins to think of Bartleby as an apparition: "The scrivener's pale form appeared to me laid out, among uncaring strangers, in its shivering winding-sheet." The narrator begins to conjure up an image if Bartleby as a spectral figure, haunting the lawyer: "he must be standing in one of those dead-wall reveries of his." The lawyer has reached the crossroads in his relationship with Bartleby.

The narrator's id, ego, and superego are in conflict as he wrestles with what to do with Bartleby. The narrator's desire (id) for compassion comes through as he expresses his sorrow at Bartleby's plight. The lawyer is sympathetic to Bartleby and desperately wants to do the right thing (superego). After much deliberation, the narrator's rational side (ego) takes over, and he decides to inform Bartleby that he must leave within six days. Business considerations have triumphed over personal sympathy. However, the narrator has underestimated Bartleby's obstinacy. The narrator finds himself back in conflict—with id, ego, and superego impulses competing for control. The superego takes over ("Turn the man out by an actual thrusting I could not do") alternating with id impulses ("'Will you, or will you not, quit me?' I now demanded in a sudden passion.") The superego wins out, temporarily, as the narrator recalls the divine injunction, "that ye love one another." Then, with another turn of the narrator's impulses, he makes a decision: "I resolved to gather all my faculties together, and forever rid me of this intolerable incubus." This stand is followed by the reemergence of his superego: "You will not thrust him, the poor, pale, passive mortal you will not thrust such a helpless creature out of our door? you will not dishonor yourself by such cruelty? No, I will not, I cannot do that." As with so many of life's internal conflicts, this one is not so easily resolved.

Throughout the story, conflicts rage among the narrator's id, ego, superego. Sometimes the narrator gives in to his rage and the id dominates; at other times, his conscience prevails; and the rest of the time, his ego moderates between the impulses of the id and ego. Because Bartleby absolutely refuses to leave the narrator's office, the lawyer eventually leaves Bartleby, but the separation between them is only physical. Bartleby still weighs heavily on the narrator's mind. Bartleby is eventually taken to the Tombs, a penitentiary, and the narrator befriends him even there, bribing the grub-man to make sure that Bartleby eats well. During a second visit, the narrator discovers Bartleby's dead body, slumped over in a corner of the Tombs. Bartleby may be "sleeping with kings and counselors," as the narrator observes, but the scrivener is very much alive in the mind of the narrator. Piqued by an obsessive, undying interest in Bartleby, the narrator researches the scrivener's background and learns that he had previously been employed in the Dead Letter Office. This discovery leads the narrator to draw some meaning from Bartleby's life and death.

Bartleby's existence, so intriguing to the narrator, leads him to conclude that the scrivener's resistance to authority (and even to life itself) derives from his miserable experience as a clerk in the Dead Letter Office, a place where language goes to die. The narrator bemoans Bartleby's fate in his concluding sigh, "Ah, Bartleby! Ah, humanity!" From a psychological perspective, this final sigh sums up the narrator's attempt (and inability) to explain one man's life and death in language, the only tools he has. The narrator's frustration in understanding (or misunderstanding) Bartleby is vented, somewhat, by his use of language to make sense out of the details of Bartleby's life. Yet in bemoaning Bartleby's fate, perhaps the narrator also bemoans his own.

WRITING YOUR ESSAY FROM A PSYCHOLOGICAL PERSPECTIVE

The following short story, "The Cask of Amontillado," is by Edgar Allan Poe (1809–1849). This narrative, like other readings in this volume, is accessible to a psychological reading. This story, like Melville's narrative, is told in the first-person voice of a narrator, but there are significant differences between Melville's narrator and Poe's narrator. You have seen that Melville's narrator is a complex mixture of sympathy, conscience, and reason. Poe's narrator, Montresor, is of a very different nature, as is so often the custom in the world of Edgar Allan Poe, inventor of the detective story. After you have read "The Cask of Amontillado," there are a series of questions to help you in the analysis of the work, as well as assisting you in writing an essay from a cultural perspective.

A SAMPLE READING

"The Cask of Amontillado" by Edgar Allan Poe (1809–1849)

The thousand injuries of Fortunato I had borne as I best could, but when he ventured upon insult I vowed revenge. You, who so well know the nature of my soul, will not suppose, however, that I gave utterance to a threat. At *length* I would be avenged; this was a point definitely settled—but the very definitiveness with which it was resolved precluded the idea of risk. I must not only punish but punish with impunity. A wrong is unredressed when retribution overtakes its redresser. It is equally unredressed when the avenger fails to make himself felt as such to him who has done the wrong.

It must be understood that neither by word nor by deed had I given Fortunato cause to doubt my good will. I continued, as was my wont, to smile in his face, and he did not perceive that my smile *now* was at the thought of his immolation.

He had a weak point—this Fortunato—although in other regards he was a man to be respected and even feared. He prided himself on his connoisseurship in wine. Few Italians have the true virtuoso spirit. For the most part their enthusiasm is adopted to suit the time and opportunity, to practise imposture upon the British and Austrian *millionaires*. In painting and gemmary, Fortunato, like his countrymen, was a quack, but in the matter of old wines he was sincere. In this respect I did not differ from him materially;—I was skillful in the Italian vintages myself, and bought largely whenever I could.

It was about dusk, one evening during the supreme madness of the carnival season, that I encountered my friend. He accosted me with excessive warmth, for he had been drinking much. The man wore motley. He had on a tight-fitting parti-striped dress, and his head was surmounted by the conical cap and bells. I was so pleased to see him that I thought I should never have done wringing his hand.

I said to him—"My dear Fortunato, you are luckily met. How remarkably well you are looking to-day. But I have received a pipe of what passes for Amontillado, and I have my doubts."   5

"How?" said he. "Amontillado? A pipe? Impossible! And in the middle of the carnival!"

"I have my doubts," I replied; "and I was silly enough to pay the full Amontillado price without consulting you in the matter. You were not to be found, and I was fearful of losing a bargain."

"Amontillado!"

"I have my doubts."

"Amontillado!"   10

"And I must satisfy them."

"Amontillado!"

"As you are engaged, I am on my way to Luchesi. If any one has a critical turn it is he. He will tell me—"

"Luchesi cannot tell Amontillado from Sherry."

"And yet some fools will have it that his taste is a match for your own."   15

"Come, let us go."

"Whither?"

"To your vaults."

"My friend, no; I will not impose upon your good nature. I perceive you have an engagement. Luchesi——"

"I have no engagement;—come."   20

"My friend, no. It is not the engagement, but the severe cold with which I perceive you are afflicted. The vaults are insufferably damp. They are encrusted with nitre."

"Let us go, nevertheless. The cold is merely nothing. Amontillado! You have been imposed upon. And as for Luchesi, he cannot distinguish Sherry from Amontillado."

Thus speaking, Fortunato possessed himself of my arm; and putting on a mask of black silk and drawing a *roquelaire* closely about my person, I suffered him to hurry me to my palazzo.

There were no attendants at home; they had absconded to make merry in honor of the time. I had told them that I should not return until the morning, and had given them explicit orders not to stir from the house. These orders were sufficient, I well knew, to insure their immediate disappearance, one and all, as soon as my back was turned.

I took from their sconces two flambeaux, and giving one to Fortunato, bowed   25
him through several suites of rooms to the archway that led into the vaults. I passed down a long and winding staircase, requesting him to be cautious as he followed. We came at length to the foot of the descent, and stood together upon the damp ground of the catacombs of the Montresors.

The gait of my friend was unsteady, and the bells upon his cap jingled as he strode.

"The pipe?" he said.

"It is farther on," said I; "but observe the white web-work which gleams from these cavern walls."

He turned towards me, and looked into my eyes with two filmy orbs that distilled the rheum of intoxication.

"Nitre?" he asked at length.   30

"Nitre," I replied. "How long have you had that cough?"

"Ugh! ugh! ugh!—ugh! ugh! ugh!—ugh! ugh! ugh!—ugh! ugh! ugh!—ugh! ugh! ugh!"

My poor friend found it impossible to reply for many minutes.

"It is nothing," he said at last.

"Come," I said, with decision, "we will go back; your health is precious. You are   35
rich, respected, admired, beloved; you are happy, as once I was. You are a man to be

missed. For me it is no matter. We will go back; you will be ill, and I cannot be responsible. Besides, there is Luchesi——"

"Enough," he said; "the cough is a mere nothing; it will not kill me. I shall not die of a cough."

"True—true," I replied; "and, indeed, I had no intentions of alarming you unnecessarily—but you should use all proper caution. A draught of this Medoc will defend us from the damps."

Here I knocked off the neck of a bottle which I drew from a long row of its fellows that lay upon the mould.

"Drink," I said, presenting him the wine.

He raised it to his lips with a leer. He paused and nodded to me familiarly, while   40
his bells jingled.

"I drink," he said, "to the buried that repose around us."

"And I to your long life."

He again took my arm, and we proceeded.

"These vaults," he said, "are extensive."

"The Montresors," I replied, "were a great and numerous family."   45

"I forget your arms."

"A huge human foot d'or, in a field azure; the foot crushes a serpent rampant whose fangs are imbedded in the heel."

"And the motto?"

"Nemo me impune lacessit."

"Good!" he said.   50

The wine sparkled in his eyes and the bells jingled. My own fancy grew warm with the Medoc. We had passed through long walls of piled bones, with casks and puncheons intermingling, into the inmost recesses of the catacombs. I paused again, and this time I made bold to seize Fortunato by an arm above the elbow.

"The nitre!" I said; "see, it increases. It hangs like moss upon the vaults. We are below the river's bed. The drops of moisture trickle among the bones. Come, we will go back ere it is too late. Your cough——"

"It is nothing," he said; "let us go on. But first, another draught of the Medoc."

I broke and reached him a flagon of De Grâve. He emptied it at a breath. His eyes flashed with a fierce light. He laughed and threw the bottle upwards with a gesticulation I did not understand.

I looked at him in surprise. He repeated the movement—a grotesque one.   55

"You do not comprehend?" he said.

"Not I," I replied.

"Then you are not of the brotherhood."

"How?"

"You are not of the masons."   60

"Yes, yes," I said; "yes, yes."

"You? Impossible! A mason?"

"A mason," I replied.

"A sign," he said.

"It is this," I answered, producing a trowel from beneath the folds of my *roquelaire*. 65

"You jest," he exclaimed, recoiling a few paces. "But let us proceed to the Amontillado."

"Be it so," I said, replacing the tool beneath the cloak and again offering him my arm. He leaned upon it heavily. We continued our route in search of the Amontillado. We passed through a range of low arches, descended, passed on, and descending again, arrived at a deep crypt, in which the foulness of the air caused our flambeaux rather to glow than flame.

At the most remote end of the crypt there appeared another less spacious. Its walls had been lined with human remains, piled to the vault overhead, in the fashion of the great catacombs of Paris. Three sides of this interior crypt were still ornamented in this manner. From the fourth side the bones had been thrown down, and lay promiscuously upon the earth, forming at one point a mound of some size. Within the wall thus exposed by the displacing of the bones, we perceived a still interior crypt or recess, in depth about four feet, in width three, in height six or seven. It seemed to have been constructed for no especial use within itself, but formed merely the interval between two of the colossal supports of the roof of the catacombs, and was backed by one of their circumscribing walls of solid granite.

It was in vain that Fortunato, uplifting his dull torch, endeavored to pry into the depth of the recess. Its termination the feeble light did not enable us to see.

"Proceed," I said; "herein is the Amontillado. As for Luchesi——" 70

"He is an ignoramus," interrupted my friend, as he stepped unsteadily forward, while I followed immediately at his heels. In an instant he had reached the extremity of the niche, and finding his progress arrested by the rock, stood stupidly bewildered. A moment more and I had fettered him to the granite. In its surface were two iron staples, distant from each other about two feet, horizontally. From one of these depended a short chain, from the other a padlock. Throwing the links about his waist, it was but the work of a few seconds to secure it. He was too much astounded to resist. Withdrawing the key I stepped back from the recess.

"Pass your hand," I said, "over the wall; you cannot help feeling the nitre. Indeed, it is *very* damp. Once more let me *implore* you to return. No? Then I must positively leave you. But I must first render you all the little attentions in my power."

"The Amontillado!" ejaculated my friend, not yet recovered from his astonishment.

"True," I replied; "the Amontillado."

As I said these words I busied myself among the pile of bones of which I have be 75 fore spoken. Throwing them aside, I soon uncovered a quantity of building stone and mortar. With these materials and with the aid of my trowel, I began vigorously to wall up the entrance of the niche.

I had scarcely laid the first tier of the masonry when I discovered that the intoxication of Fortunato had in a great measure worn off. The earliest indication I had of this was a low moaning cry from the depth of the recess. It was *not* the cry of a drunken man. There was a long and obstinate silence. I laid the second tier, and the third, and the fourth; and then I heard the furious vibrations of the chain. The noise lasted for several minutes, during which, that I might hearken to it with the more satisfaction, I ceased my labors and sat down upon the bones. When at last the clanking subsided, I resumed the trowel, and finished without interruption the fifth, the sixth, and the seventh tier. The wall was now nearly upon a level with my breast. I again paused, and holding the flambeaux over the mason-work, threw a few feeble rays upon the figure within.

A succession of loud and shrill screams, bursting suddenly from the throat of the chained form, seemed to thrust me violently back. For a brief moment I hesitated, I trembled. Unsheathing my rapier, I began to grope with it about the recess; but the thought of an instant reassured me. I placed my hand upon the solid fabric of the catacombs, and felt satisfied. I reapproached the wall; I replied to the yells of him who clamoured. I re-echoed, I aided, I surpassed them in volume and in strength. I did this, and the clamourer grew still.

It was now midnight, and my task was drawing to a close. I had completed the eighth, the ninth, and the tenth tier. I had finished a portion of the last and the eleventh; there remained but a single stone to be fitted and plastered in. I struggled with its weight; I placed it partially in its destined position. But now there came from out the niche a low laugh that erected the hairs upon my head. It was succeeded by a sad voice, which I had difficulty in recognizing as that of the noble Fortunato. The voice said—

"Ha! ha! ha!—he! he! he!—a very good joke, indeed—an excellent jest. We will have many a rich laugh about it at the palazzo—he! he! he!—over our wine—he! he! he!"

"The Amontillado!" I said.   80

"He! he! he!—he! he! he!—yes, the Amontillado. But is it not getting late? Will not they be awaiting us at the plazzo, the Lady Fortunato and the rest? Let us be gone."

"Yes," I said, "let us be gone."

"For the love of God, Montresor!"

"Yes," I said, "for the love of God."

But to these words I hearkened in vain for a reply. I grew impatient. I called   85
aloud—

"Fortunato!"

No answer. I called again—

"Fortunato!"

No answer still. I thrust a torch through the remaining aperture and let it fall within. There came forth in return only a jingling of the bells. My heart grew sick; it was the dampness of the catacombs that made it so. I hastened to make an end of my labor. I forced the last stone into its position; I plastered it up. Against the new masonry I re-erected the old rampart of bones. For the half of a century no mortal has disturbed them. *In pace requiescat!*

(1846)

Questions for Your Analysis of "The Cask of Amontillado"

1) What are some of your early impressions of the story? What is the most striking incident of the story, something that promotes an instant reaction in you?
2) This story is told in the first-person. What is your instinctive response to the form of the narration? How would you evaluate Montresor's values?
3) At what point in the narrative does the narrator's true purpose of the meeting become apparent?
4) Is there something from your personal experience that assists you in relating to any of the circumstances in the story, even if only in the psychological realm?
5) Much of the story is concerned with the encounter between Fortunato and Montresor. What do these encounters reveal about the characters, about Montresor's passionate hatred, and about Fortunato's naivete?

6) How much of Fortunato's behavior is primarily id motivated?

7) How much of Fortunato's behavior is primarily ego motivated?

8) Fortunato explains his own psychology through language, the only means he has. How does he compare himself to the Other (Fortunato)?

9) Does Montresor lack a superego? Are there circumstances in which you might be sympathetic to his hatred of Fortunato, even though you reject his actions?

10) Why does Montresor do what he does? Does he defend or explain himself rationally? What are his emotional explanations?

11) What are your observations of the narrator's obsession with revenge?

STEPS IN WRITING YOUR ESSAY

Brainstorming Your Topic

1) Identify those elements in the text (character, plot, theme, metaphor) that prompt an immediate response from you. Write down whatever impressions you have.

2) Focus on the two characters, Montresor and Fortunato. What is it about them that you do or do not like? Identify their personal traits before and during their encounter.

3) Identify elements in Montresor's narration that reveal the psychological landscape of his mind.

4) What personal experiences have you had that connect to anything in "The Cask of Amontillado"? Have you ever encountered someone obsessed with revenge? Someone who was the victim of revenge?

5) Why is the narrator so obsessed with retribution?

6) The story contains references to the past lives of all of the characters. Write down what effect(s) these references to the past have on your psychological analysis.

7) Friendship (or the appearance of friendship) plays a role in the story. How does this ironic treatment of the word shape your reading?

8) Are you satisfied with the ending? Why or why not?

9) What does the narrative show that suggests deep-rooted psychological forces at work in the narrative?

10) Unless your instructor insists that you not consult outside sources in brainstorming your topic, refer to the electronic sources listed at the end of this chapter for Edgar Allan Poe. There are many good links that will connect you to biographical sources and detailed criticism. Any ideas and words drawn directly from outside sources should be properly cited, of course. Consult the appendix for documentation procedures.

Creating an Outline

1) Collect your answers to the questions above in short two-word or three-word categories and use them as preliminary "writing points."

2) Think about the points and consider whether they add up to a central idea (for example, psychological forces at work in "The Cask of Amontillado").

3) Identify five or six main writing points that support your central idea. These points should come from the main literary elements in the story (character, plot, theme, point of view, metaphor). All of the points should provide support for your controlling idea. A good starting place is to examine the story's psychological context, the personal experiences of the author, and the cultural representations of the main characters.

4) If you have more than five or six points, try to combine one or more of them. If you have fewer than five or six points, see if some of them can be used to generate additional points. You may have some large points that include smaller issues that can stand alone as paragraph topic sentences.

5) Look for transitional devices that connect your main points of support, particularly as they connect various encounters in the story.

Preparing a Rough Draft

1) Now that you have created a working outline, you have already completed your major organizational work. Each major point is the topic of a paragraph, and your essay will have between 5 and 10 paragraphs, depending on development. These paragraphs need not be of equal length, but each one should sufficiently develop the topic sentence.

2) Now that you have your major writing points, assemble a preliminary draft by developing each topic idea with two or three sentences that discuss evidence from the text.

3) Focus on developing transitions between your paragraphs. Professional writers often begin a new paragraph with a direct reference to an idea expressed at the end of the preceding paragraph.

4) It is not too early to begin writing your concluding paragraph. Conclusions often summarize the main points of a central idea (but do not repeat word for word what has already been said). A conclusion may also refer to implications of what has been said (but what cannot be developed because of space limits). Your conclusion must examine ethical issues in the story.

5) Don't be afraid to include questions in your writing. No reader of literature can ever be absolutely certain of every observation that he or she makes, and perceptive observations often generate excellent questions, many of which are useful, even though unanswerable.

Editing Your Draft

1) At this stage, you should have a draft of a few hundred words. You have already done the most difficult work in thinking out your ideas, organizing them into an outline, and preparing a rough version of the final product. Look for ways to edit your paper that will strengthen the essay.

2) Search for repetitious wording (and ideas). Do not repeat ideas, however important, throughout the essay. Use a thesaurus to locate synonyms for terms and ideas that reappear. Attempt to emphasize variety in your language.

3) If your instructor encourages peer editing, choose someone in your class, or perhaps a roommate, and solicit advice about how your essay reads. Is it articulate, compelling, insightful, and interesting? (All of these qualities are important.) Although your peer editor may not be taking a literature class, he or she may be a very good source of feedback on how effective your writing is. Professional writers often seek feedback from peers, and not only from professional colleagues.

4) Be open to making changes in your writing, both conceptually and in specific language. Professional writers know that writing is recursive (which means that the act of writing constantly generates new ways of looking at the topic), and student writers should also take advantage of changes in thinking *as they write*. Don't be afraid to make efficient and effective changes, especially in terms of cutting out words, phrases, and sections that may not be working very well in supporting your overall idea.

5) Proofread carefully for spelling errors, punctuation problems, run-on sentences, and ambiguous or awkward constructions. You should use a solid grammar handbook to assist you in these areas.

Final Checklist

1) Make sure that your central idea (sometimes called a thesis statement) appears in the first paragraph. It is important that your reader know what major point(s) you are attempting to make.

2) Because this essay is a psychological exploration, check to see that the essay represents your analysis of psychological issues in the story. Your major points should be understandable, of course, to the community of readers to which you are writing.

3) Examine your essay for sufficient evidence. Each one of your major ideas will need illustration that comes from the text.

4) Review your conclusion to see if you have ended the essay in an effective manner, either summarizing what you have said (in different language) or suggesting some important implications of your reading.

5) Proofread one last time for errors, repetitious language, and awkward phrasing.

ELECTRONIC RESOURCES FOR HERMAN MELVILLE

http://www.melville.org/. This page has several links to biographical and analytical treatments of Melville.

http://www.gonzaga.edu/faculty/campbell/enl311/melville.htm. The site is another general introduction to Melville, which includes some of his works.

http://www.nwctc.comment.edu/fox/melville/classmaster.htm. This site focuses on historical artifacts from Melville's era.

http://www.intelligentsianetwork.com/melville/melville.htm. This page contains famous quotations of Herman Melville.

ELECTRONIC RESOURCES FOR EDGAR ALLAN POE

http://www.poedecoder.com/Qrisse/.   This site contains numerous links to information about Poe's life, works, and historical context.

http://www.poemuseum.org/.   This page connects you to the Richmond Museum of Edgar Allan Poe.

http://www.nps.gov/edal/.   This site contains information and pictures of a home that Poe lived in.

http://www.andromeda.rutgers.edu/~ehrlich/poesites.html.   This site is a comprehensive page with numerous links to biographical and bibliographical information about Poe.

chapter 9

Deconstructive Criticism

Deconstructive criticism is the most difficult chapter in this book, mainly because the principles or tools of this school are not as easily defined and explained as they are for other approaches to the interpretation of literature. The reasons why they cannot be defined with clarity will become more apparent later in this chapter, but it is fair to say that a deconstructive reading of literature relies on the basic uncertainty and ambiguity of language. Those who approach literature deconstructively must be willing to accept the position that words have many meanings and literary texts are open to a wide range of interpretation. All critical schools, of course, allow for some flexibility in the application of their principles in reading literary texts, but no other approach to interpretation begins with the premise that language, necessarily, means different things, often at the same time. Indeed, in some cases, readings are openly contradictory with one another. What is important to remember is that deconstructive reading is about exploring the different ways in which a text gives meaning rather than providing a clear, stable interpretation of what a text means. Deconstructive reading focuses on the "how" rather than the "what" of interpretation.

The term *deconstruction* comes from *destruction*, an earlier approach to interpretation, presented by the German philosopher Martin Heidegger, who emphasized that destruction is a process by which the reader "destroys" previously learned principles of interpretation that lead to "stable" meanings. To put it another way, "destruction" means to begin anew the process of interpretation, after having destroyed accepted meanings of things and ways of behaving. The process of destruction is a kind of negative analysis in which the individual wipes clean his or her traditional beliefs in order to interpret with freshness, vitality, and vigor.

The theoretical characteristics and qualities of destruction developed into deconstruction, primarily through the work of Jacques Derrida, a French philosopher, and Paul de Man, a Belgian/American literary critic. I say "characteristics" and "qualities" because these theorists resisted the notion that what they were doing could be coded in precise terms and definitions. Indeed, deconstructive critics challenge the very possibility of unambiguous rules of language and interpretation. Theorists of deconstruction resist labeling their work as that of a formal school of interpretation; their ideas and practices come to us through bits and pieces rather than through a full set of terms and principles. To interpret deconstructively is to read strategically rather than follow a carefully coded methodology.

Deconstruction, for its practitioners, involves the recognition (and practice) of the limitations of language. Professional deconstructive interpreters focus on the many layers of interpretation made possible by a wide range of meanings of words. All language, for these critics, is metaphoric, which means that all words ultimately refer to yet other words, whether we realize we are reading words as metaphors or not. To say, for example, that it is "raining cats and dogs" is an obvious metaphor, but to say that it is "raining heavily" is no less metaphoric a statement, although most individuals would not recognize this construction as an obvious metaphor.

The art of reading deconstructively also grew out of a tradition that actively opposes *logocentrism*, a view of language and reason that can be traced back to the early Greeks. Logocentrism emphasizes the primary importance of the word (*logos* in Greek) as an instrument of law and reason. (*Logos* also means reason in Greek.) "Truth" is an example of a logocentric term that has been very important in the Western tradition for over 2,000 years. The term "essence" is another master logocentric concept. Perhaps the most powerful example of logocentrism is the word "God," which represents absolute knowledge, final authority, pure essence, and an unchanging nature.

Early teachers, such as Plato and Aristotle, believed very strongly in the tradition of logocentrism, especially in the belief that words have stable meanings and the intellectual world can be understood through logic and reasoning. Indeed, their entire philosophies were built upon the belief that language is logical, stable, and predictable. Western logocentrism also relied on the assumption that concepts could sometimes be presented in their entirety, without glaring gaps, absences, or silences. Logocentrism was (and is) seen as a positive, affirmative understanding of language. It emphasizes the power of language as rational thought to provide meaning and understanding that is clear and unambiguous.

The practice of deconstruction rejects these assumptions of logocentrism. Whereas traditional Western perspectives on language view language as closed, clear, and referential, deconstructive readers perceive language as open, ambiguous, metaphoric, and necessarily incomplete, replete with gaps, absences, and silences. Deconstructive critics challenge the possibility of objective truth, replacing objectivity by embracing subjectivity (an emphasis on the mind, culture, and beliefs of the individual). However, deconstuctive readers do not recognize the relatively stable approach of reader-response criticism, where the individual mindset is critically important in acts of interpretation. Deconstructive critics are equally suspicious of those who consider cultures and mindsets of individuals and communities as definable, stable entities. Indeed, the deconstuctive mind views with suspicion all "stable" systems of interpretation, including its own. If you are confused by this apparent contradiction, you are not alone. And your confusion affirms one of deconstruction's most important assumptions: The human world is necessarily confused, ambiguous, and highly subjective. If you are able to accept ambiguities, confusions, and inconsistencies in language (as well as in life), then deconstructive interpretation is possible for you.

Here is a simple example of how a deconstructive approach to language reveals not only the complex and ambiguous nature of language, but also its instability. Beginning in the early 1930s and continuing to the present day, filmmakers have made fascinating movies about zombies, creatures that are both dead and alive, human and inhuman. In order to continue their existence (neither fully alive nor fully dead), zombies must consume living or recently killed flesh. In order to destroy a zombie, it must be killed (in spite of the fact that it is already dead). A zombie is a good illustration of deconstructive practices because it shows us something that is contradictory—neither dead nor alive; neither fully human nor fully spirit. The zombie is an ultimate uncertainty which exists between the margins of life and death. A "killed" zombie may, indeed, come back to "life." Hollywood publicity emphasizes the fact that the "nature" of the zombie is literally unbelievable. The philosophical point is that the zombie shows that categories of classification are often unreliable or contradictory. Distinctions between death and life are blurred.

The experience of deconstructive reading does not reveal what we can do to texts in interpreting them but, rather, it allows texts to expose what they do to and within themselves. The primary energy for the deconstructive act lies within texts, rather than within methods imposed from the outside. There are many strategies in deconstructive reading, but some important concepts that have generated considerable commentary include supplement, trace, and metaphor. These interpretative elements are by no means comprehensive, but they do illustrate principles and concerns shared by many deconstructive readers.

The term *supplement* refers to that which is additional, or extra: something that is added to something else. Yet a supplement often becomes a necessary part of the original. For example, the *Oxford English Dictionary* (OED) is considered by many scholars to be the most comprehensive dictionary of the

English language. Periodically, this dictionary is updated by the publication of a supplement. The supplement is something that it is added (it is not part of the original), but with the publication of the supplement, the OED is not considered "complete" without including the supplement. Therefore, the supplement is both something extra or added, yet also something essential to the original dictionary. The supplement is both integral yet not integral to the original OED. Like the zombie, the OED supplement inhabits the murky borders between one state and another. This illustration emphasizes that nothing is ever complete, closed, or defined with absolute certainty.

The concept of supplement is part of everything that is in language, according to deconstructive thought. "Thought" itself is often considered to be original, primary, and essential. Writing is often considered a supplement to thought. Writing is sometimes seen as derivative and secondary. Indeed, many writers (student and professional) strive for "original" thoughts that can be expressed in writing. The point is that thought, for deconstructionists, is necessary for writing, and writing completes thought. What is primary and original (thought) comes into expression through what is supplementary (writing). For writers, ideas that are original and essential require the supplement of writing in order to bring them into existence.

The term *trace* refers to the residue or history that every word and concept carries with it. The concept of trace reminds us that nothing ever exists in a pure, "present" state, without regard to the past or the future. To put it another way, trace is the name for what is not there. Anything that exists always refers to something else. Consider, for example, a photograph of someone you know. That photograph represents that person as she or he existed at a particular point in time, yet that photograph contains traces of what that person looked like at earlier times, perhaps even stretching back to childhood. And that photograph contains traces of what the person might look like in the near and distant future. On an intellectual level, interpreters always carry with them traces of prior experiences that shape their interpretations (as you saw in the chapter on reader-response criticism). Interpretations, literary and otherwise, shape future interpretations, as all of life's experiences contain traces of the past and hints of the future. No word can refer only to itself. All words refer to other words and concepts, all of which are interlinked traces.

Literary words and passages reveal the presence of traces (and absence, too, meaning traces that are lost, forgotten, or simply unconsidered). Consider, for example, Shakespeare's well-known play, *The Merchant of Venice*. This play focuses on the life of a moneylender, Shylock, and the experience he has living as an outsider (a Jew) in a Christian city where religious and racial prejudice are common experiences. (Indeed, Shakespeare's play eloquently calls attention to the problem of intolerance.) The word *merchant*, for most readers, means someone involved in business, a person engaged in commercial activities. This description accurately portrays Antonio, a businessman, and not Shylock, who deals in money and is not considered a merchant in the traditional sense of the term. So the title of the play raises the possibility of confusion: Shylock is not a "real" merchant, but rather a merchant of money (and all that implies, including usury or excessive interest charges). The term *merchant* comes from the Latin *mercatare*, a verb meaning to trade. Shylock is a trader, but of money and not of the kinds of goods that Renaissance merchants routinely traded. The title term of merchant, then, refers to both Antonio, a true merchant, and to Shylock, a false merchant, a trader of money but not goods. The title reveals more irony as we learn of Shylock's propensity for trading the untradable (at least in Christian Renaissance Italy and England), a pound of flesh to settle an unpaid loan.

Supplements and traces are but two issues deconstructive readers examine in interpreting texts. Metaphors are also critically important because they are everywhere in literary texts. Like supplements and traces, metaphors, resonate with meanings that may not be immediately recognized. Consider, for example, the metaphor commonly used to describe heavy rainfall: It is raining cats and dogs. Most people recognize this saying as an obvious metaphor, because it cannot be literally true. (This metaphor is particularly difficult for foreigners attempting to learn English.) However, the metaphor is indeed literally true in its earlier use. It is derived from medieval times, when animals such as dogs and cats perched on the roofs of low-lying huts. When it rained heavily, small animals were literally washed off of the roof. Hence the expression, "raining cats and dogs."

Knowing the history of language helps us to unravel metaphors such as the one just mentioned, but because we can explain a metaphor's origins (or at least the ones we know) does not mean that we have solved the metaphor and arrived at a final, literal truth. Deconstructive readers believe that there are always metaphors behind metaphors, a constant exchange of references in which metaphors refer not to concete experiences, but instead to other metaphors. (Literary critics call this movement the *turn of the trope*.) To return to "raining cats and dogs," English uses of rain trace back to rain as a gift from the gods, especially Zeus. Ancient Greeks would make sacrifices in order to please Zeus who, having been pleased, would reward loyal human subjects with rainfall for their crops. And this metaphor, too, can be unwound to reveal yet further historical sources, until the deconstructive reader runs out of decipherable references. Yet what lies beneath obvious metaphors are those metaphors of which we are unaware (but may come to surface at a later time, as we learn more about earlier cultures and traditions). To read deconstructively means to accept the infinite turn of the trope.

The deconstructive analysis of traces, supplements, and metaphors in literature all call into question the possibility of identity. Deconstructive readers come to accept the notion that literary characters are always incomplete, revealing (and hiding) traces and supplements of themselves that we can explore rigorously, but never fully understand or solve. If a reader can accept the limitations of deconstructive interpretation and recognize that a text can never be completely understood and explained, he or she is ready to enjoy the enriching experience of deconstructive reading, even with its accompanying inconclusions and frustrations. And even professional deconstructive critics are bewildered (and bothered) by the dizzying possibilities of interpretation opened up by the deconstructive approach.

What is the residue of deconstructive interpretation? It is fairly simple, at least at one level: A text necessarily has many meanings. A text cannot have only one meaning because literature always contains traces and supplements embedded within its text, and literature is rich in metaphor, where words always refer yet to other words and histories (remembered and forgotten). The ancient traces of meanings remain, sometimes hidden, in contemporary uses of language. Therefore, we can never know the complete, closed meaning of a word or a text, and this unknowability (sometimes called undecidability) is a strategic characteristic of deconstructive reading (and writing). To put it another way, the act of deconstruction is to ask a series of questions that reveal works of literature to apparently say one thing and yet mean something else (and, in turn, yet something else, again and again). Deconstructive interpretation means that we acknowledge that any act of reading is the unleashing of an infinite number of interpretive possibilities.

Does this description of deconstruction mean that we cannot find meanings in text? Absolutely not. Deconstructive readers do interpret literature; indeed, there is a large body of deconstructive interpretations available to the interested reader of literature. Paul de Man himself has produced volumes of literary interpretations. However, deconstructive readings routinely explore the ambiguities in texts, pointing out how various interpretations, sometimes equally valid from a grammatical or metaphorical point of view, contradict themselves. We might say that the mission of the deconstructive reader is to analyze the basis of various meanings in a text, not in order to arrive at a "valid" final reading, but rather to arrive at a deeper understanding of the complex forces at work within literary texts. In other words, deconstructive interpretation analyzes dimensions and problems within a text in order to articulate those forces at work. The "final product" of a deconstructive analysis is to flush out and articulate the intricacies of a text (hidden or obvious), be they traces, supplements, metaphors, grammatical constructions, or any other part of a word or literary work as a whole. The "conclusion" of deconstructive skepticism is a state of doubt (called *aporeia*, a classical Greek term), in which competing interpretations exist in a state of suspension. In other words, the end product of deconstructive reading is the act of analysis itself and not the generation of a "true" meaning of a text. Deconstructive readers do not believe that interpretation can go beyond analysis.

A SAMPLE READING

"The Blue Hotel" by Stephen Crane (1871–1900)

The Palace Hotel at Fort Romper was painted a light blue, a shade that is on the legs of a kind of heron, causing the bird to declare its position against any background. The Palace Hotel, then, was always screaming and howling in a way that made the dazzling winter landscape of Nebraska seem only a grey swampish hush. It stood alone on the prairie, and when the snow was falling the town two hundred yards away was not visible. But when the traveller alighted at the railway station he was obliged to pass the Palace Hotel before he could come upon the company of low clapboard houses which composed Fort Romper, and it was not to be thought that any traveller could pass the Palace Hotel without looking at it. Pat Scully, the proprietor, had proved himself a master of strategy when he chose his paints. It is true that on clear days, when the great transcontinental expresses, long lines of swaying Pullmans, swept through Fort Romper, passengers were overcome at the sight, and the cult that knows the brown-reds and the subdivisions of the dark greens of the East expressed shame, pity, horror, in a laugh. But to the citizens of this prairie town and to the people who would naturally stop there, Pat Scully had performed a feat. With this opulence and splendour, these creeds, classes, egotisms, that streamed through Romper on the rails day after day, they had no colour in common.

As if the displayed delights of such a blue hotel were not sufficiently enticing, it was Scully's habit to go every morning and evening to meet the leisurely trains that stopped at Romper and work his seductions upon any man that he might see wavering, gripsack in hand.

One morning, when a snow-crusted engine dragged its long string of freight cars and its one passenger coach to the station, Scully performed the marvel of catching three men. One was a shaky and quick-eyed Swede, with a great shining cheap valise; one was a tall bronzed cowboy, who was on his way to a ranch near the Dakota line; one was a little silent man from the East, who didn't look it, and didn't announce it. Scully practically made them prisoners. He was so nimble and merry and kindly that each probably felt it would be the height of brutality to try to escape. They trudged off over the creaking board sidewalks in the wake of the eager little Irishman. He wore a heavy fur cap squeezed tightly down on his head. It caused his two red ears to stick out stiffly, as if they were made of tin.

At last, Scully, elaborately, with boisterous hospitality, conducted them through the portals of the blue hotel. The room which they entered was small. It seemed to be merely a proper temple for an enormous stove, which in the centre, was humming with godlike violence. At various points on its surface the iron had become luminous and glowed yellow from the heat. Beside the stove Scully's son Johnnie was playing High-Five with an old farmer who had whiskers both grey and sandy. They were quarrelling. Frequently the old farmer turned his face toward a box of sawdust—coloured brown from tobacco juice—that was behind the stove, and spat with an air of great impatience and irritation. With a loud flourish of words Scully destroyed the game of cards, and bustled his son upstairs with part of the baggage of the new guests. He himself conducted them to three basins of the coldest water in the world. The cowboy and the Easterner burnished themselves fiery red with this water, until it seemed to be some kind of metal-polish. The Swede, however, merely dipped his fingers gingerly and with trepidation. It was notable that throughout this series of small ceremonies the three travellers were made to feel that Scully was very benevolent. He was conferring great favours upon them. He handed the towel from one to another with an air of philanthropic impulse.

Afterward they went to the first room, and, sitting about the stove, listened to   5
Scully's officious clamour at his daughters, who were preparing the midday meal. They reflected in the silence of experienced men who tread carefully amid new people. Nevertheless, the old farmer, stationary, invincible in his chair near the warmest part of the stove, turned his face from the sawdust-box frequently and addressed a glowing commonplace to the strangers. Usually he was answered in short but adequate sentences by either the cowboy or the Easterner. The Swede said nothing. He seemed to be occupied in making furtive estimates of each man in the room. One might have thought that he had the sense of silly suspicion which comes to guilt. He resembled a badly frightened man.

Later, at dinner, he spoke a little, addressing his conversation entirely to Scully. He volunteered that he had come from New York, where for ten years he had worked as a tailor. These facts seemed to strike Scully as fascinating, and afterward he volunteered that he had lived at Romper for fourteen years. The Swede asked about the crops and the price of labour. He seemed barely to listen to Scully's extended replies. His eyes continued to rove from man to man.

Finally, with a laugh and a wink, he said that some of these Western communities were very dangerous; and after his statement he straightened his legs under the table, tilted his head, and laughed again, loudly. It was plain that the demonstration had no meaning to the others. They looked at him wondering and in silence.

II

As the men trooped heavily back into the front room, the two little windows presented views of a turmoiling sea of snow. The huge arms of the wind were making attempts—mighty, circular, futile—to embrace the flakes as they sped. A gate-post like a still man with a blanched face stood aghast amid this profligate fury. In a hearty voice Scully announced the presence of a blizzard. The guests of the blue hotel, lighting their pipes, assented with grunts of lazy masculine contentment. No island of the sea could be exempt in the degree of this little room with its humming stove. Johnnie, son of Scully, in a tone which defined his opinion of his ability as a card player, challenged the old farmer of both grey and sandy whiskers to a game of High-Five. The farmer agreed with a contemptuous and bitter scoff. They sat close to the stove, and squared their knees under a wide board. The cowboy and the Easterner watched the game with interest. The Swede remained near the window, aloof, but with a countenance that showed signs of an inexplicable excitement.

The play of Johnnie and the grey-beard was suddenly ended by another quarrel. The old man arose while casting a look of heated scorn at his adversary. He slowly buttoned his coat, and then stalked with fabulous dignity from the room. In the discreet silence of all other men the Swede laughed. His laughter rang somehow childish. Men by this time had begun to look at him askance, as if they wished to inquire what ailed him.

A new game was formed jocosely. The cowboy volunteered to become the part- 10
ner of Johnnie, and they all then turned to ask the Swede to throw in his lot with the
little Easterner. He asked some questions about the game, and, learning that it wore
many names, and that he had played it when it was under an alias, he accepted the invitation. He strode toward the men nervously, as if he expected to be assaulted. Finally,
seated, he grazed from face to face and laughed shrilly. This laugh was so strange that
the Easterner looked up quickly, the cowboy sat intent and with his mouth open, and
Johnnie paused, holding the cards with still fingers.

Afterward there was a short silence. Then Johnnie said, "Well, let's get at it.
Come on now!" They pulled their chairs forward until their knees were bunched under
the board. They began to play, and their interest in the game caused the others to forget
the manner of the Swede.

The cowboy was a board-whacker. Each time that he held superior cards he
whanged them, one by one, with exceeding force, down upon the improvised table, and
took the tricks with a glowing air of prowess and pride that sent thrills of indignation
into the hearts of his opponents. A game with a board-whacker in it is sure to become
intense. The countenances of the Easterner and the Swede were miserable whenever
the cowboy thundered down his aces and kings, while Johnnie, his eyes gleaming with
joy, chuckled and chuckled.

Because of the absorbing play none considered the strange ways of the Swede.
They paid strict heed to the game. Finally, during a lull caused by a new deal, the
Swede suddenly addressed Johnnie: "I suppose there have been a good many men killed
in this room." The jaws of the others dropped and they looked at him.

"What in hell are you talking about?" said Johnnie.

The Swede laughed again his blatant laugh, full of a kind of false courage and de- 15
fiance. "Oh, you know what I mean all right," he answered.

"I'm a liar if I do!" Johnnie protested. The card was halted, and the men stared at
the Swede. Johnnie evidently felt that as the son of the proprietor he should make a direct inquiry. "Now, what might you be drivin' at, mister?" he asked. The Swede winked
at him. It was a wink full of cunning. His fingers shook on the edge of the board. "Oh,
maybe you think I have been to nowheres. Maybe you think I'm a tenderfoot?"

"I don't know nothin' about you," answered Johnnie, "and I don't give a damn
where you've been. All I got to say is that I don't know what you're driving at. There
hain't never been nobody killed in this room."

The cowboy, who had been steadily gazing at the Swede, then spoke: "What's
wrong with you, mister?"

Apparently it seemed to the Swede that he was formidably menaced. He shivered
and turned white near the corners of his mouth. He sent an appealing glance in the direction of the little Easterner. During these moments he did not forget to wear his air of
advanced pot-valour. "They say they don't know what I mean," he remarked mockingly
to the Easterner.

The latter answered after prolonged and cautious reflection. "I don't understand 20
you," he said, impassively.

The Swede made a movement then which announced that he thought he had
encountered treachery from the only quarter where he had expected sympathy, if not
help. "Oh, I see you are all against me. I see——"

The cowboy was in a state of deep stupefaction. "Say," he cried, as he tumbled
the deck violently down upon the board, "say, what are you gittin' at, hey?"

The Swede sprang up with the celerity of a man escaping from a snake on the floor. "I don't want to fight!" he shouted. "I don't want to fight!"

The cowboy stretched his long legs indolently and deliberately. His hands were in his pockets. He spat into the sawdust-box. "Well, who the hell thought you did?" he inquired.

The Swede backed rapidly toward a corner of the room. His hands were out pro- 25
tectingly in front of his chest, but he was making an obvious struggle to control his fright. "Gentlemen," he quavered, "I suppose I am going to be killed before I can leave this house! I suppose I am going to be killed before I can leave this house!" In his eyes was the dying-swan look. Through the windows could be seen the snow turning blue in the shadow of dusk. The wind tore at the house, and some loose thing beat regularly against the clapboards like a spirit tapping.

A door opened, and Scully himself entered. He paused in surprise as he noted the tragic attitude of the Swede. Then he said, "What's the matter here?"

The Swede answered him swiftly and eagerly: "These men are going to kill me."

"Kill you!" ejaculated Scully. "Kill you! What are you talkin'?"

The Swede made the gesture of a martyr.

Scully wheeled sternly upon his son. "What is this, Johnnie?" 30

The lad had grown sullen. "Damned if I know," he answered. "I can't make no sense to it." He began to shuffle the cards, fluttering them together with an angry snap. "He says a good many men have been killed in this room, or something like that. And he says he's goin' to be killed here too. I don't know what ails him. He's crazy. I shouldn't wonder."

Scully then looked for explanation to the cowboy, but the cowboy simply shrugged his shoulders.

"Kill you?" said Scully again to the Swede. "Kill you? Man, you're off your nut."

"Oh, I know," burst out the Swede. "I know what will happen. Yes, I'm crazy—yes. Yes, of course, I'm crazy—yes. But I know one thing—" There was a sort of sweat of misery and terror upon his face. "I know I won't get out of here alive."

The cowboy drew a deep breath, as if his mind was passing into the last stages of 35
dissolution. "Well, I'm doggoned," he whispered to himself.

Scully wheeled suddenly and faced his son. "You've been troublin' this man!"

Johnnie's voice was loud with its burden of grievance. "Why, good Gawd, I ain't done nothin' to 'im."

The Swede broke in. "Gentlemen, do not disturb yourselves. I will leave this house. I will go away, because"—he accused them dramatically with his glance—"because I do not want to be killed."

Scully was furious with his son. "Will you tell me what is the matter, you young divil? What's the matter, anyhow? Speak out!"

"Blame it!" cried Johnnie in despair, "don't I tell you I don't know? He—he says 40
we want to kill him, and that's all I know. I can't tell what ails him."

The Swede continued to repeat: "Never mind, Mr. Scully; never mind. I will leave this house. I will go away, because I do not wish to be killed. Yes, of course, I am crazy—yes. But I now one thing! I will go away. I will leave this house. Never mind, Mr. Scully; never mind. I will go away."

"You will not go 'way," said Scully. "You will not go 'way until I hear the reason of this business. If anybody has troubled you I will take care of him. This is my house.

You are under my roof, and I will not allow any peaceable man to be troubled here." He cast a terrible eye upon Johnnie, the cowboy, and the Easterner.

"Never mind, Mr. Scully; never mind. I will go away. I do not wish to be killed." The Swede moved toward the door which opened upon the stairs. It was evidently his intention to go at once for his baggage.

"No, no," shouted Scully peremptorily; but the white-faced man slid by him and disappeared. "Now," said Scully severely, "what does this mane?"

Johnnie and the cowboy cried together: "Why, we didn't do nothin' to 'im!"   45

Scully's eyes were cold. "No," he said, "you didn't?"

Johnnie swore a deep oath. "Why, this is the wildest loon I ever see. We didn't do nothin' at all. We were just sittin' here playin' cards, and he—"

The father suddenly spoke to the Easterner. "Mr. Blanc," he asked, "what has these boys been doin'?"

The Easterner reflected again. "I didn't see anything wrong at all," he said at last, slowly.

Scully began to howl. "But what does it mane?" He stared ferociously at his son.   50
"I have a mind to lather you for this, me boy."

Johnnie was frantic. "Well, what have I done?" he bawled at his father.

III

"I think you are tongue-tied," said Scully finally to his son, the cowboy, and the Easterner; and at the end of this scornful sentence he left the room.

Upstairs the Swede was swiftly fastening the straps of his great valise. Once his back happened to be half turned toward the door, and, hearing a noise there, he wheeled and sprang up, uttering a loud cry. Scully's wrinkled visage showed grimly in the light of the small lamp he carried. This yellow effulgence, streaming upward, coloured only his prominent features, and left his eyes, for instance, in mysterious shadow. He resembled a murderer.

"Man! man!" he exclaimed, "have you gone daffy?"

"On, no! Oh, no!" rejoined the other. "There are people in this world who know   55
pretty nearly as much as you do—understand?"

For a moment they stood gazing at each other. Upon the Swede's deathly pale cheeks were two spots brightly crimson and sharply edged, as if they had been carefully painted. Scully placed the light on the table and sat himself on the edge of the bed. He spoke ruminatively. "By cracky, I never heard of such a thing in my life. It's a complete muddle. I can't, for the soul of me, think how you ever got this idea into your head." Presently he lifted his eyes and asked: "And did you sure think they were going to kill you?"

The Swede scanned the old man as if he wished to see into his mind. "I did," he said at last. He obviously suspected that this answer might precipitate an outbreak. As he pulled on a strap his whole arm shook, the elbow wavering like a bit of paper.

Scully banged his hand impressively on the footboard of the bed. "Why, man, we're goin' to have a line of ilictric street-cars in this town next spring."

"'A line of electric street-cars,'" repeated the Swede, stupidly.

"And," said Scully, "there's a new railroad goin' to be built down from Broken   60
Arm to here. Not to mintion the four churches and the smashin' big brick school-house.
Then there's the big factory, too. Why, in two years Romper'll be a metro-*pol*-is."

Having finished the preparation of his baggage, the Swede straightened himself.
"Mr. Scully," he said, with sudden hardihood, "how much do I owe you?"

"You don't owe me anythin'," said the old man, angrily.

"Yes, I do," retorted the Swede. He took seventy-five cents from his pocket and
tendered it to Scully; but the latter snapped his fingers in disdainful refusal. However, it
happened that they both stood gazing in a strange fashion at three silver pieces on the
Swede's open palm.

"I'll not take your money," said Scully at last. "Not after what's been goin' on
here." Then a plan seemed to strike him. "Here," he cried, picking up his lamp and
moving toward the door. "Here! Come with me a minute."

"No," said the Swede, in overwhelming alarm.   65

"Yes," urged the old man. "Come on! I want you to come and see a picter—just
across the hall—in my room."

The Swede must have concluded that his hour was come. His jaw dropped and
his teeth showed like a dead man's. He ultimately followed Scully across the corridor,
but he had the step of one hung in chains.

Scully flashed the light high on the wall of his own chamber. There was revealed
a ridiculous photograph of a little girl. She was leaning against a balustrade of gorgeous
decoration, and the formidable bang to her hair was prominent. The figure was as graceful as an upright sled-stake, and, withal, it was of the hue of lead. "There," said Scully,
tenderly, "that's the picter of my little girl that died. Her name was Carrie. She had the
purtiest hair you ever saw! I was the fond of her, she——"

Turning then, he saw that the Swede was not contemplating the picture at all,
but, instead, was keeping keen watch on the gloom in the rear.

"Look, man!" cried Scully, heartily. "That's the picter of my little gal that died.   70
Her name was Carrie. And then here's the picter of my oldest boy, Michael. He's a
lawyer in Lincoln, an' doin' well. I gave that boy a grand eddication, and I'm glad for it
now. He's a fine boy. Look at 'im now. Ain't he bold as blazes, him there in Lincoln, an
honoured an' respicted gintleman! An honoured and respicted gintleman," concluded
Scully with a flourish. And, so saying, he smote the Swede jovially on the back.

The Swede faintly smiled.

"Now," said the old man, "there's only one more thing." He dropped suddenly to
the floor and thrust his head beneath the bed. The Swede could hear his muffled voice.
"I'd keep it under me piller if it wasn't for that boy Johnnie. Then there's the old
woman——Where is it now? I never put it twice in the same place. Ah, now come out
with you!"

Presently he backed clumsily from under the bed, dragging with him an old coat
rolled into a bundle. "I've fetched him," he muttered. Kneeling on the floor, he unrolled the coat and extracted from its heart a large yellow-brown whisky-bottle.

His first maneuver was to hold the bottle up to the light. Reassured, apparently,
that nobody had been tampering with it, he thrust it with a generous movement toward
the Swede.

The weak-kneed Swede was about to eagerly clutch this element of strength, but   75
he suddenly jerked his hand away and cast a look of horror upon Scully.

"Drink," said the old man affectionately. He had risen to his feet, and now stood facing the Swede.

There was a silence. Then again Scully said: "Drink!"

The Swede laughed wildly. He grabbed the bottle, put it to his mouth; and as his lips curled absurdly around the opening and his throat worked, he kept his glance, burning with hatred, upon the old man's face.

IV

After the departure of Scully the three men, with the card-board still upon their knees, preserved for a long time an astounded silence. Then Johnnie said: "That's the dod-dangedest Swede I ever see."

"He ain't no Swede," said the cowboy, scornfully.   80

"Well, that is he then?" cried Johnnie. "What is he then?"

"It's my opinion," replied the cowboy deliberately, "he's some kind of a Dutchman." It was a venerable custom of the country to entitle as Swedes all light-haired men who spoke with a heavy tongue. In consequence the idea of the cowboy was not without its daring. "Yes, sir," he repeated. "It's my opinion this feller is some kind of a Dutchman."

"Well, he says he's a Swede, anyhow," muttered Johnnie, sulkily. He turned to the Easterner: "What do you think, Mr. Blanc?"

"Oh, I don't know," replied the Eastener.

"Well, what do you think makes him act that way?" asked the cowboy.   85

"Why, he's frightened." The Easterner knocked his pipe against a rim of the stove. "He's clear frightened out of his boots."

"What at?" cried Johnnie and the cowboy together.

The Easterner reflected over his answer.

"What at?" cried the others again.

"Oh, I don't know, but it seems to me this man has been reading dime novels,   90
and he thinks he's right out in the middle of it—the shootin' and stabbin' and all."

"But," said the cowboy, deeply scandalized, "this ain't Wyoming, ner none of them places. This is Nebrasker."

"Yes," added Johnnie, "an' why don't he wait till he gits *out West?*"

The travelled Easterner laughed. "It isn't different there even not in these days. But he thinks he's right in the middle of hell."

Johnnie and the cowboy mused long.

"It's awful funny," remarked Johnnie at last.   95

"Yes," said the cowboy. "This is a queer game. I hope we don't git snowed in, because then we'd have to stand this here man bein' around with us all the time. That wouldn't be no good."

"I wish pop would throw him out," said Johnnie.

Presently they heard a loud stamping on the stairs, accompanied by ringing jokes in the voice of old Scully, and laughter, evidently from the Swede. The men around the stove stared vacantly at each other. "Gosh!" said the cowboy. The door flew open, and old Scully, flushed and anecdotal, came into the room. He was jabbering at the Swede, who followed him, laughing bravely. It was the entry of two roisterers from a banquet hall.

"Come now," said Scully sharply to the three seated men, "move up and give us a chance at the stove." The cowboy and the Easterner obediently sidled their chairs to make room for the new-comers. Johnnie, however, simply arranged himself in a more indolent attitude, and then remained motionless.

"Come! Git over, there," said Scully.   100

"Plenty of room on the other side of the stove," said Johnnie.

"Do you think we want to sit in the draught?" roared the father.

But the Swede here interposed with a grandeur of confidence. "No, no. Let the boy sit where he likes," he cried in a bullying voice to the father.

"All right! All right!" said Scully, deferentially. The cowboy and the Easterner exchanged glances of wonder.

The five chairs were formed in a crescent about one side of the stove. The Swede   105 began to talk; he talked arrogantly, profanely, angrily. Johnnie, the cowboy, and the Easterner maintained a morose silence, while old Scully appeared to be receptive and eager, breaking in constantly with sympathetic ejaculations.

Finally the Swede announced that he was thirsty. He moved in his chair, and said that he would go for a drink of water.

"I'll git it for you," cried Scully at once.

"No," said the Swede, contemptuously. "I'll get it for myself." He arose and stalked with the air of an owner off into the executive parts of the hotel.

As soon as the Swede was out of hearing Scully sprang to his feet and whispered intensely to the others: "Upstairs he thought I was tryin' to poison 'im."

"Say," said Johnnie, "this makes me sick. Why don't you throw 'im out in the   110 snow?"

"Why, he's all right now," declared Scully. "It was only that he was from the East, and he thought this was a tough place. That's all. He's all right now."

The cowboy looked with admiration upon the Easterner. "You were straight," he said. "You were on to that there Dutchman."

"Well," said Johnnie to his father, "he may be all right now, but I don't see it. Other time he was scared, but now he's too fresh."

Scully's speech was always a combination of Irish brogue and idiom, Western twang and idiom, and scraps of curiously formal diction taken from the storybooks and newspapers. He now hurled a strange mass of language at the head of his son. "What do I keep? What do I keep? What do I keep?" he demanded, in a voice of thunder. He slapped his knee impressively, to indicate that he himself was going to make reply, and that all should heed. "I keep a hotel," he shouted. "A hotel, do you mind? A guest under my roof has sacred privileges. He is to be intimidated by none. Not one word shall he hear that would prejudice him in favour of goin' away. I'll not have it. There's no place in this here town where they can say they iver took in a guest of mine because he was afraid to stay here." He wheeled suddenly upon the cowboy and the Easterner. "Am I right?"

"Yes, Mr. Scully," said the cowboy, "I think you're right."   115

"Yes, Mr. Scully," said the Easterner, "I think you're right."

V

At six-o'clock supper, the Swede fizzed like a fire-wheel. He sometimes seemed on the point of bursting into riotous song, and in all his madness he was encouraged by old

Scully. The Easterner was encased in reserve; the cowboy sat in wide-mouthed amazement, forgetting to eat, while Johnnie wrathily demolished great plates of food. The daughters of the house, when they were obliged to replenish the biscuits, approached as warily as Indians, and, having succeeded in their purpose, fled with ill-concealed trepidation. The Swede domineered the whole feast, and he gave it the appearance of a cruel bacchanal. He seemed to have grown suddenly taller; he gazed, brutally distainful, into every face. His voice rang through the room. Once when he jabbed out harpoon-fashion with his fork to pinion a biscuit, the weapon nearly impaled the hand of the Easterner, which had been stretched quietly out for the same biscuit.

After supper, as the men filed toward the other room, the Swede smote Scully ruthlessly on the shoulder. "Well, old boy, that was a good, square meal." Johnnie looked hopefully at his father; he knew that shoulder was tender from an old fall; and, indeed, it appeared for a moment as if Scully was going to flame out over the matter, but in the end he smiled a sickly smile and remained silent. The others understood from his manner that he was admitting his responsibility for the Swede's new view-point.

Johnnie, however, addressed his parent in an aside. "Why don't you license somebody to kick you downstairs?" Scully scowled darkly by way of reply.

When they were gathered about the stove, the Swede insisted on another game of High-Five. Scully gently deprecated the plan at first, but the Swede turned a wolfish glare upon him. The old man subsided, and the Swede canvassed the others. In his tone there was always a great threat. The cowboy and the Easterner both remarked indifferently that they would play. Scully said that he would presently have to go to meet the 6.58 train, and so the Swede turned menancingly upon Johnnie. For a moment their glances crossed like blades, and then Johnnie smiled and said, "Yes, I'll play."

120

They formed a square, with the little board on their knees. The Easterner and the Swede were again partners. As the play went on, it was noticeable that the cowboy was not board-whacking as usual. Meanwhile, Scully, near the lamp, had put on his spectacles and, with an appearance curiously like an old priest, was reading a newspaper. In time he went out to meet the 6.58 train, and, despite his precautions, a gust of polar wind whirled into the room as he opened the door. Besides scattering the cards, it chilled the players to the marrow. The Swede cursed frightfully. When Scully returned, his entrance disturbed a cosy and friendly scene. The Swede again cursed. But presently they were once more intent, their heads bent forward and their hands moving swiftly. The Swede had adopted the fashion of board-whacking.

Scully took up his paper and for a long time remained immersed in matters which were extraordinarily remote from him. The lamp burned badly, and once he stopped to adjust the wick. The newspaper, as he turned from page to page, rustled with a slow and comfortable sound. Then suddenly he heard three terrible words: "You are cheatin'!"

Such scenes often prove that there can be little of dramatic import in environment. Any room can present a tragic front; any room can be comic. This little den was now hideous as a torture-chamber. The new faces of the men themselves had changed it upon the instant. The Swede held a huge fist in front of Johnnie's face, while the latter looked steadily over it into the blazing orbs of his accuser. The Easterner had grown pallid; the cowboy's jaw had dropped in that expression of bovine amazement which was one of his important mannerisms. After the three words, the first sound in the room was made by Scully's paper as it floated forgotten to his feet. His spectacles had also fallen from his nose, but by a clutch he had saved them in air. His hand, grasping the spectacles, now remained poised awkwardly and near his shoulder. He stared at the card-players.

Probably the silence was while a second elapsed. Then, if the floor had been sud-denly twitched out from under the men they could not have moved quicker. The five had projected themselves headlong toward a common point. It happened that Johnnie, in rising to hurl himself upon the Swede, had stumbled slightly because of his curiously instinctive care for the cards and the board. The loss of the moment allowed time for the arrival of Scully, and also allowed the cowboy time to give the Swede a great push which sent him staggering back. The men found tongue together, and hoarse shouts of rage, appeal, or fear burst from every throat. The cowboy pushed and jostled feverishly at the Swede, and the Easterner and Scully clung wildly to Johnnie; but through the smoky air, above the swaying bodies of the peace-compellers, the eyes of the two war-riors ever sought each other in glances of challenge that were at once hot and steely.

Of course the board had been overturned, and now the whole company of cards was   125
scattered over the floor, where the boots of the men trampled the fat and painted kings and queens as they gazed with their silly eyes at the war that was waging above them.

Scully's voice was dominating the yells. "Stop now! Stop, I say! Stop, now—"

Johnnie, as he struggled to burst through the rank formed by Scully and the East-erner, was crying, "Well, he says I cheated! He says I cheated! I won't allow no man to say I cheated! If he says I cheated, he's a —— ——!"

The cowboy was telling the Swede, "Quit, now! Quit, d'ye hear——"

The screams of the Swede never ceased: "He did cheat! I saw him! I saw him——"

As for the Easterner, he was importuning in a voice that was not heeded: "Wait a   130
moment, can't you? Oh, wait a moment. What's the good of a fight over a game of cards? Wait a moment——"

In this tumult no complete sentences were clear. "Cheat"—"Quit"—"He says"— these fragments pierced the uproar and rang out sharply. It was remarkable that, whereas Scully undoubtedly made the most noise, he was the least heard of any of the riotous band.

Then suddenly there was a great cessation. It was as if each man had paused for breath; and although the room was still lighted with the anger of men, it could be seen that there was no danger of immediate conflict, and at once Johnnie, shouldering his way forward, almost succeeded in confronting the Swede. "What did you say I cheated for? What did you say I cheated for? I don't cheat, and I won't let no man say I do!"

The Swede said, "I saw you! I saw you!"

"Well," cried Johnnie, "I'll fight any man what says I cheat!"

"No, you won't," said the cowboy. "Not here."   135

"Ah, be still, can't you?" said Scully, coming between them.

The quiet was sufficient to allow the Easterner's voice to be heard. He was repeat-ing, "Oh, wait a moment, can't you? What's the good of a fight over a game of cards? Wait a moment!"

Johnnie, his red face appearing above his father's shoulder, hailed the Swede again. "Did you say I cheated?"

The Swede showed his teeth. "Yes."

"Then," said Johnnie, "we must fight."   140

"Yes, fight," roared the Swede. He was like a demoniac. "Yes, fight! I'll show you what kind of a man I am! I'll show you who you want to fight! Maybe you think I can't fight! Maybe you think I can't! I'll show you, you skin, you card-sharp! Yes, you cheated! You cheated! You cheated!"

"Well, let's go at it, then, mister," said Johnnie, coolly.

The cowboy's brow was beaded with sweat from his efforts in intercepting all sorts of raids. He turned in despair to Scully. "What are you goin' to do now?"

A change had come over the Celtic visage of the old man. He now seemed all eagerness; his eyes glowed.

"We'll let them fight," he answered, stalwartly. "I can't put up with it any longer. I've stood this damned Swede till I'm sick. We'll let them fight."   145

VI

The men prepared to go out of doors. The Easterner was so nervous that he had great difficulty in getting his arms into the sleeves of his new leather coat. As the cowboy drew his fur cap down over his ears his hands trembled. In fact, Johnnie and old Scully were the only ones who displayed no agitation. These preliminaries were conducted without words.

Scully threw open the door. "Well, come on," he said. Instantly a terrific wind caused the flame of the lamp to struggle at its wick, while a puff of black smoke sprang from the chimney-top. The stove was in mid-current of the blast, and its voice swelled to equal the roar of the storm. Some of the scarred and bedabbled cards were caught up from the floor and dashed helplessly against the farther wall. The men lowered their heads and plunged into the tempest as into a sea.

No snow was falling, but great whirls and clouds of flakes, swept up from the ground by the frantic winds, were streaming southward with the speed of bullets. The covered land was blue with the sheen of an unearthly satin, and there was no other hue save where, at the low, black railway station—which seemed incredibly distant—one light gleamed like a tiny jewel. As the men floundered into a thigh-deep drift, it was known that the Swede was bawling out something. Scully went to him, put a hand on his shoulder, and projected an ear. "What's that you say?" he shouted.

"I say," bawled the Swede again, "I won't stand much show against this gang. I know you'll all pitch on me."

Scully smote him reproachfully on the arm. "Tut, man!" he yelled. The wind tore   150
the words from Scully's lips and scattered them far alee.

"You are all a gang of——" boomed the Swede, but the storm also seized the remainder of this sentence.

Immediately turning their backs upon the wind, the men had swung around a corner to the sheltered side of the hotel. It was the function of the little house to preserve here, amid this great devastation of snow, an irregular V-shape of heavily encrusted grass, which crackled beneath the feet. One could imagine the great drifts piled against the windward side. When the party reached the comparative peace of this spot it was found that the Swede was still bellowing.

"Oh, I know what kind of a thing this is! I know you'll all pitch on me. I can't lick you all!"

Scully turned upon him panther-fashion. "You'll not have to whip all of us. You'll have to whip my son Johnnie. An' the man what troubles you durin' that time will have me to dale with."

The arrangements were swiftly made. The two men faced each other, obedient to   155
the harsh commands of Scully, whose face, in the subtly luminous gloom, could be seen set in the austere impersonal lines that are pictured on the countenances of the Roman

veterans. The Easterner's teeth were chattering, and he was hopping up and down like a mechanical toy. The cowboy stood rock-like.

The contestants had not stripped off any clothing. Each was in his ordinary attire. Their fists were up, and they eyed each other in a calm that had the elements of leonine cruelty in it.

During this pause, the Easterner's mind, like a film, took lasting impressions of three men—the iron-nerve master of the ceremony; the Swede, pale, motionless, terrible; and Johnnie, serene yet ferocious, brutish yet heroic. The entire prelude had in it a tragedy greater than the tragedy of action, and this aspect was accentuated by the long, mellow cry of the blizzard, as it sped the tumbling and wailing flakes into the black abyss of the south.

"Now!" said Scully.

The two combatants leaped forward and crashed together like bullocks. There was heard the cushioned sound of blows, and of a curse squeezing out from between the tight teeth of one.

As for the spectators, the Easterner's pent-up breath exploded from him with a   160
pop of relief, absolute relief from the tension of the preliminaries. The cowboy bounded into the air with a yowl. Scully was immovable as from supreme amazement and fear at the fury of the fight which he himself had permitted and arranged.

For a time the encounter in the darkness was such a perplexity of flying arms that it presented no more detail than would a swiftly revolving wheel. Occasionally a face, as if illumined by a flash of light, would shine out, ghastly and marked with pink spots. A moment later, the men might have been known as shadows, if it ware not for the involuntary utterance of oaths that came from them in whispers.

Suddenly a holocaust of warlike desire caught the cowboy, and he bolted forward with the speed of a broncho. "Go it, Johnnie! go it! Kill him! Kill him!"

Scully confronted him. "Kape back," he said; and by his glance the cowboy could tell that this man was Johnnie's father.

To the Easterner there was a monotony of unchangeable fighting that was an abomination. This confused mingling was eternal to his sense, which was concentrated in a longing for the end, the priceless end. Once the fighters lurched near him, and as he scrambled hastily backward he heard them breathe like men on the rack.

"Kill him, Johnnie! Kill him! Kill him! Kill him!" The cowboy's face was con-   165
torted like one of those agony masks in museums.

"Keep still," said Scully, icily.

Then there was a sudden loud grunt, incomplete, cut short, and Johnnie's body swung away from the Swede and fell with sickening heaviness to the grass. The cowboy was barely in time to prevent the mad Swede from flinging himself upon his prone adversary. "No, you don't," said the cowboy, interposing an arm. "Wait a second."

Scully was at his son's side. "Johnnie! Johnnie, me boy!" His voice had a quality of melancholy tenderness. "Johnnie! Can you go on with it?" He looked anxiously down into the bloody, pulpy face of his son.

There was a moment of silence, and then Johnnie answered in his ordinary voice, "Yes, I—it—yes."

Assisted by his father he struggled to his feet. "Wait a bit now till you git your   170
wind," said the old man.

A few paces away the cowboy was lecturing the Swede. "No, you don't! Wait a second!"

The Easterner was plucking at Scully's sleeve. "Oh, this is enough," he pleaded. "This is enough! Let it go as it stands. This is enough!"

"Bill," said Scully, "git out of the road." The cowboy stepped aside. "Now." The combatants were actuated by a new caution as they advanced toward collision. They glared at each other, and then the Swede aimed a lightning blow that carried with it his entire weight. Johnnie was evidently half stupid from weakness, but he miraculously dodged, and his fist sent the overbalanced Swede sprawling.

The cowboy, Scully, and the Easterner burst into a cheer that was like a chorus of triumphant soldiery, but before its conclusion the Swede had scuffed agilely to his feet and come in berserk abandon at his foe. There was another perplexity of flying arms, and Johnnie's body again swung away and fell, even as a bundle might fall from a roof. The Swede instantly staggered to a little wind-waved tree and leaned upon it, breathing like an engine, while his savage and flamelit eyes roamed from face to face as the men bent over Johnnie. There was a splendour of isolation in his situation at this time which the Easterner felt once when, lifting his eyes from the man on the ground, he beheld that mysterious and lonely figure, waiting.

"Are you any good yet, Johnnie?" asked Scully in a broken voice.   175

The son gasped and opened his eyes languidly. After a moment he answered, "No—I ain't—any good—any—more." Then, from shame and bodily ill, he began to weep, the tears furrowing down through the blood-stains on his face. "He was too—too—too heavy for me."

Scully straightened and addressed the waiting figure.

"Stranger," he said, evenly, "it's all up with our side." Then his voice changed into that vibrant huskiness which is commonly the tone of the most simple and deadly announcements. "Johnnie is whipped."

Without replying, the victor moved off on the route to the front door of the hotel.

The cowboy was formulating new and unspellable blasphemies. The Easterner   180 was startled to find that they were out in a wind that seemed to come direct from the shadowed arctic floes. He heard again the wail of the snow as it was flung to its grave in the south. He knew now that all this time the cold had been sinking into him deeper and deeper, and he wondered that he had not perished. He felt indifferent to the condition of the vanquished man.

"Johnnie, can you walk?" asked Scully.

"Did I hurt—hurt him any?" asked the son.

"Can you walk, boy? Can you walk?"

Johnnie's voice was suddenly strong. There was a robust impatience in it. "I asked you whether I hurt him any!"

"Yes, yes, Johnnie," answered the cowboy, consolingly: "he's hurt a good deal."   185

They raised him from the ground, and as soon as he was on his feet he went tottering off, rebuffing all attempts at assistance. When the party rounded the corner they were fairly blinded by the pelting of the snow. It burned their faces like fire. The cowboy carried Johnnie through the drift to the door. As they entered, some cards again rose from the floor and beat against the wall.

The Easterner rushed to the stove. He was so profoundly chilled that he almost dared to embrace the glowing iron. The Swede was not in the room. Johnnie sank into a chair and, folding his arms on his knees, buried his face in them. Scully, warming one foot and then the other at a rim of the stove, muttered to himself with Celtic mournfulness. The cowboy had removed his fur cap, and with a dazed and rueful air he was running one hand through his tousled locks. From overhead they could hear the creak-ing of boards, as the Swede tramped here and there in his room.

The sad quiet was broken by the sudden flinging open of a door that led toward the kitchen. It was instantly followed by an inrush of women. They precipitated them-selves upon Johnnie amid a chorus of lamentation. Before they carried their prey off to the kitchen, there to be bathed and harangued with that mixture of sympathy and abuse which is a feat of their sex, the mother straightened herself and fixed old Scully with an eye of stern reproach, "Shame be upon you, Patrick Scully!" she cried. "Your own son, too. Shame be upon you!"

"There, now! Be quiet, now!" said the old man, weakly.

"Shame be upon you, Patrick Scully!" The girls, rallying to this slogan, sniffed   190
disdainfully in the direction of those trembling accomplices, the cowboy and the East-erner. Presently they bore Johnnie away, and left the three men to dismal reflection.

VII

"I'd like to fight this here Dutchman myself," said the cowboy, breaking a long silence.

Scully wagged his head sadly. "No, that wouldn't do. It wouldn't be right. It wouldn't be right."

"Well, why wouldn't it?" argued the cowboy. "I don't see no harm in it."

"No," answered Scully, with mournful heroism. "It wouldn't be right. It was John-nie's fight, and now we mustn't whip the man just because he whipped Johnnie."

"Yes, that's true enough," said the cowboy; "but—he better not get fresh with me,   195
because I couldn't stand no more of it."

"You'll not say a word to him," commanded Scully, and even then they heard the tread of the Swede on the stairs. His entrance was made theatrics. He swept the door back with a bang and swaggered to the middle of the room. No one looked at him. "Well," he cried, insolently, at Scully, "I s'pose you'll tell me now how much I owe you?"

The old man remained stolid. "You don't owe me nothin'."

"Huh!" said the Swede, "huh! Don't owe 'im nothin'."

The cowboy addressed the Swede. "Stranger, I don't see how you come to be so gay around here."

Old Scully was instantly alert. "Stop!" he shouted, holding his hand forth, fingers   200
upward. "Bill, you shut up!"

The cowboy spat carelessly into the sawdust-box. "I didn't say a word, did I?" he asked.

"Mr. Scully," called the Swede, "how much do I owe you?" It was seen that he was attired for departure, and that he had his valise in his hand.

"You don't owe me nothin'," repeated Scully in the same imperturbable way.

"Huh!" said the Swede. "I guess you're right. I guess if it was any way at all, you'd owe me somethin'. That's what I guess." He turned to the cowboy. "'Kill him! Kill him! Kill him!'" he mimicked, and then guffawed victoriously. "'Kill him!'" He was con-vulsed with ironical humour.

But he might have been jeering the dead. The three men were immovable and   205
silent, staring with glassy eyes at the stove.

The Swede opened the door and passed into the storm, giving one derisive glance backward at the still group.

As soon as the door was closed, Scully and the cowboy leaped to their feet and began to curse. They trampled to and fro, waving their arms and smashing into the air with their fists. "Oh, but that was a hard minute!" wailed Scully. "That was a hard minute! Him there leerin' and scoffin! One bang at his nose was worth forty dollars to me that minute! How did you stand it, Bill?"

"How did I stand it?" cried the cowboy in a quivering voice. "How did I stand it? Oh!"

The old man burst into sudden brogue. "I'd like to take that Swade," he wailed, "and hould 'im down on a shtone flure and bate 'im to a jelly wid a shtick!"

The cowboy groaned in sympathy. "I'd like to git him by the neck and hammer   210
him"—he brought his hand down on a chair with a noise like a pistol shot—"hammer that there Dutchman until he couldn't tell himself from a dead coyote!"

"I'd bate 'im until he——"

"I'd show *him* some things——"

And then together they raised a yearning, fanatic cry "Oh-o-oh! if we only could——"

"Yes!"

"Yes!"   215

"And then I'd——"

"O-o-oh!"

VIII

The Swede, tightly gripping his valise, tacked across the face of the storm as if he carried sails. He was following a line of little naked, gasping trees which, he knew, must mark the way of the road. His face, fresh from the pounding of Johnnie's fists, felt more pleasure than pain in the wind and the driving snow. A number of square shapes loomed upon him finally, and he knew them as the houses of the main body of the town. He found a street and made travel along it, leaning heavily upon the wind whenever, at a corner, a terrific blast caught him.

He might have been in a deserted village. We picture the world as thick with conquering and elate humanity, but here, with the bugles of the tempest pealing, it was hard to imagine a peopled earth. One viewed the existence of man then as a marvel, and conceded a glamour of wonder to these lice which were caused to cling to a whirling, fire-smitten, ice-locked, disease-stricken, space-lost bulb. The conceit of man was explained by this storm to be the very engine of life. One was a coxcomb not to die in it. However, the Swede found a saloon.

In front of it an indomitable red light was burning, and the snowflakes were made   220
blood-colour as they flew through the circumscribed territory of the lamp's shining. The Swede pushed open the door of the saloon and entered. A sanded expanse was before him, and at the end of it four men sat about a table drinking. Down one side of the room extended a radiant bar, and its guardian was leaning upon his elbows listening to the talk of the men at the table. The Swede dropped his valise upon the floor and, smiling fraternally upon the barkeeper, said, "Gimme some whisky, will you?" The man placed a bottle, a whisky-glass, and a glass of ice-thick water upon the bar. The Swede poured himself an abnormal portion of whisky and drank it in three gulps. "Pretty bad night," remarked the bartender, indifferently. He was making the pretension of blindness which is usually

a distinction of his class; but it could have been seen that he was furtively studying the half-erased blood-stains on the face of the Swede. "Bad night," he said again.

"Oh, it's good enough for me," replied the Swede, hardily, as he poured himself some more whiskey. The barkeeper took his coin and maneuvered it through its reception by the highly nickelled cash-machine. A bell rang; a card labelled "20 cts." had appeared.

"No," continued the Swede, "this isn't too bad weather. It's good enough for me."

"So?" murmured the barkeeper, languidly.

The copious drams made the Swede's eyes swim, and he breathed a trifle heavier. "Yes, I like this weather. I like it. It suits me." It was apparently his design to impart a deep significance to these words.

"So?" murmured the bartender again. He turned to gaze dreamily at the scroll-like   225
birds and bird-like scrolls which had been drawn with soap upon the mirrors in back of the bar.

"Well, I guess I'll take another drink," said the Swede, presently. "Have something?"

"No, thanks; I'm not drinkin'," answered the bartender. Afterward he asked, "How did you hurt your face?"

The Swede immediately began to boast loudly. "Why, in a fight. I thumped the soul out of a man down here at Scully's hotel."

The interest of the four men at the table was at last aroused.

"Who was it?" said one.   230

"Johnnie Scully," blustered the Swede. "Son of the man what runs it. He will be pretty near dead for some weeks, I can tell you. I made a nice thing of him. I did. He couldn't get up. They carried him in the house. Have a drink?"

Instantly the men in some subtle way encased themselves in reserve. "No, thanks," said one. The group was of curious formation. Two were prominent local business men; one was the district attorney; and one was a professional gambler of the kind known as "square." But a scrutiny of the group would not have enabled an observer to pick the gambler from the men of more reputable pursuits. He was, in fact, a man so delicate in manner, when among people of fair class, and so judicious in his choice of victims, that in the strictly masculine part of the town's life he had come to be explicitly trusted and admired. People called him a thoroughbred. The fear and contempt with which his craft was regarded were undoubtedly the reason why his quiet dignity shone conspicuous above the quiet dignity of men who might be merely hatters, billiard-markers, or grocery clerks. Beyond an occasional unwary traveller who came by rail, this gambler was supposed to prey solely upon reckless and senile farmers, who, when flush with good crops, drove into town in all the pride and confidence of an absolutely invulnerable stupidity. Hearing at times in circuitous fashion of the despoilment of such a farmer, the important men of Romper invariably laughed in contempt of the victim, and if they thought of the wolf at all, it was with a kind of pride at the knowledge that he would never dare think of attacking their wisdom and courage. Besides, it was popular that this gambler had a real wife and two real children in a neat cottage in a suburb, where he led an exemplary home life; and when any one even suggested a discrepancy in his character, the crowd immediately vociferated descriptions of this virtuous family circle. Then men who led exemplary home lives, and men who did not lead exemplary home lives, all subsided in a bunch, remarking that there was nothing more to be said.

However, when a restriction was placed upon him as, for instance, when a strong clique of members of the new Pollywog Club refused to permit him, even as a spectator, to appear in the rooms of the organization the candour and gentleness with which he accepted the judgment disarmed many of his foes and made his friends more desperately partisan. He invariably distinguished between himself and a respectable Romper man so quickly and frankly that his manner actually appeared to be a continual broadcast compliment.

And one must not forget to declare the fundamental fact to his entire position in Romper. It is irrefutable that in all affairs outside his business, in all matters that occur eternally and commonly between man and man, this thieving card-player was so generous, so just, so moral, that, in a contest, he could have put to flight the consciences of nine tenths of the citizens of Romper.

And so it happened that he was seated in this saloon with the two prominent   235
local merchants and the district attorney.

The Swede continued to drink raw whisky, meanwhile babbling at the barkeeper and trying to induce him to indulge in potations. "Come on. Have a drink. Come on. What—no? Well, have a little one, then. By gawd, I've whipped a man to-night, and I want to celebrate. I whipped him good, too. Gentlemen," the Swede cried to the men at the table, "have a drink?"

"Ssh!" said the barkeeper.

The group at the table, although furtively attentive, had been pretending to be deep in talk, but now a man lifted his eyes toward the Swede and said, shortly, "Thanks. We don't want any more."

At this reply the Swede ruffled out his chest like a rooster. "Well," he exploded, "it seems I can't get anybody to drink with me in this town. Seems so, don't it? Well!"

"Ssh!" said the barkeeper.   240

"Say," snarled the Swede, "don't you try to shut me up. I won't have it. I'm a gentleman, and I want people to drink with me. And I want 'em to drink with me now. Now—do you understand?" He rapped the bar with his knuckles.

Years of experience had calloused the bartender. He merely grew sulky. "I hear you," he answered.

"Well," cried the Swede, "listen hard then. See those men over there? Well, they're going to drink with me, and don't you forget it. Now you watch."

"Hi!" yelled the barkeeper, "this won't do!"

"Why won't it?" demanded the Swede. He stalked over to the table, and by   245
chance laid his hand upon the shoulder of the gambler. "How about this?" he asked wrathfully. "I asked you to drink with me."

The gambler simply twisted his head and spoke over his shoulder. "My friend, I don't know you."

"Oh, hell!" answered the Swede, "come and have a drink."

"Now, my boy," advised the gambler, kindly, "take your hand off my shoulder and go 'way and mind your own business." He was a little, slim man, and it seemed strange to hear him use this tone of heroic patronage to the burly Swede. The other men at the table said nothing.

"What! You won't drink with me, you little dude? I'll make you, then! I'll make you!" The Swede had grasped the gambler frenziedly at the throat, and was dragging him from his chair. The other men sprang up. The barkeeper dashed around the corner of his bar. There was a great tumult, and then was seen a long blade in the hand of the gambler. It shot forward, and a human body, this citadel of virtue, wisdom, power, was pierced as easily as if it had been a melon. The Swede fell with a cry of supreme astonishment.

The prominent merchants and the district attorney must have at once tumbled   250
out of the place backward. The bartender found himself hanging limply to the arm of a chair and gazing into the eyes of a murderer.

"Henry," said the latter, as he wiped his knife on one of the towels that hung beneath the bar rail, "you tell 'em where to find me. I'll be home, waiting for 'em." Then he vanished. A moment afterward the barkeeper was in the street dinning through the storm for help and, moreover, companionship.

The corpse of the Swede, alone in the saloon, had its eyes fixed upon a dreadful legend that dwelt atop of the cash-machine: "This registers the amount of your purchase."

IX

Months later, the cowboy was frying pork over the stove of a little ranch near the Dakota line, when there was a quick thud of hoofs outside, and presently the Easterner entered with the letters and the papers.

"Well," said the Easterner at once, "the chap that killed the Swede has got three years. Wasn't much, was it?"

"He has? Three years?" The cowboy poised his pan of pork, while he ruminated   255
upon the news. "Three years. That ain't much."

"No. It was a light sentence," replied the Easterner as he unbuckled his spurs. "Seems there was a good deal of sympathy for him in Romper."

"If the bartender had been any good," observed the cowboy, thoughtfully, "he would have gone in and cracked that there Dutchman on the head with a bottle in the beginnin' of it and stopped all this here murderin'."

"Yes, a thousand things might have happened," said the Easterner, tartly.

The cowboy returned his pan of pork to the fire, but his philosophy continued. "It's funny, ain't it? If he hadn't said Johnnie was cheatin' he'd be alive this minute. He was an awful fool. Game played for fun, too. Not for money. I believe he was crazy."

"I feel sorry for that gambler," said the Easterner.   260

"Oh, so do I," said the cowboy. "He don't deserve none of it for killin' who he did."

"The Swede might not have been killed if everything had been square."

"Might not have been killed?" exclaimed the cowboy. "Everythin' square? Why, when he said that Johnnie was cheatin' and acted like such a jackass? And then in the saloon he fairly walked up to git hurt?" With these arguments the cowboy browbeat the Easterner and reduced him to rage.

"You're a fool!" cried the Easterner, viciously. "You're a bigger jackass than the Swede by a million majority. Now let me tell you one thing. Let me tell you something. Listen! Johnnie *was* cheating!"

"Johnnie," said the cowboy, blankly. There was a minute of silence, and then he   265
said, robustly, "Why, no. The game was only for fun."

"Fun or not," said the Easterner, "Johnnie was cheating. I saw him. I know it. I saw him. And I refused to stand up and be a man. I let the Swede fight it out alone. And you—you were simply puffing around the place wanting to fight. And then old Scully himself! We are all in it! This poor gambler isn't even a noun. He is kind of an adverb. Every sin is the result of a collaboration. We, five of us, have collaborated in the murder of this Swede. Usually there are from a dozen to forty women really involved in every murder, but in this case it seems to be only five men—you, I, Johnnie, old Scully; and that fool of an unfortunate gambler came merely as a culmination, the apex of a human movement, and gets all the punishment."

The cowboy, injured and rebellious, cried out blindly into this fog of mysterious theory: "Well, I didn't do anythin', did I?"

[1898]

ANALYZING "THE BLUE HOTEL"

The primary tools in understanding this gripping narrative involve understanding the basic elements of its historical context as well as considering major literary elements such as plot, character, tone, theme, and metaphor and imagery. Let's look at some of these elements in "The Blue Hotel," which was published in 1898.

Plot

The plot of this narrative is a version of a very old story, going back to at least the ancient Greeks: A stranger comes into town, gets into trouble, and is killed or driven off. Like Jack London's "To Build a Fire," Stephen Crane's powerful story is about the struggle for survival. An unnamed man, "the Swede," arrives in the mid-western town of Fort Romper, his head full of images of violent western life that came not from personal experience, but from reading cheap pulp fiction magazines. The story is narrated from the third-person, objective perspective. The narrator is clearly emotionally involved in the story, as indicated by his recurring ironic and sarcastic descriptions in revealing his world views. The plot line reveals numerous traces, supplements, and metaphors that together show how inhospitable a small town, and the world, is for a stranger and how difficult it is to arrive at a stable interpretation of this story. The narrative resonates with implications about human frailty, cosmic violence, and the importance of humans working together as the only hope for survival in a fundamentally hostile universe.

All literary plots reveal change over time and cause and effect relationships. "The Blue Hotel" begins with a man alone on a journey out West, stopping at a town for a night's rest. As the story develops, the main character, the Swede, arrives believing that Fort Romper is a wild and dangerous place, rich in a history of many murders, and the Swede "knows" that he will be killed in Fort Romper, as he repeats numerous times. The conclusion of the story reveals how right (and wrong) were the Swede's impressions of western life. The closing paragraphs illustrate the dire consequences (and ambiguities) of living in a hostile universe without a sense of responsibility on the part of human players.

Character

"The Blue Hotel" has long been recognized as a masterful narrative with a spellbinding plot about the plight of the stranger in a strange town, whose codes he does not know. All the Swede knows about the codes of the town are what he has read in sensational magazines and books. Although there are several major characters, usually identified by occupation or geography (cowboy, gambler, district attorney, Easterner, etc.), they are brought together in groups for social purposes (camaraderie, playing cards, passing time). Although the Swede is unnamed, we come to know him very well because of the intensely descriptive illustrations of his actions and qualities. We also learn much about the tensions of strangers coming together in a "marginal" town, one which is neither western nor eastern. We learn bits and pieces about ten or so men, mostly fragments of information that allow only superficial glimpses into their characters. This story is about a cosmic (and sometimes comic) struggle for survival, and it depicts the vulnerabilities of humans brought together by chance. The nature of their characters remains ambiguous. Indeed, at the end of the story the cowboy is thoroughly confused when the Easterner attempts to explain how the Swede's death was everyone's fault (and possibly no one particular person's fault, not even the Swede's or the gambler's).

At the beginning of the story, the Swede is tense, agitated, and extremely suspicious of the Blue Hotel and its residents. He is paranoid about being killed, and one of the great ironies of the story is that his unreasonable fear is actually realized, in part as a result of his own actions. The Swede carries with him a sense of fatalism and inevitability, which he cannot articulate convincingly to the other characters, even the sympathetic Pat Scully. The Swede's constant refrain, "I do not wish to be killed," makes him appear irrational to everyone else. The Swede reinforces this impression by telling Scully, "Yes, of course, I am crazy—yes." The ways in which the story's characters are interwoven together, often by chance, show the importance of personal and collective responsibility. As the narrative unfolds, we come to realize what the Easterner tries to tell the cowboy at the end of the story: "We are all in it!" The characters' words and actions assert the importance of human responsibility.

"The Blue Hotel" is written from the third-person, objective point of view. In some third-person accounts, there is obvious sympathy for the main character, but this does not appear to be the case in this story. In fact, there seems to be little sympathy for any of the characters. The tone of the narrator is one of irony, amusement, and sarcasm. It is as if the narrator is shocked at his own creation—characters who behave irresponsibly and often for self-serving purposes. The only remotely sympathetic character may be Mr. Blanc, the Easterner, who appears to be the only person with sympathetic insight into the cause and meaning of the Swede's death. The tone of the narrator is almost contemptuous of Fort Romper and its citizens, especially of Pat Scully, proprietor of the garish Blue Hotel, who painted his business in a color so stunning that it was "screaming and howling," contrasting sharply with the Nebraska prairie.

The tone of "The Blue Hotel" is complex, moving from moments of comic irony to moments of dead seriousness. Pat Scully is portrayed as a buffoonish "seducer," in the practical business of "catching men" to fill his hotel and its cash register. The hotel residents overhear Scully's "officious clamor at his daughters," suggesting a shallow man with one face for the paying customers and another for his workers, principally his son, daughters, and wife. In courting potential customers fresh off the train, Scully "practically made them prisoners," which suggests that his obsession with economic success clouds his judgment. Indeed, he is overly solicitous to the Swede in attempting to retain his business even after he has quarreled with others, including Johnnie. Throughout the story, the narrator creates a mood of irony, foreboding, and inevitability, illustrating the conflict between man and his fellows (and man and himself). Setting and imagery are carefully selected to create a sense of impending doom, all of which are part of the narrator's attitude and tone.

Theme

The late 1800s was a period of time in which literary naturalism flourished, and Stephen Crane was one of America's great naturalist writers. Writers like Crane believed that human beings are controlled by natural forces, heredity, environment, and fate (or chance). The world is a rugged, dangerous place in which humans are pitted against one another for survival, as well as pitted against the forces of nature. We are all instinctively brutish when our human energies are not channeled in the right direction, according to naturalism. The only way to survive, perhaps, is for humans to bond together, collectively, and help one another. Each individual shares some responsibility for the well-being of others. Without cooperation among individuals, humans are little more than animals in the universal struggle for survival.

"The Blue Hotel" is clearly a story about struggle for survival, operating on more than one level. Pat Scully struggles to maintain his meager hotel. The hotel itself, personified as a character, struggles to survive in the marketplace and against adverse weather conditions. It is painted a light blue, making it like a heron, standing "to declare its position against any background." The Swede, of course, is the most prominent example of a character caught in a struggle of life and death (partially due to his behavior, of course). A major theme in this story is the importance of individuals working together against the grim forces of nature (including the darker sides of human nature). Indeed, the story takes place against the background of a howling, violent winter storm. And it is important to remember that the Swede is a foreigner, an outsider, in Fort Romper, who finds himself in a hostile and threatening world (at least in his mind). The Swede does not fit in with the other characters from the very beginning of the narrative.

There is violence in the story, natural and human, and one of the reasons for the human violence is that the Swede does not understand the local codes of behavior in Fort Romper. His (correct) accusation of cheating by Johnnie sets in motion a series of events that result in the Swede's death. The game of High-Five was not even for money, and the accusation of cheating was far worse than the truth of dishonest play, according to local codes of conduct. The saloon scene demonstrates the Swede's lack of knowledge of correct behavior, and it costs him his life when he confronts the gambler in an unacceptable way. In the saloon, there is no friendly innkeeper, like Scully, to protect the Swede. The concluding discussion between the Easterner and the cowboy asserts the importance of human empathy. The world is a dangerous and inhospitable place, shown from the first page of the story, and at the end the Easterner points out how cold and callous the world is and accuses everyone, including himself, of responsibility: "We are all in it!" The Swede is dead and the gambler is in jail because the other characters failed to intervene. Part of the responsibility must fall, of course, on the Swede, and that is yet another interpretation of the story. A third interpretation might argue that the Swede's death is simply a result of naturalistic forces at work. All three readings are reasonable and supported by textual evidence, even though they are in some contradiction with one another. The depth, complexity, contradiction, and even confusion in "The Blue Hotel" reveal rich deconstructive possibilities.

Metaphor and Imagery

"The Blue Hotel" is rich in symbolism, metaphor, and imagery. The story begins with a sense of foreboding as the symbolic hotel stands out against the bleak backdrop of the prairie in the midst of a howling winter storm. The name itself—the Palace Hotel—wreaks of irony in referring to a modest, small hotel as "palatial," an ironic comment on its humble accommodations. It is as if the Palace Hotel is a beacon, a comic oasis on the Nebraska prairie. Indeed, the hotel is not even set within the town of Fort Romper. The narrator describes the hotel as if it were a bird in a defensive position, painted garishly, as a grim reminder of its huckster owner, Pat Scully, who "catches" his customers and mistreats his wife and children.

Irony is a pervasive metaphor in "The Blue Hotel" from the very beginning of the story. The narrator describes the modest hotel as one of "opulence and splendor." Its owner is treated ironically and almost contemptuously. He is depicted as a self-serving businessman, narrowly focused on his own economic interests. When Scully attempts to gain understanding from the Swede by showing him a photograph of his dead daughter, the episode comes across as ludicrous. The photograph is described by the narrator as "ridiculous," and the dead daughter is depicted as "graceful as an upright sledstake." The narrator further satirizes Scully by putting nonstandard pronunciations of words into his mouth as he describes his dead girl in the "picter" as having had the "purtiest hair." In describing his son, a lawyer, Scully brags about him as a "respected gintleman," who has been given by his father a "grand eddication." Scully is proud of the soon-to-come "ilictric street-cars." Other characters are satirized, too, such as the cowboy, who is given "bovine" characteristics. Yet the Swede is perhaps the story's most ironic character, with his constant refrain, "These men are going to kill me." The Swede's irrational fears turn out to come true, of course, adding yet another layer of irony to the narrative.

Other symbols and images play a significant role in this story. The raging storm outside the hotel foreshadows the storm of human violence that is about to take place. Two friendly card games serve as the backdrop for two major scenes of violence. The inaccurate image of Fort Romper as a dangerous, Wild West town (and not really in the West) turns out to be ironically true. The professional gambler, who makes his living by vice, is described as an upstanding citizen, a "thoroughbred" with "quiet dignity." To the citizens of Fort Romper, he is indistinguishable from his fellow cardplayers—the district attorney and two prominent businessmen. Perhaps one of the most powerful images is the narrator's description of the townspeople (and all of humanity by implication) as "these lice which were caused to cling to a whirling, fire-smitten, ice-locked, disease-stricken, space-lost bulb." The narrator portrays the human experience as somewhat absurd.

Questions for Your Analysis of "The Blue Hotel"

1) What are some of your early impressions of the story? In particular, what do you make of Crane's emphasis on color and sound in the first few paragraphs?
2) What are your observations of Scully and the Palace Hotel? What strikes you as unusual about the man and his hotel, and the way in which he "captures" his customers?
3) This story contains many types of characters: a gambler, an Easterner, a cowboy, and so on. What do you make of the narrator's reliance on types to tell his story? Does the use of types diminish the personal qualities of these characters? Is there any sense of "essence" to any of these characters?
4) There are many intense sensory images in this story, beginning with the description of the hotel. What do these uses of color and sound suggest to you?
5) How might you relate your personal experiences to those of the visitors to the Palace Hotel?
6) This story is laden with ironies and ambiguities, such as the Swede's entering a peaceful mid-west town believing he will be killed, only to turn out to have been right in his prediction. What are some other ironies you find in the story?
7) The narrator tells us that the Swede's body is a "citadel of virtue, wisdom, and power." This statement would seem to be not only ironic, but contemptuous of the Swede. How do you interpret this description?
8) How important is randomness or chance to this story?

9) Can you identify one element of the story and explore supplements to that element? (For example, each card game is a game of four players, which is supplemented by a fifth person.)
10) In what ways does the narrator foreshadow the end of the story?
11) How do you interpret the concluding statement of the cowboy: "Well, I didn't do anythin', did I?"

The textual issues suggested in this chapter can be appropriated to deconstructive criticism, as well as to other interpretive approaches. Please read the following sample essay on "The Blue Hotel" as an illustration of one form that deconstructive criticism might take. This essay, as you will see, focuses on elements of deconstructive reading: supplement, trace, and metaphor (or figure). All insightful criticism, whether deconstructive or any other approach, takes account of complex metaphors and multiple meanings of words.

Sample Essay on "The Blue Hotel"

"The Blue Hotel," one of the most popular American naturalist stories ever written, is set in the Nebraska town of Fort Romper around the turn of the twentieth century, a time when tales of gunfights, death, and violence in the wild West were published in dime novels (the predecessor of today's "original paperback"). From the first sentence of the story, the narrator tells the reader that this is a strange, surreal place: the Palace Hotel (which is not palatial) is painted light blue, making it look like a heron, set against the prairie background. It is significant that the hotel is neither in the open prairie nor in the town. It is nestled in no man's land between the town and open country, part of both yet, in a sense, part of neither. The hotel is essential to the town in that it houses those resting briefly before continuing on to the "real West," but it also supplements the town in that it is something added to it. The chilling narrative is told from an objective, third-person perspective, which informs the reader not only of the context of the strange hotel and its odd owner, Pat Scully, who "captures" potential guests as they exist the train, but also introduces a collection of stereotypical characters: the Swede, a cowboy, an Easterner, a gambler, and others. Some of these characters have names, but most do not, especially the central figure, the Swede. These characters, coming together by chance, are involved in a chain of events that are not easily explained. The conclusion of the narrative suggests several possible meanings, some of which contradict others. Let me begin by examining the major characters.

As we meet the various characters, it becomes apparent that there is much tension in the story, introduced early on by the Swede, who has read so many dime novels depicting the wild West and its violent way of living (and dying), he is frightened to death as soon as he steps off the train. The Swede accepts the trace of the wild West that he knows only from novels and tries to impose it on Fort Romper, hardly the counterpart of Dodge City or any other notoriously dangerous town. The concept or trace of the wild West grows in the Swede's mind until it becomes obsessive and uncontrollable. Most readers sense his instability from the very beginning. Indeed, the narrator describes him as "a shaky and quick-eyed Swede." As Scully introduces the Swede to the others, the Swede barely listens, and "His eyes continued to rove from man to man." As the Swede observes the card game, he makes a strange remark, which turns out to be prophetic: "I suppose there have been a good many men killed in this room." The statement is false, of course, but it reveals the deep paranoia of the Swede. These irrational fears are reinforced when he tells Scully, "I suppose I am going to be killed before I can leave this house." The dime novels have clearly influenced the Swede. One might even say that he has become a supplement to the wild West that he believes he has entered. It is difficult to interpret the words of a man who announces that he is not in his right mind, as the Swede tells Scully: "Yes, of course, I am crazy—yes." His erratic behavior makes him become an essential part of the violence that existed originally only in his mind.

Stereotypes common in popular magazines of the time fit the major characters, with the possible exception of the Easterner, Mr. Blanc. Most of the characters are primarily types. Scully is a fast-talking, "slick" hotel operator who lives by the principles of practical economics; the cowboy is a rough-talking hothead, whose mouth defines him; the professional gambler is a well-dressed and well-liked citizen-gentleman; the bartender fits the common stereotype of the western saloon keeper who keeps a careful eye on his customers and has seen everything over the years (he knows that the Swede is headed for trouble when he comes in). What is important about the presence of so many stereotypes is that most of these figures have no essence, no clearly definable, individual characteristics, which is important to a naturalist story because they represent a kind of herd mentality. These are men who act instinctively and out of self-preservation. Johnnie, for example, challenges the Swede to a fight as soon as his honor is questioned. The gambler kills the Swede as soon as he is accosted and dragged from his chair. The gambler punctures the Swede's body with a knife as naturally and as easily as if he had pierced a melon. Killing an adversary is instinctive to the gambler as a rite of survival, and there is a reason why he carries a knife. The gambler's coolness in dispatching the Swede is confirmed when he calmly tells the bartender, "you tell 'em where to find me. I'll be home, waiting for 'em." As a western archetypal figure, the gambler shows little variation or individuality.

What is the significance of the Swede's death, and how does it fit into the larger meaning of the story? There are multiple possibilities, none of which fit smoothly or comfortably with other explanations. Perhaps Crane is depicting a hard, cruel universe in which the Swede gets what he deserves because he fails to follow the codes of Fort Romper. The Swede accuses Johnnie of cheating, which he should have known would cause a fight, at the very least. The Swede grabs the gambler, an obvious violation of saloon decorum. From the beginning of the story, the Swede is characterized as being out of touch with the town and its people. The Swede's codes are from a different culture.

We might reasonably conclude that the Swede was killed as a result of a community of men who did not stand up for him. The Easterner clearly believes that everyone else who was there at the Palace Hotel was responsible for the Swede's death because they did not corroborate the accusation that Johnnie was cheating, which the Easterner, and probably everyone else, knew. (There are hints that Johnnie is a cheat, including two quarrels with the old man with whom he is playing cards when the others arrive.) The death of the Swede, according to the Easterner, is the inevitable result of natural forces of violence and death working their way in the natural world. The only antidote to the natural cycle of violence, according to the Easterner, is for humans to bind together to deliberately stop violence, as he attempted to do twice prior to the fight with Johnnie.

Yet another reading of the Swede's death might suggest that from the very beginning, the Swede is astutely perceptive about the violent nature of Fort Romper. Johnnie, after all, does cheat at cards and does not hesitate to fight to avenge an attack upon
his reputation. The community of men at Scully's hotel is quite comfortable in witnessing a fight that could lead to the death of one of the participants. Indeed, the cowboy
urges Johnnie to "Kill him! Kill him!" The gambler does carry a deadly weapon, and he
obviously does not hesitate to use it when the situation calls for such action. The gambler knows the codes of the saloon. Perhaps the residue of this story lies in the cowboy's
final words, "Well, I didn't do anythin', did I?" This statement might mean that he is
not responsible for killing the Swede or that he is not responsible for not preventing the
killing of the Swede, or it might just mean that he does not understand the implications
of the Easterner's explanation. It would seem to be no accident that the story ends with
a question mark.

WRITING YOUR ESSAY FROM A
DECONSTRUCTIVE PERSPECTIVE

The following short story, "Don't Delve Too Deeply," is by Alberto Moravia.
Like the other stories in his collection of short stories called *Roman Tales*,
this story is set in the city of Rome. This narrative, like "The Blue Hotel," depends heavily upon an ironic sensibility. Unlike Crane's tale, this story is told
from the first-person perspective, which makes the irony all the more profound, because much of it is self-directed at the narrator. One important
question for the reader to answer is, How seriously does one take the narrator? Is there a hint of humor in his revelation of his marital woes? The narrator Alfredo, like other characters you have met in the stories in this volume,
struggles with some major problems in his life and, like some of the characters
you have read, raises questions about the possibility of love in its fullest expression. Moravia explores emotional isolation and the frustration of everyday life, especially frustrations stemming from an unhappy marital life.
Moravia has long been considered one of Italy's premier existential writers,
who explores the day-to-day decisions individuals make and the impact they
have on their lives. Following "Don't Delve Too Deeply" is a series of questions to assist you in the analysis of the work, as well as in writing an essay
from a deconstructive perspective.

A SAMPLE READING

"Don't Delve Too Deeply" by Alberto Moravia (1907–1990)

Agnese could surely have given me some warning, instead of going away like that, without so much as telling me to go to blazes. I don't claim to be perfect, and if she had told me what it was she was needing, we could have discussed the matter. But no, not at all; in two years of married life, not a word; and then, one morning, taking advantage of a moment when I was not there, off she sneaked, like a servant-girl who has found a better place. She went; and even now, six months after she left me, I don't understand why it was.

That morning, after doing the household shopping at the little local market (I like to do the shopping myself: I know the prices, I know what I want, I like bargaining and arguing, sampling and handling, I want to know what sort of a beast my beefsteak comes from and out of which basket my apple is taken), I had gone out again to buy a yard and a half of fringe to sew on to the curtain in the dining-room. Since I did not want to spend more than so much, I went to several places before I found exactly the thing that suited me, in a little shop in the Via dell'Umiltà. It was about twenty past eleven when I got home; I went into the dining-room in order to compare the colour of the fringe with the colour of the curtain, and I at once saw, on the table, the inkstand and the pen and a letter. To tell the truth, what struck me most of all was an ink-stain on the tablecloth. "Why in the world," I thought, "does she have to be so clumsy? . . . She's made a stain on the tablecloth." I removed the inkstand, the pen and the letter, took up the tablecloth, went with it into the kitchen, and there, by dint of rubbing it hard with a lemon, managed to take out the stain. Then I went back into the dining-room and replaced the tablecloth; and only then did I remember the letter. It was addressed to me: Alfredo. I opened it and read: "I have done the housework. You can cook the lunch yourself, you're quite accustomed to it. Good-bye. I am going back to Mother's. Agnese." For a moment I understood nothing. Then I read the letter again and at last it dawned upon me: Agnese had gone away, she had left me after two years of married life. From force of habit I put the letter into the drawer of the sideboard where I keep receipts and correspondence, and sat down on a chair beside the window. I did not know what to think, I was quite unprepared and I scarcely believed it. As I sat reflecting thus, my eye fell on the floor and I saw a little white feather which must have come off the feather-brush when Agnese was doing the dusting. I picked up the feather, opened the window and threw it out. Then I took my hat and went out of the house.

As I walked along—treading, according to a special vice of mine, on every *other* paving-stone—I began to ask myself what I could have done to Agnese that she should leave me in such a very unkind way, as though with a deliberate intention of affronting me. In the first place, I thought, let us see whether Agnese can find fault with me for any kind of unfaithfulness, even the very slightest. I at once answered myself: none whatever. Indeed I have never been crazy about women, I don't understand them and they don't understand me; and, from the day I got married, it may be said that they ceased to exist for me. To such an extent, in fact, that Agnese herself used to irritate me by asking me from time to time: "What would you do if you fell in love with another woman?" And I would answer: "It's impossible: I love you and that feeling will last me

all my life." Now, thinking over it again, I seemed to recall that this "all my life" had
not given her any pleasure: on the contrary, she had pulled a long face and relapsed into
silence. Going on to an entirely different set of ideas, I was anxious to discover whether
by any chance Agnese might have left me for reasons of money and, in fact, of my treatment of her in general. But, here again, I found that my conscience was clear. With regard to money, it is true that I never gave her any except for some exceptional reason,
but then, what need had she of money? I myself was always at hand, ready to pay. And
as for the way I treated her, goodness me, there was nothing unkind about *that*: you can
judge for yourselves. The cinema twice a week; twice a week to a café, and no matter
whether she had an ice or just a cup of coffee; a couple of illustrated magazines every
month and the newspaper every day; in winter, the opera into the bargain; in summer a
holiday at Marino, at my father's house. So much for amusements; and coming on to
the question of clothes, Agnese had even less to complain about. When she needed
anything, whether it was a brassière or a pair of stockings or a handkerchief, I was always ready: I went with her to the shops, I helped her choose the article, I paid without
any fuss. It was the same with dressmakers and milliners; there was never a single occasion when she said to me: "I need a hat, I need a dress," that I did not answer: "Come
along, I'll go with you." Moreover, it must be admitted that Agnese was not exacting:
after the first year she ceased almost entirely to have any clothes made for her. It was I,
in fact, who now had to remind her that she needed this or that garment. But she used
to reply that she had the things from the year before and that it didn't matter; so that in
the end I came to think that, from this point of view, she must be different from other
women and that she didn't mind about being well-dressed.

So it had nothing to do either with affairs of the heart or with money. There remained what lawyers call "incompatibility of temperament". I now asked myself: what
incompatibility of temperament could possibly exist when, in two years, there had
never been a dispute between us, not a single one? We were always together, and if this
incompatibility had existed, it would have made itself apparent. But Agnese never con-
tradicted me, in fact it can almost be said that she never spoke. During some of the
evenings we spent at the café or at home she hardly even opened her mouth; it was I
who did all the talking. I don't deny it, I like talking and hearing myself talk, especially
if I am with a person with whom I am on terms of intimacy. My way of speaking is
quiet, uniform, with no great heights or depths, reasonable, flowing; and if I attack a
subject, I pull it to pieces, from top to bottom, in all its aspects. And the subjects I prefer are domestic ones: I like to converse about the prices of things, about the arrangement of the furniture, about the cooking and the heating, about any sort of nonsense, in
fact. I should never get tired of talking about these things; I take such a great interest in
them that I often catch myself starting all over again, with the same arguments. And—
let us be just—with a woman these are surely the right subjects of conversation:
otherwise, what would one talk about? Agnese, in any case, used to listen to me attentively—at least so it seemed to me. Only once, when I was explaining how the electric
water-heater worked, did I become aware that she had gone to sleep. I woke her up and
asked her: "Why, were you bored?" She answered at once: "No, no, I was tired, I slept
badly last night."

Husbands usually have their offices or shops or else they have nothing at all and   5
go out with their friends. But in my case, my office, my shop, my friends—were Agnese.
I never left her alone for a moment, I stayed at her side even—perhaps you will be
surprised—while she was cooking. I have a passion for cooking and every day, before

meals, I used to put on an apron and help Agnese in the kitchen. I did all sorts of things: I peeled the potatoes, shredded the French beans, prepared the stuffing, watched the saucepans. I helped her so well that she often used to say to me: "Look here, you do it . . . I've got a headache; I'm going to lie down." And then I did the cooking by myself; and, with the aid of the cookery book, I was even able to try new dishes. It was such a pity that Agnese was not greedy; in fact recently her appetite had left her altogether and she hardly touched her food. Once she said to me—just as a joke, of course: "You made a mistake in being born a man. . . . You're really a woman—a housewife, in fact." I must admit that there was some truth in this remark: as a matter of fact, besides cook- ing I like washing, ironing, sewing and even, in my leisure moments, re-doing the hem- stitching of handkerchiefs. As I say, I never left her, not even when some girl friend or her mother came to see her; not even when she took it into her head, for some reason or other, to have lessons in English: in order to be with her, I, too, made efforts to learn that extremely difficult language. I was so closely attached to her that sometimes I even made myself feel ridiculous—as on that occasion when, not having caught something she had said to me in a low voice, in a café, I followed her right to the lavatory and the attendant stopped me, telling me it was the ladies' lavatory and I could not go in. Oh yes, a husband like me is not easily found. Often she would say to me: "I've got to go to such a place, to see such-and-such a person who's of no interest to you." But I would an- swer her: "I'll come too . . . anyhow, I've got nothing to do." Then she would reply: "Come, as far as I'm concerned, but I warn you you'll be bored." But not at all, I was not in the least bored, and afterwards I told her: "You see, I wasn't bored." We were, in fact, inseparable.

Thinking over these things and wondering all the time in vain why Agnese should have left me, I arrived at my father's shop. It is a shop that sells sacred objects and it is in the neighbourhood of the Piazza Minerva. My father is a man still young, with black, curly hair, a black moustache, and, beneath the moustache, a smile I never understood. Perhaps because he is in the habit of dealing with priests and de- vout persons, he is very, very gentle, quiet, and always well-mannered. But my mother, who knows him well, says that his nerves are all hidden away inside him. Well, I went past all the glass cases full of chasubles and sacred vessels and walked straight into the room behind the shop where he has his desk. As usual he was doing his accounts, biting his moustache and meditating. Breathlessly I said to him: "Father, Agnese has left me."

He looked up and it seemed to me that he was smiling beneath his moustache; but perhaps this was just an impression. "I'm sorry," he said, "I'm very sorry. . . . But how did it happen?"

I told him the whole story. And I concluded: "Of course, I'm vexed about it. . . . But what I want to know more than anything is *why* she's left me."

Puzzled, he asked: "Don't you understand it?"

"No."

10

He remained silent for a moment and then said with a sigh: "Alfredo, I'm sorry, but I don't know what to say to you. . . . You're my son, I support you and I'm very fond of you . . . but your wife—that's your own business."

"Yes, but why has she left me?"

He wagged his head. "If I were you, I shouldn't delve too deeply," he said. "Leave it alone. . . . What does it matter to you to know the reasons?"

"It matters a great deal to me . . . more than anything."

At that moment two priests came in, and my father rose and went to meet them,   15
saying to me: "Come back later . . . we'll have a talk then . . . I'm busy now." I realized I
couldn't expect anything more from him and went out.

Agnese's mother's house was not far off, in the Corso Vittorio. I reflected that the
only person who could explain to me the mystery of her departure was Agnese herself;
so I went there. I ran upstairs, and was shown into the sitting-room. But, instead of Agnese, her mother came in. She too owned a shop, and she was a woman I could not
bear, with her dyed black hair, her florid cheeks, her smiling, sly, artificial air. She was
wearing a dressing-gown, with a rose at her breast. When she saw me, she said, with
feigned cordiality: "Oh, Alfredo, what are *you* doing here?"

"You know why I've come," I answered. "Agnese has left me."

"Yes, she's here," she said calmly. "My dear boy, what is there to be done about it?
These are things that just happen."

"What, is that the only answer you can give me?"

She considered me for a moment and then asked: "Have you told your own par-   20
ents about it?"

"Yes, I've told my father."

"And what did *he* say?"

What in the world had it to do with her, what my father had said? Unwillingly I
replied: "You know what my father's like. . . . He says I had better not delve too deeply."

"He's quite right, my dear boy. . . . Don't delve too deeply."

"But really," I exclaimed, becoming heated, "*why* is it she's left me? What have I   25
done to her? Why don't you tell me?"

While I was speaking, all angry as I was, my eye fell on the table. It was covered
with a cloth and on the cloth was an embroidered white centrepiece and on the centrepiece was a vase of red carnations. But the centrepiece was crooked. Automatically,
without knowing what I was doing, while she looked at me smiling and did not answer
me, I lifted the vase and put the centrepiece in place. Then she said: "Well done, now
the centrepiece is right in the middle. . . . I hadn't noticed it, but you saw it at
once. . . . Well done . . . and now you'd better go, my dear boy."

She had risen; meanwhile, I rose too. I wanted to ask if I might see Agnese, but I
realized it was useless; also I was afraid, if I saw her, that I might lose my head and do or
say something stupid. So I went away, and from that day to this I have never seen my
wife. Some day, perhaps, she will come back, seeing that husbands like me are not to be
met with every day of the week. But she's not going to cross the threshold of my house
unless she first explains to me why it was that she left me.

(1954)

Questions for Your Analysis of "Don't Delve Too Deeply"

1) What are some of your early impressions of the story? What is the most striking
   incident of the story, something that promotes an instant reaction in you?
2) This story is told in the first person. What is your instinctive response to the narrator? Do you find him to be a very interesting figure? Why?

3) What are your observations of the narrator's preoccupation with himself? How much insight does the narrator have into himself and his wife Agnese? Do you feel that Agnese would tell a very different story?

4) At what point in the narrative does the narrator's intensive self-focus become apparent?

5) Is there something from your personal experience that assists you in relating to any of the characters in the story? Can you sympathize with either Alfredo or Agnese?

6) Much of the story is concerned with Alfredo's explanation and defense of himself. How effective are his reasons for what has happened between him and his wife?

7) Alfredo describes himself quite clearly in portraying his essential qualities. What other traces of Alfred do you find in the narrative that he doesn't offer explicitly?

8) This story has much to do with the institution of marriage, which is often thought of as a mutually beneficial arrangement. How would you describe the two-year marriage between Alfredo and Agnese? In what way(s) has Alfredo "supplemented" his vision of marriage by his behavior and attitude?

9) What does the story say about Italian family life in the 1950s?

10) Irony and sarcasm are dominant metaphors in this story. Which statements by Alfredo are particularly ironic, and why?

11) What does the title mean to you? Why is Alfredo advised not to delve too deeply? What would happen if he did?

12) In the last sentence of the story, Alfredo demands an explanation from his wife before he will accept her back. How might this sentence serve as representative or symbolic of the story as a whole?

STEPS IN WRITING A DECONSTRUCTIVE ESSAY ABOUT ANY READING

1) Write down your impressions of key moments or settings in the story or poem that illustrate ambiguities, gaps, or silences in the text.

2) Identify traces, supplements, and metaphors in the work that reveal underlying areas of meaning.

3) Examine central characters and explore incomplete, uncertain, ambiguous (or even contradictory) circumstances within which they function. These contexts might include their background, their relations with others, and the historical setting of the story.

4) Assess the point of view of the narrator or speaker if it is a poem. Read closely for inconsistencies or ironic overtures from a narrator or speaker.

5) Detail any personal experiences you may have had that relate to themes of uncertainty, ambiguity, or inexplicability in the work.

6) Chronicle personal references in the work and look for inconsistencies in character representations.

7) Compare your ethical values with those in the work. Identify areas in which your uncertainty about moral issues differs significantly from the work's perspectives.

8) Analyze any tensions in the work that relate to issues of references to reality. Examine those tensions for representations that are contrary to your experience.
9) A good general electronic source to investigate the context of any literary reading is google.com. By typing in the title of the work, especially if it is a well-known literary work, you will locate several sources that provide background information.

STEPS IN WRITING AN ESSAY ABOUT "DON'T DELVE TOO DEEPLY"

Brainstorming Your Topic

1) Identify those elements in the text (character, plot, theme, metaphor) that prompt an immediate response from you. Write down whatever impressions you have.
2) Focus on the main character, Alfredo. What is it about him that you do or do not like? Identify his personal traits and his method of telling the reader about himself.
3) The narrator's portrait of his marriage is clearly one-sided (how could it be anything else?). Characterize, point by point, Alfredo's assessment of his marriage.
4) In the first few paragraphs, Alfredo's narration is dominated by personal pronouns ("I know what I want," etc.). Assess Alfred's obsession with himself.
5) What personal experiences have you had that connect to parts of "Don't Delve Too Deeply"? Have you ever encountered someone like Alfredo?
6) The narrator begins the story by blaming Agnese for the breakup of their marriage. What does this tell us about the narrator and his relationship with the reader? What does Alfredo assume about the reader?
7) The story contains references to the past "crimes" of Agnese and the good deeds of Alfredo. Write down what effect(s) these references to the past have on you.
8) Are you satisfied with the ending? Why or why not?
9) Identify at least one conceptualization of something that is presented as clearly and fairly stated (perhaps Alfredo's identity as described by him and through his behavior, or his overall account of his relationship with Agnese). Explore additional traces of these conceptualizations.
10) Identify at least one conceptualization of something that is presented as whole or complete (perhaps Alfredo's description of what marriage should be, especially in the area of personal responsibility). Explore additional supplements of these conceptualizations, including a perspective sympathetic to Agnese.
11) Record several instances of irony and sarcasm in the story, and list the effects they have on your reaction to the narrative.

Creating an Outline

1) Collect your answers to the questions above in short two-word or three-word categories and use them as preliminary "writing points."

2) Think about the points and consider whether they add up to a central idea (for example, the ironic face of the narrator in "Don't Delve Too Deeply").

3) Identify five or six main writing points that support your central idea. These points should come from the main literary elements in the story (character, plot, theme, point of view, metaphor). All of the points should provide support for your controlling idea. A good starting place is to examine the story's deconstructive context, beginning with the ambiguities and unreliability of character descriptions. (How can the reader really trust Alfredo?)

4) If you have more than five or six points, try to combine one or more of them. If you have fewer than five or six points, see if some of them can be used to generate additional points. You may have some large points that include smaller issues that can stand alone as paragraph topic sentences.

5) Look for transitional devices that connect your main points of support, particularly as they connect various encounters in the story.

Preparing a Rough Draft

1) Now that you have created a working outline, you have already completed your major organizational work. Each major point is the topic of a paragraph, and your essay will have between 5 and 10 paragraphs, depending on development. These paragraphs need not be of equal length, but each one should sufficiently develop the topic sentence.

2) Now that you have your major writing points, assemble a preliminary draft by developing each topic idea with two or three sentences that discuss evidence from the text.

3) Focus on developing transitions between your paragraphs. Professional writers often begin a new paragraph with a direct reference to an idea expressed at the end of the preceding paragraph.

4) It is not too early to begin writing your concluding paragraph. Conclusions often summarize the main points of a central idea (but do not repeat word for word what has already been said). A conclusion may also refer to implications of what has been said (but what cannot be developed because of space limits). Your conclusion should examine deconstructive issues in the story.

5) Don't be afraid to include questions in your writing. No reader of literature can ever be absolutely certain of every observation that he or she makes, and perceptive observations often generate excellent questions, many of which are useful, even if unanswerable.

Editing Your Draft

1) At this stage, you should have a draft of a few hundred words. You have already done the most difficult work in thinking out your ideas, organizing them into an outline, and preparing a rough version of the final product. Look for ways of editing your paper that will strengthen the essay.

2) Search for repetitious wording (and ideas). Do not repeat ideas, however important, throughout the essay. Use a thesaurus to locate synonyms for terms and ideas that reappear. Attempt to emphasize variety in your language.

3) If your instructor encourages peer editing, choose someone in your class, or perhaps a roommate, and solicit advice about how your essay reads. Is it articulate, compelling, insightful, and interesting? (All of these qualities are important.) Although your peer editor may not be taking a literature class, he or she may be a very good source of feedback on how effective your writing is. Professional writers often seek feedback from peers, and not only from professional colleagues.

4) Be open to make changes in your writing, both conceptually and in specific language. Professional writers know that writing is recursive (which means that the act of writing constantly generates new ways of looking at the topic), and student writers should also take advantage of changes in thinking *as they write*. Don't be afraid to make efficient and effective changes, especially in terms of cutting out words, phrases, and sections that may not be working very well in supporting your overall idea.

5) Proofread carefully for spelling errors, punctuation problems, run-on sentences, and ambiguous or awkward constructions. You should use a solid grammar handbook to assist you in these areas.

Final Checklist

1) Make sure that your central idea (sometimes called a thesis statement) appears in the first paragraph. It is important that your reader know what major point(s) you are attempting to make.

2) Because this essay is a deconstructive investigation, check to see that the essay represents your analysis of ambiguities in the story, especially traces, supplements, and metaphors (irony above all else). Your major points should be understandable, of course, to the community of readers to which you are writing.

3) Examine your essay for sufficient evidence. Each one of your major ideas will need illustration that comes from the text.

4) Review your conclusion to see if you have ended the essay in an effective manner, either summarizing what you have said (in different language) or suggesting some important implications of your reading.

5) Proofread one last time for errors, repetitious language, and awkward phrasing.

A SAMPLE READING

"Shall I Compare Thee to a Summer's Day?" by William Shakespeare (1564–1616)

Shall I compare thee to a summer's day?
Thou art more lovely and more temperate.
Rough winds do shake the darling buds of May,
And summer's lease hath all too short a date.
Sometime too hot the eye of heaven shines,   5

And often is his gold complexion dimmed;
And every fair from fair sometimes declines,

By chance, or nature's changing course, untrimmed.
But thy eternal summer shall not fade,
Nor lose possession of that fair thou ow'st;   10
Nor shall death brag thou wand'rest in his shade,
When in eternal lines to time thou grow'st.
    So long as men can breathe or eyes can see,
    So long lives this, and this gives life to thee.

Questions for Analyzing "Shall I Compare Thee to a Summer's Day?"

1) Write down key terms, being careful to define them and write down possible connotations. (You might begin with some of these words: "temperate," "darling," "buds," "lease," "date," "eye of heaven," "gold complexion," "dimmed," "fair," "eternal lines.")

2) Consider key moments in the poem. (For example: What is the effect of the speaker's apparent attempt to make his beloved immortal?)

3) Describe your impressions of the tone of the poem and how the tone changes, if it does. (For example: Consider the speaker's attitude toward the time.)

4) Indicate possible themes in the poem. (For example: "Life is short but beautiful.")

5) Examine key metaphors and images that appear, noting how they relate to one or more themes. (For example: Analyze the relationship between a person's life and a brief summer day.)

6) Focus on the narrating persona. Write down your impressions of what he says about himself and his beloved.

7) The speaker implies sadness and perhaps anxiety about time and what it does to summer days and humans. What inferences do you draw about time, life, and beauty from this poem?

8) The speaker says that his beloved's summer "shall not fade" yet, that cannot be literally true. What does this metaphor suggest to you?

9) Describe the personal experiences have you had, if any, that connect you to "Shall I Compare Thee to a Summer's Day?"

10) Are you satisfied with the conclusion of the poem, in which the speaker asserts that he shall achieve some kind of immortality? Why or why not? What are the deconstructive implications?

ELECTRONIC RESOURCES FOR STEPHEN CRANE

http://www.gonzaga.edu/faculty/campbell/crane/. The home page for the Stephen Crane Society.

http://www.uakron.edu/english/richards/edwards/crane1.html. This site contains biographical information, including interesting descriptions of Crane's early experiences in Ohio, written by those who knew him.

http://www.usafa.af.mil/dfeng/index.htm#craneres.htm. This site contains resources for investigation into Stephen Crane and his work.

http://www.library.utoronto.ca/utel/rp/authors/cranes.html. This site contains poems
  by Stephen Crane.
http://www.unityspot.com/arthurs/crane.html. This site allows the downloading of
  Crane's stories.

ELECTRONIC RESOURCES FOR ALBERTO MORAVIA

http://www.britannica.com/eb/article?eu=55016. *Encyclopædia Britannica* Web site for
  Moravia includes biographical information as well as links to other sites related
  to this popular Italian writer.
http://www.kirjasto.sci.fi/moravia.htm. Additional biographical and bibliographic information on Moravia.
http://www.sculoaromana.it/personag/moravia.htm and http://www.italialibri.net/autori/
  moraviaa.html. Both of these sites contain biographical information on Moravia written in Italian.

Further Readings in Deconstructive Criticism

Collins, Jeff and Bill Mayblin. *Introducing Derrida*. New York: Totem Books, 1998.
Crowley, Sharon. *A Teacher's Introduction to Deconstruction*. Urbana, IL: NCTE, 1989.
Culler, Jonathon. *On Deconstruction: Theory and Criticism After Structuralism*. Ithaca:
  Cornell UP, 1982.
De Man, Paul. "The Epistemology of Metaphor." In *On Metaphor*. Sheldon Sacks, ed.
  Chicago: U of Chicago, 1979: 11–28.
Derrida, Jacques. "The Law of Genre." In *On Narrative*, W. J. T. Mitchell, ed. (pp.).
  Chicago: U of Chicago, 1981: 51–77.
———. "The Retrait of Metaphor." *Enclitic* (2) 1978: 6–33.
———. "White Mythology: Metaphor in the Text of Philosophy." *New Literary History*
  6 (1974): 11–74.
Johnson, Barbara. *The Critical Difference*. Baltimore: Johns Hopkins UP, 1980.
Leitch, Vincent B. *American Literary Criticism from the Thirties to the Eighties*. New York:
  Columbia UP, 1988.
Neel, Jaspar. "A T(R)opological Group: Nine Terms in the Derridean Lexicon." In
  Plato, Derrida, and Writing. Carbondale: Southern Illinois UP, 1988.
Norris, Christopher. *Deconstruction: Theory and Practice*. New York: Metheun, 1982.
Powell, Jim. *Derrida for Beginners*. New York: Writers and Readers Publishing, 1997.

chapter 10

The Research Essay

A research essay is perhaps the most challenging part of a course that focuses on the analysis and evaluation of literature. The research project is a daunting task because it asks you to combine your interpretive skills with those of professional readers and arrive at an articulate, well-informed essay.

The preceding chapters encouraged you to incorporate limited secondary criticism in your papers. The research project necessarily requires that you analyze and synthesize the thought of others into your writing, and significantly more so than in the relatively short essays that appear in each chapter. Investigating your topic can and should be an enriching experience that helps you to understand the rich and complex variety of sources available to you. Once you are in the throes of your exploration, you will never feel alone in writing your paper. Scholars, living and dead, are there to assist you in developing your ideas, as well as complementing them with historical facts and interpretive opinions.

The research paper is truly a challenging investigative effort, and one of the major dimensions of library research for all writers, beginning and advanced, is the act of preliminary investigation, or brainstorming. All professional writers have experienced changes in their approaches to subjects because of ideas that surfaced while they were investigating their topic. This change is sometimes called *serendipity*, which may be defined as something that is learned by accident. (In the life sciences, medical treatments are sometimes found serendipitously.) The more vigorously you research your topic, the more surprising the results may be. And it is important to remember that where you start is not where you may wind up, a common experience among seasoned writers.

Experienced writers investigate their work in a variety of ways, so it is not possible to present one method of conducting research as clearly superior to all others. However, there are some common research characteristics shared by all accomplished writers. All research essays should contain substantial original thinking, supplemented and informed by the thought of others, generated by the use of traditional and electronic resources.

It is important to note that the research essay is not simply a longer version of the essays you have already written. A research paper provides an analysis that is a deeper penetration into a literary work and that takes into account a larger context (which may be historical, social, cultural, and so forth). The research essay involves your interpretive approach (which may include more than one critical school) *and* the critical commentary of professional readers. The inclusion of secondary sources does not mean that you necessarily agree with a critic's perspective or interpretation, but it does mean that you have familiarized yourself with what professional critics have said about a literary work. Successful researchers learn from experience where to go to locate information and how to incorporate secondary sources into their writing.

Brainstorming, as an act of early investigation, is a critical strategy to all successful writing, especially research writing where the goal is to analyze and synthesize many elements. Most writers generate substantial notes about the text that they are analyzing, and that is what brainstorming is about. The act of brainstorming allows you to randomly select ideas and points of pursuit without regard to their ultimate usefulness. Brainstorming is thinking and writing quickly, without assessing the value of the ideas that you generate. The brainstorming stage is not the time to be overly critical of the points you make. It is a time for openmindedness and it is an essential step before organization.

Organization is a critical component of the successful research investigation of a literary text. There are many ways to organize your research work, but a common approach is to read the literary text with precision, generating a list of copious notes about issues in the text that warrant further investigation. The next step is to organize them according to areas of common interest. This approach is inductive and it generates a list of particular topics and points of investigation that often come together to form a general thesis. An inductive approach usually leads to a deductive central controlling idea, which may change as you develop and explore new ideas and their implications. (Some writers begin with a tightly defined deductive premise and then search for supporting information, but this method can sometimes become rigid and lack the exploratory possibilities of beginning inductively.) Your research organization should be sufficiently flexible to allow you to develop your ideas, and not so constraining that it hinders the exploration and evaluation of new ideas that are generated by your research.

Drafting your essay is another strategic step in successful research writing. A draft should always be longer (sometimes much longer) than the final product because it is easier for most writers to edit rather than to amplify. The drafting of your essay gives you an opportunity to put together your ideas into a general format. At this stage, you should not be overly concerned about transitions, fully developed paragraphs, detailed introductions and conclusions, and so forth. The main purpose of preliminary drafting is to assemble as much information and insight as you can into a skeleton essay. Final drafting is the stage where you develop each idea to its fullest. Once you have transferred your outline of ideas into a rough draft and have developed that draft, the next step is to edit your work.

Editing is perhaps the most important segment in the writing process. This step is an opportunity for you to double check your resources and be on the lookout for the need to add additional source material and clarification. It is the first thorough check for mechanical and stylistic weaknesses. The editing stage is a good time to carefully examine phrases and sentences for fluency, logic, clarity, development, judicious use of evidence, persuasiveness, and overall achievement of purpose.

A final checklist is a mechanism that nearly all professional writers employ to give their work one final review. This step is the last opportunity to catch errors in punctuation, spelling, and grammar, as well as to fine-tune phrasing, sentence structures, transitions between paragraphs, and the effectiveness of introductions and conclusions. When you perform the final checklist, attempt to read not as the author, but rather as a reader who is reading the text for the first time. The more objective you can be in examining your own writing, the more effective an editor you will be. It is helpful to you to be your most exacting critic.

STEPS IN WRITING YOUR RESEARCH ESSAY

Beginning Your Investigation

The first step is to consider what approach, or approaches, your paper will take. Most research essays incorporate the methods of more than one critical school. Cultural criticism investigates the context and background of the text. Formalist criticism involves the close reading of the text. Reader response criticism allows you to express your personal interaction with the text. A feminist sensibility allows you an opportunity to consider gender issues. Approaching the text deconstructively gives you an opportunity to explore complex metaphors, issues of identity, and traces in the work. Reading psychologically creates an opportunity to explore the inner dimensions of characters' minds and behaviors. Ethical criticism explores issues of right and wrong, personal encounters, and issues of community responsibility. All critical approaches presented in this book offer tools to assist you in a deep probe of literature. The choice is yours as to how many, or how few, critical approaches you integrate into your overall analysis.

Steps in Brainstorming

1) Consider the historical background of the work and of the author. How do they set the stage for important elements in the text?
2) Identify those elements in the text (character, plot, theme, metaphor) that evoke an immediate response from you. Write down whatever impressions you have.
3) Examine closely the first few paragraphs of the text in order to explore clues and foreshadowing.
4) Consider narrative exposition (first- or third-person narration) and its effect on readers.
5) Focus on the main character(s). What is it about him or her or them that you do or do not like? What are their characteristics?
6) What personal experiences have you had the connect to parts of the text? Have you ever encountered individuals like the characters in the text?
7) What kinds of relationships does the text depict? What do they say about the author's "world vision"?
8) Are you satisfied with the ending? Why or why not?
9) Identify at least one conceptualization of something that is presented as objectively and fairly stated. Explore additional traces of these conceptualizations.
10) Identify at least one conceptualization of something that is presented as whole or complete. Explore additional supplements of these conceptualizations.
11) Record instances of metaphor in the story and list the effects these figures have on your reaction to the narrative.
12) Investigate major changes that take place in the story, especially to main characters.

Creating an Outline

1) Collect your answers to the questions above in short two-word or three-word categories and use them as preliminary writing points. Compare them to what professional critics have had to say about the work.
2) Think about the points and consider whether they add up to a central idea.
3) Identify 10 or 12 main writing points that support your central idea or approach, if you are able to summarize your thesis in a sentence or two. (A deconstructive reading, for example, may begin by pointing out the impossibility of posing a consistent thematic statement because of contradictory explanation of the text.)
4) Your "talking points" should come from the main literary elements in the story (character, plot, theme, point of view, metaphor). All of the points should provide support for your controlling idea.
5) Look for transitional devices that connect your main points of support, particularly as they connect various segments in the story. Be on the lookout for connections between different critical schools that help you to articulate a rigorously analytical reading.

Organizing Your Work

1) Begin to separate your notes into areas of common interest. If, for example, you are exploring gender relations in a text, place your "gender" notes in a separate category. Do the same if you are focusing, say, on ironic metaphors.

2) Once you have assembled particular points of common importance, bring them together under a larger category that may lead to a deductive position.

3) Complement your points of interpretation with scholarly support.

4) Allow your preliminary organizational pattern to be flexible enough to accommodate additions and subtractions as you learn new things and replace earlier positions.

5) If this organizational approach sounds somewhat confusing, it is because you are attempting to interrelate two tasks. First, you are compiling notes on your reading of a text. Second, you are researching the "notes" of scholarly readers and attempting to integrate them into your text, not as easy "pastes," but as salient points that relate to your positions, perhaps in agreement or in disagreement. The goal of organization is not to make everything come together as a unified, structured whole, but rather to write an articulate, compelling, and probing analysis.

Preparing a Rough Draft

1) Now that you have created a working outline, you have already completed your major organizational work. Each major point is the topic of a paragraph, and your essay may have 8 to 12 paragraphs, depending on development. These paragraphs need not be of equal length, but each one should sufficiently develop the topic sentence.

2) Now that you have your major writing points, assemble a preliminary draft by developing each topic idea with several sentences that discuss evidence from the text.

3) Focus on developing transitions between your paragraphs. Professional writers often begin a new paragraph with a direct reference to an idea expressed at the end of the preceding paragraph.

4) It is not too early to begin writing your concluding paragraph. Conclusions often summarize the main points of a central idea (but do not repeat word for word what has already been said). A conclusion may also refer to implications of what has been said (but what cannot be developed because of space limits). Your conclusion should remind the reader of the importance and implications of your analysis.

5) Don't be afraid to include questions in your writing. No reader of literature should ever be rigidly certain of every observation that he or she makes, and perceptive observations often generate excellent questions, many of which are useful even though unanswerable. Research essays, in particular, are rich sources of new questions and unexplored territory brought to light by a probing investigation.

Editing Your Draft

1) At this stage, you should have a draft of a couple of thousand words. You have already done the most difficult work in thinking out your ideas, investigating outside sources, organizing them into an outline, and preparing a rough version of the final product. Look for ways to edit your paper that will strengthen the essay.

2) Search for repetitious wording (and ideas). Do not unimaginatively repeat ideas, however important, throughout the essay. Use a thesaurus to locate synonyms for terms and ideas that reappear. Attempt to emphasize variety in your language.

3) If your instructor encourages peer editing, choose someone in your class, or perhaps a roommate, and solicit advice about how your essays reads. Is it articulate,

compelling, insightful, and interesting? (All of these qualities are important.) Although your peer editor may not be taking a literature class, he or she may be a very good source of feedback on how effective your writing is. Professional writers often seek feedback from peers, and not only from professional colleagues.

4) Be open to make changes in your writing, both conceptually and in specific language. Professional writers know that writing is recursive (which means that the act of writing constantly generates new ways of looking at the topic), and student writers should also take advantage of changes in thinking *as they write*. Don't be afraid to make efficient and effective changes, especially in terms of cutting out words, phrases, and sections that may not be working very well in supporting your overall idea.

5) Proofread carefully for spelling errors, punctuation problems, run-on sentences, and ambiguous or awkward constructions. You should use a reputable grammar handbook to assist you in these areas.

Final Checklist

1) Make sure that your central idea (sometimes called a thesis statement) appears in the first paragraph. It is important that your reader know what major point(s) you are attempting to make, even if you actively challenge them (as one might do in a deconstructive essay).

2) Because this essay is a research investigation, check to see that the essay represents your full and rigorous incorporation of outside information. Your major points should be understandable, of course, to the community of readers to which you are writing, and you should avoid jargon, even if you encounter it in the criticism you find.

3) Examine your essay for sufficient evidence. Each one of your major ideas will need illustration that comes from the text.

4) Review your conclusion to see if you have ended the essay in an effective manner, either summarizing what you have said (in different language) or suggesting some important implications of your reading.

5) Proofread one last time for errors, repetitious language, and awkward phrasing.

Following the sample reading of James Joyce's "The Dead" is a section to further assist you in researching your topic, using traditional library research methods as well as electronic resources.

SAMPLE READING

"The Dead" by James Joyce (1882–1941)

Lily, the caretaker's daughter, was literally run off her feet. Hardly had she brought one gentleman into the little pantry behind the office on the ground floor and helped him off with his overcoat than the wheezy hall-door bell clanged again and she had to scamper along the bare hallway to let in another guest. It was well for her she had not to attend to the ladies also. But Miss Kate and Miss Julia had thought of that and had converted the bathroom upstairs into a ladies' dressing-room. Miss Kate and Miss Julia were there, gossiping and laughing and fussing, walking after each other to the head of the stairs, peering down over the banisters and calling down to Lily to ask her who had come.

It was always a great affair, the Misses Morkan's annual dance. Everybody who knew them came to it, members of the family, old friends of the family, the members of Julia's choir, any of Kate's pupils that were grown up enough, and even some of Mary Jane's pupils too. Never once had it fallen flat. For years and years it had gone off in splendid style, as long as anyone could remember; ever since Kate and Julia, after the death of their brother Pat, had left the house in Stoney Batter and taken Mary Jane, their only niece, to live with them in the dark, gaunt house on Usher's Island, the upper part of which they had rented from Mr. Fulham, the corn-factor on the ground floor. That was a good thirty years ago if it was a day. Mary Jane, who was then a little girl in short clothes, was now the main prop of the household, for she had the organ in Haddington Road. She had been through the Academy and gave a pupils' concert every year in the upper room of the Antient Concert Rooms. Many of her pupils belonged to the better-class families on the Kingstown and Dalkey line. Old as they were, her aunts also did their share. Julia, though she was quite grey, was still the leading soprano in Adam and Eve's, and Kate, being too feeble to go about much, gave music lessons to beginners on the old square piano in the back room. Lily, the caretaker's daughter, did housemaid's work for them. Though their life was modest, they believed in eating well; the best of everything: diamond-bone sirloins, three-shilling tea and the best bottled stout. But Lily seldom made a mistake in the orders, so that she got on well with her three mistresses. They were fussy, that was all. But the only thing they would not stand was back answers.

Of course, they had good reason to be fussy on such a night. And then it was long after ten o'clock and yet there was no sign of Gabriel and his wife. Besides they were dreadfully afraid that Freddy Malins might turn up screwed. They would not wish for worlds that any of Mary Jane's pupils should see him under the influence; and when he was like that it was sometimes very hard to manage him. Freddy Malins always came late, but they wondered what could be keeping Gabriel: and that was what brought them every two minutes to the banisters to ask Lily had Gabriel of Freddy come.

"O, Mr. Conroy," said Lily to Gabriel when she opened the door for him, "Miss Kate and Miss Julia thought you were never coming. Good-night, Mrs. Conroy."

"I'll engage they did," said Gabriel, "but they forget that my wife here takes three 5 mortal hours to dress herself."

He stood on the mat, scraping the snow from his goloshes, while Lily led his wife to the foot of the stairs and called out:

"Miss Kate, here's Mrs. Conroy."

Kate and Julia came toddling down the dark stairs at once. Both of them kissed Gabriel's wife, said she must be perished alive, and asked was Gabriel with her.

"Here I am as right as the mail, Aunt Kate! Go on up. I'll follow," called out Gabriel from the dark.

He continued scraping his feet vigorously while the three women went upstairs,   10 laughing, to the ladies' dressing-room. A light fringe of snow lay like a cape on the shoulders of his overcoat and like toecaps on the toes of his goloshes; and, as the buttons of his overcoat slipped with a squeaking noise through the snow-stiffened freeze, a cold fragrant air from out-of-doors escaped from crevices and folds.

"Is it snowing again, Mr. Conroy?" asked Lily.

She had preceded him into the pantry to help him off with his overcoat. Gabriel smiled and the three syllables she had given his surname and glanced at her. She was a slim, growing girl, pale in complexion and with hay-coloured hair. The gas in the pantry made her look still paler. Gabriel had known her when she was a child and used to sit on the lowest step nursing a rag doll.

"Yes, Lily," he answered, "and I think we're in for a night of it."

He looked up at the pantry ceiling, which was shaking with the stamping and shuffling of feet on the floor above, listened for a moment to the piano and then glanced at the girl, who was folding his overcoat carefully at the end of a shelf.

"Tell me, Lily," he said in a friendly tone, "do you still go to school?"   15

"O no, sir," she answered. "I'm done schooling this year and more."

"O, then," said Gabriel gaily, "I suppose we'll be going to your wedding one of these fine days with your young man, eh?"

The girl glanced back at him over her shoulder and said with great bitterness:

"The men that is now is only all palaver and what they can get out of you."

Gabriel coloured, as if he felt he had made a mistake and, without looking at her,   20 kicked off his goloshes and flicked actively with his muffler at his patent-leather shoes.

He was a stout, tallish young man. The high colour of his checks pushed upwards even to his forehead, where it scattered itself in a few formless patches of pale red; and on his hairless face there scintillated restlessly the polished lenses and the bright gilt rims of the glasses which screened his delicate and restless eyes. His glossy black hair was parted in the middle and brushed in a long curve behind his ears where it curled slightly beneath the groove left by his hat.

When he had flicked luster into his shoes he stood up and pulled his waistcoat down more tightly on his plump body. Then he took a coin rapidly from his pocket.

"O Lily," he said, thrusting it into her hands, "it's Christmas-time, isn't it? Just . . . here's a little. . . ."

He walked rapidly towards the door.

"O no, sir!" cried the girl, followed him. "Really, sir, I wouldn't take it."   25

"Christmas-time! Christmas-time!" said Gabriel, almost trotting to the stairs and waving his hand to her in deprecation.

The girl, seeing that he had gained the stairs, called out after him:

"Well, thank you, sir."

He waited outside the drawing-room door until the waltz should finish, listening to the skirts that swept against it and to the shuffling of feet. He was still discomposed by the girl's bitter and sudden retort. It had cast a gloom over him which he tried to dispel by arranging his cuffs and the bows of his tie. He then took from his waistcoat pocket a little paper and glanced at the headings he had made for his speech. He was undecided about the lines from Robert Browning, for he feared they would be above the heads of his hearers. Some quotation that they would recognise from Shakespeare or from the Melodies would be better. The indelicate clacking of the men's heels and the shuffling of their soles reminded him that their grade of culture differed from his. He would only make himself ridiculous by quoting poetry to them which they could not understand. They would think that he was airing his superior education. He would fail with them just as he had failed with the girl in the pantry. He had taken up a wrong tone. His whole speech was a mistake from first to last, an utter failure.

Just then his aunts and his wife came out of the ladies' dressing-room. His aunts were two small, plainly dressed old women. Aunt Julia was an inch or so the taller. Her hair, drawn low over the tops of her ears, was grey; and grey also, with darker shadows, was her large flaccid face. Though she was stout in build and stood erect, her slow eyes and parted lips gave her the appearance of a woman who did not know where she was or where she was going. Aunt Kate was more vivacious. Her face, healthier than her sister's, was all puckers and creases, like a shrivelled red apple, and her hair, braided in the same old-fashioned way, had not lost its ripe nut colour.   30

They both kissed Gabriel frankly. He was their favorite nephew, the son of their dead elder sister, Ellen, who had married T. J. Conroy of the Port and Docks.

"Gretta tells me you're not going to take a cab back to Monkstown tonight, Gabriel," said Aunt Kate.

"No," said Gabriel, turning to his wife, "we had quite enough of that last year, hadn't we? Don't you remember, Aunt Kate, what a cold Gretta got out of it. Cab windows rattling all the way, and the east wind blowing in after we passed Merrion. Very jolly it was. Gretta caught a dreadful cold."

Aunt Kate frowned severely and nodded her head at every word.

"Quite right, Gabriel, quite right," she said. "You can't be too careful."   35

"But as for Gretta there," said Gabriel, "she'd walk home in the snow if she were let."

Mrs. Conroy laughed.

"Don't mind him, Aunt Kate," she said. "He's really an awful bother, what with green shades for Tom's eyes at night and making him do the dumbbells, and forcing Eva to eat the stir-about. The poor child! And she simply hates the sight of it! . . . O, but you'll never guess what he makes me wear now!"

She broke out into a peal of laughter and glanced at her husband, whose admiring and happy eyes had been wandering from her dress to her face and hair. The two aunts laughed heartily, too, for Gabriel's solicitude was a standing joke with them.

"Goloshes!" said Mrs. Conroy." That's the latest. Whenever it's wet underfoot I must put on my goloshes. Tonight even, he wanted me to put them on, but I wouldn't. The next thing he'll buy me will be a diving suit."   40

Gabriel laughed nervously and patted his tie reassuringly, while Aunt Kate nearly doubled herself, so heartily did she enjoy the joke. The smile soon faded from Aunt Julia's face and her mirthless eyes were directed towards her nephew's face. After a pause she asked:

"And what are goloshes, Gabriel?"

"Goloshes, Julia!" exclaimed her sister. "Goodness me, don't you know what goloshes are? You wear them over your . . . over your boots, Gretta, isn't it?"

"Yes," said Mrs. Conroy. "Guttapercha things. We both have a pair now. Gabriel says everyone wears them on the Continent."

"O, on the Continent," murmured Aunt Julia, nodding her head slowly.   45

Gabriel knitted his brows and said, as if he were slightly angered:

"It's nothing very wonderful, but Gretta thinks it very funny because she says the word reminds her of Christy Minstrels."

"But tell me, Gabriel," said Aunt Kate, with brisk tact. "Of course, you've seen about the room. Gretta was saying . . ."

"O the room is all right," replied Gabriel. "I've taken one in the Gresham."

"To be sure," said Aunt Kate, "by far the best thing to do. And the children,   50
Gretta, you're not anxious about them?"

"O, for one night," said Mrs. Conroy. "Besides, Bessie will look after them."

"To be sure," said Aunt Kate again. "What a comfort it is to have a girl like that, one you can depend on! There's that Lily, I'm sure I don't know what has come over her lately. She's not the girl she was at all."

Gabriel was about to ask his aunt some questions on this point, but she broke off suddenly to gaze after her sister, who had wandered down the stairs and was craning her neck over the banisters.

"Now, I ask you," she said almost testily, "where is Julia going? Julia! Julia! Where are you going?"

Julia, who had gone half way down one flight, came back and announced blandly: 55
"Here's Freddy."

At the same moment a clapping of hands and a final flourish of the pianist told that the waltz had ended. The drawing-room door was open from within and some couples came out. Aunt Kate drew Gabriel aside hurriedly and whispered into his ear:

"Slip down, Gabriel, like a good fellow and see if he's all right, and don't let him up if he's screwed. I'm sure he's screwed. I'm sure he is."

Gabriel went to the stairs and listened over the banisters. He could hear two persons talking in the pantry. Then he recognised Freddy Malins' laugh. He went down the stairs nosily.

"It's such a relief," said Aunt Kate to Mrs. Conroy, "that Gabriel is here. I always   60
feel easier in my mind when he's here. . . . Julia, there's Miss Daly and Miss Power will take some refreshment. Thanks for your beautiful waltz, Miss Daly. It made lovely time."

A tall wizen-faced man, with a stiff grizzled moustache and swarthy skin, who was passing out with his partner, said:

"And may we have some refreshment, too, Miss Morkan?"

"Julia," said Aunt Kate summarily, "and here's Mr. Browne and Miss Furlong. Take them in, Julia, with Miss Daly and Miss Power."

"I'm the man for the ladies," said Mr. Browne, pursing his lips until his moustache bristled and smiling in all his wrinkles. "You know, Miss Morkan, the reason they are so fond of me is———"

He did not finish his sentence, but, seeing that Aunt Kate was out of earshot, at   65
once led the three young ladies into the back room. The middle of the room was occupied by two square tables placed end to end, and on these Aunt Julia and the caretaker were straightening and smoothing a large cloth. On the sideboard were arrayed dishes and plates, and glasses and bundles of knives and forks and spoons. The top of the

closed square piano served also as a sideboard for viands and sweets. At a smaller sideboard in one corner two young men were standing, drinking hop-bitters.

Mr. Browne led his charges thither and invited them all, in jest, to some ladies'
punch, hot, strong and sweet. As they said they never took anything strong, he opened
three bottles of lemonade for them. Then he asked one of the young men to move
aside, and, taking hold of the decanter, filled out for himself a goodly measure of
whisky. The young men eyed him respectfully while he took a trial sip.

"God help me," he said, smiling, "it's the doctor's orders."

His wizened face broke into a broader smile, and the three young ladies laughed
in musical echo to his pleasantry, swaying their bodies to and fro, with nervous jerks of
their shoulders. The boldest said:

"O, now, Mr. Browne, I'm sure the doctor never ordered anything of the kind."

Mr. Browne took another sip of his whisky and said, with sidling mimicry: 70

"Well, you see, I'm like the famous Mrs. Cassidy, who is reported to have said:
'Now, Mary Grimes, if I don't take it, make me take it for I feel I want it.'"

His hot face had leaned forward a little too confidentially and he had assumed a
very low Dublin accent so that the young ladies, with one instinct, received his speech
in silence. Miss Furlong, who was one of Mary Jane's pupils, asked Miss Daly what was
the name of the pretty waltz she had played; and Mr. Browne, seeing that he was ignored, turned promptly to the two young men who were more appreciative.

A red-faced young woman, dressed in pansy, came into the room, excitedly clapping her hands and crying:

"Quadrilles! Quadrilles!"

Close on her heels came Aunt Kate, crying: 75

"Two gentlemen and three ladies, Mary Jane!"

"O, here's Mr. Bergin and Mr. Kerrigan," said Mary Jane. "Mr. Kerrigan, will you
take Miss Power? Miss Furlong, may I get you a partner, Mr. Bergin. O, that'll just do
now."

"There ladies, Mary Jane," said Aunt Kate.

The two young gentlemen asked the ladies if they might have the pleasure, and
Mary Jane turned to Miss Daly.

"O, Miss Daly, you're really awfully good, after playing for the last two dances,   80
but really we're so short of ladies tonight."

"I don't mind in the least, Miss Morkan."

"But I've a nice partner for you, Mr. Bartell D'Arcy, the tenor. I'll get him to sing
later on. All Dublin is raving about him."

"Lovely voice, lovely voice!" said Aunt Kate.

As the piano had twice begun the prelude to the first figure Mary Jane led her re-
cruits quickly from the room. They had hardly gone when Aunt Julia wandered slowly
into the room, looking behind her at something.

"What is the matter, Julia?" asked Aunt Kate anxiously. "Who is it?"   85

Julia, who was carrying in a column of table-napkins, turned to her sister and
said, simply, as if the question had surprised her:

"It's only Freddy, Kate, and Gabriel with him."

In fact right behind her Gabriel could be seen piloting Freddy Malins across the
landing. The latter, a young man of about forty, was of Gabriel's size and build, with
very round shoulders. His face was fleshy and pallid, touched with colour only at the

thick hanging lobes of his ears and at the wide wings of his nose. He had coarse features, a blunt nose, a convex and receding brow, tumid and protruded lips. His heavy-lidded eyes and the disorder of his scanty hair made him look sleepy. He was laughing heartily in a high key at a story which he had been telling Gabriel on the stairs and at the same time rubbing the knuckles of his left fist backwards and forwards into his left eye.

"Good-evening, Freddy," said Aunt Julia.

Freddy Malins bade the Misses Morkan good-evening in what seemed an off-   90
hand fashion by reason of the habitual catch in his voice and then, seeing that Mr. Browne was grinning at him from the sideboard, crossed the room on rather shaky legs and began to repeat in an undertone the story he had just told to Gabriel.

"He's not so bad, is he?" said Aunt Kate to Gabriel.

Gabriel's brows were dark, but he raised them quickly and answered:

"O, no hardly noticeable."

"Now, isn't he a terrible fellow!" she said. "And his poor mother made him take the pledge on New Year's Eve. But come on, Gabriel, into the drawing-room."

Before leaving the room with Gabriel she signalled to Mr. Browne by frowning   95
and shaking her forefinger in warning to and fro. Mr. Browne nodded in answer and, when she had gone, said to Freddy Malins:

"Now, then. Teddy, I'm going to fill you out a good glass of lemonade just to buck you up."

Freddy Malins, who was nearing the climax of his story, waved the offer aside impatiently but Mr. Browne, having first called Freddy Malins' attention to a disarray in his dress, filled out and handed him a full glass of lemonade. Freddy Malins' left hand accepted the glass mechanically, his right hand being engaged in the mechanical readjustment of his dress. Mr. Browne, whose face was once more wrinkling with mirth, poured out for himself a glass of whisky while Freddy Malins exploded, before he had well reached the climax of his story, in a kink of high-pitched bronchitic laughter and, setting down his untasted and overflowing glass, began to rub the knuckles of his left fist backwards and forwards into his left eye, repeating words of his last phrase as well as his fit of laughter would allow him.

Gabriel could not listen while Mary Jane was playing her Academy piece, full of runs and difficult passages, to the hushes drawing-room. He liked music but the piece she was playing had no melody for him and he doubted whether it had any melody for the other listeners, though they had begged Mary Jane to play something. Four young men, who had come from the refreshment-room to stand in the doorway at the sound of the piano, had gone away quietly in couples after a few minutes. The only persons who seemed to follow the music were Mary Jane herself, her hands racing along the keyboard or lifted from it at the pauses like those of a priestess in momentary imprecation, and Aunt Kate standing at her elbow to turn the page.

Gabriel's eyes, irritated by the floor, which glittered with beeswax under the heavy chandelier, wandered to the wall above the piano. A picture of the balcony scene in *Romeo and Juliet* hung there and beside it was a picture of the two murdered princes in the Tower which Aunt Julia had worked in red, blue and brown wools when she was a girl. Probably in the school they had gone to as girls that kind of work had been taught for one year. His mother had worked for him as a birthday present a waistcoat of purple tabinet, with little foxes' heads upon it, lined with brown satin and having round mulberry buttons. It was strange that his mother had had no musical talent though Aunt Kate used to call her the brains carrier of the Morkan family. Both she and Julia had always seemed a little proud of their serious and matronly sister. Her photograph stood before the pierglass. She held an open book on her knees and was pointing out something in it to Constantine who, dressed in a man-o'-war suit, lay at her feet. It was she who had chosen the name of her sons for she was very sensible of the dignity of family life. Thanks to her, Constantine was now senior curate in Balbriggan and, thanks to her, Gabriel himself had taken his degree in the Royal University. A shadow passed over his face as he remembered her sullen opposition to his marriage. Some slighting phrases she had used still rankled in his memory; she had once spoken of Gretta as being country cute and that was not true of Gretta at all. It was Gretta who had nursed her during all her last long illness in their house at Monkstown.

He knew that Mary Jane must be near the end of her piece for she was playing   100
again the opening melody with runs of scales after every bar and while he waited for the end the resentment died down in his heart. The piece ended with a trill of octaves in the treble and a final deep octave in the bass. Great applause greeted Mary Jane as, blushing and rolling up her music nervously, she escaped from the room. The most vigorous clapping came from the four young men in the doorway who had gone away to the refreshment-room at the beginning of the piece but had come back when the piano had stopped.

Lancers were arranged. Gabriel found himself partnered with Miss Ivors. She was a frank-mannered talkative young lady, with a freckled face and prominent brown eyes. She did not wear a low-cut bodice and the large brooch which was fixed in the front of her collar bore on it an Irish device and motto.

When they had taken their places she said abruptly:

"I have a crow to pluck with you."

"With me?" said Gabriel.

She nodded her head gravely.   105

"What is it?" asked Gabriel, smiling at her solemn manner.

"Who is G. C.?" answered Miss Ivors, turning her eyes upon him.

Gabriel coloured and was about to knit his brows, as if he did not understand, when she said bluntly:

"O, innocent Amy! I have found out that you write for *The Daily Express*. Now, aren't you ashamed of yourself?"

"Why should I be ashamed of myself?" asked Gabriel, blinking his eyes and trying   110
to smile.

"Well, I'm ashamed of you," said Miss Ivors frankly. "To say you'd write for a paper like that. I didn't think you were a West Briton."

A look of perplexity appeared on Gabriel's face. It was true that he wrote a literary column every Wednesday in *The Daily Express*, for which he was paid fifteen shillings. But that did not make him a West Briton surely. The books he received for review were almost more welcome than the paltry cheque. He loved to feel the covers and turn over the pages of newly printed books. Nearly every day when his teaching in the college was ended he used to wander down the quays to the second-hand booksellers, to Hickey's on Bachelor's Walk, to Web's or Massey's on Aston's Quay, or to O'Clohissey's in the by-street. He did not know how to meet her charge. He wanted to say that literature was above politics. But they were friends of many years' standing and their careers had been parallel, first at the University and then as teachers: he could not risk a grandiose phrase with her. He continued blinking his eyes and trying to smile and murmured lamely that he saw nothing political in writing reviews of books.

When their turn to cross had come he was still perplexed and inattentive. Miss Ivors promptly took his hand in a warm grasp and said in a soft friendly tone:

"Of course, I was only joking. Come, we cross now."

When they were together again she spoke of the University question and Gabriel   115 felt more at ease. A friend of hers had shown her his review of Browning's poems. That was how she had found out the secret: but she liked the review immensely. Then she said suddenly:

"O, Mr. Conroy, will you come for an excursion to the Aran Isles this summer? We're going to stay there a whole month. It will be splendid out in the Atlantic. You ought to come. Mr. Clancy is coming, and Mr. Kilkelly and Katheleen Kearney. It would be splendid for Gretta too if she'd come. She's from Connacht, isn't she?"

"Her people are," said Gabriel shortly.

"But you will come, won't you?" said Miss Ivors, laying her warm hand eagerly on his arm.

"The fact is," said Gabriel, "I have just arranged to go——"

"Go where?" asked Miss Ivors.   120

"Well, you know, every year I go for a cycling tour with some fellows and so——"

"But where?" asked Miss Ivors.

"Well, we usually go to France or Belgium or perhaps Germany," said Gabriel awkwardly.

"And why do you go to France and Belgium," said Miss Ivors, "instead of visiting your own land?"

"Well," said Gabriel, "it's partly to keep in touch with the languages and partly   125 for a change."

"And haven't you your own language to keep in touch with—Irish?" asked Miss Ivors.

"Well," said Gabriel, "if it comes to that, you know, Irish is not my language."

Their neighbors had turned to listen to the cross-examination. Gabriel glanced right and left nervously and tried to keep his good humour under the ordeal which was making a blush invade his forehead.

"And haven't you your own land to visit," continued Miss Ivors, "that you know nothing of, your own people, and your own country?"

"O, to tell you the truth," retorted Gabriel suddenly, "I'm sick of my own country,   130 sick of it!"

"Why?" asked Miss Ivors.

Gabriel did not answer for his retort had heated him.

"Why?" repeated Miss Ivors.

They had to go visiting together and, as he had not answered her, Miss Ivors said warmly:

"Of course, you've no answer."   135

Gabriel tried to cover his agitation by taking part in the dance with great energy. He avoided her eyes for he had seen a sour expression on her face. But when they met in the long chain he was surprised to feel his hand firmly pressed. She looked at him from under her brows for a moment quizzically until he smiled. Then, just as the chain was about to start again, she stood on tiptoe and whispered into his ear:

"West Briton!"

When the lancers were over Gabriel went away to a remote corner of the room where Freddy Malins' mother was sitting. She was a stout feeble old woman with white hair.

Her voice had a catch in it like her son's and she stuttered slightly. She had been told that Freddy had come and that he was nearly all right. Gabriel asked her whether she had had a good crossing. She lived with her married daughter in Glasgow and came to Dublin on a visit once a year. She answered placidly that she had had a beautiful crossing and that the captain had been most attentive to her. She spoke also of the beautiful house her daughter kept in Glasgow, and of all the friends they had there. While her tongue rambled on Gabriel tried to banish from his mind all memory of the unpleasant incident with Miss Ivors. Of course the girl or woman, or whatever she was, was an enthusiast but there was a time for all things. Perhaps he ought not to have answered her like that. But she had no right to call him a West Briton before people, even in joke. She had tried to make him ridiculous before people, heckling him and staring at him with her rabbit's eyes.

He saw his wife making her way towards him through the waltzing couples. When she reached him she said into his ear:

"Gabriel, Aunt Kate wants to know won't you carve the goose as usual. Miss Daly   140
will carve the ham and I'll do the pudding."

"All right," said Gabriel.

"She's sending in the younger ones first as soon as this waltz is over so that we'll have the table to ourselves."

"Were you dancing?" asked Gabriel.

"Of course I was. Didn't you see me? What row had you with Molly Ivors?"

"No row. Why? Did she say so?"   145

"Something like that. I'm trying to get that Mr. D'Arcy to sing. He's full of conceit, I think."

"There was no row," said Gabriel moodily, "only she wanted me to go for a trip to the west of Ireland and I said I wouldn't."

His wife clasped her hands excitedly and gave a little jump.

"O, do go, Gabriel," she said. "I'd love to see Galway again."

"You can go if you like," said Gabriel coldly.   150

She looked at him for a moment, then turned to Mrs. Malins and said:

"There's a nice husband for you, Mrs. Malins."

While she was threading her way back across the room Mrs. Malins, without adverting to the interruption, went on to tell Gabriel what beautiful places there were in Scotland and beautiful scenery. Her son-in-law brought them every year to the lakes and they used to go fishing. Her son-in-law was a splendid fisher. One day he caught a beautiful big fish and the man in the hotel cooked it for their dinner.

Gabriel hardly heard what she said. Now that supper was coming near he began to think again about his speech and about the quotation. When he saw Freddy Malins coming across the room to visit his mother Gabriel left the chair free for him and retired into the embrasure of the window. The room had already cleared and from the back room came the clatter of plates and knives. Those who still remained in the drawing-room seemed tired of dancing and were conversing quietly in little groups. Gabriel's warm trembling fingers tapped the cold pane of the window. How cool it must be outside! How pleasant it would be to walk out alone, first along by the river and then through the park! The snow would be lying on the branches of the trees and forming a bright cap on the top of the Wellington Monument. How much more pleasant it would be there than at the supper-table!

He ran over the headings of his speech: Irish hospitality, sad memories, the Three   155
Graces, Paris, the quotation from Browning. He repeated to himself a phrase he had

written in his review: "One feels that one is listening to a thought-tormented music." Miss Ivors had praised the review. Was she sincere? Had she really any life of her own behind all her propagandism? There had never been any ill-feeling between them until that night. It unnerved him to think that she would be at the supper-table, looking up at him while he spoke with her critical quizzing eyes. Perhaps she would not be sorry to see him fail in his speech. An idea came into his mind and gave him courage. He would say, alluding to Aunt Kate and Aunt Julia: "Ladies and Gentlemen, the generation which is now on the wane among us may have had its faults but for my part I think it had certain qualities of hospitality, of humour, and of humanity, which the new and very serious and hypereducated generation that is growing up around us seems to me to lack." Very good: that was one for Miss Ivors. What did he care that his aunts were only two ignorant old women?

A murmur in the room attracted his attention. Mr. Browne was advancing from the door, gallantly escorting Aunt Julia, who leaned upon his arm, smiling and hanging her head. An irregular musketry of applause escorted her also as far as the piano and then, as Mary Jane seated herself on the stool, and Aunt Julia, no longer smiling, half turned so as to pitch her voice fairly into the room, gradually ceased. Gabriel recognised the preclude. It was that of an old song of Aunt Julia's—*Arrayed for the Bridal*. Her voice, strong and clear in tone, attacked with great spirit the runs which embellish the air and though she sang very rapidly she did not miss even the smallest of the grace notes. To follow the voice, without looking at the singer's face, was to feel and share the excitement of swift and secure flight. Gabriel applauded loudly with all the others at the close of the song and loud applause was borne in from the invisible supper-table. It sounded so genuine that a little colour struggled into Aunt Julia's face as she bent to replace in the music-stand the old leather-bound songbook that had her initials on the cover. Freddy Malins, who had listened with his head perched sideways to hear her better, was still applauding when everyone else had ceased and talking animatedly to his mother who nodded her head gravely and slowly in acquiescence. At last, when he could clap no more, he stood up suddenly and hurried across the room to Aunt Julia whose hand he seized and held in both his hands, shaking it when words failed him or the catch in his voice proved too much for him.

"I was just telling my mother," he said, "I never heard you sing so well, never. No, I never heard your voice so good as it is tonight. Now! Would you believe that now? That's the truth. Upon my word and honour that's the truth. I never heard your voice sound so fresh and so . . . so clear and fresh, never."

Aunt Julia smiled broadly and murmured something about compliments as she released her hand from his grasp. Mr. Browne extended his open hand towards her and said to those who were near him in the manner of a showman introducing a prodigy to an audience:

"Miss Julia Morkan, my latest discovery!"

He was laughing very heartily at this himself when Freddy Malins turned to him   160 and said:

"Well, Browne, if you're serious you might make a worse discovery. All I can say is I never heard her sing half so well as long as I am coming here. And that's the honest truth."

"Neither did I," said Mr. Browne. "I think her voice has greatly improved."

Aunt Julia shrugged her shoulders and said with meek pride:

"Thirty years ago I hadn't a bad voice as voices go."

"I often told Julia," said Aunt Kate emphatically, "that she was simply thrown   165
away in that choir. But she never would be said by me."

She turned as if to appeal to the good sense of the others against a refractory child
while Aunt Julia gazed in front of her, a vague smile of reminiscence playing on her
face.

"No," continued Aunt Kate, "she wouldn't be said or led by anyone, slaving there
in that choir night and day, night and day. Six o'clock on Christmas morning! And all
for what?"

"Well, isn't it for the honour of God, Aunt Kate?" asked Mary Jane, twisting
round on the piano-stool and smiling.

Aunt Kate turned fiercely on her niece and said:

"I know all about the honour of God, Mary Jane, but I think it's not at all hon-   170
ourable for the pope to turn out the women out of the choirs that have slaved there all
their lives and put little whipper-snappers of boys over their heads. I suppose it is for the
good of the Church if the pope does it. But it's not just, Mary Jane, and it's not right."

She had worked herself into a passion and would have continued in defence of
her sister for it was a sore subject with her but Mary Jane, seeing that all the dancers
had come back, intervened pacifically:

"Now, Aunt Kate, you're giving scandal to Mr. Browne who is of the other persuasion."

Aunt Kate turned to Mr. Browne, who was grinning at this allusion to his religion, and said hastily:

"O, I don't question the pope's being right. I'm only a stupid old woman and
I wouldn't presume to do such a thing. But there's such a thing as common everyday po-
liteness and gratitude. And if I were in Julia's place I'd tell that Father Healey straight
up to his face . . ."

"And besides, Aunt Kate," said Mary Jane, "we really are all hungry and when we   175
are hungry we are all very quarrelsome."

"And when we are thirsty we are also quarrelsome," added Mr. Browne.

"So that we had better go to supper," said Mary Jane, "and finish the discussion
afterwards."

On the landing outside the drawing-room Gabriel found his wife and Mary Jane
trying to persuade Miss Ivors to stay for supper. But Miss Ivors, who had put on her hat
and was buttoning her cloak, would not stay. She did not feel in the least hungry and
she had already overstayed her time.

"But only for ten minutes, Molly," said Mrs. Conroy. "That won't delay you."

"To take a pick itself," said Mary Jane, "after all your dancing."   180

"I really couldn't," said Miss Ivors.

"I am afraid you didn't enjoy yourself at all," said Mary Jane hopelessly.

"Ever so much, I assure you," said Miss Ivors, "but you really must let me run off
now."

"But how can you get home?" asked Mrs. Conroy.

"O, it's only two steps up the quay."   185

Gabriel hesitated a moment and said:

"If you will allow me, Miss Ivors, I'll see you home if you are really obliged to go."

But Miss Ivors broke away from them.

"I won't hear it," she cried. "For goodness' sake go in to your suppers and don't
mind me. I'm quite well able to take care of myself."

"Well, you're the comical girl, Molly," said Mrs. Conroy frankly.   190

"*Beannacht libh*," cried Miss Ivors, with a laugh, as she ran down the staircase.

Mary Jane gazed after her, a moody puzzled expression on her face, while Mrs. Conroy leaned over the banisters to listen for the hall-door. Gabriel asked himself was he the cause of her abrupt departure. But she did not seem to be in ill humour: she had gone away laughing. He stared blankly down the staircase.

At the moment Aunt Kate came toddling out of the supper-room, almost wringing her hands in despair.

"Where is Gabriel?" she cried. "Where on earth is Gabriel? There's everyone waiting in there, stage to let, and nobody to carve the goose!"

"Here I am, Aunt Kate!" cried Gabriel, which sudden animation, "ready to carve   195
a flock of geese, if necessary."

A fat brown goose lay at one end of the table and at the other end, on a bed of creased paper strewn with sprigs of parsley, lay a great ham, stripped of its outer skin and peppered over with crust crumbs, a neat paper frill round its shin and beside this was a round of spiced beef. Between these rival ends ran parallel lines of side-dishes: two little ministers of jelly, red and yellow; a shallow dish full of blocks of blancmange and red jam, a large green leaf-shaped dish with a stalk-shaped handle, on which lay bunches of purple raisins and peeled almonds, a companion dish on which lay a solid rectangle of Smyrna figs, a dish of custard topped with grated nutmeg, a small bowl full of chocolates and sweets rapped in gold and silver papers and a glass vase in which stood some tall celery stalks. In the centre of the table there stood, as sentries to a fruit-stand which up-held a pyramid of oranges and American apples, two squat old-fashioned decanters of cut glass, one containing port and the other dark sherry. On the closed square piano a pudding in a huge yellow dish lay in waiting and behind it were three squads of bottles of stout and ale and minerals, drawn up according to the colours of their uniforms, the first two black, with brown and red labels, the third and smallest squad white, with transverse green sashes.

Gabriel took his seat boldly at the head of the table and, having looked to the edge of the carver, plunged his fork firmly into the goose. He felt quite at ease now for he was an expert carver and liked nothing better than to find himself at the head of a well-laden table.

"Miss Furlong, what shall I send you?" he asked. "A wing or a slice of the breast?"

"Just a small slice of the breast."

"Miss Higgins, what for you?"   200

"O, anything at all, Mr. Conroy."

While Gabriel and Miss Daly exchanged plates of goose and plates of ham and spiced beef Lily went from guest to guest with a dish of hot floury potatoes wrapped in a white napkin. This was Mary Jane's idea and she had also suggested apple sauce for the goose but Aunt Kate had said that plain roast goose without any apple sauce had always been good enough for her and she hoped she might never eat worse. Mary Jane waited on her pupils and saw that they got the best slices and Aunt Kate and Aunt Julia opened and carried across from the piano bottles of stout and ale for the gentlemen and bottles of minerals for the ladies. There was a great deal of confusion and laughter and noise, the noise of orders and counter-orders, of knives and forks, of corks and glass-stoppers. Gabriel began to carve second helpings as soon as he had finished the first round without serving himself. Everyone protested loudly so that he compromised by taking a long draught of stout for he had found the carving hot work. Mary Jane settled down quietly to her supper but Aunt Kate and Aunt Julia were still toddling round the table, walking on each other's heels, getting in each other's way and giving each other unheeded orders. Mr. Browne begged of them to sit down and eat their suppers and so did Gabriel but they said there was time enough, so that, at last Freddy Malins stood up and, capturing Aunt Kate, plumped her down on her chair amid general laughter.

When everyone had been well served Gabriel said, smiling:

"Now, if anyone wants a little more of what vulgar people call stuffing let him or her speak."

A chorus of voices invited him to begin his own supper and Lily came forward   205
with three potatoes which she had reserved for him.

"Very well," said Gabriel amiably, as he took another preparatory draught, "kindly forget my existence, ladies and gentlemen, for a few minutes."

He set to his supper and took no part in the conversation with which the table covered Lily's removal of the plates. The subject of talk was the opera company which was then at the Theatre Royal. Mr. Bartell D'Arcy, the tenor, a dark-complexioned young man with a smart moustache, praised very highly the leading contralto of the company but Miss Furlong thought she had a rather vulgar style of production. Freddy Malins said there was a Negro chieftain singing in the second part of the Gaiety pantomime who had one of the finest tenor voices he had ever heard.

"Have you heard him?" he asked Mr. Bartell D'Arcy across the table.

"No," answered Mr. Bartell D'Arcy carelessly.

"Because," Freddy Malins explained, "now I'd be curious to hear your opinion of   210
him. I think he has a grand voice."

"It takes Teddy to find out the really good things," said Mr. Browne familiarly to the table.

"And why couldn't he have a voice too?" asked Freddy Malins sharply. "Is it because he's only a black?"

Nobody answered this question and Mary Jane led the table back to the legitimate opera. One of her pupils had given her a pass for *Mignon*. Of course it was very fine, she said, but it made her think of poor Georgina Burns. Mr. Browne could go back farther still, to the old Italian companies that used to come to Dublin—Tietjens, Ilma de Murzka, Campanini, the great Trebelli, Giuglini, Ravelli, Aramburo. Those were the days, he said, when there was something like singing to be heard in Dublin. He told too of how the top gallery of the old Royal used to be packed night after night, of how one night an Italian tenor had sung five encores to *Let Me Like a Soldier Fall*, introducing a high C every time, and of how the gallery boys would sometimes in their enthusiasm unyoke the horses from the carriage of some great prima donna and pull her themselves through he streets to her hotel. Why did they never play the grand old operas now, he asked, *Dinorah, Lucretia Borgia*? Because they could not get the voices to sing them: that was why.

"Oh, well," said Mr. Bartell D'Arcy, "I presume there are as good singers today as there were then."

"Where are they?" asked Mr. Browne defiantly.   215

"In London, Paris, Milan," said Mr. Bartell D'Arcy warmly. "I suppose Caruso, for example, is quite as good, if not better than any of the men you have mentioned."

"Maybe so," said Mr. Browne. "But I may tell you I doubt it strongly."

"O, I'd give anything to hear Caruso sing," said Mary Jane.

"For me," said Aunt Kate, who had been picking a bone, "there was only one tenor. To please me, I mean. But I suppose none of you ever heard of him."

"Who was he, Miss Morkan?" asked Mr. Bartell D'Arcy politely.   220

"His name," said Aunt Kate, "was Parkinson. I heard him when he was in his prime and I think he had then the purest tenor voice that was ever put into a man's throat."

"Strange," said Mr. Bartell D'Arcy. "I never even heard of him."

"Yes, yes, Miss Morkan is right," said Mr. Browne. "I remember hearing of old Parkinson but he's too far back for me."

"A beautiful, pure, sweet, mellow English tenor," said Aunt Kate with enthusiasm.

Gabriel having finished, the huge pudding was transferred to the table. The clat- 225 ter of forks and spoons began again. Gabriel's wife served out spoonfuls of the pudding and passed the plates down the table. Midway down they were held up by Mary Jane, who replenished them with raspberry or orange jelly or with blancmange and jam. The pudding was of Aunt Julia's making and she received praises for it from all quarters. She herself said that it was not quite brown enough.

"Well, I hope, Miss Morkan," said Mr. Browne, "that I'm brown enough for you because, you know, I'm all brown."

All the gentlemen, except Gabriel, ate some of the pudding out of compliment to Aunt Julia. As Gabriel never ate sweets the celery had been left for him. Freddy Malins also took a stalk of celery and ate it with his pudding. He had been told that celery was a capital thing for the blood and he was just then under doctor's care. Mrs. Malins, who had been silent all through the supper, said that her son was going down to Mount Melleray in a week or so. The table then spoke of Mount Melleray, how bracing the air was down there, how hospitable the monks were and how they never asked for a penny-piece from their guests.

"And do you mean to say," asked Mr. Browne incredulously, "that a chap can go down there and put up there as if it were a hotel and live on the fat of the land and then come away without paying anything?"

"O, most people give some donation to the monastery when they leave," said Mary Jane.

"I wish we had an institution like that in our Church," said Mr. Browne candidly. 230

He was astonished to hear that the monks never spoke, got up at two in the morning and slept in their coffins. He asked what they did it for.

"That's the rule of the order," said Aunt Kate firmly.

"Yes, but why?" asked Mr. Browne.

Aunt Kate repeated that it was the rule that was all. Mr. Browne still seemed not to understand. Freddy Malins explained to him, as best he could, that the monks were trying to make up for the sins committed by all the sinners in the outside world. The explanation was not very clear for Mr. Browne grinned and said:

"I like that idea very much but wouldn't a comfortable spring bed do them as well 235 as a coffin?"

"The coffin," said Mary Jane, "is to remind them of their last end."

As the subject had grown lugubrious it was buried in a silence of the table during which Mrs. Malins could be heard saying to her neighbour in an indistinct undertone:

"They are very good men, the monks, very pious men."

The raisins and almonds and figs and apples and oranges and chocolates and sweets were now passed about the table and Aunt Julia invited all the guests to have either port or sherry. At first Mr. Bartell D'Avery refused to take either but one of his neighbours nudged him and whispered something to him upon which he allowed his glass to be filled. Gradually as the last glasses were being filled the conversation ceased.

A pause followed, broken only by the noise of the wine and by unsettlings of chairs. The Misses Morkan, all three, looked down at the tablecloth. Someone coughed once or twice and then a few gentlemen patted the table gently as a signal for silence. The silence came and Gabriel pushed back his chair and stood up.

The patting at once grew louder in encouragement and then ceased altogether.   240
Gabriel leaned his ten trembling fingers on the tablecloth and smiled nervously at the company. Meeting a row of upturned faces he raised his eyes to the chandelier. The piano was playing a waltz tune and he could hear the skirts sweeping against the drawing-room door. People, perhaps, were standing in the snow on the quay outside, gazing up at the lighted windows and listening to the waltz music. The air was pure there. In the distance lay the park where the trees were weighted with snow. The Wellington Monument wore a gleaming cap of snow that flashed westward over the white field of Fifteen Acres.

He began:

"Ladies and Gentlemen,

"It has fallen to my lot this evening, as in years past, to perform a very pleasing task but a task for which I am afraid my poor powers as a speaker are all too inadequate."

"No, no!" said Mr. Browne.

"But, however that may be, I can only ask you tonight to take the will for the   245
deed and to lend me your attention for a few moments while I endeavour to express to you in words what my feelings are on this occasion.

"Ladies and Gentlemen, it is not the first time that we have gathered together under this hospitable roof, around this hospitable board. It is not the first time that we have been the recipients—or perhaps, I had better say, the victims—of the hospitality of certain good ladies."

He made a circle in the air with his arm and paused. Everyone laughed or smiled at Aunt Kate and Aunt Julia and Mary Jane who all turned crimson with pleasure. Gabriel went on more boldly:

"I feel more strongly with every recurring year that our country has no tradition which does it so much honour and which it should guard so jealously as that of its hospitality. It is a tradition that is unique as far as my experience goes (and I have visited not a few places abroad) among the modern nations. Some would say, perhaps, that with us it is rather a failing than anything to be boasted of. But granted even that, it is, to my mind, a princely failing, and one that I trust will long be cultivated among us. Of one thing, at least, I am sure. As long as this one roof shelters the good ladies aforesaid—and I wish from my heart it may do so for many and many a long year to come—the tradition of genuine warm-hearted courteous Irish hospitality, which our forefathers have handed down to us and which we in turn must hand down to our descendants, is still alive among us."

A hearty murmur of assent ran round the table. It shot through Gabriel's mind that Miss Ivors was not there and that she had gone away discourteously: and he said with confidence in himself:

"Ladies and Gentlemen,   250

"A new generation is growing up in our midst, a generation actuated by new ideas and new principles. It is serious and enthusiastic for these new ideas and its enthusiasm, even when it is misdirected, is, I believe, in the main sincere. But we are living in a skeptical and, if I may use the phrase, a thought-tormented age: and sometimes I fear that this new generation, educated or hypereducated as it is, will lack those qualities of humanity, of hospitality, of kindly humour which belonged to an older day. Listening tonight to the names of all those great singers of the past it seemed to me, I must confess, that we were living in a less spacious age. Those days might, without exaggeration, be called spacious days: and if they are gone beyond recall let us hope, at least, that in gatherings such as this we shall still speak of them with pride and affection, still cherish in our hearts the memory of those dead and gone great ones whose fame the world will not willingly let die."

"Hear, hear!" said Mr. Browne loudly.

"But yet," continued Gabriel, his voice falling into a softer inflection, "there are always in gatherings such as this sadder thoughts that will recur to our minds: thoughts of the past, of youth, of changes, of absent faces that we miss here tonight. Our path through life is strewn with many such sad memories: and were we to brood upon them always we could not find the heart to go on bravely with our work among the living. We have all of us living duties and living affections which claim, and rightly claim, our strenuous endeavours.

"Therefore, I will not linger on the past. I will not let any gloomy moralising intrude upon us here tonight. Here we are gathered together for a brief moment from the bustle and rush of our everyday routine. We are met here as friends, in the spirit of good-fellowship, as colleagues, also to a certain extent, in the true spirit of *camaraderie*, and as the guests of—what shall I call them—the Three Graces of the Dublin musical world."

The table burst into applause and laughter at this allusion. Aunt Julia vainly   255
asked each of her neighbours in turn to tell her what Gabriel had said.

"He says we are the Three Graces, Aunt Julia," said Mary Jane.

Aunt Julia did not understand but she looked up, smiling, at Gabriel, who continued in the same vein:

"Ladies and Gentlemen,

"I will not attempt to play tonight the part that Paris played on another occasion. I will not attempt to choose between them. The task would be an invidious one and one beyond my poor powers. For when I view them in turn, whether it be our chief hostess herself, whose good heart, whose too good heart, has become a byword with all who know her, or her sister, who seems to be gifted with perennial youth and whose singing must have been a surprise and a revelation to us all tonight, or, last but not least, when I consider our youngest hostess, talented, cheerful, hard-working and the best of nieces, I confess, Ladies and Gentlemen, that I do not know to which of them I should award the prize."

Gabriel glanced down at his aunts and, seeing the large smile on Aunt Julia's face   260
and the tears which had risen to Aunt Kate's eyes, hastened to his close. He raised his glass of port gallantly, while every member of the company fingered a glass expectantly, and said loudly:

"Let us toast them all three together. Let us drink to their health, wealth, long life, happiness and prosperity and may they long continue to hold the proud and self-won position which they hold in their profession and the position of honour and affection which they hold in our hearts."

All the guests stood up, glass in hand, and turning towards the three seated ladies, sang in unison, with Mr. Browne as leader:

For they are jolly gay fellows,
For they are jolly gay fellows,
For they are jolly gay fellows,
Which nobody can deny.

Aunt Kate was making frank use of her handkerchief and even Aunt Julia seemed moved. Freddy Malins beat time with his pudding-fork and the singers turned towards one another, as if in melodious conference, while they sang with emphasis:

Unless he tells a lie,
Unless he tells a lie,

Then, turning once more towards their hostesses, they sang:

For they are jolly gay fellows,
For they are jolly gay fellows,
For they are jolly gay fellows,
Which nobody can deny.

The acclamation which followed was taken up beyond the door of the supper-room by many of the other guests and renewed time after time, Freddy Malins acting as officer with his fork on high.

The piercing morning air came into the hall where they were standing so that Aunt Kate said:

"Close the door, somebody, Mrs. Malins will get her death of cold."

"Browne is out there, Aunt Kate," said Mary Jane.

"Browne is everywhere," said Aunt Kate, lowering her voice.

Mary Jane laughed at her tone.

"Really," she said archly, "he is very attentive."

"He has been laid on here like the gas," said Aunt Kate in the same tone, "all during the Christmas."

She laughed herself this time good humouredly and then added quickly:

"But tell him to come in, Mary Jane, and close the door. I hope to goodness he didn't hear me."

At that moment the hall-door was opened and Mr. Browne came in from the doorstep, laughing as if his heart would break. He was dressed in a long green overcoat with mock astrakhan cuffs and collar and wore on his head an oval fur cap. He pointed down the snow-covered quay from where the sound of shrill prolonged whistling was borne in.

"Teddy will have all the cabs in Dublin out," he said.

Gabriel advanced from the little pantry behind the office, struggling into his overcoat and, looking round the hall, said:

"Gretta not down yet?"

"She's getting on her things, Gabriel," said Aunt Kate.

"Who's playing up there?" asked Gabriel.

"Nobody. They're all gone."

"O no, Aunt Kate," said Mary Jane. "Bartell D'Arcy and Miss O'Callaghan aren't gone yet."

"Someone is fooling at the piano anyhow," said Gabriel.

Mary Jane glanced at Gabriel and Mr. Browne and said with a shiver:

"It makes me feel cold to look at you two gentlemen muffled up like that. I wouldn't like to face your journey home at this hour."

"I'd like nothing better this minute," said Mr. Browne stoutly, "than a rattling fine walk in the country or a fast drive with a good spanking goer between the shafts."

"We used to have a very good horse and trap at home," said Aunt Julia sadly. "The never-to-be-forgotten Johnny," said Mary Jane, laughing.

Aunt Kate and Gabriel laughed too.

"Why, what was wonderful about Johnny?" asked Mr. Browne.

"The late lamented Patrick Morkan, our grandfather, that is," explained Gabriel,   290 "commonly known in his later years as the old gentleman, was a glue-boiler."

"O, now, Gabriel," said Aunt Kate, laughing, "he had a starch mill."

"Well, glue or starch," said Gabriel, "the old gentleman had a horse by the name of Johnny. And Johnny used to work in the old gentleman's mill, walking round and round in order to drive the mill. That was all very well; but now comes the tragic part about Johnny. One fine day the old gentleman thought he'd like to drive out with the quality to a military review in the park."

"The Lord have mercy on his soul," said Aunt Kate compassionately.

"Amen," said Gabriel. "So the old gentleman, as I said, harnessed Johnny and put on his very best tall hat and his very best stock collar and drove out in grand style from his ancestral mansion somewhere near Back Lane, I think."

Everyone laughed, even Mrs. Malins, at Gabriel's manner and Aunt Kate said: 295

"O, now, Gabriel, he didn't live in Back Lane, really. Only the mill was there."

"Out from the mansion of his forefathers," continued Gabriel, "he drove with Johnny. And everything went on beautifully until Johnny came in sight of King Billy's statue and whether he fell in love with the horse King Billy sits on or whether he thought he was back again in the mill, anyhow he began to walk round the statue."

Gabriel paced in a circle round the hall in his goloshes amid the laughter of the others.

"Round and round he went," said Gabriel, "and the old gentleman, who was a very pompous old gentleman, was highly indignant. 'Go on, sir! What do you mean, sir? Johnny! Johnny! Most extraordinary conduct! Can't understand the horse!'"

The peal of laughter which followed Gabriel's imitation of the incident was inter-   300 rupted by a resounding knock at the hall door. Mary Jane ran to open it and let in Freddy Malins. Freddy Malins, with his hat well back on his head and his shoulders humped with cold, was puffing and steaming after his exertions.

"I could only get one cab," he said.

"O, we'll find another along the quay," said Gabriel.

"Yes," said Aunt Kate, "Better not keep Mrs. Malins standing in the draught."

Mrs. Malins was helped down the front steps by her son and Mr. Browne and, after many manoeuvers, hoisted into the cab. Freddy Malins clambered in after her and spent a long time settling her on the seat, Mr. Browne helping him with advice. At last she was settled comfortably and Freddy Malins invited Mr. Browne into the cab. There was a good deal of confused talk, and then Mr. Browne got into the cab. The cabman settled his rug over his knees, and bent down for the address. The confusion grew greater and the cabman was directed differently by Freddy Malins and Mr. Browne, each of whom had his head out through a window of the cab. The difficulty was to know where to drop Mr. Browne along the route, and Aunt Kate, Aunt Julia and Mary Jane helped the discussion from the doorstep with cross directions and contradictions and abundance of laughter. As for Freddy Malins he was speechless with laughter. He popped his head in and out of the window every moment to the great danger of his hat, and told his mother how the discussion was progressing, till at last Mr. Browne shouted to the bewildered cabman above the din of everybody's laughter:

"Do you know Trinity College?" 305

"Yes, sir," said the cabman.

"Well, drive bang up against Trinity College gates," said Mr. Browne, "and then we'll tell you where to go. You understand now?"

"Yes, sir," said the cabman.

"Make like a bird for Trinity College."

"Right, sir," said the cabman. 310

The horse was whipped up and the cab rattled off along the quay amid a chorus of laughter and adieus.

Gabriel had not gone to the door with the others. He was in a dark part of the hall gazing up the staircase. A woman was standing near the top of the first flight, in the shadow also. He could not see her face but he could see the terra-cotta and salmon-pink panels of her skirt which the shadow made appear black and white. It was his wife. She was leaning on the banisters, listening to something. Gabriel was surprised at her stillness and strained his ear to listen also. But he could hear little save the noise of laughter and dispute on the front steps, a few chords struck on the piano and a few notes of a man's voice singing.

He stood still in the gloom of the hall, trying to catch the air that the voice was singing and gazing up at his wife. There was grace and mystery in her attitude as if she were a symbol of something. He asked himself what is a woman standing on the stairs in the shadow, listening to distant music, a symbol of. If he were a painter he would paint her in that attitude. Her blue felt hat would show off the bronze of her hair against the darkness and the dark panels of her skirt would show off the light ones. *Distant Music* he would call the picture if he were a painter.

The hall-door was closed; and Aunt Kate, Aunt Julia and Mary Jane came down the hall, still laughing.

"Well, isn't Freddy terrible!" said Mary Jane. "He's really terrible." 315

Gabriel said nothing but pointed up the stairs towards where his wife was standing. Now that the hall-door was closed the voice and the piano could be heard more clearly. Gabriel held up his hand for them to be silent. The song seemed to be in the old Irish tonality and the singer seemed uncertain both of his words and of his voice. The voice, made plaintive by distance and by the singer's hoarseness, faintly illuminated the cadence of the air with words expressing grief:

O, the rain falls on my heavy locks
And the dew wets my skin,
My babe lies cold . . .

"O," exclaimed Mary Jane. "It's Bartell D'Arcy singing and he wouldn't sing all the night. O, I'll get him to sing a song before he goes."

"O, do, Mary Jane," said Aunt Kate.

Mary Jane brushed past the others and ran to the staircase, but before she reached it the singing stopped and the piano was closed abruptly.

"O, what a pity!" she cried. "Is he coming down, Gretta?" 320

Gabriel heard his wife answer yes and saw her come down towards them. A few steps behind her were Mr. Bartell D'Arcy and Miss O'Callaghan.

"O, Mr. D'Arcy," cried Mary Jane, "it's downright mean of you to break off like that when we were all in raptures listening to you."

"I have been at him all the evening," said Miss O'Callaghan, "and Mrs. Conroy, too, and he told us he had a dreadful cold and couldn't sing."

"O, Mr. D'Arcy," said Aunt Kate, "now that was a great fib to tell."

"Can't you see that I'm as hoarse as a crow?" said Mr. D'Arcy roughly.   325

He went into the pantry hastily and put on his overcoat. The others, taken aback by his rude speech, could find nothing to say. Aunt Kate wrinkled her brows and made signs to the others to drop the subject. Mr. D'Arcy stood swathing his neck carefully and frowning.

"It's the weather," said Aunt Julia, after a pause.

"Yes, everybody has colds," said Aunt Kate readily, "everybody."

"They say," said Mary Jane, "we haven't had snow like it for thirty years; and I read this morning in the newspapers that the snow is general all over Ireland."

"I love the look of snow," said Aunt Julia sadly.   330

"So do I," said Miss O'Callaghan. "I think Christmas is never really Christmas unless we have the snow on the ground."

"But poor Mr. D'Arcy doesn't like the snow," said Aunt Kate, smiling.

Mr. D'Arcy came from the pantry, fully swathed and buttoned, and in a repentant tone told them the history of his cold. Everyone gave him advice and said it was a great pity and urged him to be very careful of his throat in the night air. Gabriel watched his wife, who did not join in the conversation. She was standing right under the dusty fanlight and the flame of the gas lit up the rich bronze of her hair, which he had seen her drying at the fire a few days before. She was in the same attitude and seemed unaware of the talk about her. At last she turned towards them and Gabriel saw that there was colour on her cheeks and that her eyes were shining. A sudden tide of joy went leaping out of his heart.

"Mr. D'Arcy," she said, "what is the name of that song you were singing?"

"It's called *The Lass of Aughrim*," said Mr. D'Arcy, "but I couldn't remember it   335
properly. Why? Do you know it?"

"*The Lass of Aughrim*," she repeated. "I couldn't think of the name."

"It's a very nice air," said Mary Jane. "I'm sorry you were not in voice tonight."

"Now, Mary Jane," said Aunt Kate, "don't annoy Mr. D'Arcy. I won't have him annoyed."

Seeing that all were ready to start she shepherded them to the door, where good-night was said:

"Well, good-night, Aunt Kate, and thanks for the pleasant evening."   340

"Good-night, Gabriel. Good-night, Gretta!"

"Good-night, Aunt Kate, and thanks ever so much. Good-night, Aunt Julia."

"O, good-night, Gretta. I didn't see you."

"Good-night, Mr. D'Arcy. Good-night, Miss O'Callaghan."

"Good-night, Miss Morkan."   345

"Good-night, again."

"Good-night, all. Safe home."

"Good-night. Good night."

The morning was still dark. A dull, yellow light brooded over the houses and the river; and the sky seemed to be descending. It was slushy underfoot; and only streaks and patches of snow lay on the roofs, on the parapets of the quay and on the area railings. The lamps were still burning redly in the murky air and, across the river, the palace of the Four Courts stood out menacingly against the heavy sky.

She was walking on before him with Mr. Bartell D'Arcy, her shoes in a brown   350
parcel tucked under one arm and her hands holding her skirt up from the slush. She had no longer any grace of attitude, but Gabriel's eyes were still bright with happiness. The blood went bounding along his veins: and the thoughts went rioting through his brain, proud, joyful, tender, valorous.

She was walking on before him so lightly and so erect that he longed to run after her noiselessly, catch her by the shoulders and say something foolish and affectionate into her ear. She seemed to him so frail that he longed to defend her against something and then to be alone with her. Moments of their secret life together burst like stars upon his memory. A heliotrope envelope was lying beside his breakfast-cup and he was caressing it with his hand. Birds were twittering in the ivy and the sunny web of the curtain was shimmering along the floor: he could not eat for happiness. They were standing on the crowded platform and he was placing a ticket inside the warm palm of her glove. He was standing with her in the cold, looking in through a grated window at a man making bottles in a roaring furnace. It was very cold. Her face, fragrant in the cold air, was quite close to his; and suddenly he called out to the man at the furnace:

"Is the fire hot, sir?"

But the man could not hear with the noise of the furnace. It was just as well. He might have answered rudely.

A wave of yet more tender joy escaped from his heart and went coursing in warm flood along his arteries. Like the tender fire of stars moments of their life together, that no one knew of or would ever know of, broke upon and illumined his memory. He longed to recall to her those moments, to make her forget the years of their dull existence together and remember only their moments of ecstasy. For the years, he felt, had not quenched his soul or hers. Their children, his writing, her household cares had not quenched all their souls' tender fire. In one letter that he had written to her then he had said: "Why is it that words like these seem to me so dull and cold? Is it because there is no word tender enough to be your name?"

Like distant music these words that he had written years before were borne to-   355
wards him from the past. He longed to be alone with her. When the others had gone away, when he and she were in the room in the hotel, then they would be alone together. He would call her softly:

"Gretta!"

Perhaps she would not hear at once: she would be undressing. Then something in his voice would strike her. She would turn and look at him. . . .

At the corner of Winetavern Street they met a cab. He was glad of its rattling noise as it saved him from conversation. She was looking out of the window and seemed tired. The others spoke only a few words, pointing out some building or street. The horse galloped along wearily under the murky morning sky, dragging his old rattling box after his heels, and Gabriel was again in a cab with her, galloping to catch the boat, galloping to their honeymoon.

As the cab drove across O'Connell Bridge Miss O'Callaghan said:

"They say you never cross O'Connell Bridge without seeing a white horse."   360

"I see a white man this time," said Gabriel.

"Where? asked Mr. Bartell D'Arcy.

Gabriel pointed to the statue, on which lay patches of snow. Then he nodded familiarly to it and waved his hand.

"Good-night, Dan," he said gaily.

When the cab drew up before the hotel, Gabriel jumped out and, in spite of Mr.   365
Bartell D'Arcy's protest, paid the driver. He gave the man a shilling over his fare. The
man saluted and said:

"A prosperous New Year to you, sir."

"The same to you," said Gabriel cordially.

She leaned for a moment on his arm in getting out of the cab and while standing
at the curbstone, bidding the others good-night. She leaned lightly on his arm, as
lightly as when she had danced with him a few hours before. He had felt proud and
happy then, happy that she was his, proud of her grace and wifely carriage. But now,
after the kindling again of so many memories, the first touch of her body, musical and
strange and perfumed, sent through him a keen pang of lust. Under cover of her silence
he pressed her arm closely to his side; and, as they stood at the hotel door, he felt that
they had escaped from their lives and duties, escaped from home and friends and run
away together with wild and radiant hearts to a new adventure.

An old man was dozing in a great hooded chair in the hall. He lit a candle in the
office and went before them to the stairs. They followed him in silence, their feet
falling in soft thuds on the thickly carpeted stairs. She mounted the stairs behind the
porter, her head bowed in the ascent, her frail shoulders curved as with a burden, her
skirt girt tightly about her. He could have flung his arms about her hips and held her
still, for his arms were trembling with desire to seize her and only the stress of his nails
against the palms of his hands held the wild impulse of his body in check. The porter
halted on the stairs to settle his guttering candle. They halted, too, on the steps below
him. In the silence Gabriel could hear the falling of the molten wax into the tray and
the thumping of his own heart against his ribs.

The porter led them along a corridor and opened a door. Then he set his unstable   370
candle down on a toilet-table and asked at what hour they were to be called in the
morning.

"Eight," said Gabriel.

The porter pointed to the tap of the electric-light and began a muttered apology,
but Gabriel cut him short.

"We don't want any light. We have light enough from the street. And I say," he
added, pointing to the candle, "You might remove that handsome article, like a good
man."

The porter took up his candle again, but slowly, for he was surprised by such a
novel idea. Then he mumbled good-night and went out. Gabriel shot the lock to.

A ghastly light from the street lamp lay in a long shaft from one window to the   375
door. Gabriel threw his overcoat and hat on a couch and crossed the room towards the
window. He looked down into the street in order that his emotion might calm a little.
Then he turned and leaned against a chest of drawers with his back to the light. She
had taken off her hat and cloak and was standing before a large swinging mirror, un-
hooking her waist. Gabriel paused for a few moments, watching her, and then said:

"Gretta!"

She turned away from the mirror slowly and walked along the shaft of light towards him. Her face looked so serious and weary that the words would not pass Gabriel's
lips. No, it was not the moment yet.

"You looked tired," he said.

"I am a little," she answered.

"You don't feel ill or weak?"   380

"No, tired: that's all."

She went on to the window and stood there, looking out. Gabriel waited again and then, fearing that diffidence was about to conquer him, he said abruptly:

"By the way, Gretta!"

"What is it?"

"You know that poor fellow Malins?" he said quickly.   385

"Yes. What about him?"

"Well, poor fellow, he's a decent sort of chap, after all," continued Gabriel in a false voice. "He gave me back that sovereign I lent him, and I didn't expect it, really. It's a pity he wouldn't keep away from that Browne, because he's not a bad fellow, really."

He was trembling now with annoyance. Why did she seem so abstracted? He did not know how he could begin. Was she annoyed, too, about something? If she would only turn to him or come to him of her own accord! To take her as she was would be brutal. No, he must see some ardour in her eyes first. He longed to be master of her strange mood.

"When did you lend him the pound?" she asked, after a pause.

Gabriel strove to restrain himself from breaking out into brutal language about   390 the sottish Malins and his pound. He longed to cry to her from his soul, to crush her body against his, to overmaster her. But he said:

"O, at Christmas, when he opened that little Christmas-card shop in Henry Street."

He was in such a fever of rage and desire that he did not hear her come from the window. She stood before him for an instant, looking at him strangely. Then, suddenly raising herself on tiptoe and resting her hands lightly on his shoulders, she kissed him.

"You are a very generous person, Gabriel," she said.

Gabriel, trembling with delight at her sudden kiss and at the quaintness of her phrase, put his hands on her hair and began smoothing it back, scarcely touching it with his fingers. The washing had made it fine and brilliant. His heart was brimming over with happiness. Just when he was wishing for it she had come to him of her own accord. Perhaps her thoughts had been running with his. Perhaps she had felt the impetuous desire that was in him, and then the yielding mood had come upon her. Now that she had fallen to him so easily, he wondered why he had been so diffident.

He stood, holding her head between his hands. Then, slipping one arm swiftly   395 about her body and drawing her towards him, he said softly:

"Gretta, dear, what are you thinking about?"

She did not answer nor yield wholly to his arm. He said again, softly:

"Tell me what it is, Gretta. I think I know what is the matter. Do I know?"

She did not answer at once. Then she said in an outburst of tears:

"O, I am thinking about that song, *The Lass of Aughrim*."   400

She broke loose from him and ran to the bed and, throwing her arms across the bed-rail, hid her face. Gabriel stood stock-still for a moment in astonishment and then followed her. As he passed in the way of the cheval-glass he caught sight of himself in full length, his broad, well-filled shirt-front, the face whose expression always puzzled him when he saw it in a mirror, and his glimmering gilt rimmed eyeglasses. He halted a few paces from her and said:

"What about the song? Why does that make you cry?"

She raised her head from her arms and dried her eyes with the back of her hand like a child. A kinder note than he had intended went into his voice.

"Why, Gretta?" he asked.

"I am thinking about a person long ago who used to sing that song."   405

"And who was the person long ago?" asked Gabriel, smiling.

"It was a person I used to know in Galway when I was living with my grandmother," she said.

The smile passed away from Gabriel's face. A dull anger began to gather again at the back of his mind and the dull fires of his lust began to glow angrily in his veins.

"Someone you were in love with?" he asked ironically.

"It was a young boy I used to know," she answered, "named Michael Furrey. He   410
used to sing that song, *The Lass of Aughrim*. He was very delicate."

Gabriel was silent. He did not wish her to think that he was interested in this delicate boy.

"I can see him so plainly," she said, after a moment. "Such eyes as he had: big, dark eyes! And such an expression in them—an expression!"

"O, then, you are in love with him?" said Gabriel.

"I used to go out walking with him," she said, "when I was in Galway."

A thought flew across Gabriel's mind.   415

"Perhaps that was why you wanted to go to Galway with that Ivors girl?" he said coldly.

She looked at him and asked in surprise:

"What for?"

Her eyes made Gabriel feel awkward. He shrugged his shoulders and said:

"How do I know? To see him, perhaps."   420

She looked away from him along the shaft of light towards the window in silence.

"He is dead," she said at length. "He died when he was only seventeen. Isn't it a terrible thing to die so young as that?"

"What was he?" asked Gabriel, still ironically.

"He was in the gasworks," she said.

Gabriel felt humiliated by the failure of his irony and by the evocation of this   425
figure from the dead, a boy in the gasworks. While he had been full of memories of their secret life together, full of tenderness and joy and desire, she had been comparing him in her mind with another. A shameful consciousness of his own person assailed him. He saw himself as a ludicrous figure, acting as a pennybox for his aunts, a nervous, well-meaning sentimentalist, orating to vulgarians and idealising his own clownish lusts, the pitiable fatuous fellow he had caught a glimpse of in the mirror. Instinctively he turned his back more to the light lest she might see the shame that burned upon his forehead.

He tried to keep up his tone of cold interrogation, but his voice when he spoke was humble and indifferent.

"I suppose you were in love with this Michael Furey, Gretta," he said.

"I was great with him at that time," she said.

Her voice was veiled and sad. Gabriel, feeling now how vain it would be to try to lead her whither he had purposed, caressed one of her hands and said, also sadly:

"And what did he die of so young, Gretta? Consumption, was it?"   430

"I think he died for me," she answered.

A vague terror seized Gabriel at this answer, as if, at that hour when he had hoped to triumph, some impalpable and vindictive being was coming against him, gathering forces against him in its vague world. But he shook himself free of it with an effort of reason and continued to caress her hand. He did not question her again, for he felt that she would tell him of herself. Her hand was warm and moist: it did not respond to his touch, but he continued to caress it just as he had caressed her first letter to him that spring morning.

"It was in the winter," she said, "about the beginning of the winter when I was going to leave my grandmother's and come up here to the convent. And he was ill at the time in his lodgings in Galway and wouldn't be let out, and his people in Oughterard were written to. He was in decline, they said, or something like that. I never knew rightly."

She paused for a moment and sighed.

"Poor fellow," she said. "He was very fond of me and he was such a gentle boy.   435
We used to go out together, walking, you know, Gabriel, like the way they do in the country. He was going to study singing only for his health. He had a very good voice, poor Michael Furey."

"Well; and then?" asked Gabriel.

"And then when it came to the time for me to leave Galway and come up to the convent he was much worse and I wouldn't be let see him so I wrote him a letter saying I was going up to Dublin and would be back in the summer, and hoping he would be better then."

She paused for a moment to get her voice under control, and then went on:

"Then the night before I left, I was in my grandmother's house in Nuns' Island, packing up, and I heard gravel thrown up against the window. The window was so wet I couldn't see, so I ran downstairs as I was and slipped out the back into the garden and there was the poor fellow at the end of the garden, shivering."

"And did you not tell him to go back?" asked Gabriel.   440

"I implored of him to go home at once and told him he would get his death in the rain. But he said he did not want to live. I can see his eyes as well! He was standing at the end of the wall where there was a tree."

"And did he go home?" asked Gabriel.

"Yes, he went home. And when I was only a week in the convent he died and he was buried in Oughterard, where his people came from. O, the day I heard that, that he was dead!"

She stopped, choking with sobs, and, overcome by emotion, flung herself face downward on the bed, sobbing in the quilt. Gabriel held her hand for a moment longer, irresolutely, and then, shy of intruding on her grief, let it fall gently and walked to the window.

She was fast asleep.   445

Gabriel, leaning on his elbow, looked for a few moments unresentfully on her tangled hair and half-open mouth, listening to her deep-drawn breath. So she had had that romance in her life: a man had died for her sake. It hardly pained him now to think how poor a part he, her husband, had played in her life. He watched her while she slept, as though he and she had never lived together as man and wife. His curious eyes rested long upon her face and on her hair: and, as he thought of what she must have been then, in that time of her first girlish beauty, a strange, friendly pity for her entered his soul. He did not like to say even to himself that her face was no longer beautiful, but he knew that it was no longer the face for which Michael Furey had braved death.

Perhaps she had not told him all the story. His eyes moved to the chair over which she had thrown some of her clothes. A petticoat string dangled to the floor. One boot stood upright, its limp upper fallen down: the fellow of it lay upon its side. He wondered at his riot of emotions of an hour before. From what had it proceeded? From his aunt's supper, from his own foolish speech, from the wine and dancing, the merry-making when saying goodnight in the hall, the pleasure of the walk along the river in the snow. Poor Aunt Julia! She, too, would soon be a shade with the shade of Patrick Morkan and his horse. He had caught that haggard look upon her face for a moment when she was singing *Arrayed for the Bridal*. Soon, perhaps, he would be sitting in that same drawing-room, dressed in black, his silk hat on his knees. The blinds would be drawn down and Aunt Kate would be sitting beside him, crying and blowing her nose and telling him how Julia had died. He would cast about in his mind for some words that might console her, and would find only lame and useless ones. Yes, yes: that would happen very soon.

The air of the room chilled his shoulders. He stretched himself cautiously along under the sheets and lay down beside his wife. One by one, they were all becoming shades. Better pass boldly into that other world, in the full glory of some passion, than fade and wither dismally with age. He thought of how she who lay beside him had locked in her head for so many years that image of her lover's eyes when he had told her that he did not wish to live.

Generous tears filled Gabriel's eyes. He had never felt like that himself towards any woman, but he knew that such a feeling must be love. The tears gathered more thickly in his eyes and in the partial darkness he imagined he saw the form of a young man standing under a dripping tree. Other forms were near. His soul had approached that region where dwell the vast hosts of the dead. He was conscious of, but could not apprehend, their wayward and flickering existence. His own identity was fading out into a grey impalpable world: the solid world itself, which these dead had one time reared and lived in, was dissolving and dwindling.

A few light taps upon the pane made him turn to the window. It had begun to   450
snow again. He watched sleepily the flakes, silver and dark, falling obliquely against the lamplight. The time had come for him to set out on his journey westward. Yes, the newspapers were right: snow was general all over Ireland. It was falling on every part of the dark central plain, on the treeless hills, falling softly upon the Bog of Allen and, farther westward, softly falling into the dark mutinous Shannon waves. It was falling, too, upon every part of the lonely churchyard on the hill where Michael Furey lay buried. It lay thickly drifted on the crooked crosses and headstones, on the spears of the little gate, on the barren thorns. His soul swooned slowly as he heard the snow falling faintly through the universe and faintly falling, like the descent of their last end, upon all the living and the dead.

RESOURCES IN INVESTIGATING YOUR RESEARCH ESSAY

When beginning any research project, it is critically important to locate as much background information on your subject as you can. Even before you choose a specific topic, just reading various reference and critical texts will help you place your subject in its historical context and give you an idea about the significant aspects of the literary text. The research paper rarely contains a single approach to a piece of literature, like formalist or reader response, but will often include various strategies for interpretation and discussion. For example, you may begin by citing historical information about a text, suggesting biographical parallels in text, and end with a deconstructive or formalist reading of the piece. In order to move from the general to the specific, you must choose a manageable topic that uses the primary text as its foundation, support by secondary texts for background and authority, and your own creative addition to the established literary conversation.

In a class that emphasizes imaginative literature, you will probably begin your research project with a primary text and an assignment. For example, the sample essay in this chapter uses James Joyce's "The Dead" as its primary text. If you look at the works cited page of the essay, you will see in it secondary sources, used to support and add to positions and interpretations made in the paper. While finding a copy of the primary text should be easy—your instructor probably gave it to you—the secondary sources require leg and finger work. While the Internet's popularity shows no signs of waning, you will still find it necessary to use your library's resources for a well-written and thorough research essay. However, you need not begin with the library anymore. The Internet and your library's databases provide an efficient method of gathering information about your primary text and help you to begin to narrow your focus. If you plan to do this initial research at home, be sure you consult your library's policies about off-campus connections. See if the library requires any specific proxy settings for connection, if there are any time limits, or if there are any other unexpected hoops to jump through. Every library will be different, so an initial visit to your library to collect this information will only make your first day of research more productive.

Free Internet Sources for Tertiary References

The Internet is a superb tool to use when beginning your research, providing you with general background and historical information about your topic, sources I call tertiary texts. You will find Internet resources to be vast, sometimes overwhelmingly so. For example, a search for "james joyce" on Google (*http://www.google.com.*) gave me 868,000 hits. However, the first few that Google turned up were golden. Internet search engines, like Google, Yahoo!, and Excite, offer excellent ways to begin researching your topic. Google is an example of a "meta" search engine; that is, it uses "spiders" to hunt through servers on the Internet, and its catalogs Web pages it finds on them. While the meta search engines will provide you with the most results, they are often the most daunting, especially for beginning researchers. Google is the first search engine I turn to, but others prefer Yahoo!'s categorization approach. Yahoo!'s database of Web sites, unlike Google's, is comprised of sites submitted by Web site authors; for example, if you create a site about James Joyce and want to share it with the Internet community at large, you could fill out a brief form and submit it for categorization on Yahoo!. While this process presents no challenges other than filling out a form, it can sometimes take in excess of a year for your Web's site's listing to appear on Yahoo!. Therefore, while engines like Yahoo! do not overwhelm researchers with hundreds of thousands of choices, their databases never seem to be as current as the meta engines. For an introduction to Internet search engines and tips for using them successfully, see the Internet Public Library's "Web Searching" at *http://www. ipl.org/ref/websearching.html*.

The early results from Google were excellent places to start my investigation of "The Dead." Some of the results were as follows:

1) Work in Progress: A James Joyce Website
   http://www.2street.com/joyce/

   A comprehensive site, "Work in Progress" offers historical, biographical, critical, and geographical information about James Joyce and Dublin. Links to articles, groups, and other sites devoted to Joyce are easily found on this well-constructed site.

2) James Joyce Web Page
   http://members.ozemial.com.au/~caveman/Joyce/

   Charles Cave presents personal resources that have influenced his readings of Joyce. This site also contains links to other resources and reading recommendations.

3) James Joyce Resource Center
   http://www.cohums.ohio-state.edu/english/organizations/ijjf/jrc/default.htm.

   This site presents historical and biographical information and has individual sections for various critical approaches to Joyce, like Marxist, feminist, and psychoanalytic criticism.

This list on Google continues, but as you begin looking deeply into these sites, you will find that they begin pointing to each other, just as a bibliography refers to other related work. Since I was researching a story that appears in Joyce's collection *Dubliners*, I wanted to concentrate on looking for references to this collection in general and to "The Dead" specifically. When I searched Yahoo! for "joyce dubliners," I got a specific category match for "Dubliners," which contained links to "The Dead" specifically. Yet the results were disappointing: I got an excerpt from the text, a (broken) link to the Grateful Dead's site, and the full e-text of "The Dead." Searching Google with the same parameters generates the following links:

1) The James Joyce Papers
   http://www.themodernword.com/joyce/joyce_papers.html

Mostly a collection of links to papers about Joyce, with a section that addresses *Dubliners* specifically.

2) World Wide *Dubliners*
http://www.stg.brown.edu/~rog/WWD/

Here there are numerous links to e-texts and notes on "Araby" and "The Dead." Wallace Gray's annotations provide an excellent reading accompaniment for "The Dead."

As you can see, many resources for James Joyce exist on the Internet. For a list of some others, see Chapter 2. Further, examining these resources will un-cover others that the search engines did not find, or that are buried too far down the list of results. If your first search does not uncover many good sources, you might want to vary your search criteria. I could also have tried "joyce dead" or "joyce dubliners dead" to limit my search even further.

Let us suppose that you do not have a primary text from which to start your research. Well, help is available for you, too. Some sites provide a compre-hensive list of literary resources. One of the best is "Voice of the Shuttle: Web Page for Humanities Research." While spanning the humanities, VOS has ex-cellent sections on literature in English, literature in other languages, and liter-ary theory. Clicking on the former links you to historical, genre, and miscellaneous classifications of literature: from medieval to contemporary; drama to poetry; teaching resources to cultural studies. A quick click on "Mod-ern British" shows a list of Internet resources beginning with Auden and con-tinuing through Yeats. Looking at the Joyce resources presents many others not found in my Google or Yahoo! searches. Other general literary sites exist on the Web and are worth a look.

1) Voice of the Shuttle: Web Page for Humanities Research
http://vos.ucsb.edu/

2) Annotated Webliography of Literary Sources
http://www2gasou.edu/facstaff/dougt/weblio.htm

This "Webliography" points to other general English-related collections of mate-rials, such as VOS. It also links to various collections of e-texts, e-journals, and hypertexts.

3) The EServer: Accessible Online Publishing
http://eserver.org/

Formerly the "English Server," the more cyber-sounding "EServer" contains arti-cles and essays relating to cultural studies. This site has links to e-journals, a *very* good list, and various English-related sites on the Internet. Again, another great site for general browsing.

4) Internet Public Library: Online Literary Criticism
http://www.ipl.org/ref/litcrit/

This page pulls together resources from all over the Internet into national and historical categories. Not limited to essays, this resource links to general reference material and specific resources about authors, movements, and periods.

While not exhaustive in the least, these sites should give you a good start in reference and background information on your chosen topic, or give you more direction about how to pursue a topic. While these sources are designed to help give you a general entre into your topic, none of them should be listed in a works cited page. These tertiary references are to point you to more scholarly, detailed sources that should help you directly through quotations and paraphrases in your research paper. With general information in hand, you need to begin looking for more specific resources. This is not to say that first-rate secondary resources cannot be found freely on the Internet, but they are few and are often shoddily edited. When evaluating an online site, consider the accuracy and detail of the information provided, the qualifications of the author, and the timeliness of the information. For other tips about evaluating Internet sources, see "Evaluating Information Found on the Internet" at *http://milton/mse/jhu.edu:8001/research/education/net.html*. To begin narrowing your search, you must turn to more specific sources found both in your library and online: secondary texts. Generally, what distinguishes these sources from those above is the price tag.

Subscription Internet Sources: Secondary Texts

Secondary resources—that is, sources talking about your primary source, or the literary text itself—generally take two forms: books and journals. Since these sources go through a rigorous evaluation and editing process, they cost money to produce and distribute. These funds are provided by publishing companies, like university presses, that publish specialized journals and book-length studies on specific literary figures, genres, or historical periods and by the individuals and institutions that purchase books and subscribe to journals. While distribution of these books and periodicals have traditionally been in book form, many future-looking editors have begun to look to the Internet as a more economical and efficacious means of dissemination. However, while the Internet does differ in some costs, these efforts must still be supported by the end user: you.

You are not on your own, fortunately, in searching electronic sources. Working with publishers, university libraries are involved in the ongoing process of making what was once only available as a physical commodity that sat on a bookshelf and that only one person at a time could use into a digital resource available to many more users at the same time, regardless of locale. These electronic resources are paid for partially by the university, partially through other means, and partially through your tuition. So what you could once obtain only by walking into the library and scanning the stacks, you may now readily access electronically, as long as you are a student. Also note that all libraries and their holdings will differ, depending on funds, interest, and knowledge of databases. Therefore, sources discussed in this section may not be available at your institution, but if your librarians are anything like most college librarians, they would love to hear your suggestions.

Like the tertiary Internet sources listed previously, other general resources may be found through a digital subscription. Try these for starters:

1) *Oxford English Dictionary (OED)*
   http://dictionary.oed.com/

   The *OED* can help trace the etymology of key words and how they have been used in practical and literary contexts over the years.

2) Gale Group
   http://galenet.gale.com/m/mcp/prodlist

   Series like *Contemporary Literary Criticism*, *Twentieth-Century Literary Criticism*, and the *Dictionary of Literary Biography* are published by Gale. Their online database combines these resources into single searches delineated by themes, titles, authors, topics, movements, and other criteria.

Some of these expansive multivolume series, like the *Masterplots* series that can help with general plot details, are not yet available in an electronic form, but can help with various background information in your research. Like other tertiary sources, these should not appear in your list of works cited.

Once you have your topic, or at least the name of the primary text or author that you'd like to address in your research, you should turn to the MLA Bibliography. Probably the most useful resource for locating specific secondary sources is the Modern Language Association's (MLA) Bibliography, available through electronic subscription to FirstSearch. The MLA Bibliography was one of the first to be released as a CD-ROM version, but since that was restricted to one computer in the library, it was not much better than the printed volume. FirstSearch has made the MLA Bibliography, as well as many others, available via the familiar interface of a Web site. Searches now take a matter of seconds, and results can be printed, or better yet, e-mailed directly to the researcher's e-mail account. As a major source for research in English Studies, the MLA Bibliography lists multiple-language books, journal articles, dissertations, and other resources, some of which are full-text. The MLA Bibliography should be the first place you look for secondary literary scholarship. Like the MLA Bibliography, other lists of secondary texts are available:

1) Academic Index

   A searchable index of over 1,000 journals in subjects ranging from popular culture to feminist theory. Many resources are available in full text.

2) Dissertation Abstracts International

   A FirstSearch database that includes bibliographic entries from and abstracts of completed doctoral dissertations from over 500 universities worldwide.

3) Project Muse

One of my favorites, Project Muse is comprised of over 40 scholarly journals published by Johns Hopkins University Press, including: *Configurations*, *Postmodern Culture*, and *ELH (English Literary History)*. You might not want to begin a search here, but the full-text journals and the search engine make this a strong model for the future of research and scholarship.

4) Wilson Selects

Another FirstSearch database, Wilson Selects contains indexes and abstracted articles from over 430 journals.

5) WorldCat

Touting itself as the largest bibliographic database in the world, WorldCat's database includes bibliographic records of anything a library might catalog. This database contains some full-text articles.

This group is obviously not an exhaustive list of databases, but based on the number of times FirstSearch comes up, its service is becoming integral in English studies' research.

Once you have compiled a list of entries from your secondary sources research, it is time to locate and read those texts. If you find full-text documents, many can be e-mailed to you and others can be read on or printed from a Web browser. Here's a tip: Instead of printing, read the articles online and cut and paste interesting or appropriate sections of the essays into a word processing document. This way, when you have finished reading your selections, you have the pith of those sources in one file. Don't forget to clearly label each quotation with its source (volume, issue, and year), author, URL (the universal resource locator, usually beginning with "http"), and paragraph number(s) (if available). You will need these references later.

For print sources, you will need to make a sacrifice and actually go to the library. While many researchers do not use note cards themselves, a strong strategy when reading your sources is to copy down pertinent quotations and paraphrases from the text as you read, as you did with the cut-and-pasted electronic sources. This way, you needn't spend the money or waste trees to photocopy each article, and the juicy sections of each essay can now be easily referenced from your cards. Alternately, if you have a laptop computer, you can use it in place of note cards: Just keep adding to your research file that you began with your electronic sources. Still another strategy involves photocopying each article so that it can be annotated as you read it. Although this process is not the most environmentally responsible practice, I prefer it because I like to keep copies of the articles for future projects. Remember to keep track of sources while taking notes, including author, source (volume, issue, and date), title, and page numbers. Be sure to label each quotation or paraphrase with the specific page number you took it from.

When you locate your initial set of secondary texts, you will naturally derive other sources from those articles' references that you will want to examine. Be sure you write these additional references down so that you can retrieve them the next time you go to the library or are browsing the Internet.

The following essay is a sample research paper, which illustrates the major components of the research essay.

Sample Essay on James Joyce's "The Dead"

James Joyce's complex and powerful short story, "The Dead," is the last story in a collection titled *Dubliners*. The volume was first published in 1914 as part of a collection of stories about the residents and settings of Dublin, Ireland. Since the publication of "The Dead," scholars have been fascinated by the richness of the text, and each year brings new and fresh readings of this master short story. Indeed, some critics believe "The Dead" to be perhaps the greatest short story ever written. There is no lack of innovative and challenging interpretations.

This story is dominated by interesting characters, especially Gabriel Conroy, the story's protagonist. Some critics have explored "The Dead" as Joyce's concern with an individual's continuing reconsideration of his life. Richard Ellmann, for example, states that Joyce's approach to "The Dead" is one of revision and reexamination (230). Ellmann's view is supported by his historical research into various "indulgent" views in Joyce's letters, wherein he muses that he may have been "unnecessarily harsh" is not presenting any of Dublin's "ingenious insularity and its hospitality" (Ellmann 231). Joyce's own estimation of his harsh images of Dubliners may have led to his somewhat sympathetic, yet no less poignant, characterizations.

This powerful story, completed in 1907, differs from the others in that it is more elaborate and dense, offering both "summary and climax" to *Dubliners* (Tindall 42). This essay concentrates on the character of Gabriel Conroy who, as Ellmann and other critics point out, shares characteristics and historical parallels with Joyce himself as he developed as an artist. "The Dead" traces a "possibility for renewal" in the character of Gabriel through his encounters with three women at his aunts' annual dance held on the Feast of the Epiphany, Twelfth Night, or January 6, 1907 (Schwarz 8; Brunsdale 38). These women—Lily, Miss Ivors, and Gabriel's wife Gretta—force Gabriel to acknowledge his own lack of humanity in his personal relationships with the people in his life and promote his recognition that he, too, is one of the "living dead," one of the story's most moving metaphors. We learn that Gabriel must take action to renounce his overly intellectual and condescending attitudes toward others and Ireland in order to rediscover life and love. In other words, Gabriel must become more human, like some of the other characters who inhabit "The Dead."

Gabriel is not presented as a very likable character, once one digs beneath his surface gentility and comforting manners. When Gabriel makes his tardy, yet predictable, appearance at the Morkans' residence, he blames "his wife" (at present, little more than a nameless possession of his) for his lack of punctuality. He appears condescending and supercilious when addressing Lily, the caretaker's daughter. Joyce's language, as Hugh Kenner observes, calls immediate attention to Lily's deficient education through the "Uncle Charles Principle" that allies the narrator with his or her subject's idiom (Kenner 18): "Lily, the caretaker's daughter, was literally run off her feet" (Joyce 175). The narrator's alliance illustrates Lily's incorrect, but colloquial, use of "literal," subtly informing the reader of her class realities as a servant in the "best of everything" Morkan household (Joyce 176). This wonderful introductory metaphor is also an example of a statement that announces its impossibility. Indeed, Lily was run "off her feet" only figuratively. The narrator deftly warns us, early on, of the dangers of reading literary language without caution and precision.

Gabriel's treatment of Lily makes their class distinctions explicit and presents his condescending attitude toward her class: He "smiled at the three syllables she had given his surname" (Joyce 177). In their time-filling discussion of the weather, Gabriel attempts to narrate Lily's life for her. Since she is no longer attending school, she must soon be getting married, according to Gabriel's sense of propriety. (Indeed, that progression is only "natural.") Her retort is filled with bitterness: "The men that is now is only all palaver and what they can get out of you" (Joyce 178). Gabriel attempts to cover his embarrassment at her response by giving, not a gift, but a tip for the servant girl. This action further solidifies their relationship and Gabriel's own sense of superiority (Brunsdale 38).

It becomes clear by now that pride is one of Gabriel's weaknesses. Brunsdale argues, for example, that Gabriel also blames his subsequent feeling of inferiority on those whose "culture differed from his," which includes nearly everyone at the party (Joyce 38). While contemplating the speech he prepared for that evening, he wonders if he may be going "above the heads of his hearers" if he includes the quotation from Browning rather than someone more popular, like Shakespeare: "He would only make himself ridiculous by quoting poetry to them which they could not understand. . . . He would fail with them just as he had failed with the girl in the pantry" (Joyce 179). Lily is now just "the girl" as Gabriel moves to his next encounter, although a little less sure of himself.

Gabriel next reveals his superiority in his encounter with Miss Molly Ivors, who also refuses to fit into his sense of "proper" young women. According to William Handy, Miss Ivors' chides represent less of a hostile attack and more of a flirtatious banter appropriate for a party (47–8). Perhaps because of his perceived failing with Lily, Gabriel misreads Miss Ivors' irony as an aggressiveness typical of the "frank-mannered talkative young lady" who is a zealous supporter of Ireland (Joyce 187). Because he sees her as his intellectual equal, "he could not risk a grandiose phrase with her" and becomes agitated with her conversation. After she invites him to go west to the Aran Islands with her, and reminds him that Gretta is from the western Connacht, he decides that he has had enough of the "uppity" Miss Ivors:

—And why do you go to France or Belgium, said Miss Ivors, instead of visiting your own land?

—Well, said Gabriel, it's partly to keep in touch with the languages and partly for a change.

—And haven't you your own language to keep in touch with—Irish? asked Miss Ivors.

—Well, said Gabriel, if it comes to that, you know, Irish is not my language. . . .

—And haven't you your own land to visit, continued Miss Ivors, that you know nothing of, your own people, and your own country?

—O, to tell you the truth, retorted Gabriel suddenly, I'm sick of my own country, sick of it! (Joyce 189)

As she takes her leave, Molly can't help but get in one more jab at Gabriel by calling him a "West Briton," or an Anglicized Irishman (Joyce 190). Gabriel later recalls this nickname with the story of his grandfather Patrick Morkan and his horse Johnny. Although the anecdote is told for the departing guests' amusement, the joke seems to be on Gabriel and his support of the British ruling class (Brunsdale 39). Like Johnny circling the stature of the Protestant King William III, whose total subjugation of Ireland began after he defeated them at the Battle of the Boyne in 1690, Gabriel's work for *The Daily Express* makes him the Irish mouthpiece for British ideology (Blumberg): "Round and round he went" (Joyce 208). So far, Gabriel is portrayed as being uncomfortable with himself, his "inferiors," and his country (which he sees as inferior). As the story develops, his discomfort with his family (wife Gretta) adds to the list of his discomforts.

Gabriel's work for the pro-English newspaper has a parallel in Joyce's life and influences. A supporter of the Irish nationalist leader Charles Parnell, Joyce's ire attacked those who removed Parnell from Irish Parliamentary Delegation because of his relationship with the wife of Captain O'Shea. Along with Parnell, the Irishmen and artists Yeats, Swift, and Wilde also influenced the young Joyce, yet the latter believed that Ireland should not separate itself from the broader intellectual and cultural traditions of Europe, a trend he saw in much of Yeats' work, but neither should it become a broken "court jester to the English," a fate Joyce saw in Wilde's life (Schwarz 6). Like Joyce, Gabriel places Ireland and himself in a larger cultural tradition, which did not limit itself strictly to Ireland.

The banquet speech is one of the high moments of the story and illustrates Gabriel's role as the leading gentleman-intellectual of the evening. Although still agitated by Miss Ivors, Gabriel nevertheless gives his speech, in which he compares his aunts and his nieces to the three graces, for the gathered company. Yet this decorum is but a show, since Gabriel's true feelings about his aunts were shown in his excited state after his encounter with Miss Ivors: "What did he care that his aunts were only two ignorant old women?" (Joyce 192). His speech restores his rightful place as head of the table and authority; the habitual triumph of his speech briefly returns his complacency (Tindall 43). However, his ease will soon be disrupted by the image of Gretta listening to Mr. Bartell D'Arcy sing. Gabriel looks penetratingly at his wife and tries to imagine what she symbolizes, as if she were a literary object, rather than his loving wife (Joyce 209–10). Her position on the stairs above recalls the picture of Romeo and Juliet he saw earlier, foreshadowing the eminent tragic scene to come.

Perhaps the most important encounter of the evening is the final one between Gabriel and Gretta. She tells him the story of Michael Furey, her now dead lover from the west. The narrative told by Gretta parallels one told by Nora Joyce to her husband. In Galway, Michael "Sonny" Bodkin courted the young Nora Barnacle before the latter knew and married Joyce. Sonny contracted tuberculosis and was confined to bed, but on hearing of Nora's plans to move to Dublin, he braved the rainy weather to sing to Nora under an apple tree. He died shortly after this incident. Nora's first attraction to Joyce, she later confided in him, was a result of his resemblance to Sonny Bodkin (Ellmann 243). Joyce's reaction to Nora's confession provoked a jealousy fed by the fact that she had an interest in a boy before she met him. This fact annoyed Joyce in that Nora's heart could still be moved by a dead man, and he felt as if he must compete with the ghost of Sonny Bodkin (Ellmann 243–44). Surely Joyce drew on this personal fact from his life along with Thomas Moore's lyric "O, Ye Dead!" to suggest that the living and the dead are jealous of each other, and Gabriel seems to long to live as Michael Furey lives in Gretta's memory (Ellmann 244).

Gabriel's longing turns to terror as he realizes that the pretensions of his life make him one of the walking dead: "He saw himself as a ludicrous figure, acting as pennyboy for his aunts, a nervous well-meaning sentimentalist, orating to vulgarians and idealizing his own clowning lusts, the pitiable fatuous fellow he had caught a glimpse of in the mirror" (Joyce 220). The image of the well-off, well-fed, and comfortable man contrasts sharply with that of the sick and dying Michael, a contrast that Gabriel fears his wife has made all the years they were married, resulting from her "secret life" (Joyce 219). The cold, calculating Gabriel realizes that he has never loved like the passionate Michael, and the former wonders at the "poor . . . part he, her husband, played in her life" (Joyce 222). This self-realization crushes the normally stable, self-controlled intellectual.

There would seem to be little doubt that Gabriel has come to know himself and does not like what he has found. His epiphany, a "showing forth, or revelation," is one that consciously aligns him with the dead (Scholes 253). Gabriel realizes that he has been nothing but the living dead in an equally dead society when compared to the living ghost of Michael Furey (Walzl 17): "He had never felt like that himself towards any woman but he knew that such a feeling must be love" (Joyce 223). Gabriel is not guilty of keeping love from Gretta, but entirely lacking it (Tindall 43). With this realization, Gabriel figuratively dies as he "approached that region where dwell the vast hosts of the dead," which causes him to begin to relinquish his own superiority and detachedness: "His own identity was fading out into a grey impalpable world" (Joyce 223). He then makes a conscious decision to rejoin the community of his people: "The time had come for him to make his journey westward" (223). In a literary tradition, the move westward could signify death, but its specific significance to "The Dead" points to a journey of rebirth in the provincial Ireland of Michael Furey and Gretta's childhood—away from the "West Britain" influences in Dublin.

The final image of "The Dead" is of the "cosmic" snow that covers and unifies "all the living and the dead" (Joyce 224). Gabriel's sacrifice of his superiority and ego is necessary for an unencumbered journey westward, to see the world apart from his own narrow subjectivity (Handy 61). His stunning epiphany shows Gabriel that his wife is more than just an object to be interpreted and exploited and that other human beings exist apart from his estimation of them (Brunsdale 40). Gabriel's epiphany may have been very much Joyce's as well. Joyce's change in attitude toward Ireland as a place of paralysis, frustration, and inaction to one of hope and community seems evident even in the ambiguous snow image of the ending (Brunsdale 47, Walzl 17). The possibility for renewal for a lapsed soul lies perhaps in the rediscovery of humanity and escape from the drab, brown Dublin (Schwarz 8, 10). Further, Schwarz suggests that Joyce "is regarding his egoism with poignance and sympathy" through the character of Gabriel, and later through that of Stephen Dedalus in A Portrait of an Artist as a Young Man (12). While escaping the subjectivity of the ego might be a useless endeavor, Gabriel's hard-won lesson to see beyond the individual held the key to Joyce's success as an artist and might help in creating a more sympathetic and compassionate humanity. In a sense, Gabriel must die to live and live to die to earn the knowledge he has painfully purchased by story's end.

Works Cited

Blumberg, Roger B. and Wallace Gray. "Wallace Gray's Notes for James Joyce's 'The Dead.'" *World Wide Dubliners*. Draft 97:1: World Wide Web. 7 May 2001. Available http://www.stg.brown.edu/~rog/WWD/WWDdead.notes.html.

Brunsdale, Mitizi M. *James Joyce: A Study of the Short Fiction*. New York: Twayne, 1993.

Ellmann, Richard. *James Joyce*. New and Revised Edition. New York: Oxford UP, 1982.

Handy, William J. *Modern Fiction: A Formalist Approach*. Carbondale: U of Illinois P, 1971.

Joyce, James. *Dubliners: Text, Criticism, and Notes*. Eds. Robert Scholes and A. Walton Litz. New York: Viking Penguin, 1969.

Kenner, Hugh. *Joyce's Voices*. Berkeley: U of California P, 1978.

Schwarz, Daniel R., Ed. *The Dead*. Boston: Bedford, 1994.

Tindall, William York. *A Reader's Guide to James Joyce*. New York: Syracuse UP, 1959.

Walzl, Florence L. "Gabriel and Michael: The Conclusion of 'The Dead.'" *James Joyce Quarterly* 4, Fall 1966. 17–31.

Credits

Index

Note: Boldface page numbers indicate the text of the readings.